THE POPULAR ENCYCLOPEDIA OF CHURCH HISTORY

ED HINDSON
DAN MITCHELL
GENERAL EDITORS

HARVEST HOUSE PUBLISHERS
EUGENE, OREGON

THE POPULAR ENCYCLOPEDIA OF CHURCH HISTORY
Copyright © 2013 by Ed Hindson and Daniel R. Mitchell
Published by Harvest House Publishers
Eugene, Oregon 97402
www.harvesthousepublishers.com

Library of Congress Cataloging-in-Publication Data
    The popular encyclopedia of church history / Ed Hindson and Dan Mitchell, general editors.
        pages cm
    Includes bibliographical references.
    ISBN 978-0-7369-4806-7
    1. Church history—Encyclopedias. I. Hindson, Edward E., editor of compilation. II. Mitchell, Dan (Daniel R.) editor of compilation.
    BR95.P67 2013
    270.03—dc23

                                                                                    2012046795

Printed in the United States of America

13 14 15 16 17 18 19 20 21 / LB-CD / 10 9 8 7 6 5 4 3 2 1

*To our students,
the future church history makers
of the 21st century
who will prove against the winds of time
that God's church still stands
and the gates of hell
will not prevail against it.*

CONTENTS

✠

Will Honeycutt, DMin,
Trinity Evangelical Divinity School

Barbara Hubbard, MDiv,
Liberty Baptist Theological Seminary

Thomas Ice, ThD,
Tyndale Theological Seminary

Jerry Ireland, MA,
Global University

Kevin King, PhD,
Pretoria University (South Africa)

Benjamin Laird, MLitt,
University of St. Andrews (Scotland)

Steve Lemke, PhD,
Southwestern Baptist Theological
Seminary

Douglas Mann, PhD,
University of Georgia

Edward Martin, PhD,
Purdue University

Troy Matthews, EdD,
Argosy University

Dennis McDonald, PhD,
Dallas Theological Seminary

Christopher Moody, PhD,
Southwestern Baptist Theological
Seminary

Ramon Moran, PhD,
Regent University

John D. Morrison, PhD,
University of Virginia

Ken Nehrbass, PhD,
Biola University

Mark Nickens, PhD,
Southern Baptist Theological Seminary

David Pettus, PhD,
Baylor University

Karen Swallow Prior, PhD,
State University of New York

Thomas Provenzola, PhD,
Trinity Evangelical Divinity School

Stephen Putney, DMin,
Trinity Evangelical Divinity School

David Roberts, DMin,
Southeastern Baptist Theological Seminary

Daryl Rodriguez, DMin,
Southern Evangelical Seminary

Daniel Russell, PhD,
New Orleans Baptist Theological
Seminary

Jon Tyler Scarlett, DMin,
Southeastern Baptist Theological Seminary

Roger Schultz, PhD,
University of Arkansas

Gary Shultz, Jr., PhD,
Southern Baptist Theological Seminary

C. Fred Smith, PhD,
Southwestern Baptist Theological Seminary

Ed Smither, PhD,
University of Wales (Britain)

Joe Super, PhD (candidate),
West Virginia University

A. Chadwick Thornhill, PhD (candidate),
Liberty Baptist Theological Seminary

Mark Tinsley, ThM,
Liberty Baptist Theological Seminary

Elmer Towns, DMin,
Fuller Theological Seminary

Paul Weaver, ThM,
Dallas Theological Seminary

Vernon Whaley, PhD,
University of Oklahoma

PREFACE

The history of Christianity is the story of a man, Jesus of Nazareth, and a people who call themselves his disciples. Their faith is based upon his life, teachings, sacrificial death, and triumphal resurrection. His followers are the fulfillment of his own "great prediction," "I will build My church, and the gates of Hades shall not prevail against it" (Matthew 16:18). From the moment the Holy Spirit came upon the original 120 believers in the upper room, until today, that prophecy has continued to be fulfilled with amazing results.

The eminent church historian Kenneth Scott Latourette observed that Christianity has not only become the world's largest religious faith, but "measured by its effects, Christianity has become the most potent single force in the life of mankind."* In the nearly 2000 years since its inception, Christianity has multiplied into thousands of churches, schools, hospitals, and orphanages worldwide. Today, Christianity claims two billion followers of Jesus Christ. These include North Americans, Latin Americans, Native Americans, Europeans, Asians, Africans, and those on the far-flung islands of the globe.

Christian churches can be found on every inhabited continent of the world. These faith assemblies meet in everything from warehouses to cathedrals, from private homes to public arenas, and from grass huts to towering skyscrapers. The diversity of global Christianity is the most unique of all the religions of humankind. While Christians may differ in how they worship and where they worship, they all claim to worship Jesus Christ as Savior, Lord, and God.

In order to help these laymen and pastors alike, we have assembled a team of scholars from both the resident and online faculties of Liberty University to provide a series of succinct articles on major people, events, and movements in this *Popular Encyclopedia of Church History*. We have endeavored to select topics of interest to evangelical readers in particular, while also acquainting readers with everything from the church

---

* K.S. Latourette, *A History of Christianity* (New York: Harper Collins, 1953), xii-xiii.

fathers, Catholic theologians, medieval monks, the Protestant Reformation, the evangelical revivals, global missions, and more. By the limitation of space, we have had to be selective in this process. But it is our sincere prayer and desire that what we have included will inform your mind, bless your heart, and stir your soul.

Jonathan Hill writes, "The story of Christianity, its transformation from an illegal sect to the religion of emperors, kings and presidents, and its spread across the globe, is an endlessly fascinating one…it is a story not just of how Christianity has changed the world, but how the world has changed Christianity…as it has spread to virtually every culture on earth."* As Philip Schaff, the father of American church history, has observed, it is a story that has two sides: the human and the divine.† It is the story of fallible human beings who dared attempt to represent the will and purpose of the infallible God. May a glimpse into their lives, hopes, dreams, and concerns challenge you with a passion to fulfill God's purpose in your life and your own generation.

Edward E. Hindson, and Daniel R. Mitchell, General Editors
Liberty University, Virginia

---

* J. Hill, *Zondervan Handbook on the History of Christianity* (Grand Rapids: Zondervan, 2006), 12.

† P. Schaff, *History of the Christian Church* (New York: Scribner's Sons, 1890), 1:2.

ca. 30	Death and resurrection of Jesus Christ
ca. 30	Birth of the church
ca. 45–48	Paul's missionary journeys
ca. 49	Council of Jerusalem determines Gentiles are not required to observe Jewish law
70	Roman destruction of the temple in Jerusalem
ca. 90	Gnostic heresies begin to spread
ca. 95	John exiled to Patmos
107	Martyrdom of Ignatius of Antioch
180	Irenaeus of Lyons writes *Against Heresies*
ca. 230	Origen of Alexandria founds school, writes
313	Edict of Milan legalizes Christianity, ends persecution
325	Council of Nicaea condemns Arianism and other heresies
380	Theodosius establishes Christianity as state religion
420	Augustine of Hippo writes *City of God*
451	Council of Chalcedon addresses heresies about divine and human natures of Christ
537	Hagia Sophia cathedral at Constantinople dedicated by Emperor Justinian
590	Gregory the Great becomes Pope
630	Muslim conquests of Palestine and Syria begin
691	Dome of the Rock built on the Temple Mount
800	Pope Leo III crowns Charlemagne as emperor of the Roman Empire
1054	Great Schism between Catholic and Orthodox Churches
1095	Pope Urban II authorizes First Crusade
1099	Crusaders capture Jerusalem
1187	Muslim general Saladin recaptures Jerusalem
1210	Francis of Assisi founds Franciscans

1216	Dominic founds Dominican order
1273	Thomas Aquinas writes *Summa Theologica*
1305	Clement V moves papacy to Avignon, France
1377	Gregory XI condemns John Wycliffe
1387	Great papal schism between competing popes
1414	Papacy returns to Rome
1453	Constantinople falls to Ottoman Turks
1480	Spanish Inquisition begins
1517	Martin Luther's 95 Theses
1521	Diet of Worms condemns Luther
1534	Henry VIII establishes Church of England
1540	Ignatius of Loyola founds Society of Jesus (Jesuits)
1542–1549	Francis Xavier's missionary endeavors in India and Japan
1545–1563	Council of Trent rejects Protestant reforms
1559	John Calvin's *Institutes of the Christian Religion* published
1560	Geneva Bible published; John Knox begins Reformed Church in Scotland
1572	Massacre of Protestant Huguenots in Paris
1588	Spanish Armada fails to conquer England
1611	King James Bible published
1618–1619	Synod of Dort condemns Arminianism
1626	Basilica of St. Peter's completed in Rome
1646	Westminster Confession adopted in England, Scotland
1642–1651	English civil wars; Puritan revolution
1739	John Wesley founds Methodism
1740	George Whitefield preaches in America; Great Awakening begins
1775–1783	American Revolution
1786	Thomas Jefferson urges religious freedom in Virginia
1787–1805	Second Great Awakening in America
1793	William Carey arrives in India

1807	William Wilberforce convinces English Parliament to abolish slavery
1809	Napoléon invades Papal States
1813	Adoniram Judson arrives in Burma
1851–1873	David Livingstone's mission to Africa
1861–1865	US Civil War
1865	William Booth begins Salvation Army
1870	First Vatican Council affirms papal infallibility
1873–1875	D.L. Moody's evangelistic campaigns in Britain
1901	Boxer Rebellion in China; large numbers of missionaries and Christians killed
1906	Azusa Street Revival; early beginnings of Pentecostalism
1910–1915	*Fundamentals* published; giving rise to American Fundamentalism
1920s	Fundamentalist-Modernist controversy
1931	C.S. Lewis converted to Christianity
1932	Karl Barth begins publishing *Church Dogmatics*
1933	Adolf Hitler enforces Nazi-dominated Reich Church
1945	Dietrich Bonhoeffer executed by Nazis
1945–1947	Communist governments begin suppression of Christianity in Eastern Europe
1947	First Billy Graham crusade
1948	Discovery of the Dead Sea Scrolls
1962–1965	Second Vatican Council
1968	Martin Luther King Jr. assassinated
1970s	Television evangelism expands
1978	John Paul II becomes Pope
1979	Jerry Falwell founds the Moral Majority
1989–1991	Collapse of Communism in Eastern Europe
2000	Evangelical Christianity continues to expand rapidly in Asia, Africa, and Latin America; persecution of Christians also continues, most notably in Muslim-dominant regions

✠

AUGUSTINE OF HIPPO
Christian Theologian
354–430

ABELARD, PETER (1079–1142)

Peter Abelard was a medieval philosopher and theologian born near modern Nantes in western France. He entered the cathedral school of Notre Dame in Paris at an early age and soon emerged as one of the most astute and controversial figures, aggressively advocating the use of reason and logic to debate the philosophical and theological topics that occupied the brightest minds of his day. Abelard was likely the most daring of the new dialecticians, applying what was known of Aristotelian logic, found in Boethius's (ca. 480–525) translations of Aristotle's *Categories* and *On Interpretation* from Greek to Latin, to the proper relationship between philosophy and theology. In what came to be viewed suspiciously by many as the new rationalism in theology, Abelard championed the method of subjecting the articles of the faith to rigorous logical analysis, doing this to the point that some critics, such as Bernard of Clairvaux, considered him to have so seriously misused his logical arguments that he ended up favoring heretical views such as tritheism over traditional conceptions of the Trinity and abandoning the adopted Anselmian notion of the substitutionary atonement of Christ in favor of the moral influence theory, which taught that Christ's sacrifice was not intended to pay the debt for human sin, but instead, to move people to love of God because of Christ's example.

Abelard's famous *Sic et Non* (*Yes and No*), written around 1122, in which contrasting and apparently contradictory opinions of the church fathers were placed side by side without resolution, was intended to demonstrate the methodological inadequacy of merely citing authorities when it came to determining theological truth. Abelard was not seeking to undermine the credibility of Christian beliefs, but to showcase the way rationally autonomous persons could critique the arguments of others and come to their own conclusions, even if that meant challenging ideas long held sacrosanct by the church.

Abelard, in applying his method to one of the central philosophical debates of his day, the doctrine of universals put forth by Boethius, recovered some of the ground he lost on the theological side. Traditional realism considered universals—that is, the repeatable characteristics and qualities that can be exemplified in the many particular things of the world, such as the roundness of two separate balls or the redness of

A

two separate roses—to be extra-mental realities. This position was under considerable attack by the newly emerging nominalists, who argued instead that universals were mere words that expressed the characteristics that particular things have in common. Abelard argued for a middle ground between the two positions, stressing critical distinctions between a word that corresponds to a thing in the world, the particular thing itself, and the concept of the thing in the mind. Rather than viewing universals as extra-mental realities as the extreme realists maintained, or considering them to be mere words or sounds, as the nominalists insisted, Abelard expanded the horizons of the possible categories of reality by suggesting that universals gain their objective reality as a result of concepts of the mind derived from the process of mental abstraction.

Thomas Provenzola

Bibliography

Abelard, Peter. *Ethical Writings: 'Ethics' and 'Dialogue between a Philosopher, a Jew, and a Christian.'* Translated by Paul Vincent Spade. Indianapolis, IN: Hackett, 1995.

———. *Sic et Non*. Edited by B.B. Boyer and R.P. McKean. Chicago: University of Chicago Press, 1978.

Bower, Jeffery E., and Kevin Guilfoy, eds. *The Cambridge Companion to Abelard*. Cambridge, UK: Cambridge University Press, 2004.

Clanchy, M.T. *Abelard: A Medieval Life*. Malden, MA: Wiley-Blackwell, 1999.

Marenbon, John. *The Philosophy of Peter Abelard*. Cambridge, UK: Cambridge University Press, 1999.

ADOPTIONISM

Adoptionism names a problematic attempt to explain the Christian doctrine of the incarnation of the Word (John 1:1,14,18) by claiming that Jesus was just a human being who, for different reasons, was deified and/or given divine powers, and so "adopted" as God's Son. In whatever form, adoptionism is directly related to the doctrine of Christ and more indirectly related to the doctrine of God.

In the early second century, while the new church was wrestling with how to work out its dual commitments to monotheism (inherited from Judaism) and its worship of Jesus as truly God (and truly human), it was inevitable that, for a time, adoptionist-like theories would arise. The very early *Shepherd of Hermas* seems to teach that the Redeemer was a virtuous man chosen by God, and to whom the Spirit was united at his baptism. He therefore could do the work God called him to do and, because he was faithful, God "adopted" him as his Son with great power. Another early second-century position represented a Jewish-Christian sect (Ebionites) who taught that Jesus, though virgin-born, was only a human being. He kept the Mosaic Law perfectly, and so was made (adopted as) the Messiah and God's Son at his baptism by the coming of God's Spirit upon him. The early church regarded this as heresy.

The position that most emphatically embodied the heresy of adoptionism, according to the early church synods and councils (and to the present), was the teaching brought to Rome about AD 190 by a learned Byzantine leather merchant named Theodotus. He held that Jesus was conceived by the Holy Spirit but lived an ordinary human life, with the exception that he was surpassingly virtuous. It was at Jesus' baptism that the Christ-Spirit came upon him, and from that moment, he became the Christ, and though not yet divine, he was "adopted" as God's Son. It was only at the resurrection that Jesus was deified. This view, improperly named *dynamic monarchianism*, continued for the next century and was represented most prominently by Paul of Samosata (mid third century). Such adoptionism was condemned as heresy at the synod of Antioch (268).

Later forms of this heresy broke out in the eighth century in both Spain and northern Europe. Under Charlemagne's leadership, these were condemned as heresy. It should be added that numerous adoptionistic-like views of Christ have arisen from and since the eighteenth-century Enlightenment. These views assumed a Newtonian universe in which God cannot directly act. Hence, for these liberal or neoliberal Christians, Jesus cannot be the pre-existent Son/Word of God incarnate, but rather only a mere human being who was uniquely "dependent" on God, or "open" to God, thereby he "became" a central source of human transformation.

As noted, this is *directly* a Christological heresy and *indirectly* a problem for the doctrine of God. Christologically, the adoptionist wants to "explain away" the Christian teaching of the divine and human natures in Jesus Christ and how they relate. Yet while trying to "sound" somehow trinitarian via an *adopted* "Son" via the "Spirit," all these assume a *Unitarian* view of God, not trinitarian.

John Douglas Morrison

Bibliography

Epiphanius. *Nicene Fathers*, chapter 54.

Gonzalez, J. *A History of Christian Thought*. New York: Harper & Row, 1984.

Grillmeier, A. *Christ in Christian Tradition*. Louisville, KY: Westminster John Knox, 1988.

Kelly, J.N.D. *Early Christian Doctrines*. Harrisburg, PA: Continuum, 2000.

Pelikan, Jaroslav. *The Christian Tradition: A History of the Development of Doctrine*, vols. 1-2. Chicago: University of Chicago Press, 1975, 1977.

A

ADVENTISTS

The term *Adventists* is often used in a broad sense to refer to various Christian groups who believe in the imminent and literal second advent of Christ. However, it is more specifically used to define Seventh Day Adventists (SDA) and other splinter groups including the Church of God (Abrahamic Faith) and the Adventist Christian Church. The General Conference of Seventh Day Adventists acknowledges 27 fundamental beliefs that include generally orthodox views mixed with doctrines that are unique to SDA. Among their distinctive teachings are the strict observance of the Saturday Sabbath, belief that SDA is the "remnant" church of the last days, the prophetic ministry of Ellen G. White, the "continuing and authoritative truth" of her writings, and the beginning of "investigative judgment" of Christ's heavenly ministry in 1844.

Around 1818, William Miller (1782–1849) became convinced that Christ would return in 1843. He arrived at his calculation by interpreting the 2300 days in Daniel 8:14 as referring to 2300 years beginning in 457 BC and culminating in AD 1843 with the return of Christ to "cleanse the temple," which Miller understood to be the church. When 1843 passed without the advent of Christ, Miller was persuaded to recalculate the date as October 22, 1844 (the Day of Atonement). When Christ did not return on that day, Miller abandoned any further predictions. However, Adventist Hiram Edson claimed to have a vision of Christ entering the Holy of Holies in heaven on that day, explaining that the great Day of Disappointment was really the great Day of Atonement. In the meantime, Ellen G. White (1827–1915) claimed to have a series of prophetic visions that affirmed Edson's view and also focused on the importance of strict observance of the Saturday Sabbath.

SDA eschatology tends to hold a historicist view of biblical prophecy, interpreting various historical events (earthquakes, solar eclipses, meteoric showers, and so on) as fulfillments of predicted events. SDA also tend to view the 1260 days of Revelation 11:3 as 1260 years of papal dominance by the Roman Catholic Church, which would then be "wounded," but not exterminated, by the Protestant Reformation. Most SDA teach that a resurgence of the papacy will lead to a last-days apostasy that can be resisted only by those who "keep the commandments of God" (Revelation 14:12). SDA generally abstain from alcohol, drugs, tobacco, and most meats, preferring a vegetarian diet as means of attaining optimum health for the believer. As a result, SDA are significantly involved in efforts relating to healthy lifestyles and the medical sciences. Among the many SDA institutions nationwide are Andrews University (Michigan) and Loma Linda University (California).

Ed Hindson

A

Bibliography

Hoekema, Anthony. *The Four Major Cults*. Grand Rapids: Eerdmans, 1984.

Martin, Walter. *Kingdom of the Cults*. Minneapolis: Bethany Fellowship, 1965.

Paxton, G.J. *The Shaking of Adventism*. Grand Rapids: Baker, 1977.

Seventh-Day Adventists Believe. Silver Spring, MD: General Conference of SDA, 1988.

Tucker, Ruth. *Another Gospel*. Grand Rapids: Zondervan, 1989.

AFRICAN METHODIST EPISCOPAL CHURCH

The African Methodist Episcopal Church (AME Church) is an African-American Methodist denomination founded in 1816 in Philadelphia. In 2011, there were 2.5 million members in attendance at churches in 31 countries and territories.

Richard Allen and other free blacks created the Free African Society in 1787. The Society's purpose was to provide for the various needs of Philadelphia's African American community. This Society provided a backdrop for the creation of the AME Church. Prior to 1787, Allen and others were members of the biracial St. George's Methodist Episcopal Church in Philadelphia. While attending a worship service during that year, Allen and other free blacks were told to move from an area reserved for white members to an area reserved for blacks. Allen and the others decided to leave the church immediately.

They used the Free African Society as a springboard to develop a worshipping community for themselves. Yet because of the Methodist leadership structure they retained, this new African-American church was subservient to St. George's. A few of the black members of the new church (including Allen) purchased a blacksmith shop and turned the building into a church in 1794. In that same year, the church was dedicated by Francis Asbury. Then in 1799, Allen was ordained by Asbury. In 1816, out of a meeting with over 1000 African-Americans, the AME Church was formed. It was the first African-American denomination founded in the USA. The original church was rebuilt in 1890 and is today known as Mother Bethel Church. The property it sits on is the oldest parcel of land in the US that has been owned continuously by African-Americans.

Through the formation of a denomination, the AME Church withdrew from the white Methodist Episcopal (today's United Methodist) denomination. It still retained the structure of the Methodist Episcopal denomination and its moral and scriptural

A focus, and it continued to use the *Book of Discipline*, although some sections were altered. Basically it developed as the African-American alternative to the white Methodist Episcopal Church. Over the next 50 years the AME Church developed a publishing house (1818, the first created and owned by African-Americans), sent missionaries to Canada and Haiti (1827), founded a university (Wilberforce in 1856), ordained the first African-American chaplain (1863), and began working with ex-slaves in the South (1864).

After the Civil War, the AME Church expanded its numbers and churches in the South. Many Methodist ex-slaves left the white-dominated Methodist Episcopal Church and joined the AME Church (along with many joining the AME Zion Church as well as creating the Colored ME Church, now the Christian ME, or CME, Church). Since the Civil War, the AME Church has continued its emphasis on education by opening colleges and seminaries in the US and schools in Liberia and South Africa. It continues to operate *The Christian Recorder*, which it began in 1848 and is the longest-running publication operated by African-Americans in the US.

Mark Nickens

Bibliography

Gregg, Howard D. *History of the African Methodist Episcopal Church: The Black Church in Action.* Nashville, TN: AME Sunday School Union, 1980.

Lincoln, C. Eric, and Lawrence H. Mamiya. *The Black Church in the African American Experience.* Durham, NC: Duke University Press, 1995.

Pinn, Anne H., and Anthony B. Pinn. *Fortress Introduction to Black Church History.* Minneapolis: Fortress Press, 2002.

ALBIGENSIANS

An eleventh- and twelfth-century dualistic form of Christianity based on Manichean beliefs with regard to the struggle between good and evil, *Albigensians* (sometimes called *Cathari* or *Bogomiles*) believed that salvation was attained by gradual self-purification from matter. They condemned marriage, procreation, most foods, and the use of any materials in acts of worship. Because of their disdain for the body, they rejected the ideas of a literal heaven or hell. One of the last surviving holdouts of Arianism, they flourished in the region of Provence in southern France until they were crushed by a papal crusade in 1209–1229.

The Albigensians were divided into the *perfecti* (clergy) and the *credentes* (believers). The *perfecti* lived by rigid asceticism and the *credentes* tried to become *perfecti* by receiving their only sacrament, the *consolamentum*. For those who failed to live by their rigid standards, friends could ensure their salvation by self-starvation, a ceremonial death called *endura*. Count Raymond VI of Toulouse protected the Abigensians until his agents killed a papal legate, which provoked a papal reprisal that led to the crusade against the Albigensians.

Ed Hindson

Bibliography

Costen, Michael. *The Cathars and the Albigensian Crusade*. Manchester Medieval Studies. Manchester, UK: Manchester University Press, 1997.

Oldenburg, Zoe. *Massacre at Montsegur: A History of the Albigensian Crusade*. London: Phoenix Press, 2001.

Sumption, Jonathan. *The Albigensian Crusade*. London: Faber & Faber, 2000.

ALEXANDRIAN SCHOOL

The Alexandrian school generally refers to the approach to interpreting Scripture taken by some key exegetes from Alexandria, Egypt, beginning in the second and third centuries. This school held to the allegorical approach to biblical interpretation, in contrast to the Antiochene school, which emphasized a more historical and grammatical approach to Scripture.

Allegory, which literally means "another proclamation," refers to finding a figurative meaning in a text of Scripture. This interpretive tool was not unique to Christian theologians in the ancient world as Homer and Cicero made use of it, while the Jewish exegete Philo also interpreted the Hebrew Scriptures in this manner. It seems that both Jewish and Christian interpreters favored this approach because they were influenced by the neo-Platonic worldview of their day—a worldview that saw God as completely other, without emotion, and incapable of being described by human qualities. Thus, when early Christian exegetes read Bible passages that spoke of God's wrath or of God having humanlike qualities (i.e., hands or feet), they were compelled to find a figurative meaning behind the words.

The most well-known Alexandrian biblical scholar was Origen (184–254). In the fourth book of his *De Principiis* (*On First Principles*), Origen outlined his rationale

A

for interpreting Scripture allegorically and defined three levels of interpretation: the bodily level, which was a basic literal interpretation; a soulish level, which pointed to the moral or ethical meaning in a text; and the spiritual level, the ever-present mystical meaning that points to Christ and relationship with God. For Origen, the spiritual level was the most important and was only accessed by a spiritually attuned exegete. In addition to these levels of interpretation, Origen emphasized reading Scripture Christologically, believing that all Scripture pointed in some way to Christ. Finally, he was a champion of typology and held that the accounts and stories of the Old Testament prefigured the realities and promises of the New Testament.

While Alexandrian exegesis originated in the Greek-speaking church, the allegorical approach to Scripture figured prominently in both the Eastern and Western Church in the Patristic period. The allegorical method was further employed by Latin fathers such as Ambrose, Augustine, Jerome, and Gregory the Great.

Edward Smither

Bibliography

Bray, Gerald L. *Biblical Interpretation: Past & Present.* Downers Grove, IL: InterVarsity, 2000.

Origen. *De Principiis (On First Principles). Ante-Nicene Fathers,* vol. 4. Edited by A. Roberts and J. Donaldson. Peabody, MA: Hendrickson, 2004.

Trigg, Joseph. *Origen (The Early Church Fathers).* London: Routledge, 1998.

Young, Frances. "Alexandrian and Antiochene Exegesis." *A History of Biblical Interpretation,* vol. 1. Edited by Alan J. Hauser. Grand Rapids: Eerdmans, 2003.

AMBROSE, SAINT (340–397)

Ambrose of Milan was born in Trier (modern Germany), where his father served as an official in the Roman government. After receiving a liberal arts education in Rome, Ambrose also pursued a career in politics and was appointed governor of Aemilia-Liguria (in northern Italy) in 370. In 374, he intervened in a disputed episcopal election in Milan and, following an unusual turn of events, ended up leaving his role with the state and becoming the city's new bishop. According to his biographer Paulinus, the new bishop was baptized barely a week before his consecration. Despite this intriguing beginning, Ambrose continued to serve as bishop of Milan until his death in 397.

Having inherited a church in a region that was greatly affected by the Arian heresy,

Ambrose's primary task as bishop was preaching. In addition, he served as a metropolitan bishop, meaning that he oversaw the ministries of the bishops of northern Italy. Part of this role included participation in regional church councils that addressed theological matters as well as church practices. In particular, he played an influential role at the councils of Sirmium (378–379) and Aquileia (381), at which Arian thought was confronted.

Ambrose's key writings include *On the Faith*, a summary of the Christian faith addressed to the Emperor Gratian; *On the Mysteries,* a teaching for new Christians on baptism and the Lord's Supper; and *On the Duties of Ministers,* a manual for clergy that emphasized the character of a church leader. In addition, he penned 91 letters, many of which served to mentor other church leaders in theology and the work of ministry.

Aside from a commitment to doctrinal purity in the face of Arian teaching, Ambrose's career was marked by other key contributions. First, he believed that the government existed to serve the church, and when there was conflict between church and state, he took a firm stand. For instance, in 385, he staged a sit-in at the Portian basilica in Milan after the government attempted to give the building to the Arians. And in 390, after Emperor Theodosius I ordered a massacre in Thessalonica, Ambrose excommunicated the emperor until he repented. Second, he was innovative in making the singing of hymns a regular part of corporate worship in Milan. Third, he interpreted and preached the Scriptures allegorically, emphasizing the spiritual sense of the biblical text. Finally, he was instrumental in leading Augustine of Hippo to faith in Christ when Augustine came to Milan to pursue a teaching career. In fact, it was Ambrose's preaching and use of hymns that helped Augustine to discover the gospel.

Edward Smither

Bibliography

Ambrose, (Selected Works and Letters), *Nicene and Post-Nicene Fathers*, series 2, vol. 10. http://www.ccel.org/fathers.html.

Ramsey, Boniface. *Ambrose.* London: Routledge, 1997.

Smither, Edward L. *Augustine as Mentor: A Model for Preparing Spiritual Leaders.* Nashville, TN: Broadman & Holman Academic, 2008.

A

AMISH

A Christian sect numbering about 250,000 in North America, the Amish separated from the Mennonites in 1693 under the leadership of Jakob Ammann. Often recognized by external factors such as plain clothing, the use of horses and buggies for transportation, and their refusal to adopt various modern amenities, the spiritual reasons behind these choices are far more significant. With roots in the Anabaptist movement of the sixteenth and seventeenth centuries, the Amish were familiar with persecution. This led to a general distrust of the world as well as the various state churches of Europe. As Anabaptists, they also carried the ideas of the Reformation, but to even more conservative conclusions, with an emphasis on humility, separation from the world, nonviolence, hard work, and individual responsibility.

Though all these characteristics are shared by the Mennonites, by the end of the seventeenth century, some felt that the Mennonites were compromising with the world, particularly by not exercising church discipline as often or as completely as they ought. Eventually a confrontation ruptured between Jakob Ammann and Hans Reist in the spring of 1693. Those who sided with Ammann became known as Ammannish Mennonites, then later, simply as the Amish (Nolt, 39-45).

During the eighteenth and early nineteenth centuries the Amish experienced periods of persecution as well as favor from various civil and religious entities in France, Switzerland, Germany, and other parts of Europe. Both persecution in Europe and the promise of opportunity in the New World drew many Amish to North America. The virtual absence of persecution in Canada and the Colonies made it more difficult to remain separate from the world, thus many of the early Amish emigrants melded into the broader culture. Some, however, feared the loss of such biblical truths as "love not the world" and sought a new round of reforms aimed at preserving their application of the Christian doctrine of being a plain and separated people. Such efforts led to what is now known as the Old Order Amish.

The nineteenth century also brought challenges to and tensions among the Amish. While some accepted elements of the genteel life, others rejected them as superfluous or as expressions of pride and self-accomplishment, and thus evil. While the Amish were certainly against slavery and were often involved in abolitionist efforts, they were also reluctant to go to war for the cause because of their strong convictions about nonviolence. Agricultural machinery, household appliances, and other fruits of the industrial revolution have brought tensions among the Amish as well. Some reject all such developments as worldly, while others cautiously accept them provided there is no entanglement with the government or other worldly institutions. Even today some Amish are not so much interested in maintaining a certain antiquated lifestyle as they

are in maintaining a simple life free from entanglements with the world. However, **A**
tight internal controls, such as the practice of shunning (cutting off all social interaction with a sinning community member) are viewed as extreme and excessive by
many evangelicals.

Timothy Faber

Bibliography

Kraybill, Donald B, Steven M. Nolt, and David L. Weaver-Zercher. *The Amish Way:
Patient Faith in a Perilous World*. San Francisco: Jossey-Bass, 2010.

Nolt, Steven M. *A History of the Amish*. Intercourse, PA: Good Books, 1992.

AMYRAUT, MOÏSE (1596–1664)

A French theologian in the Calvinist tradition, Moïse Amyraut was noted for his
distinctive defense of the doctrine of unlimited atonement. Abandoning the classical
Calvinist view that Christ died only for the elect whom God has chosen beforehand
for salvation, Amyraut taught a conditional universalism. In addition to predesti-
nating the elect to salvation unconditionally, he argued that God has predestinated all
humans to salvation conditionally—that is, if they believe. This universal predestination does not actually save anyone; only those whom God has individually chosen for
salvation really come to belief. Nonetheless, claimed Amyraut, God can desire, and
sincerely does desire, the salvation of all humans, since all have a natural ability to
believe. However, because by themselves humans are morally incapable of exercising
faith, only the elect are actually saved:

> However, this act of divine love does not go beyond the point of pro-
> viding salvation to people if they do not refuse it. If they do refuse, *he
> removes this hope from them*, and by their unbelief they aggravate their
> condemnation. And thus the statement "God desires all people to be
> saved" necessarily includes this proviso: "if they believe." If they do
> not believe, God does not desire their salvation. God wills to make
> the grace of salvation universal and common for all humans; but this
> will is conditional: unless the condition is met, it is entirely ineffec-
> tive. We see, then, on what the fulfillment of the condition depends,
> and consequently we see the *particular* efficacy of God's *universal* grace
> (*Brief Traitté de la predestination*, 89-90).

A Amyraut's theology was not Arminian. For him, *God's initiative alone* ultimately determines who will be saved, whereas for Arminians the *individual's response* is decisive. Still, Amyraut's doctrine immediately met strong opposition among Calvinists. He was tried for heresy three times (and was acquitted each time). Charles Hodge's verdict may fairly represent the judgment of most theologians: Amyraut's teaching was "designed to take a middle ground between Augustinianism and Arminianism" but "is liable to the objections which press on both systems" (*Systematic Theology*, vol. 2, 322).

Because Scripture states that God "desires all people to be saved" (1 Timothy 2:4), Amyraut's viewpoint has remained influential, and other defenders of unlimited atonement are often considered his followers. These so-called *Amyraldians* have not always accepted Amyraut's central notion of hypothetical universalism. The nineteenth-century dispensationalist J.N. Darby, for example, suggested that Jesus offered himself as an unconditionally *universal* propitiation and a *limited* substitute: "He is a propitiation for the whole world. All has been done that is needed…But it will never be found in Scripture that Christ bore the sins of all. Had he done so, they never could be mentioned again, nor men judged according to their works" ("Propitiation and Substitution," 278).

As an instructor at the Protestant Academy at Saumur in France and a popular writer, Amyraut was an influential voice for Christian unity. His most famous student was William Penn, whose Pennsylvania *Charter of Liberties* (1701) is a landmark in the progress of American religious freedom.

Greg Enos

Bibliography

Amyraut, Moïse. *Brief traitté de la prédestination et ses principales dependences*. Saumur, France: Jean Lesnier & Isaac Desbordes, 1634, (available online).

Armstrong, Brian G. *Calvinism and the Amyraut Heresy: Protestant Scholasticism and Humanism in Seventeenth-Century France*. Eugene, OR: Wipf & Stock, 2004.

Darby, John Nelson. "Propitiation and Substitution." *The Collected Writings of J.N. Darby*, vol. 29, 286-288. Edited by William Kelly. London: G. Morrish, 1879.

Hodge, Charles. *Systematic Theology*. Grand Rapids: Eerdmans, 1977 (1872).

ANABAPTISTS

A

Continental reformers who rejected infant baptism and insisted upon believer's baptism were called *Anabaptists* (rebaptizers, or antipaedo Baptists) on account of their practice of baptizing believers upon their profession of faith. Because they did not accept the validity of infant baptism, they required believers to be rebaptized as adults. They have also been called the left wing of the Reformation (because they rejected more of the status quo of the medieval church than the other reformers), the stepchildren of the Reformation (because they were the children of mother church, but not of father state), or the radical reformers (because they sought to build a church like that of the first century without the traditions added to it in subsequent centuries).

Early Reformation historians made the mistake of supposing that some radical millenarians, as at Munster in 1535, or some rationalists, as Servetus (1511–1553), who was burned at the stake in John Calvin's Geneva for rejecting the eternality of Christ, were the essence of the Anabaptist movement. However, the true essence of the movement is to be found in the Swiss Brethren in Zurich, the Hutterites in Moravia, and the Mennonites in the Netherlands.

The Swiss Brethren arose under Ulrich Zwingli in Zurich, Switzerland. When their convictions led them to adopt believer's baptism, Zwingli's movement began to persecute them. Felix Manz, one of the earliest of them, was the first martyr of the Protestant Reformation to die at the hands of other Protestants when he was drowned in the Limmat River in Zurich in 1527. Perhaps the most influential of the Swiss Brethren was Balthazar Hubmaier (1481–1528), who authored *The Christian Baptism of Believers*. The Swiss Brethren laid the foundation for later Anabaptists.

Hubmaier was influential in the rise of the Anabaptists who came to be known as the Hutterites. They were named after Jacob Hutter, who was martyred in 1536, and were best known for their practice of the community of goods, patterned after Acts 2:44-45. They still exist today. The Mennonites, led by Menno Simons (1496–1561), gathered the remnants of the Munster fiasco, weaned them of their radical excesses, and built a movement best known for its practice of discipline, or shunning. They are the largest and best known of existing Anabaptists today.

The Anabaptists accepted the doctrines of the other reformers: the sole authority of the Scriptures, grace and faith alone for salvation, and the priesthood of the believer. To these they added the supremacy of the New Testament as the authority for Christian living and church order, the gathered (voluntary) church, believer's baptism, strict discipleship, pacifism, and religious freedom (secured by the separation of church and

A state). They also had an influence on the rise of English Baptists. This connection to the Baptists was most obvious in the rise of the General Baptists, but is also apparent with the Particular Baptists as well.

Carl Deimer

Bibliography

Estep, William R. *The Anabaptist Story*. 3d ed. Grand Rapids: Eerdmans, 1995.

Littell, Franklin H. *The Origins of Sectarian Protestantism*. New York: Macmillan, 1964.

Verdiun, Leonard, and Franklin Littell. *The Reformers and Their Stepchildren*, 14. The Dissent and Nonconformity Series. Paris, AR: The Baptist Standard Bearer, 2001.

Williams, George H. *The Radical Reformation*. 3d ed. Kirksville, MO: Truman State University Press, 2000.

ANGLICANISM

Anglicanism is a global Christian fellowship that finds its roots in the Church of England. English Christianity was clearly organized by the fourth century when several British bishops were sent as representatives to the Council of Arles in 314. In 597, Pope Gregory the Great appointed a Benedictine monk named Augustine as the first archbishop of Canterbury to promote the growth and development of Christianity in England. As the Catholic Church in England grew, a steady national identity began to take hold, with clear evidences of resistance to Rome's authority emerging as early as the fourteenth century. In the sixteenth century, Henry VIII (ruled 1509–1547) claimed sovereignty over the church as well as the state, establishing himself as "supreme head in Earth of the Church of England," and later the "supreme governor." Henry's daughter, Mary I (ruled 1553–1558), restored papal authority in England, but then her sister, Queen Elizabeth I (ruled 1558–1603), was a part of a political landscape that saw the emergence of a *via media*, or middle way, between the early Protestants and Rome, which came to characterize Anglicanism. The episcopacy was retained in the new Church of England, but most of the leadership in the new church no longer considered it to have divine origins.

From the time of the Protestant Reformation, the Church of England's influence spread in conjunction with British exploration and colonization, with an early colonial presence in India and North America, among other places. Churches in these areas, **A** though independent and guided by local authorities, were nevertheless joined in communion by a mutual commitment and respect for one another, a common loyalty to the see of Canterbury, and an alignment with the faith and worship of the Church of England. Today, Anglicanism refers to the fellowship of Christians who are part of the Anglican Communion, a conglomeration of autonomous national churches that has no central authority figure or board. The communion between these churches is created by a common respect for the leadership of the archbishop of Canterbury and a common liturgy rooted in the various versions of the *Book of Common Prayer* (BCP). Originally published in 1549, the BCP serves as the distinct locus of Anglican doctrine and practice.

The first Anglican church in America was built in 1607 in Jamestown, Virginia. Out of the pressures of the American Revolution, the Protestant Episcopal Church in the United States of America emerged and was clearly organized as a national Anglican church in communion with the see of Canterbury by 1789. It would later officially change its name to the Episcopal Church in the United States of America in 1979. Since Anglicans have no Pope or chief authority, they continue to rely on dialogue and consensus in matters of faith and practice, with Scripture, tradition, and reason serving as guiding forces. Consensus on theological matters has often eluded the Anglican Communion, and some sects continue to establish unaffiliated regional and national organizations.

Recent years have seen a number of conservative congregations withdraw from the Anglican Communion over issues such as the ordination of openly practicing homosexuals. Other congregations have withdrawn from acknowledgment of the Archbishop of Canterbury over theological issues and preferred to align with the more conservative Anglican fellowships.

Brian Goard

Bibliography

Dickens, A.G. *The English Reformation*. 2d ed. University Park, PA: Pennsylvania State University Press, 1989.

McGrath, Alister E. *The Renewal of Anglicanism*. Harrisburg, PA: Morehouse, 1993.

Neill, Stephen, *Anglicanism*. 4th ed. Oxford: Oxford University Press, 1978.

Sykes, Stephen, John Booty, and Jonathan Knight. *The Study of Anglicanism*. Rev. ed. Minneapolis: Fortress Press, 1998.

ANSELM OF CANTERBURY (CA. 1033–1109)

Anselm of Canterbury was a medieval scholastic theologian born in Aosta, near modern Turin in northwest Italy, who studied under the learned Lanfranc (ca. 1005–1089) at the monastery of Bec in Normandy. He went on to great acclaim as one of the ablest practitioners of the dialectic method prior to Thomas Aquinas (1225–1274). Considered to be the father of scholastic theology, Anselm's approach argued for the rational credibility of Christian belief. It is this approach that gives rise to natural theology, which insists that, while drawing on the apparent necessary truths of reason, and without appeal to divine revelation or one's experiences with the concrete things of reality, one could arrive at certain objective truths about the world, including at least knowledge of God's existence and perhaps some of his other essential attributes, such as his goodness.

For nearly 30 years after succeeding Lanfranc as abbot of Bec, Anselm wrote and perfected his craft, ultimately producing his two celebrated works, notably the *Monologion* (1076) and the *Proslogion* ("Address"), written between 1077–1078 and containing his famous ontological proof for the existence of God. Throughout the *Proslogion*, Anselm was consciously guided by the maxim and subtitle of his work, "faith seeking understanding" (*fides quaerens intellectum*), and the phrase "I believe so that I may understand" (*credo ut intelligam*), reflecting the influence of Augustine of Hippo on his thought. Anselm argued in the ontological proof that persons have in their minds the idea of the greatest conceivable being, and that this being must be none other than the Christian God. Such a being must exist in reality as well as in the mind, and if such a being existed in the mind alone, he could be superseded by a being who existed in reality as well. Consequently, God must exist, since it's impossible to have the idea of the greatest conceivable being that does not include the notion that such a being must exist in reality apart from the mind.

Subsequent to his appointment as archbishop of Canterbury in 1093, Anselm produced his treatise *Cur Deus Home* ("Why God Became Man"), in which he attempted to prove by necessary reasons why the Christian account of the incarnation and atonement is rational to believe. Anselm first answered the objections of those who see the incarnation as contrary to reason, and then went on to use the same approach, apart from any appeal to revealed truth, to argue for the impossibility of redemption apart from the atoning work of Christ.

In constructing such arguments, Anselm attempted to show that faith and reason can work together in arriving at truth, and while reason alone cannot discover the truth of such claims as the incarnation and atonement, it can and does argue for their rational support.

Thomas Provenzola

Bibliography

Anselm, St. *Anselm of Canterbury: The Major Works*. Edited by Brian Davies and G.R. Evans. New York: Oxford University Press, 2008.

Davies, Brian, and Brian Leftow, eds. *The Cambridge Companion to Anselm*. Cambridge: Cambridge University Press, 2005.

Southern, Richard W. *Saint Anselm: A Portrait in Landscape*. Cambridge: Cambridge University Press, 1992.

Visser, Sandra, and Thomas Williams. *Anselm*. Oxford: Oxford University Press, 2008.

APOSTLES' CREED

Recited weekly in worship services around the world by congregations in the liturgical tradition, the text of the Apostles' Creed reads:

> I believe in God the Father almighty;
> Creator of heaven and earth,
> and in Christ Jesus his only Son, our Lord;
> who was conceived of the Holy Spirit, born of the virgin Mary,
> suffered under Pontius Pilate, was crucified, died and was buried,
> he descended into hell;
> on the third day he rose again from the dead,
> he ascended into heaven,
> and is seated as the right hand of God the Father almighty,
> whence he shall come to judge the living and the dead;
> I believe in the Holy Spirit,
> the holy catholic church,
> the communion of saints,
> the forgiveness of sins,
> the resurrection of the body,
> and life everlasting. Amen.

Though the declaration in this form dates to the eighth century, its contents can be traced to the second-century church at Rome and its worship practices. The term *creed* (from the Latin *credo*), literally means "I believe," and the Apostles' Creed was, in a sense, an oral exam for new believers as they entered the waters of baptism. According to his second-century worship manual *Apostolic Tradition,* Hippolytus of Rome (170–235) originally posed many of the lines of the Apostles' Creed as questions for new

A

believers. For instance, he would ask, "Do you believe in God the Father?" to which the candidate would reply, "I believe." In the third century, Cyprian of Carthage followed a similar practice. Later, this tradition of interrogation developed into an affirmation of faith for churches in the Western Roman Empire.

While the primary purpose of the Apostles' Creed was to declare what a Christian believed, it also contains propositions that were designed to counter heretical thinking. For instance, the statements that Jesus was "born of the virgin Mary" and "under Pontius Pilate, was crucified, died and was buried" probably challenged docetic and Gnostic claims that Jesus was merely a phantom and lacked a real body and authentic humanity. Such teaching was also countered by the Rule of Faith that was developing in the second and third centuries.

Edward Smither

Bibliography

Ferguson, Everett. *Early Christians Speak.* Abilene, TX: Abilene Christian University, 1987.

Kelly, J.N.D. *Early Christian Creeds.* London: Longmans, 1972.

Schaff, Philip. *Creeds of Christendom.* http://www.ccel.org/ccel/schaff/creeds1.i.html.

APOSTOLIC FATHERS

The name *Apostolic Fathers* is applied generally to Christian writers of the first and second centuries who were considered to have been personally acquainted with one or another of the apostles. There is no single ancient collection that contains all their works as a group. Their writings consist of primitive Christian literature prior to the apologists of the latter second century, forming a bridge between the latter and the writings of the New Testament.

Although there has not always been unanimous agreement among scholars as to which writers to include among the *patrum apostolicorum*, or "Apostolic Fathers," there is little doubt among scholars that Clement of Rome (ca. 97), Ignatius of Antioch (ca. 110–117), and Polycarp of Smyrna (ca. 110–120) were personally acquainted with the apostles, as attested by Irenaeus (*Adv. Haer.*, III, iii, 3, 4) and Eusebius (*Hist. Eccl.* III.36; v, 20). Other extant postapostolic writers include the author of the *Didache* ("Teachings of the Twelve Apostles," ca. 80–100), the *Epistle of Barnabas* (96–98), *The Shepherd of Hermas* (ca. 150), and *Expositions of the Discourses of the Lord* by Papias (ca.

150). *The Letter to Diogenes's* (ca. 130) is also included. Geographically, they represent a fairly large footprint, including Rome (Clement and Hermas), Smyrna (Polycarp and Ignatius), Hierapolis in Phrygia (Papias), and Egypt (author of the *Didache*[?] and Barnabas).

Like the writers of the canonical New Testament documents, the Apostolic Fathers wrote epistles, or letters, written to assuage the concerns or needs of particular individuals or local assemblies. They had a fairly wide appeal in the second century and later, as reported by Eusebius (*Hist. Eccl.* III. 16; IV.23) and attested by their inclusion in some of the earliest collections of the canonical writings, including the Codex Alexandrinus and the Codex Sinaiticus.

The letters of the Apostolic Fathers were never intended to be scholarly treatises on matters of doctrine or philosophy. Nevertheless, they are extremely valuable, attesting to the teachings of the earliest Christian communities. The writings were produced at a time when the New Testament canon was a long way from being fixed, and nearly every book of the New Testament (except 3 John and Philemon) is cited directly or indirectly. Among the doctrinal teachings presented are the Trinitarian formula, the deity and humanity of Christ, the redemptive work of Christ, his high priestly ministry, and his shed blood offered as a vicarious ransom for our sins. Other teachings include eternal life for the believer, justification by faith, and the importance of good works. Clement, for example, considered the teachings of Paul and James concerning faith and works to be complementary, in turn testifying against the thesis of a conflict between Jewish and Gentile assemblies in early Christianity.

Daniel R. Mitchell

Bibliography

Ehrman, Bart D. *The Apostolic Fathers*. 2 vols. Loeb Classical Library. Cambridge: Harvard University Press, 2003.

Gebhardt, Oscar de, Adolfus Harnack, and Theodorus Zahn. *Patrum Apostolicorum Opera*. Lipsiae: J.C. Hinrichs, 1877.

Lightfoot, J.B. *The Apostolic Fathers*. 5 vols. London: Macmillan, 1893. Updated by Holmes, Michael, *The Apostolic Fathers: Greek Texts and English Translations*. 3d rev. ed. Grand Rapids: Baker, 2007.

AQUINAS, THOMAS (1225–1274)

Thomas Aquinas was an influential theologian of the Roman Catholic Church during the medieval period. He emphasized the need for reason in the exercise of faith. Born to noble parents, Count Landolfo d'Aquino and Countess Teodora of Chieti, his father was lord of Rocca Secca (a part of the kingdom of Naples). He was educated at the Benedictine monastery of Monte Cassino and the University of Naples (1239), where he studied liberal arts under Peter of Ireland. Thomas became a Dominican sometime between 1240 and 1243. His family disapproved of this decision and had him imprisoned at the castle of Rocca Secca for two years.

Aquinas later went to Cologne in 1244–1245 to study under Albert the Great. Thomas became a priest in 1250 and eventually regent master of the University of Paris in 1257. His methodology is representative of the tradition of scholasticism. He was called the "Angelic Doctor" (*Doctor Agelicus*) due to his fidelity to calling. Medieval scholasticism fostered the notion that religious ideas were best preserved, developed, and defended through critical thinking and the application of the dialectical method of investigation, a method which engages an argument's point(s) of tension by the critical appraisal of contradicting sides.

Aquinas's main literary contribution to scholasticism and Roman Catholic theology was his *Summa Theologica*. Thomas's system of thought, sometimes called "Thomism," adapted Aristotelian philosophy to delineate between reason and faith. The resultant natural theology suggested that ideas about God can and should be formulated by the deductive study of all levels of science as building blocks to achieve the final beatific vision of who God really is. Thomas rejected special illumination and effectively modeled the discipline of theological discourse as both a subordinated and deductive science rather than a movement of divine revelation from above to below. Through human effort and analogies concerning the essence of created things (*analogia entis,* "analogy of being"), the academy of sacred scholars could arrive at a proper understanding of the church's beliefs.

Aquinas wrote more than 60 texts of different kinds, most notably his two summaries, *Summa Theologica* and *Summa Contra Gentiles*. He also authored a commentary on the works of Aristotle in addition to his numerous scriptural commentaries (Job, Gospel of John, Ephesians, Galatians, Hebrews, Philippians, Thessalonians). Thomas was declared a saint in 1323 and the patron of Catholic schools in 1880.

Christopher Moody

A

Bibliography

Aquinas, Thomas. *The Summa Theologica*. Translated by Fathers of the English Dominican Province. Westminster, PA: Christian Classics, 1981.

———. *Summa Contra Gentiles*. Edited by Joseph Kenny and Anton C. Pegis, et al. New York: Hanover House, 1957.

Cairns, Alan. *Dictionary of Theological Terms*, 78-79, 488. 3d ed. Greenville, SC: Ambassador Emerald International, 2002.

Melton, J. Gordon. *Religious Leader of America*. 2d ed. Detroit, MI: The Gale Group, 1999.

Weisheipl, James A. "Thomas Aquinas." *Dictionary of Christian Biography*. Edited by Michael Walsh. Collegeville, MN: Liturgical Press, 2001.

ARIUS AND ARIANISM

Arius (ca. 250–336), probably born in Libya (North Africa), studied under Lucian in Antioch. The theological schools in Antioch and Alexandria had become rivals in the third century and disagreed about issues pertaining to biblical interpretation and Christology. Arius left Antioch to become a deacon and later a priest at a church in Alexandria. Arius was a popular preacher who often put his thoughts to memorable tunes for the people. He is described as tall, thin, and bearing the physical marks of his asceticism.

Alexander, Bishop of Alexandria, preached the sermon "The Great Mystery of the Trinity in Unity," which, in Arius's opinion, equivocated about the relationship between the Father and the Son. This sparked a lively debate that spilled into the streets of Alexandria and eventually to the Christian schools and churches across the Roman Empire. Regarding the origin of the Son, Arius maintained that "there was [a time] when He was not"—that the Son was the first of God's created beings, and the Son became the creator of the rest of the universe for the Father. Arius explained that sonship implies a beginning and that the titles of "Lord" and "God"—as applied by the apostles to Jesus—referred to Jesus' lordship over the apostles, not Jesus' equality with God. In response, Alexander defended the Son's eternal existence and full divinity and had Arius deposed from his church. Arius appealed, and eventually Emperor Constantine stepped in to call the very first ecumenical conference to bring about peace among the Christian churches and settle this doctrinal dispute.

More than 300 bishops from across the empire accepted the emperor's invitation to the Council of Nicæa (325). Since Arius was not a bishop himself, his friend

A Eusebius, Bishop of Nicomedia, represented Arius's views. When Eusebius claimed that Jesus was a creature, the majority of those participating in the council swung firmly in favor of Alexander and drafted a creed that absolutely opposed Arianism. The council considered Arians to be heretics, Arianism as unorthodox, and the emperor had the few Arian bishops exiled from their cities. This new cooperation between church and state brought about many consequences in the centuries to come.

In the time between this ecumenical council and the next in Constantinople (381), Arians and Nicenes experienced waxing and waning popularity, church positions, and state sanction. Arian and Nicene bishops and clergy were deposed and restored several times depending on who had the upper hand. Eventually, due in no small part to the steadfast work of Athansius (Bishop of Alexandria) and the Cappadocian Fathers (Basil the Great, Gregory of Nazianzus, and Gregory of Nyssa), the Nicene Creed was reaffirmed at the Council of Constantinople, and what few Arian leaders remained ended up moving northward to do missionary work among the Germanic tribes. When those tribes returned to conquer the Roman Empire in the next century, they were generally known as Aryans—a racial term still used today.

Arianism became associated with heretical movements that denied the eternity of the Son of God. These movements generally denied the eternal triune nature of God, insisting that Christ had a temporal beginning and was the creator only in an intermediate sense. The Jehovah's Witnesses, like the heretical Arians, also deny the eternality of the Son of God and the doctrine of the Trinity, and instead view the existence of Christ (the Logos) as an intermediate being between the Father (Creator) and the creation.

Kenneth Cleaver

Bibliography

Hanson, R.P.C. *The Search for the Christian Doctrine of God: The Arian Controversy, 318–381.* Grand Rapids: Baker Academic, 2005.

Wiles, Maurice. *Archetypal Heresy: Arianism through the Centuries.* New York: Oxford University Press, 2001.

Williams, Rowan. *Arius: Heresy and Tradition.* Grand Rapids: Eerdmans, 2002.

ARMINIANISM

Arminianism is a theological system named for Dutch theologian Jacob Arminius (1560–1609), whose theological development is found in the Reformed doctrines of eternal predestination. Arminius was a famous preacher in Amsterdam and occupied an important chair of theology at the University of Leyden from 1603 to 1609. As a Reformed theologian, Arminius was troubled by the views he imbibed under the tutelage of Theodore Beza and the famed school at Geneva. From his detailed studies of Scripture and early Christian writings, Arminius concluded that certain Calvinist doctrines of predestination were contrary to the nature of God.

Following John Calvin's death, Reformed scholasticism departed in some ways from the teachings of the great systematic theologian. With an emphasis on philosophy, the Protestant scholastics attempted to construct perfectly logical and coherent systems of doctrine. Efforts were made to resolve tensions found in some portions of Scripture, but the resulting conclusions created other problems. A key pressure point concerned the decrees of God. In his teachings on providence, Calvin emphasized that God works in all things. He wrote that the fall, election to salvation, and damnation were all encompassed in God's decree. God foreknows all that will happen because he foreordains all things, and he foreordains all things by his eternal decree. Theologians after Calvin, particularly Beza, became fascinated with the order of God's decrees and attempted to define them not chronologically, but logically. This logical priority attempted to answer things like why God created the world, and what God's ultimate purpose for humanity is.

In his scheme, Beza devised *supralapsarianism* to preserve God's glorifying of himself in preordaining some people to eternal life and others to eternal damnation. *Supra* indicates logical priority, and *lapsarian* refers to the fall of humanity. *Supralapsarianism,* then, literally means "something prior to the fall." In this case it is God's decree to predestine some to heaven or hell before his decree to create humanity and allow people to fall into sin. It was this outworking of doctrine against which Arminius rebelled. In his *Declaration of Sentiments*, Arminius proposed four alternative decrees: First, that God decreed to appoint Jesus Christ as mediator and redeemer of humanity. Second, that those who repent and believe in Christ will be saved. Third, God has given grace sufficiently and efficaciously for repentance and faith to all people. Fourth, God's decree is rooted from eternity past in his foreknowledge of those who would, by prevenient grace believe, and by subsequent grace persevere unto salvation (cf. *Works of Arminius*, 1:653-54).

For Arminius, to conclude that God had predestined some to heaven and others to hell was unthinkable. What of God's love for all humanity? What of God's expressed will that none should perish but that all should come to repentance? What of the call to "whosoever will"? What of the universality of the cross? In his preaching, Arminius attempted to find a balance between God's sovereign grace and the free will of humanity. In this Arminianism rejected unconditional election and irresistible grace. Election referred not to individuals, but to classes of people, believer or unbeliever. Election is conditioned not on God's will of decree, but on God's foreknowledge of free human actions. In addition, grace works with the human will, not against it.

For many Calvinists, this smacked of Roman Catholic synergism (the belief that salvation is the work of both God and man). A bitter debate ensued in Amsterdam chiefly resulting from a barrage of attacks levied against Arminius by his fellow chair of theology at Leyden, Franciscus Gomarus. This debate went on until Arminius's death in 1609. After Arminius's death, leading Dutch ministers and laymen penned the "Remonstrance," which summarized Arminian doctrine in five points. It was these five points that inspired the more widely recognized Calvinistic response codified at the Synod of Dort in the acronym TULIP (1618–1619). The Synod of Dort, a meeting of Reformed divines, was conducted in response to the work of the Arminian Remonstrants and canonized as official Reformed Church doctrine exactly opposite what the Arminians had previously stated.

Using the five points as a guide, Arminianism teaches depravity, but not to such a degree that a person is totally incapable of some response to God. Still, Arminianism acknowledges the effects of sin on the human constitution and the necessity of God's prevenient grace to restore humanity. Election is not based merely on God's sovereign choice, but is conditioned on the legitimate, personal response of faith. In this, election is according to God's foreknowledge as noted previously in the divine decrees. Given this, the extent of the atonement is universal in scope, general, rather than particular. This means that we may legitimately say that Christ died for all people, not simply the elect, but only believers will be saved. As God draws the elect, grace is not irresistible, as Calvin claimed. God's grace works cooperatively with the human spirit, drawing and wooing the necessary response, but always in such a way as to preserve the legitimacy of human responsibility before God. Salvation remains, however, only for those who persevere. It is possible within Arminian doctrine that one may fall away from the faith, grieving the Spirit of God and being condemned in sin.

The bitterest controversies over Arminianism in the Netherlands would eventually die down following an official tolerance granted in 1631, and Arminian influences would spread throughout the world in Protestant churches. John Wesley became the most influential Arminian, holding to a stronger view of total depravity and thus a highlighted need for God's grace. A type of synergism was retained in which Christ's sacrifice delivered all people from the initial effects of the fall and granted sufficient grace to allow repentance and faith. This theological move shifted some of the Reformed emphasis on God's act to a more pietistic stress on human response. This stress motivates evangelistic fervor and the persistent need to call all people to respond to God by believing the gospel.

Keith Church

Bibliography

Arminius, Jacob. *Works of Jacob Arminius*. 3 vols. Translated by James Nichols and William Nichols. Grand Rapids: Baker, 1986.

Bangs, Carl. *Arminius: A Study in the Dutch Reformation*. 2d ed. Grand Rapids: Zondervan, 1985.

González, Justo. *The Story of Christianity: The Early Church to the Present Day*. Peabody, MA: Prince, 1999.

Muller, Richard A. *God, Creation, and Providence in the Thought of Jacob Arminius*. Grand Rapids: Baker, 1985.

Olson, Roger. *The Story of Christian Theology*. Downers Grove, IL: InterVarsity, 1999.

ARMINIUS, JACOB (JACOBUS) (1559–1609)

A Dutch theologian born the same year John Calvin published the final edition of his *Institutes*, Jacob Arminius is best known as the namesake of Arminianism, the antithesis of Calvinistic doctrine. Arminius was, however, a thoroughly trained Calvinist in the Reformed tradition. An astute student, he studied at Leyden, Basle, and Geneva under Theodore Beza. At a time when Reformation doctrine was taking shape, Arminius became a clear theological voice and gained great influence as a preacher from his famous pulpit in Amsterdam. Because of his solid reputation, the church in Amsterdam asked him to refute the views of Dirck Koornhert, a theologian who had challenged certain Calvinist doctrines of predestination. Arminius, however, under careful study of Scripture and the writings of the early church, concluded that Koornhert was in fact correct.

In 1603, Arminius became professor at the University of Leiden. From one of two important chairs of theology, his opinions became the matter of much debate. Occupying the other chair of theology at Leiden was Francis Gomarus. Almost immediately

A

Gomarus began attacking Arminius for his views on human freedom in the acts of belief and repentance. Gomarus followed the supralapsarian doctrine of predestination, which states that God decreed the fall before creation, which, to Arminius, made God the author of sin. Thus the battle lines were drawn with followers rallying around these two banner bearers.

The issue at stake was not whether there was divine predestination, but rather the basis on which predestination takes place. Arminius concluded predestination was the result of God's foreknowledge based on those who God foresaw would at some point in time place their faith in Christ. In contrast, Gomarus held that faith was the result of predestination such that whether a person would or would not receive Christ was based on God's decree before the foundation of the world. For Arminius, the sovereign decree was that Jesus Christ would be the redeemer of humanity, not that some would be saved and some would perish. The later conclusion seemed to diminish the doctrine of God's love and revealed will that none should perish, but that all would come to repentance. In most every other way, Arminius was a strict Calvinist. Interestingly the conflict turned out to be an internecine debate. Arminius died in 1609, and thus never saw the issuance of the "Remonstrance," the five articles against Calvinism, in 1610.

Arminius published many treatises, which were put together in three large volumes. His primary doctrinal works related to the Arminian controversy over God's decrees, providence, and predestination. They are *Examination of Dr. Perkins's Pamphlet on Predestination* (1602), *A Declaration of Sentiments* (1608), *A Letter Addressed to Hippolytus A Collibus* (1608), and *Certain Articles to Be Diligently Examined and Weighed* (nd). Arminius wrote many other important works related to his pastoral duties, as well as commentaries on Romans 7 and 9.

Keith Church

Bibliography

Arminius, Jacob. *Works of Jacob Arminius*. 3 vols. Translated by James Nichols and William Nichols. Grand Rapids: Baker, 1986.

Bangs, Carl. *Arminius: A Study in the Dutch Reformation*. 2d ed. Grand Rapids: Zondervan, 1985.

González, Justo. *The Story of Christianity: The Early Church to the Present Day*. Peabody, MA: Prince Press, 1999.

Muller, Richard A. *God, Creation, and Providence in the Thought of Jacob Arminius*. Grand Rapids: Baker, 1985.

Olson, Roger. *The Story of Christian Theology*. Downers Grove, IL: InterVarsity, 1999.

ASBURY, FRANCIS (1745–1816)

Born in 1745 near Birmingham, England, American Methodist bishop Francis Asbury apprenticed as a metalworker when the British Isles stood on the brink of the Industrial Revolution. He began attending Methodist class and band meetings, and at age 17, while still an apprentice, became a local preacher. He became a full-time minister in 1768, when he was admitted into full connection and given his own circuit.

In 1771, Asbury arrived in Philadelphia, part of a second wave of preachers chosen by John Wesley himself to provide more guidance to the growing Methodist movement in the colonies. Unlike others, who saw the American movement as but an extension of the English, Asbury believed the unique social and political situation of America would help create a distinct form of Methodism (*American Saint,* 72). But because Methodism was still technically a movement within the Anglican Church at that time, Asbury and his fellow ministers were supposed to unify the fledgling American movement and bring it into closer connection with its English counterpart.

The Revolutionary War constituted the biggest impediment to this task. Asbury's standing in America increased during this time, as he was one of two Wesley appointees to remain in the country during the war. Nevertheless, authority was difficult to assert, as the spirit of independence ran high among American Methodists, especially those in the South, who owed very little to Asbury or any other Wesley lieutenants. It was not until 1780 that American Methodists recognized Asbury's authority. Four years later, John Wesley finally agreed to the establishment of a separate Methodist Church in America, also with an episcopal form of government. Asbury was appointed, again by Wesley, as one of two superintendents, the other being Thomas Coke. In order to ensure true separation from Wesley and English Methodism, Asbury refused to accept his ordination unless it was voted on and approved by a conference of American preachers. This occurred at the Christmas Conference in December 1784, and soon he and Coke took the title of bishop (*Taking Heaven by Storm,* 140).

While Asbury ensured that American Methodism would retain its connectional structure, he contended with certain circumstances unique to the United States that both challenged his authority and reshaped Methodism in the new nation. Following the rest of English Methodism, Asbury was ardently antislavery. However, efforts made at the General Conferences of 1784 and 1800 to forbid Methodists from holding slaves failed. This topic remained contentious until the Civil War. The camp meeting, however, served as a unifying factor. During the Cane Ridge Revival of 1801 in Kentucky, Asbury encouraged the use of mass extended gatherings, which fit in nicely with the existing system of Methodist quarterly meetings.

Although a bishop, Asbury maintained an itinerant lifestyle, traveling thousands of miles on horseback or carriage, including several trips across the Appalachian Mountains. He maintained a journal of his travels and records of his correspondences throughout his ministry in America. In 1816, while en route to the General Conference in Baltimore, he died at a private home in Spotsylvania County, Virginia.

Joseph Super

Bibliography

Clark, Elmer T., J. Manning Potts, and Jacob S. Payton, eds. *The Journal and Letters of Francis Asbury.* 3 vols. Nashville, TN: Abingdon Press, 1958.

Salter, Darius L. *America's Bishop: The Life of Francis Asbury.* Nappanee, IN: Francis Asbury Press, 2003.

Wigger, John. *American Saint: Francis Asbury and the Methodists.* New York: Oxford University Press, 2009.

———. *Taking Heaven by Storm: Methodism and the Rise of Popular Christianity in America.* Chicago: University of Illinois Press, 1998.

ASSEMBLIES OF GOD

The Assemblies of God, USA (AG) began in 1914 in Hot Springs, Arkansas, as a gathering of like-minded Pentecostals, mostly from the South. Today, the Assemblies of God is the largest Pentecostal denomination in the United States (though the group prefers the designation *fellowship* over *denomination*) with more than three million adherents. Several Protestant movements already underway in America at the beginning of the twentieth century helped give rise to the AG—they included Wesleyan perfectionism, premillennialism, restorationist movements like that of John Alexander Dowie, Charles F. Parham, and Frank Sanford, and the Keswick higher life movement that began in England in 1875. The Azusa Street Revival led by William J. Seymour, which began in Los Angeles in 1906, played a key role in the growth of American Pentecostalism and the birth of the AG.

Beginning in 1913, Pentecostal papers across the country began to run an advertisement announcing a call for a general council to be held in Hot Springs, Arkansas, in April of 1914. More than 300 people responded. Four specific purposes were given for the event. Organizers described their goals as follows: (1) to come to a consensus on doctrinal beliefs, (2) to "conserve the work," (3) to establish better means of supporting missionaries, and (4) to provide their ministers with legal standing. Organizers labeled the event a "general assembly of God," which was meant to allay fears about denominationalism. In the years that followed, especially from 1914 to 1918, the council would continue to meet to address doctrinal differences, especially as they related to sanctification, the Trinity, and tongues speaking. The AG allowed for divergent views regarding the precise nature of sanctification, but developed a harder stance against Oneness teaching. Oneness Pentecostalism, also known as "Jesus Only," was the first theological controversy confronting the AG in 1914, and was officially denounced in 1917. In 1916, the AG formulated its Statement of Fundamental Truths, which was designed to clarify the group's Pentecostal beliefs.

The primary doctrinal belief that sets the AG apart from the rest of evangelicalism is the doctrine of initial physical evidence, which teaches that speaking in tongues is the initial, outward, and visible evidence of a person having received Spirit baptism (usually defined as subsequent and separate from conversion initiation and based on Acts 2:8; 10:46; 19:6). Since the early days of the AG, the doctrine of initial physical evidence has been controversial, and one early leader in the AG resigned over the issue. Challenges to this doctrine continue to come from both Pentecostals and non-Pentecostals alike (see James D.G. Dunn's *Baptism in the Holy Spirit*, 1970; Max Turner's *The Holy Spirit and Spiritual Gifts*, 1996; Gordon Fee, *Gospel and Spirit*, 1991).

One of the chief reasons for launching the AG related to world missions and the need to better support missions efforts that had been a central feature of the Pentecostal movement. The baptism in the Holy Spirit and gift of tongues that many had received was often interpreted as empowerment for world evangelization. One early Pentecostal leader, John W. Welch, once declared that the AG was "never meant to be an institution," but only "a missionary agency." Missionaries were sent out immediately, with 27 going to overseas assignments in 1914. By 1925, that number had risen to 250, many of them single women.

The AG has often had an uneasy relationship with the larger evangelical community, particularly due to its emphasis on tongues speaking. Ironically, many early members of the AG considered themselves Fundamentalists, even though most Fundamentalists in the past held to a generally negative view of Pentecostals. This over time led to Pentecostals associating themselves with the National Association of Evangelicals (NAE) in 1943. Today, most AG churches hold to evangelical and premillennial theology and practice baptism by immersion.

J.M. Ireland

A Bibliography

Blumhoffer, Edith L. *The Assemblies of God*. 2 vols. Springfield, MO: Gospel Publishing House, 1989.

Burgess, Stanley M., and Eduard M. van der Maas. *The International Dictionary of Pentecostal and Charismatic Movements*. Grand Rapids: Zondervan, 2002.

Dayton, Donald W. *Theological Roots of Pentecostalism*. Peabody, MA: Hendrickson, 1987.

McGee, Gary B. *People of the Spirit: The Assemblies of God*. Springfield, MO: Gospel Publishing House, Kindle edition 2004.

ATHANASIUS (CA. 293–373)

The early monastic theologian Athanasius, bishop of Alexandria, was born near Alexandria, Egypt, around 293–298 and died there May 2, 373. His enduring legacy was his intrepid defense of the deity of Christ against Arianism. This battle would occupy five decades of his life until his death, and would virtually equate his work with the development of Christian thought in the fourth century.

Born to Christian parents, Athanasius was drawn very early to clerical life. A fragment of a Coptic "Ecomium" written by a contemporary of Bishop Theophilus (d. 412) records that Athanasius served six years as a reader, and by the time of the outbreak of Arianism he was already a deacon. It is now thought that during this time, Athanasius wrote his two earliest works, *Contra Gentes* (*Against the Heathens*) and *De Incarnatione* (*On the Incarnation*). In them the young theologian articulated the two defining truths of Christianity against which he would later evaluate the destructive influences of Arianism. These two doctrines, as Gonzalez reports, were Christian monotheism and salvation as a new creation of fallen humanity. He would later liken Arianism to polytheism because in that system of thought, the Son is worshipped as a lesser god. Likewise, Christ's role in salvation is vitiated because it is said that only the creator God can bring about a new creation.

Working alongside Bishop Alexander, Athanasius played a key role at the Council of Nicea (325). Largely due to the forcefulness of Athanasius, the Council affirmed the full deity of Christ against Arianism. Alexander died the following year, and Athanasius (who was barely 30 years of age) succeeded him as bishop. However, Athanasius's enemies, led by the semi-Arian Eusebius of Nicomedia, set out to reverse Nicea by discrediting Athanasius. While they failed to prove his alleged crimes, Emperor Constantine nevertheless considered him a hindrance to peace and banished him in

335 to Treves, Germany. When Constantine died in May 337, Athanasius returned to Alexandria in November of the same year. He would incur four more exiles—under Contantius (339–346) in Rome, again for six more years (356–362), and later under Julian the Apostate (362–363) in the Egyptian desert, then finally under Valens (365–366) in his father's tomb.

Athanasius was the first bishop to actively promote the monastic life. His relationships with the ascetics is well documented in his classic *The Life of Anthony*, which helped spread the ascetic ideal in both Eastern and Western Christianity. He was a prolific writer albeit not an armchair theologian. He wrote as a pastor to address issues of his day. Important among these include his *Festal Letters*, some of which have bearing on the New Testament canon, the four *Letters to Serapion*, which defended the deity of the Holy Spirit, and *Four Orations Against the Arians*, his dogmatic masterpiece.

Daniel R. Mitchell

Bibliography

Athanasius. *On the Incarnation*. New rev. ed. Yonkers, NY: St. Vladimir's Seminary Press, 1996.

Chadwick, Henry. *Early Church History*. Rev. ed. New York: Penguin Putnam, 1993.

Gonzalez, Justo. *The Story of Christianity*, vol. 1. New York: HarperCollins, 1984.

AUGUSTINE OF HIPPO (354–430)

Christian theologian Augustine was born in Thagaste (modern Souk Ahras, Algeria) in 354. His mother, Monica, was a committed Christian, while his father, Patricius, a local Roman official, was a pagan who converted to Christianity just before his death. Though Augustine was raised by a Christian mother, for most of his youth he strayed from the faith and even spent about a decade as a follower of the Manichean sect. After studying rhetoric (communication), Augustine worked as a teacher of rhetoric in Carthage, Rome, and Milan. It was at Milan that Augustine met Bishop Ambrose and became attracted to his biblical teaching that satisfied many of Augustine's questions about the gospel. Following a dramatic conversion (recorded in Book 8 of his *Confesssions*), Augustine was baptized on Easter of 387 in Milan. Later, he returned to Thagaste, where he established a type of monastery prior to being ordained a presbyter at Hippo in 391, and then later he became the city's bishop in 395.

Augustine was a prolific author who wrote some 117 books. His most famous

A theological works include the treatise *On the Trinity,* his book *The City of God* (a Christian philosophy of history in light of the fall of Rome), and doctrinal works refuting Manichean, Donatist, and Pelagian thought. While many of his earlier works were philosophical in nature (e.g., the Cassiciacum dialogues), his later works, written after his ordination in Hippo, were pastoral in nature (*On Teaching Christianity, Instructing Beginners,* and some 252 letters). His most famous work was *Confessions,* an extended prayer that recounted his journey to faith in Christ and his ongoing struggles as he followed the Lord.

Augustine's key contributions to church history were many. First, he influenced the development of theology in a number of areas. Against the Donatists, he argued that the church was universal and should not be divided, even if it did have many imperfections in the earthly context. Against the Pelagians, he argued strongly for divine sovereignty in the work of salvation. Against the Manicheans, he proposed a Christian solution to the problem of evil. Second, as a monk who became a bishop, he helped to further the blending of these two roles in the medieval church. Third, as a pastor in Hippo for nearly 40 years, he set a new standard for preaching, invested in and mentored other church leaders, and did theology in the context of and for the church.

Edward Smither

Bibliography

Brown, Peter. *Augustine of Hippo: A Biography.* Berkeley, CA: University of California Press, 1967, 2000.

Fitzgerald, Allen D. *Augustine Through the Ages: An Encyclopedia.* Grand Rapids: Eerdmans, 2009.

Smither, Edward L. *Augustine as Mentor: A Model for Preparing Spiritual Leaders.* Nashville, TN: B&H Academic, 2008.

The Works of Saint Augustine: A Translation for the 21st Century. Hyde Park, NY: New City Press, 1990– .

BACH, JOHANN SEBASTIAN (1685–1750)

A classical Christian musician, Johann Sebastian Bach was known as much for his deeply spiritual and pious life as he was distinguished as a world-class composer and performer of the organ, harpsichord, and clavichord. Orphaned at the age of ten, most of his adult life was given to promoting and serving the Lutheran Church through music. His wife, Maria Barbara, died unexpectedly in May of 1720, leaving the young organist-composer with the responsibility of rearing their children alone. A year later, Bach married Anna Magdalena Wilcken, and together they had 13 children. Two of Bach's children, Wilhelm Friedemann Bach and Johann Christian Bach, followed in his footsteps to become world-class organist-composers.

Bach spent his entire career in the regions of Weimar, Leipzig, Thuringia, and Saxony, Germany. Considered by many to be the greatest composer of Western music ever (Wilson-Dickson, 93), Bach was known for his craftsmanship in composition, impeccable improvisational ability, innovations in musical style and form, and an unwavering commitment to Pietism. Bach was highly influenced by Luther's theology and his own (1) personal relationship with Christ, (2) commitment to "the priesthood of believers," (3) deep love and appreciation for the Bible, and (4) use of biblical and extrabiblical texts as resource material for his cantatas and sacred songs (Wilson-Dickson, 97).

Paul Rumrill identified four qualities that set Bach apart as a dedicated and committed believer: (1) he studied Scripture and theology passionately; (2) he enthusiastically sought to excel in every musical area for God's glory; (3) he relentlessly worked to compose, arrange, and create worship music for his own church's services; and (4) as part of his weekly responsibilities, he actively taught Christian devotion and music-making to his family and the next generation. In fact, Bach wrote the initials S.D.G. at the beginning and end of all his church compositions, which stands for *Soli Deo gloria,* a Latin phrase that translates to "glory to God alone" (Butt, 52).

Among Bach's many contributions to sacred music for the German Protestant liturgy were preludes, more than 200 cantatas, *St. John Passion* (1723), *Christmas Oratorio* (1734), and *Mass in B minor* (1749). One of the most outstanding contributions of Bach's composition technique to modern Christian music was his fondness of music with a strong pulse—most often seen in his use of a "walking" or "running" bass line to notes of equal value (Wilson-Dickson, 99). This technique was a precursor to jazz, black gospel, and much of the late twentieth- and early twenty-first-century contemporary Christian music. Bach was perhaps one of few musicians who owed his living almost entirely to work in the church. Today, Bach's music serves as a model for church musicians around the world.

Vernon M. Whaley

Bibliography

Butt, John, ed. *The Cambridge Companion to Bach*. London: Cambridge University Press, 1997.

Rumrill, Paul. "Master Course: 5 Lessons Every Worship Leader Can Learn from Bach." *Worship Leader Magazine* 19:1 (January-February 2010): 34-35.

Wilson-Dickson, Andrew. *The Story of Christian Music: From Gregorian Chant to Black Gospel*. Minneapolis: Fortress Press, 1992.

BAPTISTS

Baptists represent one of the largest Protestant denominations in the world and are known for their emphasis on the doctrines of biblical authority, religious liberty, and believer's baptism. Unlike other Protestant denominations, Baptists cannot claim a founder of their denomination as can other Protestants (as is the case with Lutherans and Martin Luther). Consequently, there is a considerable difference of opinion concerning their origin. Some claim that the Baptists began in the first century with the apostles. This view holds to an unbroken succession of Baptists from the first century to the present. In America, this opinion is represented by the Landmark movement and is held by the American Baptist Association. However, most Baptist historians reject this successionist view, recognizing that history seems to support the view that Baptists arose out of the influence of the Continental Anabaptists and the Puritan English Separatists of the seventeenth century, who were Puritans who separated from the Anglican Church.

The first Baptist church on English soil was founded in England in 1612. Although John Smyth was the original leader of this group, it was Thomas Helwys who led them back to England after Smyth had led them previously to Holland to escape persecution in England. This church was considered to be the beginning of the General Baptists, so called because they held to a general atonement, or the view that salvation is generally available to all people. They were significantly influenced by the Anabaptists, but less so by English Separatism. Another Baptist church, founded in 1641, was the beginning of the Particular Baptists, so called because they held to a particular atonement, or the view that salvation is available only to the elect. They were significantly influenced by the English Separatists, but less so by the Anabaptists. In most other respects, these two groups held similar views that came to be seen as Baptist distinctives.

Baptist distinctives include the following emphases: the supremacy of the New Testament for determining matters of Christian living and church order, regenerate church membership, believer's baptism, religious liberty, and discipleship. Baptists differed from Anabaptists in that they required baptism by immersion and rejected pacifism.

Some of the more famous English Baptists were William Carey (1761–1834), often called the father of the modern missions movement, and Charles Haddon Spurgeon (1834–1892), a conservative evangelical who led the largest Baptist church of the nineteenth century in London.

Although Baptists can be found in most countries in the world today, they have achieved their greatest success in America. Beginning with the First Baptist Church in America in Providence, Rhode Island, in 1639, founded by Roger Williams (1603–1683), they experienced persecution in New England, much as they had in England previously. Baptists experienced their most remarkable growth in the southern portion of the United States, resulting in the Southern Baptist Convention (founded in 1845). Among the more notable early Baptists in America were Isaac Backus of Massachusetts (1724–1806) and James Leland of Virginia (1754–1841), who led the struggle for religious freedom, and Adoniram Judson (1788–1850), who pioneered the missions endeavor. Recent well-known Baptists include Billy Graham, Jerry Falwell, and W.A. Criswell.

Carl Deimer

Bibliography

Hobbs, Herschel H. *What Baptists Believe*. Nashville, TN: Broadman & Holman, 1964.

Lumpkin, William L., and Bill J. Leonard. *The Baptist Confessions of Faith*. 2d rev. ed. Philadelphia: Judson, 2011.

———. *Baptist Foundations in the South Tracing Through the Separates the Influence of the Great Awakening, 1754–1787*. Eugene, OR: Wipf & Stock, 2006.

McBeth, H. Leon. *The Baptist Heritage*. Nashville, TN: Broadman, 1987.

Underwood, Alfred C. *A History of the English Baptists*. Np: Baptist Union Publications, 1947.

BARTH, KARL (1886–1968)

B

A Swiss theologian, Karl Barth was perhaps the most significant and influential European theologian of the twentieth century. He was born in Basel, Switzerland, the oldest son of a moderately orthodox Swiss Reformed pastor and New Testament professor (at Basel and Berne). He later trained in theology at Swiss and German universities in the classic (Ritschlian) theological liberalism of the day and, for a time, was a modified advocate of such liberalism. However, a series of events related to the German War effort (1914–1918) and his own study of Scripture, especially the book of Romans, and of his preaching duties at Safenwil, Switzerland, led to his rejection of liberal theology. Specifically, Barth saw the moral, spiritual, and theological bankruptcy of liberal theology and saw in the New Testament, especially Paul, the glory and transcendence of God, the fallen corruption of humanity and culture, and the unique centrality of Jesus Christ.

This first stage of Barth's break from liberalism led to the first edition of his theological commentary *The Epistle to the Romans* (1919). Finding that edition still too much given over to human questions (like liberalism), Barth rewrote the commentary with the expressive, conceptual help of Christian existentialist Søren Kierkegaard, and the result was the profound, potent, and disruptive second edition, which promoted Barth's expression of neo-orthodoxy, or better, dialectical theology, which remains a highly constructive influence, advancing and renewing many classical Christian concerns in the context of theologically liberal Europe.

Barth eventually taught theology at the universities of Göttingen (1921), Munster (1925), and Bonn (1930) until he was expelled from Germany by the Nazis. He then returned to Basel, where he taught until he retired in 1962. Barth became increasingly unsatisfied with the way he "did" theology (method). Though he was a university professor of theology, he knew that what he had learned as a preacher still applied to doing theology, and he sought a way to *do* theology in accord with the Word of God. In 1930, with the help of medieval theologian Anselm (1033–1109), he found a way to do theology objectively in accord with God's incarnate Word, Jesus Christ, via Scripture. From this point onward, the previous dialectical way of doing theology was increasingly extracted from Barth's theology.

Though Barth wrote over 500 books, articles, and papers, it was the work that resulted from his "Anselm discovery" for which he is most famous, his four-volume *Church Dogmatics*. Therein, while still emphasizing the transcendence and sovereignty of God, human (and cultural) sinfulness, and the powerful redemptive Word of God to helpless persons, Barth's now clear and consistent Christocentricity, and hence emphatic trinitarianism, modified his earlier overemphasis on God's transcendence, which had led almost to deism. For Barth, John 1:14, "the Word (who is God) became flesh and dwelt among us," became the center and circumference of all Christian doctrines.

Barth was a powerful voice against theologians who placed human experience or any human "addition" into the redemptive kingdom purposes of God in Christ. Barth's Christocentricity is succinctly embodied in the Barmen Declaration, essentially written by Barth for the Confessing Church in its struggle against the Nazis and the German church that they dominated in the 1930s. For his anti-Nazi activities Barth was deported back to Basel, where he taught and lived for the rest of his life.

Barth's theology was occasionally controversial and often misunderstood, even by those claiming to be followers. For example, the particular Christocentric direction he applied to the issue of predestination *seems* to lead logically to universal human redemption, though Barth never advocated that conclusion. Also, many evangelicals have criticized Barth's view of Scripture (e.g., that Scripture is said to "become" the Word of God if God chooses to use it by the Spirit) and the fact that he did not overtly defend the inerrancy of Scripture. Despite this, Barth was vehement against all natural theology, seeing such formulations as human attempts to "get to God behind the back of Jesus." He acknowledged general revelation, but pointed out that fallen humans always distort such into idolatry, preferring to focus on God's specific revelation through Jesus Christ.

John Douglas Morrison

Bibliography

Barth, Karl. *Dogmatics in Doctrine.* Louisville, KY: Westminster John Knox, 1994.

———. *Evangelical Theology.* Grand Rapids: Eerdmans, 1992.

Eberhard, Busch. *Karl Barth.* London: SCM, 2011.

Parker, T.H.L. *Karl Barth.* Grand Rapids: Eerdmans, 1970.

Torrance, Thomas F. *Karl Barth: An Introduction to His Early Theology.* London: T&T Clark, 2001.

Van Til, Cornelius. *Christianity and Barthianism.* Philadelphia: P&R Publishing, 1962.

BASIL THE GREAT (CA. 330–379)

Basil, a fourth-century monastic leader, was born into a large, wealthy Christian family in Cæsarea, the capital of Cappadocia, in the eastern portion of modern Turkey. Educated by his father in Cæsarea, Basil left for further schooling in Constantinople under the teaching of Libanius, the famous Sophist. Basil then went on to Athens in the early 350s to study rhetoric, philosophy, and math. Two of his colleagues of note in Athens were a future emperor, Julian the Apostate, and Basil's lifelong friend and ministry partner, Gregory of Nazianzus. Following his studies in Athens, Basil returned home to Cæsarea, where he was vigorously persuaded by his sister, Macrina, to follow an ascetic life.

Basil researched desert monks by traveling to Syria, Palestine, and Egypt. It was in Egypt that he discovered Pachomius's well-organized system of monasticism. The Egyptian monks settled in communities of hundreds and thousands to escape the world and improve their own spiritual lives. Basil returned to Cappadocia, dispersed his property to the poor, and found a secluded, serene place in Pontus to begin his own monastic community. He persuaded his friend, Gregory of Nazianzus, to join him there, and they began to study, pray, and engage in manual labor. Together they created an organized set of plans for smaller communities of monks (usually 30 or so per cloister).

Unlike their Egyptian counterparts, the Cappadocian cloisters would operate with and under the authority of their local churches. Basil's *Rules* for monasteries continue to be the standard practice for all Eastern monastic communities. Basil would also have an others-centered ministry focus. His monastic communities included hospitals, schools, food kitchens, lodging for strangers, and other means to help the poor and needy. He was personally involved in these types of ministry, being known to cook and serve food in the kitchen and to touch the lepers in his hospitals when no one else would. Though he was not seeking fame from these good deeds, fame found him.

In 364, Basil reluctantly accepted a call to become an elder in the church in Cæsarea, and upon the bishop's death six years later, Basil became the Bishop of Cæsarea (and therefore the metropolitan of all Cappadocia). The main reason he took on these pastoral roles was to fight back against the state-sponsored Arianism that had crept into the Eastern churches. Basil, his younger brother Gregory of Nyssa, and his friend Gregory of Nazianzus together became known as the Cappadocian Fathers—they wrote and preached against Arianism even when the Arian Emperor, Valens, tried to persecute them and their churches. Basil and his brother wrote a set of books titled *Against Eunomius,* a response to a leader among the more extreme Arians in Cappadocia. Basil also defended the Nicene definition of the Trinity, dealing especially with the deity of the Holy Spirit in works written against the Pneumatomachians (those who denied the deity of the Holy Spirit). Basil died in 379, two years before the Council of Constantinople would forever cement the legacy of the Cappadocian Fathers as staunch defenders of orthodox theology.

Kenneth Cleaver

Bibliography

Basil, St. Bp. of Cæsarea in Cappadocia. *Letters and Select Works, Nicene and Post-Nicene Fathers.* Series 2., vol. 14. Peabody, MA: Henrickson, 1995.

Lowther, William. *St. Basil the Great: A Study in Monasticism.* Toronto: University of Toronto Press, 2011.

Rousseau, Philip. *Basil of Caesarea.* Los Angeles: University of California Press, 1994.

BAXTER, RICHARD (1615–1691)

English Reformed pastor Richard Baxter was born in the year 1615, in Rowton, England. His humble beginnings included an education that was generally informal and never let him rise above the position of parish pastor. He lived in a time of great political, social, and moral upheaval and for much of his life, he suffered poor health. Some of his ministry took place during the years of the English Civil War, in which the armies of the king fought against the armies of the Parliament to see who would assert the ultimate authority in England. Much of Baxter's ministry occurred at St. Mary's Church in Kidderminster, his only pastorate.

Baxter was ordained as a deacon in 1638 and then an assistant minister in 1639. Two years later, at the age of 26, he became curate at St. Mary's Church in Kidderminster, a town located southwest of Birmingham, England. He served there from 1641 to 1642 and then again from 1647 to 1661. Following his time in Kidderminster, he moved to London, serving and preaching wherever he could, but never again having a church of his own.

When Baxter arrived in Kidderminster, he found a town that was largely unregenerate. By 1661, the majority of the town had come to a true saving knowledge of Christ. This can be attributed to the Lord working through the preaching of Baxter, as well as through his practice of spending two days each week visiting homes, evangelizing unbelievers, and discipling believers.

Baxter's writings are warm, challenging, and devotional in nature. He was a prolific writer, penning nearly 200 books. *The Saints' Everlasting Rest* was his first major work, written in a time of prolonged illness during which he stared death in the face while keeping his eyes fixed on Christ and the eternal rest that awaits God's people. *The Reformed Pastor* was written to instruct and encourage pastors to have a reformed or revived ministry, becoming shepherds who do the work of the ministry seriously and prayerfully.

A Christian Directory is certainly one of the most important books ever written about practical Christianity. In it, Baxter wrote about an enormous number of subjects that believers face in day-to-day living for Christ, providing sound biblical counsel for each matter. *Reliquiae Baxterianae* (Baxter's autobiography) is the best source of information about his life. Baxter has been called a Puritan and a nonconformist, but he never truly separated from the parish churches that were part of the Church of England. He was actually a peacemaker who never wanted to leave the Church of England, despite being persecuted and even imprisoned at one point by the Church. He sought to bring together those who were in the Church of England, the Presbyterians, and nonconformists. His works are still in print and widely read today.

Baxter was a leader on the nonconformist side of the Savoy Conference in 1661. He spoke passionately for moderation and fairness and often held a mediating position between Episcopalianism and Presbyterianism, Calvinism and Arminianism. He welcomed the restoration of the monarchy and was appointed chaplain to Charles II and was offered the bishopric of Bedford, which he declined. Excluded from a pastorate in the Church of England, after the Act of Uniformity in 1662, Baxter continued to preach and write extensively. As he himself said, he "preached as never sure to preach again, and as a dying man to dying men."

Stephen Putney

Bibliography

Baxter, Richard. *The Practical Works of Richard Baxter*. 4 vols. Morgan, PA: Soli Deo Gloria Publications, 2000.

Beeke, Joel R., and Randall J. Pederson. *Meet the Puritans*. Grand Rapids: Reformation Heritage, 2006.

Loane, Marcus L. *Makers of Puritan History*. Grand Rapids: Baker, 1980.

Martin, Hugh. *Puritanism and Richard Baxter*. London: SCM, 1954.

Thomas, J.M. Lloyd, abridged by. *The Autobiography of Richard Baxter*. London: Guernsey Press, 1985.

BECKET, THOMAS (CA.1120 –1170)

Born in London of middle-class Norman parents, murdered by four of King Henry II's knights at the cathedral in Canterbury, and immortalized in Geoffrey Chaucer's *Canterbury Tales* (1475), Thomas Becket's story of transformation from worldly courtier into the staunch Catholic archbishop who zealously resisted the king's attempts to meddle in ecclesiastical affairs is one that continues to be surrounded by mystery and intrigue.

Around the year 1141, Becket's natural talents, solid education, and unusual abilities eventually brought him into the service of Theobald, archbishop of Canterbury, where he quickly excelled and was called upon by the archbishop to handle highly sensitive negotiations between church and state, including diplomatic missions to Rome. He was even given a year's leave of absence to study civil and canon law at Bologna and Auxerre, ultimately resulting in Theobald's ordaining him a deacon in 1154.

The year 1154 was pivotal for Becket in more ways than one when Henry II, who had that same year ascended the throne of England, upon the recommendation of Theobald, made Becket his chancellor. This set into motion a seemingly bizarre series of circumstances that would eventually lead to Becket's martyrdom. Although some recent scholarship challenges the long-held assumption that the two eventual rivals were once close friends, the consensus is that Becket likely became the second-most-powerful subject under Henry II's reign, working with the throne in administrating reforms and even riding with the king to lead the English army into battle. It was only natural, then, that upon the death of Theobald, Henry II appointed Becket the new archbishop of Canterbury.

The king's friendship with his archbishop was put under strain when it became clear that Becket, who as chancellor had earned a reputation as a cruel military commander with extensive materialistic gains, had inexplicably transformed himself from a pleasure-loving courtier into a serious and ascetic cleric who had no intentions of conceding ecclesiastical rights into the hands of Henry II. A number of protracted disputes with the king over land, taxes, and other clerical rights soon followed. In the year 1170, Becket excommunicated the archbishop of York and other leading churchmen who had supported Henry II's policies. Henry, who was in Normandy when he heard the news of Becket's most recent edict, is said to have shouted in a fit of rage, "Will no one rid me of this turbulent priest?" In response to what they believed to be a genuine request on the king's part, four of his valiant knights traveled to Canterbury to bring their swords down on Becket's head and so end the cleric's insolence against king and country. The martyr's bones, supposedly held in a jewel-encrusted shrine, soon became the focus of pilgrimages to the cathedral at Canterbury. Becket was canonized as a saint by the Roman Catholic Church in 1173.

Thomas Provenzola

Bibliography

Barlow, Frank. *Thomas Becket.* Berkeley: University of California Press, 1990.

Ellis, Jerry. *Walking to Canterbury: A Modern Journey through Chaucer's Medieval England.* New York: Ballantine, 2003.

Guy, John. *Thomas Becket: Warrior, Priest, Rebel.* New York: Random House, 2012.

Staunton, Michael. *The Lives of Thomas Becket.* Manchester, UK: Manchester University Press, 2001.

BEDE, SAINT (CA. 673–735)

Bede, referred to as "the Venerable," was an English monk. As church historians frame the Patristic period from about AD 100 to 750, Bede is regarded by many as the last church father in the Latin-speaking world. Born around 673, Bede lived most of his life at the monasteries of Wearmouth and Jarrow. Entering the community at the age of 7, where he was educated by the monks, he was later ordained as a deacon at age 19, and then a priest at 30. Living his entire life in England, Bede never ventured beyond the kingdom of Northumbria in northeast England.

Bede's greatest contributions to the church came through his writing—works that were originally intended to edify friends and students. He wrote commentaries on many of the books of the Old and New Testaments. Probably his most famous exegetical work was his *Commentary on the Catholic Epistles*; today termed the general or non-Pauline epistles. Bede does not appear to have been an innovative biblical commentator, as his exegesis largely followed that of the doctors of the Latin church: Ambrose (340–397), Jerome (347–420), Augustine (354–430), and Gregory the Great (ca. 540–604). Thus, his hermeneutics included a combination of allegorical, historical, and grammatical methods of reading Scripture.

In addition to his commentaries, Bede also left behind a corpus of sermons and hymns, a number of sacred biographies remembering the lives of saints such as Athanasius (ca. 293–373), and even some scientific books. His most famous book was historical in nature—*The Ecclesiastical History of the English People*. Ultimately, this work was groundbreaking because it served as an early compilation of the history of Christianity in the British Isles.

Edward Smither

Bibliography

Bede. *The Ecclesiastical History of the English People.* Oxford: Oxford University Press, 1994, 2008.

Bruce, F.F. *The Spreading Flame: The Rise and Progress of Christianity from Its First Beginnings to the Conversion of the English.* Grand Rapids: Eerdmans, 1973.

Moorman, John R.H. *A History of the Church in England.* New York: Morehouse, 1980.

BENEDICT, SAINT (CA. 480–547)

Saint Benedict, a Catholic monastic also known as Benedict of Nursia, was born near Nursia, in Umbria, Italy, and was the founder of the order of Benedictines, father of Western monasticism, and creator of the *Rule of Saint Benedict.* Born in an upper-class family, he lived and studied in Rome but was dismayed by the immorality he saw there. So he sought solitude by living in a cave near Rome. He founded 12 monasteries with 12 monks each. Jealousy arose amongst the local priests, so in 529 he moved to Monte Cassino (between Rome and Naples) to found what became a famous monastery. By 540, Benedict developed his *Rule,* which was based on rules by Basil and John Cassian. Benedict's *Rule* (Latin, *Regula)* was adopted by all Western monasteries by 670.

Famous for his phrase *ora et labora,* "pray and work," Benedict's *Rule* stressed order and discipline rather than learning. Indeed, the longest section of *Regula* is "On Humility," detailing 12 steps to spiritual growth of fruitful virtue. His "On Humility" sounds like Aristotle on virtues: "[A]fter ascending all of these steps of humility…he will now begin to observe without effort, as though naturally, from habit, no longer out of fear of hell, but out of love for Christ, good habit and delight in virtue. All this the Lord will by the Holy Spirit graciously manifest in his workman now cleansed of vices and sins" (RB 7:67-70).

The *Rule* directs and fosters reflection: one does something *unless* there is reason or utility to do otherwise; the abbot must seek the elders' opinion here, making reasonable decisions "for the goodness" of each monk. The abbot must own all things, and the monk, nothing. No stylus, book, bread crumb, undergarment, bed, clothing is one's own; all are designated to the abbot. Frequent checks in monks' cells ensured that no items were withheld as one's own—"in order that this vice of private ownership may be completely uprooted, the abbot is to provide all things necessary" (BR 55.16).

Why strictly forbid ownership? Benedict employed Acts 4:35 here: "Distribution was made to each one as he had need" (BR 34.1; and again in BR 55.20). If coheirship with Christ comes only by sharing his sufferings, then asceticism/monasticism is a proactive path to a sort of self-persecution and separation from sinful culture to please God. Benedict saw one way this might happen: that humans needed a strict "taskmaster"—yet compassionate and tender father (cf. *abba*)—in the person of the abbot. Monks and nuns today are still guided by this *Rule*, which testifies of the enduring importance and legacy of this noteworthy monastic founder.

Edward N. Martin

Bibliography

Benedict, St. *The Rule of St. Benedict in English*. Edited by Timothy Fry. Collegeville, MN: Liturgical Press, 1982.

De Waal, Esther. *Seeking God: The Way of St. Benedict*. Collegeville, MN: Liturgical Press, 1984.

Knowles, David. *The Benedictines*. New York: Macmillan, 1930.

BERNARD OF CLAIRVAUX (1090–1153)

Bernard of Clairvaux was a medieval mystic, defender of Rome, prophet of the Reformation, and crusader for the defense of the Holy Land. Said to be the greatest preacher since Gregory the Great, Bernard also anticipated Calvin and Luther, both of whom held him in high esteem. Educated at Chatillon-sur-Seine, he was a bright student with a magnetic personality and strong character. He was especially fond of his mother, whose death induced a crisis that was a turning point in his young life. In 1113, he joined the newly formed Cistercian monastery at Cîteaux, enthusiastically adopting the disciplines of St. Benedict with such zeal that he nearly ruined his health. In 1115, he was made abbot of a new house at Clairvaux. Within a decade his fame and influence would thrust him into prominence in the Cistercian community and throughout Europe. While the cloistered life was his passion, it was not to be his destiny. Rather, in an illustrious career, he would be called upon to advise princes and clerics at the highest levels.

In 1128, Bernard attended the Synod of Troyes, where he spoke in favor of the Knights Templar and is credited with outlining the first rule of the order. In 1130, he was called upon to adjudicate the schism between Innocent II and Anacletus II in favor of Innocent II. Over the next eight years he would have to defend this decision against supporters of Anacletus throughout France, Germany, and Italy.

In 1139, Bernard took on one of the greatest intellectual minds of his time. Against Peter Abelard's moral-influence theory of the atonement, Bernard defended the cardinal doctrine of the substitutionary atonement of Christ for sin. Abelard was summoned to the Council of Sens in 1141, where his teachings were condemned by Innocent II when he refused to defend himself against Bernard.

In 1146, Pope Eugenius III enlisted Bernard to promote the Second Crusade. In time this would prove disastrous and "no one felt the blow more keenly than Bernard, who with prophetical authority to speak had predicted a favorable issue" (Deutsch, 63). In 1147, Bernard traveled throughout southern France preaching against the Albigensian heresy.

Many of Bernard's teachings both reflect the dogma of his time and anticipate future Protestant developments. He was strongly devoted to the saints and to Mary, although he opposed the doctrine of her immaculate conception. In terms echoed later in the Reformation, he affirmed salvation by grace alone apart from works, and faith as the means by which God's grace is secured (Deutsch, 64). His mysticism would also escape the censure of Luther inasmuch as it was deemed the pure contemplation of Christ, free from any form of pantheism. Many know Bernard today through his hymns, such as "O Sacred Head, Now Wounded," "Jesus, the Very Thought of Thee," and "Jesus, Thou Joy of Loving Hearts."

Daniel R. Mitchell

Bibliography

Bernard of Clairvaux. *Bernard of Clairvaux: Selected Works*. Translated by G.R. Evans. Mahwah, NJ: Paulist Press, 1987.

Deutsch, S.M. "Bernard of Clairvaux." *The New Schaff-Herzog Religious Encyclopedia*. Edited by S.M. Jackson. Grand Rapids: Baker, 1952.

Storrs, Richard S. *Bernard of Clairvaux*. London: Hodder & Stoughton, 1892.

BEZA, THEODORE (1519–1605)

A Protestant Reformer, Theodore Beza spent most of life in Switzerland, where he worked closely with John Calvin. He preached at Calvin's funeral service and became the leader of the Reformed movement until his death and burial in Geneva.

Beza was born in France and studied under Melchior Wolmar in Paris and then in Bourges, then a center of Protestant thought, before moving to Orleans and studying law. Through an illness he became increasingly aware of his spiritual condition and left the Catholic faith to become a Protestant. He then moved to Geneva in 1548. At that point Geneva was known as a city of refuge for French Protestants, and Calvin was its ecclesial leader.

Beza visited his mentor Wolmar (who also taught Greek to John Calvin) at the academy in Lausanne, Switzerland, in 1549, where he was appointed professor of Greek. Calvin established his academy in Geneva in 1559 and invited Beza to teach Greek there. Beza accepted the position and taught until declining health forced him to stop in 1597. He was pastor of the church in Geneva from 1559 (Calvin died in 1564) to 1605.

While Beza was no equal to Calvin, he served as a stabilizing factor in Geneva and to Calvin's followers elsewhere. He contributed to the Reformed tradition through his many theological writings, shaping its subsequent scholastic development. Through his writings and travels, including many trips into Catholic France, he encouraged the faithful and helped to spread Calvinism throughout Europe. Beza's works also include a biography of Calvin and New Testaments in Greek and Latin. A fifth-century codex that was once in Beza's possession is known today as Codex Bezae.

Mark Nickens

Bibliography

Baird, Henry Martyn. *Theodore Beza: The Counselor of the French Reformation, 1519–1605.* New York: G.P. Putnam's Sons, 1899; reprint New York: Elibron Classics Series, 2005.

Mallinson, Jeffrey. *Faith, Reason, and Revelation in Theodore Beza (1519–1605).* New York: Oxford University Press, 2003.

Steinmetz, David C. *Reformers in the Wings: From Geiler von Keysersberg to Theodore Beza.* New York: Oxford University Press, 2001.

BONHOEFFER, DIETRICH (1906–1945)

A German Lutheran pastor and theologian, one biographer notes that "Dietrich Bonhoeffer has become a man with mystique" (Roark, 13). As a teenager, to the dismay of his parents and siblings, Bonhoeffer chose to study theology instead of chasing after more worldly pursuits. Always his own man, he rejected the pervasive liberalism of the time and aligned (not uncritically) with Karl Barth. In 1927, at age 21, he submitted his dissertation at Berlin, entitled *Sanctorum Communio*. Published three years later, Barth praised it as a "theological miracle" (Roark, 15). After serving two years as associate pastor in Barcelona, Spain, in 1930, Bonhoeffer submitted his inaugural dissertation, *Act and Being*, requisite to a faculty position in theology at Berlin. That same year, he came to study at Union Theological Seminary in New York. Unimpressed with American theologians and the lack of interest in theology among his fellow students, he was, however, highly influenced by their social activism.

Bonhoeffer joined with Frank Fisher, a black seminarian, to serve in a Baptist church in Harlem. While in the United States he also met Jean Lasserre whose pacifism and ecumenical interests markedly influenced the young theologian. Upon his return to Berlin, Bonhoeffer's ideas were warmly received by students but not by his liberal colleagues. In 1931, Bonhoeffer met and cultivated what would become an enduring friendship with Karl Barth. He also became affiliated with the World Alliance of Churches and became actively involved in ministry with at-risk youth in the community.

The year 1933 saw the fateful rise of Nazi power, and Bonhoeffer was at the center of the firestorm against the pro-Nazi national church, identifying instead with the evangelical Confessing Church. In anticipation of the Nazi takeover of Germany, he took a leave of absence to pastor in London.

Sternly chided by Karl Barth for leaving, Bonhoeffer returned in 1935 to assume leadership of an underground seminary in Finkenwalde. Denounced as a pacifist and enemy of the state, Bonhoeffer's authorization to teach in Berlin was revoked. In 1937, the underground seminary was closed and many of its pastors and students arrested. Against this backdrop Bonhoeffer wrote *Life Together* and *The Cost of Discipleship*, in which he harshly criticized "cheap grace."

First accepting and then declining an invitation by Reinhold Niebuhr at Union, Bonhoeffer returned to Germany in 1939. To escape military conscription he joined the Abwehr, the German Military Intelligence Service, as a courier. It was there that he learned the full scope of the Nazi atrocities taking place in Europe. In 1943, he was implicated in an attempt on Hitler's life and arrested. While awaiting trial, he engaged in correspondence with Eberhard Bethge, a former student from Finkenwalde. These writings would later be published as *Letters and Papers from Prison*.

On April 9, 1945, only days before the collapse of Berlin, Bonhoeffer and six fellow conspirators were hanged. As he was led to his death, he asked a British prisoner to remember him to Bishop George Bell of Chichester and to say, "This is the end— for me the beginning of life" (Bethge, 927).

Daniel R. Mitchell

Bibliography

Bethge, Eberhard. *Dietrich Bonhoeffer: A Biography*. Minneapolis: Fortress, 2000.

Metaxas, Eric. *Bonhoeffer: Pastor, Martyr, Prophet, Spy*. Nashville, TN: Thomas Nelson, 2011.

Roark, Dallas M. *Dietrich Bonhoeffer*. Waco, TX: Word, 1972.

BOOTH, WILLIAM (1829–1912)

The founder of the Salvation Army, William Booth was born in Nottingham, England, on April 10, 1829, the third son of Samuel and Mary (Moss) Booth. Growing up in the spiritual turmoil of nineteenth-century England fostered in Booth an unquenchable desire to serve the Lord and his fellow men in vocational ministry. As an itinerant Methodist preacher in England, Booth quickly gained the reputation of being a fiery, brash, single-minded, and even obstinate purveyor of the gospel (Hattersley, 2). However, Booth's best-known trait was perhaps his hyperpracticality in ministry. He was not one to become embroiled in theological debates or the nuances of philosophy (Hattersley, 2-3). His was a determined effort simply to reach the underprivileged masses with the message of the cross and the work of social reform (Cairns, 407).

Booth was supported in ministry by his wife, Catherine (Mumford) Booth, from 1855 until her death in 1890. Although in many ways surpassing Booth in intellectual capacity and spiritual maturity, Catherine never sought to overshadow her husband or otherwise disrupt his ministerial endeavors (Hattersley, 4). By all accounts, Catherine was a devoted and loving wife in the highest traditions of Victorian social decorum. Even as her reputation as a social reformer began to broaden, she never wavered in her dedication to Booth or his gospel mission to the "submerged tenth" of society— i.e., those occupying the lowest rung of England's socioeconomic ladder.

B

The Booths toured England in the early 1860s preaching for such denominations as the British Wesleyan Methodists, the Wesleyan reformers, and the Methodist New Connexion (*Eerdmans' Handbook*, 516). However, they were quickly disillusioned with the "death-charged atmosphere" of English Christianity (Hattersley, 3), and thus in 1865 established their own quasidenomination known as the Christian Mission (*Eerdmans' Handbook*, 516). By 1878, the Christian Mission had been rechristened The Salvation Army and was well on its way to becoming the legacy for which Booth is best known today (*Encyclopedia of Religious Revivals*, 380).

In 1890 Booth published *In Darkest England and the Way Out*, which became his clarion call for social and religious reform in England. However, the central notions of *In Darkest England* and, accordingly, The Salvation Army were not muted at England's coastline. To the contrary, Booth's messages of grace, mercy, love, and Christian service reverberated worldwide. By the time of his death in 1912, The Salvation Army had migrated around the globe, and its "soldiers" were well-known for their evangelistic fervor and staunch commitment to the poor and needy.

The Booths were strongly influenced by John Wesley's views of entire sanctification and personal holiness; thus, the Salvation Army has generally held to an Arminian-Holiness theology. In addition to their aggressive street evangelism, military uniforms, and personal discipline, the Salvation Army is known for its extensive humanitarian work and practical philanthropy. They have a training college in Atlanta, Georgia, and are especially known for their volunteer "bell ringers" who raise funds during the Christmas holidays.

At the beginning of the twenty-first century, The Salvation Army numbered some two million members in 109 countries, with a fund-raising income of over $1 billion annually (*Encyclopedia of Religious Revivals*, 381). Although many historians dispute the person and motivations of William Booth, few can argue with the successes of The Salvation Army and the mighty work this organization has done to spread the gospel of Jesus Christ.

Mark Tinsley

Bibliography

Briggs, J.H.Y. "The Salvation Army," 516-18. *Eerdmans' Handbook to the History of Christianity*. Grand Rapids: Eerdmans, 1982.

Cairns, Earle E. *Christianity Through the Centuries: A History of the Christian Church*. Grand Rapids: Zondervan, 1996.

Dieter, Melvin E. *Encyclopedia of Religious Revivals in America*. Westport, CT: Greenwood Press, 2007. S.v. "Salvation Army."

Hattersley, Roy. *Blood and Fire: William and Catherine Booth and Their Salvation Army*. New York: Doubleday, 2000.

B

BRAINERD, DAVID (1718–1747)

American Missionary David Brainerd's life lasted less than three decades but his impact has been felt for over two-and-a-half centuries. By the time Brainerd was 14, both of his parents had died. Scholars believe that Brainerd experienced his conversion on July 12, 1739, based on his own now-famous diary (*The Life and Diary of David Brainerd*, 69-70). Shortly after this experience, Brainerd enrolled at Yale. During his third year at Yale, Brainerd was expelled for statements that he made about officials at the school. Tensions had been brewing at the school during the time of the Great Awakening, and the faculty considered the spiritual enthusiasm of the students, who had been influenced by preachers such as George Whitefield, to be excessive. The school decided to punish students who made negative statements about school officials, and Brainerd was overheard making a statement about a faculty member's prayer as having "no more grace than this chair" (*The Life of David Brainerd*, 155-56).

Not graduating meant that Brainerd could not, by law, be a minister in Connecticut. He was later licensed to preach by an association of ministers in eastern Connecticut (*The Life of David Brainerd*, 30). After this, he was appointed as a missionary to the Indians by the Scottish Society for Propagating Christian Knowledge (*The Life of David Brainerd*, 189). For the next five years until his death, Brainerd worked as a missionary to the Housatonic, Delaware, and Crossweeksung Indians, traveling over 3000 miles by horseback to fulfill his ministry duties. In 1747, David Brainerd died in the home of Jonathan Edwards from complications related to tuberculosis.

Those who measure greatness by the number of converts in their ministry may not immediately understand the influence of David Brainerd, which has been greater after his life than during it. Jonathan Edwards wrote a biography about Brainerd that is still in print today. Above all else, Brainerd is known for his diaries, which serve as records of his dedication to prayer and fasting, and his steadfastness in the midst of difficulties. Brainerd remains an inspiration to aspiring missionaries and ministers today.

John Cartwright

Bibliography

Brainerd, David, Jonathan Edwards, and Philip Eugene Howard. *The Life and Diary of David Brainerd*. Chicago: Moody Press, 1949.

Edwards, Jonathan. *The Life of David Brainerd, Missionary to the Indians*. New York: The Christian Alliance, 1925.

Edwards, Jonathan. *The Life of David Brainerd*. New Haven, CT: Yale University Press, 1985.

B

BRETHREN

The term *Brethren of the Common Life* arose in the fourteenth century in Germany and Holland under the influence of Gerhard Groote (1340–1384), and speaks of groups of churches that emphasize Christian brotherhood, mystical lay piety, the inner life of the soul, and imitating the life of Christ. The Brethren were self-supporting and self-educated. Thomas à Kempis was influenced by them in writing his *Imitation of Christ*, a work that to this day is still a devotional classic.

Later, the term *Brethren* became associated with German Pietists (from the Anabaptist tradition) led by Alexander Mack at Schwarzenau, Germany, in 1708. They were pacifist Pietists who practiced trine-immersion (believer's baptism three times face forward), foot washing, communion, love feasts, and anointing the sick. American Brethren groups include the Church of the Brethren (Elgin, Illinois), the Brethren Church (Ashland, Ohio), and the National Fellowship of Brethren Churches, often called the Grace Brethren (Winona Lake, Indiana). All together, the Brethren churches number about 300,000 members.

The Brethren in Christ churches were organized between 1775 and 1788 in Lancaster County, Pennsylvania, under the leadership of Jacob and John Engel, who were formerly Swiss Mennonite Anabaptists. Originally simply called Brethren, they were later known as River Brethren, and by 1862, they officially became the Brethren in Christ. They are affiliated with the Mennonite Central Committee, the National Association of Evangelicals, and the National Holiness Association. Their headquarters is in Nappanee, Indiana.

Various Brethren groups range from Arminian to Calvinistic. The latter are often identified with the Grace Brethren associated with Grace College and Grace Theological Seminary (Indiana), founded by Alva McClain (a dispensational premillennialist). Creationist Dr. John Whitcomb, coauthor of *The Genesis Flood* (1961), theologian Dr. Herman Hoyt, Old Testament scholar Dr. John Davis, and New Testament scholar Dr. Homer Kent Jr. were among the major proponents of moderately Pietistic/Calvinistic dispensational theology.

Ed Hindson

Bibliography

Clouse, Robert. "Church of the Brethren." *The New International Dictionary of the Christian Church*. Edited by J.D. Douglas. Grand Rapids: Zondervan, 228.

Kent, Sr., H.A. *250 Years Conquering Frontiers: A History of the Brethren Church*. Winona Lake, IN: BMH Press, 1958.

B

BRIGHT, WILLIAM "BILL" (1921–2003)

William Rohl "Bill" Bright was the founder of Campus Crusade for Christ (now called Cru as of 2012), a major evangelistic ministry to students on university campuses. He started the ministry at University of California, Los Angeles (UCLA), in 1951, and it has since spread abroad to 191 countries and expanded to include 29 different ministries to such areas as inner cities, the armed forces, athletes, secular leaders, and families (Cru Press Kit, 2012).

Before founding Campus Crusade, Bill Bright worked as a successful business owner of his own company, Bright's California Confections, until his conversion through the ministry of Hollywood Presbyterian Church. His seminary education moved him from one coast to the other; he attended both Princeton Theological Seminary and then Fuller Theological Seminary. In 1948, he married Vonette Zachary, a young lady he knew from his hometown of Coweta, Oklahoma. The call of full-time ministry led Bill to quit Fuller Theological Seminary in his last year, sell his business, and move near the UCLA campus to begin offering and leading evangelistic Bible studies for college students, especially those involved in athletics and fraternities. The success of those early efforts, at least partially due to Bill's authoring of a gospel tract titled *Have You Heard of the Four Spiritual Laws?*, eventually led to the suggestion that he expand the ministry to other campuses.

In just eight short years the ministry grew to 109 staff members on 40 campuses in 15 states, in part because of the support of evangelist Billy Graham. After six decades of ministry, Cru now employs more than 25,000 full-time staff—most of whom raise their own support—and over 225,000 trained volunteer staff in 191 countries. The ministry serves 1140 campuses across America. Bright authored over 100 books and booklets, including *Revolution Now* (1969), *Come Help Change Our World* (1979), *Ten Basic Steps Toward Christian Maturity* (1968), and *Handbook of Concepts for Living* (1981). Another shining achievement of this international ministry was the production of the *Jesus* film in 1979, which has been distributed worldwide in many different languages.

Christopher Moody

Bibliography

Cru Press Kit. "Profile: Bill and Vonette Bright, Founders of Campus Crusade for Christ International." Cru Newsroom. http://www.demossnews.com/ccci/additional/profile_bill_and_vonette_bright_founders_of_campus_crusade_for_christ_inter. Accessed August 30, 2012.

Melton, J. Gordon. *Religious Leaders of America*, 79-80. 2d ed. Detroit, MI: The Gale Group, 1999.

Richardson, Michael. *Amazing Faith: The Authorized Biography of Bill Bright, Founder of Campus Crusade for Christ.* Colorado Springs: Waterbrook Press, 2011.

BRYAN, WILLIAM JENNINGS (1860–1925)

William Jennings Bryan was born in Salem, Illinois, to Silas and Mariah Jennings Bryan. When he was 14, he went to a revival at which he became a Christian, was baptized, and became a member of the Cumberland Presbyterian Church. Until age ten he was homeschooled, but thereafter he attended Whipple Academy and eventually entered its parent school—Illinois College in Jacksonville, Illinois. Bryan went on to obtain a law degree from Union Law College in Chicago, where he met and married fellow lawyer Mary Baird in 1884. Bryan practiced law back in Jacksonville (1883–1887) and later in Lincoln, Nebraska, where he began his political career.

Bryan joined the Democratic Party and was elected to represent Nebraska in the United States Congress for two terms (1891–1895). He lost a US Senate race in 1894, and despite being the party's nomination for president of the United States three times (1896, 1900, and 1908), he lost all three races to the Republican candidates William McKinley, Theodore Roosevelt, and William Howard Taft. He also served as Woodrow Wilson's Secretary of State (1913–1915). Bryan was very influential in US politics. Many crowds came to hear him speak on the Chautauqua Lecture Circuit between political campaigns. He fought for the rights of the common American, campaigned for a silver standard of currency, promoted women's suffrage, pushed for prohibition, and spoke for those in the rural and Western portions of America.

Of all the things Bryan is remembered for, none will compare to his tireless work against the public schools' teaching of Darwin's theory of evolution as if it were established scientific fact. Bryan maintained that to deny the existence of God is to deny his creation of the world and therefore his authority over it. Without God, there is no basis for moral law. Bryan eventually agreed to serve on the prosecution against a high school teacher in Dayton, Tennessee, who broke a state law by teaching evolution in a public school. The Scopes Monkey Trial (1925) attracted great interest around the country. While Bryan won the case, the cause eventually lost popular support in America, though it is still widely debated today. Bryan died five days after the conclusion of the trial from a combination of diabetes and exhaustion. Before he died, he cast a vision for the creation of a college in Dayton that would teach creationism. His friends raised support for William Jennings Bryan College, which opened its doors in 1930 and continues to offer a Christian liberal arts education on a hill overlooking Dayton's Rhea County Courthouse.

Kenneth Cleaver

Bibliography

Bryan, William Jennings, and Mary Baird Bryan. *Memoirs of William Jennings Bryan, by Himself and His Wife*. 2 vols. Chicago: John C. Winston, 1925.

Cherny, Robert W. *A Righteous Cause: The Life of William Jennings Bryan*. Boston: Little & Brown, 1985.

Kazin, Michael. *A Godly Hero: The Life of William Jennings Bryan*. New York: Alfred A. Knopf, 2006.

Koenig, Louis W. *Bryan: A Political Biography of William Jennings Bryan*. New York: Putnam, 1971.

BULLINGER, HEINRICH (1504–1575)

Protestant Reformer Heinrich Bullinger has been called "the common shepherd of all Christian churches" for his multifaceted ministry that began following the death of Ulrich Zwingli on the battlefield of Kappel (1531). Bullinger was a scholar (author of *The Second Helvetic Confession*), rector of a theological academy, preacher, and during the plague of 1564, his sacrificial care for those in Zurich exemplified the best of pastoral care (Sharf, 3). He worked tirelessly toward the unification of the various factions among the reformers. There are 15,000 extant letters that he wrote that spread across every corner of the Protestant world at the time. As a local pastor, he preached six to seven times a week for more than 40 years. He negotiated the *Consensus Tigurinus* (1549) with John Calvin and William Farel (the *Consensus* unified Reformed churches with regard to the Lord's Supper). He also provided much-needed hospitality to the Protestants who fled the persecution in England under Queen Mary I, which enabled him to develop valuable relationships with England's future church leaders, and he defended the teachings of the reformers (Pine, 33-34).

Born to a priest in 1504 in Bremgarten (a small town about ten miles west of Zurich), Bullinger was sent to Cologne University in the hopes he would follow his father's footsteps. While there, his interest in theology was aroused with the burning of Martin Luther's books in the wake of Luther's excommunication. The years of 1520–1522 were pivotal for Bullinger. It was during this time that he discovered the Fathers, read for the first time Matthew's Gospel, and then through reading Melanchthon's *Loci Communes* came to embrace the evangelical faith. He would write that "I discovered that salvation came from God through Christ" (Berthoud, 10-11).

Bullinger graduated from Cologne in 1522 with a master's degree and began teaching at Cistercian monastery at Kappel in 1523. There, he abolished the Mass in 1525 and replaced it with a reformed rite in March of 1526 (Trueman, 90).

The most significant development for Bullinger during this period was meeting Zwingli. He attended the January 1525 Zurich Disputation, became the clerk of the next two disputations, and then in 1527 studied under Zwingli in Zurich. In 1528, Bullinger, along with Leo Jud, drafted a clerical and synodal constitution that was approved by the Zurich Council in 1532 and remained as the foundation for religious life in Zurich for centuries (Wood, 8). Bullinger married in 1529, and his home served as a model, just like his pastoral ministry would, of Reformation principles. In the same year, Bullinger also succeeded his father as pastor in Bremgarten. Upon the death of Zwingli in 1531, Bullinger succeeded Zwingli as the chief pastor of Zurich. For the next 44 years, Bullinger directed the development of the Reformation in Zurich and displayed the heart of a pastor as he worked as a moderating influence with the Reformed communion.

Kevin L. King Sr.

Bibliography

Berthoud, Jean-Marc. "Heinrich Bullinger (1504–1575) and the Reformation: A Comprehensive Faith." The Evangelical Library Annual Lecture 2004, 10-11. http://www.elib.org.uk/lectures/el_2004_bullinger.pdf. Accessed September 3, 2012.

Pine, Leonard W. "Henrich Bullinger: The Common Shepherd of All Christian Churches." *WRS Journal* 3:2 (August 1996): 33-35.

Sharf, Greg R. "Was Bullinger Right About the Preached Word?" *Trinity Journal* 26NS (2005): 3-10.

Trueman, Carl R. "Bullinger, Heinrich (1504–1575)." *The Dictionary of Historical Theology.* Edited by Trevor A. Hart and Richard Bauckham. Milton Keynes, UK: Authentic Media, 2000.

Wood, Jon Delmas. "Heinrich Bullinger's Sermons Syondales: New Light on the Transformation of Reformation Zurich." PhD dissertation, Princeton Theological Seminary, 2008.

BUNYAN, JOHN (1628–1688)

B

Puritan Baptist preacher and author John Bunyan was born at Elstow, near Bedford, England, in the fall of 1628. Greaves observes, "Bunyan's life spanned that tumultuous period of English history extending from the Petition of Right in 1628 to the Glorious Revolution of 1688" (Greaves, 15). Stunned by the death of his mother in 1644 and his father's abrupt remarriage, Bunyan joined the Parliamentary Army, where he was exposed to the preaching captain of Cromwell's Ironsides (troopers in the Parliamentarian cavalry). After Bunyan received his discharge, he married a devout Protestant woman whose father gave him two books that were instrumental in Bunyan's subsequent conversion and influenced his own writings. These were Arthur Dent's *The Plain Man's Pathway to Heaven* (1601) and Lewis Bayly's *The Practice of Piety* (ca. 1613).

Bunyan originally worked as a tinker, mending pots, grinding knives, and repairing various metal implements. During a visit to Bedford he was spiritually impressed by the testimonies of some women who were members of John Gifford's Puritan Congregational Free Church, later the Baptist Church of Bedford. In time, Gifford's preaching and Bunyan's reading of Luther's commentary on Galatians led to Bunyan's conversion. In 1653, Bunyan joined the nonconformist church, which was comprised of both Congregational and Baptist members. By 1657, he was appointed a deacon and began preaching while still working as a tinker. His earliest works were polemics against Quaker teaching, entitled *Some Gospel-Truths Opened* (1656) and *A Few Sighs from Hell* (1658). His first theological work was *The Doctrine of Law and Grace Unfolded* (1659).

Bunyan's wife died in 1658, and he remarried a year later. By 1660, the restoration of the monarchy ended the era of Puritan tolerance, and Bunyan was imprisoned for two periods of six years from 1660 to 1672 for his nonconformist views. During these years of imprisonment, he wrote *Grace Abounding to the Chief of Sinners* (1666) and *A Defense of the Doctrine of Justification* (1672). Released from prison in 1672 by the Act of Pardon, Bunyan was chosen as the pastor of the church he had attended at Bedford. From then until his death in 1688 he produced his greatest literary works, including *Pilgrim's Progress* (1678 and 1684), *The Life and Death of Mr. Badman* (1680), and *The Holy War* (1682).

While Bunyan's theology centered upon the Puritan and Calvinist view of grace, he was a separatist Baptist in his views of baptism and the church. Beyond his personal ministry in Bedford, he is most remembered for his narrative and allegory. His incredible word pictures and poetic style are seen in the many characters of *Pilgrim's Progress* and his descriptions of the Hill of Difficulty, the Slough of Despond, the Delectable Mountains, the City of Destruction, and heavenly Mount Zion. Bunyan's allegories so resonated with common English readers that *Pilgrim's Progress* became the best-selling book after the Bible in all of England.

Ed Hindson

Bibliography

Bacon, E.W. *John Bunyan: Pilgrim and Dreamer*. Grand Rapids: Baker, 1983.

Brown, John. *John Bunyan: His Life, Times, and Work*. New York: Houghton Mifflin, 1888.

Duffield, G.E. "Bunyan." *The New International Dictionary of the Christian Church*. Edited by J.D. Douglas. Grand Rapids: Zondervan, 1978.

Greaves, R.L. *John Bunyan*. Grand Rapids: Eerdmans, 1969.

BYZANTINE CHRISTIANITY

The Eastern Orthodox churches and cultures were associated with Constantinople of the ancient Byzantine Empire. On May 11, 330, the Roman emperor Constantine christened his new capital at Constantinople. Most historians mark this as the beginning of the Byzantine Empire. Constantine considered himself to be the representative of God on earth. Having authorized the legitimacy of the Christian religion by the Edict of Milan in 313, he presided over the Council of Nicea in 325 and viewed himself as *pontifex maximus*. In the years that followed, Constantine rivaled Rome as the most important city in Christendom. The Byzantine Orthodox Church acknowledged seven ecumenical councils held between 325–787, which condemned Arianism and Monophysitism, and affirmed the doctrine of the Trinity. During those centuries, religion permeated all aspects of life in the Byzantine Empire, which saw the building of the Church of the Holy Sepulcher in Jerusalem and the Hagia Sophia church in Constantinople. The Byzantine period also saw extensive copies of the Greek New Testament circulated, which later became known as the Byzantine Text, which underlies the *Textus Receptus* used in early English translations of the Bible.

Ed Hindson

Bibliography

Mango, Cyril. *Byzantium: The Empire of New Rome*. New York: Scribner's Sons, 1930.

✠

JOHN CALVIN
Protestant Reformer
1509–1564

CALVIN, JOHN (1509–1564)

John Calvin was a French Reformer born at Noyon in Picardy, France, in 1509. He was the son of Gérard Cauvin, who was an administrative assistant to the bishop of Noyon, a connection that would pave the way for young Calvin to enter the minor orders and continue his education in Paris. It was here that Calvin developed his distaste for the obscurity of scholastic theology and came under humanist influences that would so impact his writing. At the request of his father, Calvin moved in 1528 to Orléans, then Bourges, to study law. Following his father's death in 1531, Calvin moved back to Paris in pursuit of classical literature studies. At some point between 1527 and 1534, Calvin had a sudden conversion experience. Little is known about the particulars of this event, but by 1533, he was clearly advocating church reform.

As the French Reformation heated up, the persecution aimed at Protestants in Paris became unbearable. Calvin fled to Basel, Switzerland, where he wrote the first edition of his *Institutes of the Christian Religion*, published in 1536. The *Institutes* became an immediate success and established a new theological direction for Reformation doctrine. Calvin's early genius lent just the right voice to Protestants who, with Ulrich Zwingli dead and Desiderius Erasmus dying, needed a new impetus to keep the movement going. Calvin preferred scholarship, but providence had other plans. An unexpected stop in Geneva for Calvin led to his staying there for two years, making the connection that would mark his life.

After Calvin was ousted from Geneva over an issue of church discipline, he traveled to Strasbourg, where he spent three productive and enjoyable years as pastor of a small French congregation. He became a teacher of Scripture and published a new edition of the *Institutes* in 1539, roughly triple the size of his original work. That same year he published his first commentary, which was on the book of Romans. In all, Calvin wrote voluminous commentaries on most of the Old Testament and all of the New Testament except for 2–3 John and Revelation. His commentaries set the standard for biblical exposition for centuries to come.

In 1541, at the invitation of the city councilors in Geneva, Calvin reluctantly returned there to continue his work. He struggled for many years to apply, to the community, the principles of the Christian faith he had so eloquently set down on paper. Geneva was to be a holy city (theocracy) under God's rule through church and state.

This ideal led to what is perhaps the greatest criticism of Calvin, when he accepted the execution by burning at the stake of Michael Servetus in 1533 for denying the Trinity.

Calvin's *Institutes* went through eight editions from 1536 to 1559. Calvin was never completely satisfied with his work until the final edition, a volume consisting of four books: *The Knowledge of God the Creator; The Knowledge of God the Redeemer; The Way in Which We Receive the Grace of Christ, Its Benefits and Effects;* and *The External Means by Which God Invites Us into the Society of Christ.* Calvin's chief intent was to set down a biblical theology that would lead his readers into a deeper understanding of the faith. Yet his literary output was extensive and included numerous sermons, tracts, treatises, and letters, which had a deep impact on many. Those who follow his theology are generally known as Calvinists.

Calvin's influence not only dominated Geneva in the sixteenth century, but he also became, along with Martin Luther, the dominant influence in the Protestant Reformation in general. Calvin preached regularly to a congregation at Geneva without holding an official government position. However, his concept of church government by representation (elected elders) became the basis of the Puritan and Presbyterian influence on American democracy. Many of Calvin's ideas influenced Western thought in the areas of aesthetics, science, and history as well as religion. Calvin wrote and worked extensively until his death at age 53 on May 27, 1564.

Keith Church

Bibliography

Calvin, John. *Institutes of the Christian Religion*, Library of Christian Classics, vol. 20. Edited by John T. McNeill. Translated by Ford L. Battles. Louisville, KY: Westminster John Knox, 1960.

George, Timothy. *Theology of the Reformers.* Nashville, TN: Broadman & Holman, 1988.

Hesselink, I. John. "Calvin's Theology." *The Cambridge Companion to John Calvin.* Edited by Donald K. McKim. Cambridge, UK: Cambridge University Press, 2004.

Parker, T.H.L. *John Calvin: A Biography.* Philadelphia: Westminster, 1975.

Wendel, François. *Calvin: Origins and Development of His Religious Thought.* Translated by Philip Mairet. Durham, NC: Labyrinth Press, 1963.

CALVINISM

Calvinism properly refers to the theological system of John Calvin, one of the leaders of the second generation of the Protestant Reformation in the sixteenth century, particularly as found in his *Institutes of the Christian Religion*. The term *Calvinism* is often used, however, to refer to the theological systems of all Reformed churches and individuals that base their thinking upon the *Institutes* and confessions such as the Heidelberg Catechism (1563) and the Westminster Confession and Catechisms (1647–1648). The latter use of the term implies that all Reformed thought is essentially the thought of Calvin, and this is inaccurate, as Calvin's ideas were often modified by his successors.

Others use the term *Calvinism* in reference to an individual's beliefs concerning the so-called five points of Calvinism as summarized in the popular acronym TULIP (standing for the doctrines of total depravity, unconditional election, limited atonement, irresistible grace, and perseverance of the saints). These points are based on the five articles of the Synod of Dort (1618–1619). It is debatable, however, whether Calvin himself held to all five of these doctrines as they are explained by the Synod of Dort. Regardless, there is much more to Calvin's theology than these five doctrines.

The formal principle of Calvinism is found in the Latin phrase *sola Scriptura* (Scripture only). Calvin was a biblical theologian who insisted that the words of the Bible be understood in their literal sense based upon their historical context. His *Institutes* were an attempt to systematically communicate the teachings of Scripture. Calvin taught that the Bible is the sole moral and religious authority for humanity because it is the inspired Word of God. God does communicate through creation and providence, but these communications are properly understood solely through the worldview that Scripture provides. Calvin also emphasized the need for the Holy Spirit's "internal testimony" to impress the Bible's teaching and authority upon the hearts of believers if they are to truly understand and obey the Scriptures.

The Scriptures point to the God who inspired them, and Calvin held to the orthodox doctrine of God's tri-unity. God is Father, Son, and Holy Spirit, and the three persons of the one Godhead are the same in substance and glory. Calvin stressed the sovereignty of God, which for him meant that God is completely perfect, powerful, and holy, as well as eternal and self-sufficient. God is beyond human comprehension outside of what he has revealed of himself. As the sovereign God, he is the creator of everything that exists, and he created freely according to his own good plan and purpose. God did not create and then leave his creation alone, however; he continues moment by moment to sustain its existence through the continual work of the Holy

Spirit. God is actively guiding all things in his creation, including the free actions of humanity, to accomplish his ultimate purpose of glorifying himself in all things.

According to Calvin, God created human beings in a state of innocence, which meant they were completely free to obey or disobey God's commands. This changed when Adam and Eve disobeyed God and fell into sin. Because of the fall, human beings are now by nature sinners, which means that they only will and do sin, and because they are sinners they are under the just condemnation of God. God's sovereignty, however, means that the entrance of sin into his creation did not frustrate his will or plan. In eternity past, based on nothing but his mercy and grace, God chose a large number of his fallen people to be saved. God the Father also purposed to send God the Son to redeem these chosen elect through an atoning sacrifice for sin. Believers in the Old Testament looked forward to Christ's promised redemption for their salvation, while believers in the New Testament look back to what Christ accomplished on the cross for their salvation.

The heart of Calvin's theology of salvation is union with Christ through the Holy Spirit, which happens solely through faith. The only way condemned sinners are able to trust Christ and his atonement for them is through the effectual work of the Holy Spirit upon them. When the Holy Spirit saves someone, he does so by uniting them to Christ, meaning that all the benefits of Christ's sinless life, penal substitutionary death, and victorious resurrection become the believer's through his or her relationship to Christ. From beginning to end, salvation is a work of God upon the believer.

Once saved, believers become citizens of God's kingdom and serve him together as the church. The church is made up of all believers from both the Old and New Testament eras, as well as their children. Baptism signifies the entrance of believers and their children into the visible body of the church, and the Lord's Supper is a continuing sacrament that bestows grace upon those in the church who partake of it in faith. Calvin taught what has become known as the Presbyterian model of church government, which concentrates the authority of the church in elders elected by the congregation. Calvin also believed that the state should be subject to the church. The church looks forward to the second coming of Jesus Christ and will continue for all eternity.

It is almost impossible to overestimate the influence of Calvinism. All Reformed and Presbyterian churches base their doctrines upon Calvin's teachings. Theologians such as Theodore Beza, John Owen, Jonathan Edwards, Abraham Kuyper, Herman Bavinck, Charles Hodge, B.B. Warfield, J. Gresham Machen, Karl Barth, and J.I. Packer are among those who have elaborated upon and developed Calvin's thought over the last 400 years.

Calvinism has spread throughout the world due to Calvinist missionary activity. Beyond the theological sphere, Calvin's thought has decisively influenced politics, art, philosophy, science, economics, and social reform, particularly in Europe and North America. Despite the fact there are many who reject the basic principles of Calvinism, Calvin's theology continues to influence millions of Christians today.

Gary L. Shultz Jr.

C

Bibliography

Calvin, John. *Institutes of the Christian Religion.* Edited by John T. McNeill. Translated by Ford Lewis Battles. Library of Christian Classics, vols. 20-21. Philadelphia: Westminster, 1960.

Horton, Michael. *For Calvinism.* Grand Rapids: Zondervan, 2011.

Kuyper, Abraham. *Lectures on Calvinism.* Grand Rapids: Eerdmans, 1943.

Stewart, Kenneth J. *Ten Myths About Calvinism: Restoring the Breadth of the Reformed Tradition.* Downers Grove, IL: InterVarsity, 2011.

CAMPBELL, ALEXANDER (1788–1866)

Christian Restorationist Alexander Campbell was the principle leader of a powerful nineteenth-century church reform effort centered in America. His goal was the restoration of Christianity to what he perceived to be the pure and primitive New Testament faith and practice. Though he detested denominations and party spirit, he is paradoxically seen as one of the key leaders in founding the Christian Church tradition in the United States.

Alexander Campbell was born in Ireland in 1788. His father, Thomas Campbell, emigrated to America in 1808 and became the pastor of Brush Run Church, a Presbyterian congregation in Pennsylvania. When Alexander and the rest of the family tried to follow later, nearly all of them were lost at sea in a shipwreck off Scotland. Alexander himself experienced the call to ministry in this crisis and was able to spend a packed year of theological study at the University of Glasgow as his family rested and refitted for a second attempted passage. It was during this time that Alexander first began to have doubts about certain beliefs and practices of the Presbyterians, who were at that time fragmented into several competing synods in Scotland and Ireland.

Upon arriving in America in the fall of 1809, Campbell discovered that his father had been censured by the Presbyterian Synod and, as a result, had withdrawn his church from their fellowship. Both of them determined to work together in the matter of a new reformation with the goal being the restoration of primitive Christianity as modeled in the New Testament. One of the key issues that surfaced early in the

C

reform effort was the matter of infant baptism. Like many Baptists before them, the Campbells came to the conclusion that the New Testament knew only of the baptism of believers. That decision led to a season of affiliation with the Baptists, including active involvement in the Redstone Baptist Association.

As time went on, however, Alexander came to see the Baptists as just another sect that stood in the way of a genuine restoration of primitive New Testament Christianity and separated from them as well. Throughout his career, Campbell's beliefs continued to evolve, usually in the direction of ever more minimalistic expressions of his faith. He came to reject all use of creeds, choosing instead only to speak on topics directly addressed in Scripture and even to limit his thoughts about those things to that which could be expressed in words lifted from Scripture itself.

It was from such a woodenly literalistic framework that Alexander Campbell and his followers came to propound what has been seen as one of the key distinctives of the Christian Church tradition: a belief in the necessity of believers' baptism in order to be saved (based on their understanding of Mark 16:16). That belief, more than any other, created almost open warfare on the American religious scene as Baptists and others took strong issue with this teaching, which they saw as undercutting the doctrine of salvation by faith alone. Campbell's personal magnetism and tireless efforts in publishing, preaching, and debating continued to grow a following that was made all the larger by union with other reform-minded groups and leaders like Barton Stone of the Disciples of Christ.

Paul Brewster

Bibliography

Foster, Douglas, et al. *The Encyclopedia of the Stone-Campbell Movement*. Grand Rapids: Eerdmans, 2005.

Richardson, Robert. *Memoirs of Alexander Campbell: Embracing a View of the Origin, Progress and Principles of the Religious Reformation Which He Advocated*. 2 vols. Philadelphia: J.B. Lippincott, 1868–1871.

Wrather, Eva Jean. *Alexander Campbell: Adventurer in Freedom, a Literary Biography*. Edited by D. Duane Cummins. 3 vols. Fort Worth: Texas Christian University Press and the Disciples of Christ Historical Society, 2005–2009.

CAREY, WILLIAM (1761–1834)

Baptist missionary William Carey was born in Northampton, England, in 1761. The son of a weaver, Carey worked as a shoemaker until age 28 while also serving as a lay pastor in two Baptist churches. After reading *Captain Cooke's Voyages,* Carey's heart became inflamed for the world and he was unable to shake the conviction that the church's central mission should be making disciples of all nations. Much of this theology of missions, which was contrary to that of many Protestant Christians in his day, was articulated in his 1792 work *An Enquiry into the Obligations of Christians to Use Means for the Conversion of the Heathens.* In the same year, Carey preached this message to a gathering of Baptist ministers in Nottingham—a message summarized by the theme "expect great things from God; attempt great things for God." Shortly thereafter the Baptist Missionary Society was formed, and Carey volunteered to go. He and his wife, Dorothy, went to India in 1793. After some stints in West Bengal and the interior of the country, they moved to Serampore in 1800 and based their mission there.

Carey's pioneering work made several lasting contributions in efforts related to world missions. First, through his *Enquiry,* he initiated a paradigm shift in missions, arguing that the church in every generation is responsible for fulfilling the Great Commission. Second, he was an innovator in Bible translation. Though not formally trained in linguistics, Carey oversaw the translation work for complete Bibles in Bengali, Sanskrit, and Marathi; New Testament translation in 23 languages; and portions of Scripture in ten other languages. The work of translating the Bible and other Christian literature was facilitated by the printing press, a technological tool highly valued by Carey and the Serampore mission team. Third, Carey believed in saturation evangelism, church planting, and raising up national leaders. Finally, he valued doing contextual studies on the peoples of India so he could proclaim the gospel with as little intrusion as possible from Western culture. In the process, Carey became an Orientalist and was invited to teach at the university level.

Carey's faith and tangible contributions have earned him the title "the father of modern missions." Indeed, Carey's ministry inaugurated the "great century" of nineteenth-century Protestant missions.

Edward Smither

Bibliography

Carey, William. *An Enquiry into the Obligations of Christians to Use Means for the Conversion of the Heathens.* http://www.wmcarey.edu/carey/enquiry/enquiry.html.

George, Timothy. *Faithful Witness: The Life and Mission of William Carey.* Birmingham, AL: Christian History Institute, Samford University, 1998.

Mangawaldi, Vishal and Ruth. *The Legacy of William Carey: A Model for the Transformation of Culture.* Wheaton, IL: Crossway, 1999.

Tucker, Ruth A. *From Jerusalem to Irian Jaya: A Biographical History of Christian Missions.* Grand Rapids: Zondervan, 1983, 2004.

CHAFER, LEWIS SPERRY (1871–1952)

Lewis Sperry Chafer was a musician, evangelist, writer, theologian, and Bible teacher, and he was best known as the primary founder, theologian, and longtime president of Dallas Theological Seminary. Born in Rock Creek, Ohio, Chafer was the son of a Congregational minister who died of tuberculosis when Lewis was 11. Chafer didn't get a college education, but he did attend a Conservatory of Music in Oberlin, Ohio, for three semesters. Chafer and his wife, Ella Lorraine Case, served for a number of years as musicians with traveling evangelists, including times when Chafer did the preaching. Chafer was discipled by C.I. Scofield, who aided him in making the transition from evangelist to Bible teacher. Chafer was ordained to the ministry by the Presbyterian Church (USA) in 1912, and he aided Scofield in founding the Philadelphia School of the Bible in 1913 by writing the curriculum.

Among Chafer's significant works were *True Evangelism* (1911), *The Kingdom in History and Prophecy* (1915), *He That Is Spiritual* (1918), *Satan: His Motive and Methods* (1919), *Grace: The Glorious Theme* (1922), and *Major Bible Themes* (1926). Chafer's most significant written contribution was his eight volume *Systematic Theology* (1947–1948), which became the first comprehensive systematic expression of dispensational theology and was viewed for many years as the definitive statement of dispensational theology.

Chafer was the primary founder of the Evangelical Theological College, which became Dallas Theology Seminary in 1936. In 1922, Chafer had moved to Dallas to pastor First Congregational Church, where he succeeded C.I. Scofield. Chafer, who had moved his ordination to the Presbyterian Church, founded the new seminary with the help of First Congregational Church and First Presbyterian Church of Dallas in 1924. He served as president and professor of systematic theology at the school from 1924 until his death in 1952.

Dallas Theological Seminary was a blend of moderate Calvinism; the development of an English Bible exposition department from the Bible Conference movement in which Chafer had been greatly involved; and a dispensational view of Israel, the church, and eschatology. Before World War II most of the graduates went into the Presbyterian Church, but after the war they increasingly became the backbone of the newly emerging Bible Church movement. Chafer's school went on to become a leading conservative seminary in America, producing a multitude of well-known pastors, scholars, and Christian leaders who have greatly impacted evangelicalism throughout the world.

Prominent Dallas graduates who have influenced American evangelicalism include Charles Swindoll, David Jeremiah, Bruce Wilkinson, John F. Walvoord, Charles Ryrie, and J. Dwight Pentecost.

Grace is said by Chafer to be at the core of his theology; however, he is probably best known for his systemization of Scofield's dispensationalism. He taught that the gospel of grace should be simply and clearly presented and then one should simply challenge the sinner to believe God's message. The results should be left to God the Holy Spirit to bring conviction and perhaps conversion. Chafer was also known for his distinct view of the Christian life.

Critics of Chafer's theology often objected to his "believe only" approach to the gospel and his criticism of the public invitations given in many evangelical churches. His most positive contributions to American evangelicalism were his emphases on Bible exposition, expository preaching, and dispensational eschatology.

Thomas Ice

Bibliography

Hannah, John D. "The Social and Intellectual History of the Origins of the Evangelical Theological College." PhD dissertation. Dallas: University of Texas, 1988.

———. An Uncommon Union: Dallas Theological Seminary and American Evangelicalism. Grand Rapids: Zondervan, 2009.

Renfer, Rudolf A. "A History of Dallas Theological Seminary." PhD dissertation. Dallas: University of Texas, 1959.

Richards, Jeffrey J. The Promise of Dawn: The Eschatology of Lewis Sperry Chafer. Lanham, MD: University Press of America, 1991.

CHALCEDON, THE COUNCIL OF (451)

Chalcedon was officially the fourth ecumenical council of the Christian church. It sought to clarify the church's faith regarding the doctrine of Christ in the face of new issues, questions, and heresies. This council was called by the emperor of the Eastern Roman Empire, Marcian, to establish doctrinal unity, especially in the Eastern Church, wherein opposing Alexandrian and Antiochene views of Christ were creating much conflict. The final formulation or definition of Christology by this council has long been the standard of Christian orthodoxy regarding the two natures and single person of Christ.

Yet Chalcedon can only be properly evaluated in light of what had been concluded in the three previous ecumenical councils, Nicaea, Constantinople, and Ephesus. The Nicene Creed (325), which gave basic definitive form to Trinitarian doctrine, was centered on the relation of the Father and Son. Nicaea concluded also that Father and Son were of the "same essence" (Greek, *homoousion*); hence, the Son is fully God as is the Father, contra Arius and the Arian heresy, which said the Son was utterly different from the Father and so not truly God at *all*. At Constantinople (381) the Nicene Creed, regarding the Trinity and the Father-Son relation, clarified also the *homoousion* of the Spirit (implicit at Nicaea), and rejected the Christological heresy known as Apollinarianism (which denied Christ's true humanity, claiming that Christ's human soul was replaced by the Word/Logos). Later, the Council of Ephesus (431) condemned both Nestorianism and Eutychianism. Through this period, significant church conflicts continued between the Alexandrian (Word-flesh) Christology and the Antiochene (Word-human) Christology. A Christological outcome that united the best insights of both was needed, and to that end substantial help came from the Western church in the form of what is often called (Pope) Leo's Tome.

Marcian became emperor in the Eastern Roman Empire in 450, and an immediate concern was the achievement of church unity regarding Christ's oneness and two natures. At the Chalcedonian council, Leo's Tome, which sought to affirm and amalgamate the Antiochene (two natures) and Alexandrian (one person) contributions, was read and acknowledged as essentially defining the Christological concerns. Also accepted were definitive letters from Cyril to Nestorius (previously received at Ephesus) as well as the earlier Nicene and Constantinopolitan statements. Most at the council wanted to go no further, but Marcian perceived that a fourth defining statement was crucial to begin to unify the prominent schools of Christological formulation, both theologically and in terms of church relations.

Officially, the bishops at Chalcedon finally fulfilled the council's mandate and more fully defined the church's faith regarding Christology. To accomplish the latter, the council had to carefully deal with two major questions/concerns: maintaining the oneness/unity of Christ's person, and simultaneously affirming that Jesus Christ existed in two "natures." The council's final statement, expressed largely in negative terms, regarded the one-nature view of Christ (Eutychus, extreme Alexandrian) to be in error, and affirmed the orthodoxy of the two-nature view (Antiochene). It also accepted the propriety of the title *God-bearer* (Greek, *Theotokos*), an indirect way of referring to Christ's oneness that was popular among Alexandrians.

Christ was thereby said to be of one nature with the Father as to deity, and of one nature with us as to humanity. The unity of the two natures—the full deity of Christ and the full humanity of Christ—were said to exist "without confusion, without change, without division, without separation," coalescing in one person (*prosopon*) and one substance (*hypostasis*). Having God's redemption of human beings in Christ as their first concern, the council knew that only a Christ who was truly God and truly human could truly save.

John Douglas Morrison

Bibliography

Gonzalez, Justo L. *A History of Christian Thought*. New York: Harper & Row, 1984.

Grillmeier, Aloys. *Christ in Christian Tradition*. Louisville, KY: Westminster John Knox, 1988.

Kelly, J.N.D. *Early Christian Creeds*. London: Continuum, 2006.

Sellers, R.V. *The Council of Chalcedon*. London: SPCK, 1961.

CHAMBERS, OSWALD (1874–1917)

Oswald Chambers was an evangelical Christian born in Aberdeen, Scotland, where his father was a Baptist pastor. Chalmers himself was personally converted to Christ upon hearing Charles Spurgeon. He later studied art in London and Edinburgh and entered Dunoon College in 1897 to train for ministry. During this time he was greatly influenced by William Quarrier, from whom he learned the power of prayer and faith. In 1907 Chambers traveled to Japan and America as an evangelist for the Pentecostal League of Prayer founded by Reader Harris. From 1911 to 1915 he served as principal of the Bible Training College at Clapham Common, London. He is best remembered for his devotional classic *My Utmost for His Highest*, which combines Bible readings with devotional comments.

Ed Hindson

Bibliography
J.G. Norman. "Chambers, Oswald." *The New International Dictionary of the Christian Church*. Edited by J.D. Douglas. Grand Rapids: Zondervan, 1978.

CHARISMATIC MOVEMENT

Historically, the Charismatic movement forms amorphous strata of Christianity consisting of congregations with a theology and praxis that places emphasis on being *filled* or *baptized* with the Holy Spirit. The nomenclature *Charismatic movement* was first used in 1963 to distinguish the Renewal movement flowing through the Anglican, Catholic, Orthodox, and mainline Protestant churches. Since its formative development, other renewal streams such as the healing revivals and Faith movement have identified and merged with the Charismatic movement. It includes clergy and lay people from all walks of life, including many converted youth from the Jesus movement of the 1960s, which, in turn, had an impact on the development of contemporary Christian music.

Distinguished from what is known today as classical Pentecostalism, Charismatics share with Pentecostals an emphasis on the Holy Spirit for recovering the spiritual vitality of the church. Despite evident theological differences, Charismatics tend to speak a common language. Charismatic church ministry and distinctives are shaped by a pneumatology having its point of departure in the directive of Christ to be filled with the Holy Spirit in preparation for the mission of world evangelization (Acts 1:2,4-8; Luke 24:48-49). Theologically, the doctrine of baptism in the Holy Spirit is understood as the Holy Spirit's operation in equipping Christians to evangelize and to live empowered lives.

Today, fewer established churches self-identify with the label of Charismatic, except for adherents of the Catholic Charismatic renewal. The term *charismatic* was coined from the Greek word *charisma* (*charismata*—plural), which appears in the New Testament 17 times when referring to the gifts of the Spirit and other "grace gifts." There are nine lists or varieties of gifts in the New Testament, but nine *pneumatic* gifts are considered normative in renewal church services. From Pauline teaching (1 Corinthians 12:3-11) it is determined that the purpose of the manifestation of the Spirit is for God to be present in and among his people and for the edification of the church. Classical Pentecostalism has classified the gifts as the *vocal* gifts: tongues (*glossolalia*), interpretation of tongues, and prophecy; the *revelatory* gifts: the word of knowledge, the word of wisdom, and the discernment of spirits; and the *power* gifts: the gift of healing, the gift of miracles (or powers), and the gift of faith.

Variations of Charismatic theology are found along descriptive lines (e.g., prosperity teachings, dominion theology, and so on) and prescriptive teachings that address the essential nature and expression of the charismata. For instance, the prescriptive view of the Holy Spirit Baptism (HSB) is that it is not required for salvation; however, views differ on how the infilling is manifested subsequent to the conversion experience. Some espouse the view that the HSB is *evidenced* either by speaking in tongues or by the manifestation of any gift of the Spirit. There are also variant views on how to receive the baptism of the Holy Spirit, ranging from deliberate conscious prayer to God to the belief that the gifting of the Spirit is received at salvation and subsequently manifested during occasions of being filled with the Spirit.

Historically, the Charismatic movement is understood by some scholars to make up the *Second Wave* of Christian renewal that began in the early 1960s. Classical Pentecostals are linked to the *First Wave* of the Pentecostal movement in the early 1900s, with the *Third Wave* of Charismatics streaming in from the evangelical churches in the 1980s (Synan; Barrett), including those influenced by the Toronto Blessing. Demographically speaking, the early classical Pentecostals are generally made up of those in the working class, and the new Charismatics reflect the largely middle-class character of most evangelical churches. Unlike conventional Charismatics, Third-Wave Charismatics usually congregate as independent church groups and in non- or interdenominational churches. Third-Wave Charismatics came into prominence concurrently with John Wimber's teaching of MC510 (a course on signs and wonders) at Fuller Theological Seminary. Wimber (1934–1997), known among evangelicals for his teachings on the gifts of the Spirit and divine healing, eventually cofounded the Association of Vineyard Churches. By the year 2000, Third-Wavers were credited with 295 million members worldwide (Barrett, et al).

Since its inception, the Charismatic movement has been associated with leaders instrumental in introducing the Renewal movement in their respective denominations and at the national level. Dennis Bennett, the rector of St. Mark's Episcopal Church in Van Nuys, California, captured national headlines for the nascent Charismatic movement in the mainline Protestant churches when in 1960 he publicly shared his Spirit baptism experience with his congregation. This led to other Protestant clergy becoming vocal about their own Charismatic experiences. For example, in the Lutheran denomination, this included the prominent ministers Larry Christenson and Harold

C

Bredesen (Dutch Reformed), who befriended the Baptist minister Pat Robertson. In 1960, Robertson launched the popular *700 Club* TV program, which showcases individual testimonials of physical healing or conversion to Christ. Other important leaders of the Charismatic movement include Demos Shakarian (1913–1993, the organizer of the Full Gospel Businessmen's Fellowship International or FGBMFI), Agnes Sandford (of the Inner Healing movement), Gerald Derstine (a Mennonite), Katherine Kulhman (a notable Methodist evangelist, 1907–1976), and the Reverend David du Plessis (a South African minister who at the inception of the Charismatic movement was instrumental in reaching mainline churches with his teaching of the Holy Spirit's renewal ministry).

The extent of the Charismatic movement's organizing ability can be seen in the founding of many parachurch organizations such as the Christian Broadcasting Network (CBN), Rhema Institute, Mike Bickle's International House of Prayer (IHOP), Trinity Broadcasting Network (TBN), Oral Roberts University, and major missions agencies such as Teen Mania and Youth with a Mission (YWAM).

Ramon Moran

Bibliography

Barrett, David B., George T. Kurian, and Todd M. Johnson. *World Christian Encyclopedia*, vol. 1. Oxford: Oxford University Press, 2001.

Burgess, Stanley M. *Encyclopedia of Pentecostal and Charismatic Christianity*. New York: Routledge, 2006.

Hamilton, Michael, ed. *The Charismatic Movement*. Grand Rapids: Eerdmans, 1975.

Harrell, David Edwin. *All Things Are Possible: The Healing and Charismatic Revivals in Modern America*. Bloomington, IN: Indiana University Press, 1975.

Hummel, Charles. *Fire in the Fireplace: Charismatic Renewal in the Nineties*. Downers Grove, IL: InterVarsity, 1993.

Poewe, Karla. *Charismatic Christianity as a Global Culture*. Columbia, SC: University of South Carolina, 1994.

Synan, Vinson. *The Century of the Holy Spirit*. Nashville, TN: Thomas Nelson, 2001.

CHESTERTON, GILBERT KEITH (1874–1936)

Born in London of Anglican parents and unable to read at the age of nine, English author G.K. Chesterton overcame his inauspicious beginnings to go on to become one of the most influential English writers and Christian apologists of the early twentieth century. Although he is likely best known for his Father Brown murder mysteries (1911–1935), in addition to the thousands of essays and columns he regularly produced for various newspapers and magazines, he wrote, among other things, insightful pieces on philosophy, poetry, fantasy, biographies, and especially works in Christian apologetics.

Whether writing a scathing social and political critique on materialism and scientific determinism's inability to adequately address the dilemmas of the modern human condition, or whether publically debating his close friend George Bernard Shaw on the conceptual inconsistencies of fascism, agnosticism, and moral relativism, what attracted readers and audiences alike was Chesterton's endearing humility and wit— together with his artful use of proverbs and Christian allegory, and most especially, his inimitable use of logic and paradox in casting aspersions on the various forms of secular humanism and evolutionary naturalism that so characterized the intellectual and social attitudes of his day. Quite intriguingly, although he had already produced a rich output of seminal pieces in Christian apologetics that included such works as *Orthodoxy* (1908), *The Man Who Was Thursday* (1908), and *What's Wrong with the World* (1910), Chesterton converted to Roman Catholicism in 1922, insisting that it was the only institution in which true humanism could develop and flourish.

Critical to the form of humanism for which Chesterton so skillfully argued is a conception of the human person that can be seen against the backdrop of his high view of the majesty of man. In *Everlasting Man* (1925), for example, Chesterton argued against a reductionist and materialist view of man, insisting, among other things, that man's intrinsic value, which is divinely imputed to him, is evidenced in man's use of language, art, imagination, and creativity. These very features in the human person set us apart from brutes in both kind and degree. Like C.S. Lewis, who named *Everlasting Man* as a critical piece that shaped his worldview, Chesterton's writings, and the characters he used to tell his stories, are presented with clear metaphysical convictions that express this divinely imputed feature in man. Similarly, in his *Orthodoxy*, Chesterton appealed to the intrinsic value of man and used this seemingly undeniable feature in arguing for a conscious reaction against the pessimism of life.

Another aspect of Chesterton's giftedness can be found in his unusual ability to use virtue and allegory as a Christian apologetic. In his *What's Wrong with the World*

C

(1910), rather than casting aspersions on the classical masculine and feminine virtues, he argued instead that it is precisely such unique characteristics that bring so much value to our human identity. Equally, in his *The Man Who Was Thursday*, Chesterton showed us with almost matchless skill that allegory can have its place in extolling virtue and the uniqueness of man in story.

Thomas Provenzola

Bibliography

Ahlquist, Dale, ed. *In Defense of Sanity: The Best Essays of G.K. Chesterton*. San Francisco: Ignatius Press, 2011.

Barker, Dudley. *G.K. Chesterton: A Biography*. New York: Stein & Day, 1975.

Maycock, A.L. *The Man Who Was Orthodox*. London: Dennis Dobson, 1963.

Pearce, Joseph Chilton. *Wisdom and Innocence: A Life of G.K. Chesterton*. London: Hodder & Stoughton, 1996.

Ward, Maisie. *Gilbert Keith Chesterton*. London and Lanham, MD: Sheed & Ward, 1942; reprinted, 2005.

CHO, DAVID YONGGI (1936–   )

David Yonggi Cho founded and pastored the Full Gospel Church in Seoul, South Korea, which at one time claimed over one million members/followers. The church operates a large metropolitan hospital, one of the city's largest newspapers, Prayer Mountain (a sanctuary for meditation and intercession), Hansei University, and Elim Town (a humanitarian organization for the homeless).

Cho was raised a Buddhist but converted to Christianity at age 19 when a Christian girl visited him daily because he had contracted tuberculosis. When this happened, Cho said he had the Pentecostal experience of the baptism of the Holy Ghost, spoke in tongues, and saw Jesus in a vision. Because Cho felt God calling him into ministry, he enrolled in the Full Gospel Bible College, graduating in March 1958.

Cho began a church in the home of a friend with only five in attendance at the first service. With the help of door-to-door evangelism, attendance reached 400 members, and when the church built a 1500-seat auditorium in 1961, the attendance quickly reached 3000. Cho appointed both men and women leaders, and eventually had 20,000 cell meetings with women leading approximately half of them. In 1968, Cho purchased land for the church on Yeoui Island, a sandbar in the middle of the Han

River that ran through the city of Seoul. He was criticized for selecting this location, but many government buildings were there, and in time, the location became the center of the city. (It was there on a mall that Billy Graham spoke to over one million people in 1973.) Cho then built an 8000-seat auditorium, and later doubled its size. Cho continued to set goals—100,000 in 1972; 250,000 in 1978; 500,000 in 1984. In 1992, the church offered seven services each Sunday, and in 2000, Cho began satellite services, reaching over 50 congregations with his teaching. He retired from active ministry in 2008.

Cho originally called himself Paul Yonggi Cho because of his admiration for the apostle Paul. Later in life he changed his name to David Yonggi Cho to emphasize his shepherd nature. Cho's theology reflects a Pentecostal belief in healing, wellness, and prosperity as evidence of God's blessing. However, his teaching on the "fourth dimension" of visions and dreams has been criticized by American and British evangelicals. Despite criticism of Cho, no one can deny he built the world's largest church in the twentieth century and perhaps in all the history of Christianity. His model of cell evangelism has been copied all around the globe as an effective means of evangelism. He has fed the hungry, offered medical care to the sick, educated his followers, and left a monumental work in South Korea.

Elmer Towns

Bibliography

Cho, David Yonggi. *The Fourth Dimension,* vol. 1. Gainesville, FL: Bridge-Logos Publishers, 1979.

Horton, Michael. *The Selling Out of the Evangelical Church.* Chicago: Moody Press, 1997.

Towns, Elmer L., John N. Vaughan, and David J. Seifert. *The Complete Book of Church Growth.* Wheaton, IL: Tyndale House, 1981.

CHRISTIAN SCIENCE

Christian Science falls under the general category of what are known as the Mind Sciences. It has been observed that Christian Science is neither truly Christian nor a true physical science. Founded by Mary Baker Eddy (1821–1910), Christian Science is a monistic (i.e., all is spiritual) and pluralistic religion that denies all matter, sin, sickness, and death. The intellectual father of mind science was Phineas Parkhurst Quimby, whose ideas formed much of the foundation of Christian Science. Eddy "discovered"

C

Christian Science for herself in 1866, when she claimed she was miraculously healed from a fall. In 1875, Eddy published her book *Science and Health with Key to the Scriptures,* and in 1879 she officially founded The Church of Christ, Scientist (the official name) in Boston, Massachusetts.

Many Christian Science teachings come from *Science and Health*, which is considered divinely inspired. Christian Science uses the Bible, but it is viewed as inferior to Eddy's writings, and unreliable in and of itself. The only way to gain true meaning from the Bible is to interpret it "spiritually" with the assistance of *Science and Health*. God is defined as the Divine Mind or Divine Principle, and is an impersonal "all-in-all." Since God is all, everything is divine and nothing is material. The Holy Spirit is not a person, but the Divine Science—the universal expression or teaching of Christian Science. The Trinity is defined as the triple Divine Principle of Life, Truth, and Love.

Christian Science also distinguishes between *Jesus* and *Christ*. Jesus is seen as a mere human who demonstrated the Divine Idea (of God). Christ is the divine manifestation of God, who apparently came to the flesh to destroy fleshly error. Jesus did not die on the cross, and there was no bodily resurrection of his body. Man is viewed as the compound idea of infinite Spirit—that is, the spiritual image and likeness of God. Since God is the all-in-all, man is actually part of God. Hence, man is perfect, without sin, and eternal. Eddy said that all matter, evil, sin, disease, and death are unreal. Jesus is seen merely as our "way-shower" to salvation, and mankind must save itself by ceasing to believe in the illusion of sin and death. Heaven is the total reign of Divine Science, and there is no literal hell.

Christian Science stands in complete contrast to evangelical Christianity, which holds that the Bible alone is inspired by God, and that there is no justification for randomly spiritualizing the plain meaning of the Scriptures. The Christian God is one God made up of three eternal, distinct, and equal persons—the Father, the Son, and the Holy Spirit. The God of the Bible is separate from his creation; by contrast, the God of Christian Science is essentially a semipantheistic "idea." Eddy's denial of matter, sin, and death does not correspond to reality. Merely believing that these things do not exist does not make it so. Finally, Christianity does not espouse a view of self-attained salvation, but insists that salvation is solely by God's grace through faith in Christ. Christ is not merely a way-shower but the Way (John 14:6).

Daryl Rodriguez

Bibliography

Cather, Willa, and Georgine Milmine. *The Life of Mary Baker G. Eddy and the History of Christian Science.* Lincoln, NE: University of Nebraska Press, 1993.

Eddy, Mary Baker. *Science and Health with Key to the Scriptures.* Boston: Trustees Under the Will of Mary Baker G. Eddy, 1934.

Ehrenborg, Todd. *Mind Sciences.* Zondervan Guide to Cults and Religious Movements. Grand Rapids: Zondervan, 1995.

Rhodes, Ron. *The Challenge of the Cults and New Religions.* Grand Rapids: Zondervan, 2001.

C

CHRYSOSTOM, JOHN (CA. 347–407)

Chrysostom is primarily known as one of the greatest preachers of the early church. People loved his sermons so much they gave him the title "Golden Mouth." The Roman Catholic and Orthodox Churches consider him a saint. He is much more prominent in art, theology, and liturgy in the Eastern Church than the Western Church.

Chrysostom was born in Antioch and baptized around the age of 20. He was ordained as a deacon in 381, and as a priest in 386. It was then that he began to gain prominence. His primary responsibility over the 12 years he spent as a priest was to preach, and in this he excelled to such a degree that this is when he became known as "Golden Mouth." His preaching style was one of a homily, in which he read a biblical passage and then provided commentary on it. He preached consecutively through the books of the Bible and explained the theological and practical implications in ways that the common people appreciated and understood. His theological output rivaled that of other teachers in his day; Jerome, writing in 392, referred to Chrysostom's outstanding contribution to theology. In addition, Chrysostom undertook a reform of the liturgy, which resulted in a number of popularly used liturgies.

Chrysostom was unexpectedly made bishop of Constantinople in 397 by Emperor Theodosius I. While he continued to write, his focus changed to that of a religious leader in a large city. He spent much time on resolving ecclesiastical matters. He alienated the emperor's wife by his actions in several highly public matters, which eventually led to his banishment in 403 at the Synod of the Oak. One of the charges against him was that he was an Origenist heretic, which was false. Chrysostom later died during a forced march into exile in a distant land.

Chrysostom's writings include hundreds of commentaries on both the Old and New Testaments, and treatises on the monastic life, the priesthood, catechumens, and theology. The Divine Liturgy of St. John Chrysostom is still used by the Eastern Orthodox Churches.

Mark Nickens

Bibliography

Kelly, J.N.D. *The Story of John Chrysostom: Ascetic, Preacher, Bishop*. Ithaca, NY: Cornell University Press, 1995.

Maxwell, Jaclyn L. *Christianization and Communication in Late Antiquity*. New York: Cambridge University Press, 2006.

Mayer, Wendy, and Pauline Allen. *John Chrysostom*. New York: Routledge, 2000.

CHURCH GROWTH MOVEMENT (1950–2000)

The church growth movement began in the heart and vision of its modern-day founder, Donald McGavran. In the 1950s as a missionary in India, McGavran saw some examples of inept attempts of Christian churches to evangelize the lost. Slowly, McGavran formed several hypotheses that, with time, proved to be the foundational concepts of what was to become the modern church growth movement. These have generally been identified as (1) focus on people groups, (2) social receptivity, (3) numerical growth, (4) scientific research, and (5) methodology. McGavran emphasized the need to analyze and develop strategic approaches to effective evangelism, which he believed would produce measurable results—hence, church growth.

In time, the work of the church growth movement has developed three distinctive elements. First, church growth measures observable, countable, repeatable phenomena. Second, church growth involves church planting based on reaching specific social and ethnic groups. Third, it provides scientific research that is data-driven with the purpose of discovering principles that are most effective in evangelizing new people groups.

When the church growth movement was growing rapidly during the 1970s, it was not without its critics, who accused church growth proponents of stressing numerical growth, proselytism, priority of the church over interdenominational agencies, priority of evangelism over ministry, overemphasis on removing barriers that prohibited evangelism, pragmatism versus scriptural authority, and manipulative evangelism and/or unbiblical motivation. Also, some criticized the "homogeneous unit principle" of church growth theory as cultural exclusivism rather than understanding it as an evangelistic outreach strategy.

The positive contributions of the church growth movement of the late twentieth century include its emphases on effective evangelistic strategies, targeting specific social groups, measuring numerical results, and encouraging the growth of local churches.

Elmer Towns

Bibliography

Towns, Elmer L., gen. ed. *A Practical Encyclopedia of Evangelism and Church Growth*. Ventura, CA: Regal Books, 1995. Note articles on church growth.

_____, John Vaughan, and David Seifert. *The Complete Book of Church Growth*. Wheaton, IL: Tyndale House, 1981.

Wagner, C. Peter. *Our Kind of People: The Ethical Dimensions of Church Growth in America*. Atlanta, GA: John Knox, 1979.

C

CHURCH OF GOD

The Church of God (Cleveland, Tennessee) traces its origins to a tiny band of believers at Barney Creek in Monroe County, Tennessee. Richard G. Spurling and his son, Richard G. Spurling Jr., two Baptists concerned about the lack of spiritual vitality in major denominations and seeking renewed holiness, led a small group to form the Christian Union in 1886. The elder Spurling intended this new church to be a reform movement, reclaiming the purity of primitive Christianity. He also sought to unite all denominations in a true quest for holy living and the pursuit of God.

For the first ten years, the Christian Union existed as a Holiness group and made negligible gains in membership. In 1896, it merged with a similar group in Camp Creek, North Carolina. That same year a revival broke out, during which time about 100 people claimed to speak in tongues. This marked the transition of the body to Pentecostalism. This would mean the Pentecostal movement started here and not during the Azusa Street Revival in Los Angeles in 1906, a claim very hotly contested ("Holiness in the Highlands," 246).

In the early 1900s, more congregations were added and the movement became known as the Holiness Church. A centralized church government with an episcopal structure was established to organize an increasingly large network of local congregations. The headquarters moved to Cleveland, Tennessee, where it currently remains, when A.J. Tomlinson, formerly a Quaker, took over executive leadership and added his own congregation to the Christian Union. The first General Assembly convened in 1906, and in 1907, the name *Church of God* was adopted to signify the twin emphases of Christian unity and holiness.

Under Tomlinson's leadership, the Church of God split in 1923. Ousted from control over allegations of financial malfeasance, Tomlinson led the small faction in the schism to form yet another Pentecostal denomination, which came to be called the Church of God of Prophecy.

The episcopal polity is balanced with an egalitarian theology. While speaking in tongues is considered the initial sign of the baptism of the Holy Spirit, such an occurrence is only the beginning of sanctification. All church members are also expected to pursue a life of holiness and separation from the world. Early in its history, the Church of God eschewed so-called man-made creeds, such as the "five fundamentals" (of Fundamentalists), even though it held to the doctrinal positions taught in those fundamentals. This also prompted the church to avoid any kind of interdenominational cooperation. By the middle of the twentieth century, however, these positions had changed. The body became a charter member of the National Association of Evangelicals, and went on to publish increasingly detailed doctrinal statements.

Like other evangelical denominations, the Church of God demonstrates a commitment to missions. As a result, the church has spread to nearly 200 countries. Currently the Church of God is one of the largest Pentecostal denominations in world, with most of its members living outside the United States. Of those living in North America, about one-third reside in Appalachia.

Joseph Super

Bibliography

Anderson, Robert Mapes. *Vision of the Disinherited: The Making of American Pentecostalism*. New York: Oxford University Press, 1979.

Bowdle, Donald N. "Holiness in the Highlands: A Profile of the Church of God." *Christianity in Appalachia*, 243-56. Edited by Bill Leonard. Knoxville: The University of Tennessee Press, 1999.

Conn, Charles W. *Like a Mighty Army: A History of the Church of God, 1886–1995*. Cleveland, TN: Pathway Press, 1996.

Crews, Mickey. *The Church of God: A Social History*. Knoxville: University of Tennessee Press, 1990.

Synan, Vinson. *The Holiness-Pentecostal Movement in the United States*. Grand Rapids: Eerdmans, 1971.

CHURCH OF GOD IN CHRIST

Charles Harrison Mason and Charles Price Jones, two black Baptist preachers, founded the Church of God in Christ (COGIC) in Mississippi in 1897. They started this group after a revival in which they advocated complete sanctification as a distinct, second work of grace accomplished by the baptism of the Holy Spirit. This doctrine was associated with the emerging Holiness movement, which owed much to Methodism. The Holiness message they preached was inconsistent with Baptist teachings, and so both men broke away from the Baptists. Taking with them those who were converted during the protracted revival meeting, they formed a new denomination, which initially was called the Church of God. Because so many groups of believers were separating themselves from mainline denominations under the name Church of God, Mason decided to rename the body the Church of God in Christ.

The Church of God in Christ reflects the relationship between the Holiness movement and Pentecostalism in the late nineteenth and early twentieth centuries. For roughly the first decade, the church continued to adhere to standard Holiness ideas of the pursuit and practice of the sinless life. Gifts of the Spirit, such as speaking in tongues and faith healing, played at best a minor role in denominational life and practice. However, reports of a special outpouring of the Spirit and speaking in tongues at the Azusa Street Revival in Los Angeles attracted the attention of Mason, Jones, and other COGIC leaders. Mason, J.A. Jeter, and D.J. Young traveled to Southern California to investigate for themselves. While there, Mason claimed to speak in tongues (Butler, 29-31)

Upon returning East, Mason began to preach that speaking in tongues was the initial evidence of the baptism of the Holy Spirit, although not everyone was convinced. At a convention in Jackson, Mississippi, in 1907, Jones and Jeter rejected these ideas, asserting simply that speaking in tongues was but one of many possible evidences of true holiness. Division ensued, resulting in Mason's expulsion. Undeterred, Mason immediately reformed the Church of God in Christ in Memphis, Tennessee—this time as a Pentecostal denomination. D.J. Young, one of the emissaries to the Azusa Street Revival, joined him. After a legal battle with the Jones/Jeter faction, Mason won the right to use the name Church of God in Christ. The former group continued as a Holiness church under the name Church of Christ (Holiness).

Initially, Mason's new church was concentrated in just a few states in the South, but it quickly spread throughout the region. Black migration to the north and west during the first half of the twentieth century helped spread the COGIC to the rest of the country, especially to urban areas. Historically, the church has been, and continues to

C

be, predominately black. It is currently one of the largest Pentecostal denominations in the world, with a presence in 60 countries, and is the fifth-largest Christian denomination in the United States. Like many other Pentecostal groups, the Church of God in Christ has an episcopal form of church government.

Joseph Super

Bibliography

Butler, Anthea D. *Women in the Church of God in Christ: Making a Sanctified World.* Chapel Hill, NC: University of North Carolina Press, 2007.

Clemmons, Ithiel. *Bishop C.H. Mason and the Roots of the Church of God in Christ.* Bakersfield, CA: Pneuma Life Publishing, 1997.

Robeck Jr., Cecil. *The Azusa Street Mission and Revival.* Nashville, TN: Thomas Nelson, 2006.

Wacker, Grant. *Heaven Below: Early Pentecostals and American Culture.* Cambridge, MA: Harvard University Press, 2003.

CHURCHES OF CHRIST

The Churches of Christ is an association of nondenominational churches that was established in 1906. It was formerly a part of a larger restoration movement known as the Christian Church (Disciples of Christ). This restoration movement was comprised of Christians who left their various denominations (Baptist, Presbyterian, and Methodist) to begin a movement focused on restoring (1) the church to its New Testament origins, and (2) unity within the body of Christ. Richard Hughes made a strong argument that the freedoms won during the French and American Revolutionary Wars caused people to want "a new kind of institutional church premised on the self-evident principle of republicanism" (Hatch, 13-14). It was believed that these were not mutually exclusive tasks, and that it was possible to accomplish both. It was also believed that both were essential for the hastening of the coming kingdom (this group initially held to a postmillennial interpretation of Bible prophecy).

It became increasingly apparent that one group of its members (which later became known as the Disciples of Christ), held a stronger allegiance to the idea of unity and ecumenicalism, whereas another group (known today as the Churches of Christ) had a greater commitment to restoring Christianity to what was perceived to be its original state. Despite these disparities, the primary reason given for the initial split was a disagreement over participation with missionary societies and the use of musical instruments during worship. The splintering group, which took on the name Churches of Christ, saw no New Testament precedent for mission agencies or the use of music in worship.

The Churches of Christ reject doctrinal creeds and theological systems such as Calvinism and Arminianism, and strongly adhere to the authority of Scripture as their only true guide. Churches of Christ believe in and cherish unity and believe there is only one true church. In their view, because denominations, creeds, and theological systems cause disunity, denominations and creeds should be discarded. They stress a strict following of the New Testament pattern of all things, from worship to church organization to mission efforts apart from work with mission agencies. They practice the New Testament model of baptism by immersion, and maintain that baptism is necessary for the remission of sins. They observe communion weekly, and the more conservative branches still do not allow for music, although some have adapted to modern church practice. It is estimated that there are approximately 1,200,000 members in more than 10,000 churches (Mead, et al, 254).

Paul Weaver

Bibliography

Dunnavant, Anthony L. "Churches of Christ." *Encyclopedia of Religious Controversies in the United States*, 100-102. Edited by George H. Shriver and Bill J. Leonard. Westport, CT: Greenwood, 1997.

Hatch, Nathan O. "The Christian Movement and the Demand for a Theology of the People." *American Origins of Churches of Christ: Three Essays on Restoration History*. Abilene, TX: ACU Press, 2000.

Hughes, Richard T. *Reviving the Ancient Faith: The Story of Churches of Christ in America*. Grand Rapids: Eerdmans, 1996.

Hughes, Richard, Nathan O. Hatch, and David Edwin Harrell Jr. *American Origins of Churches of Christ: Three Essays on Restoration History*. Abilene, TX: ACU Press, 2000.

Hughes, Richard T., and R.L. Roberts. *The Churches of Christ*. Westport, CT: Greenwood, 2001.

Mead, Frank S., Samuel S. Hill, and Craig D. Atwood. *Handbook of Denominations in the United States*. 13th ed. Nashville, TN: Abingdon, 2010.

CONGREGATIONALISM

Congregationalism is a term used to refer to both (1) a form of church government, and (2) a name used by some independent and autonomous churches that adhere to the core principles of the form of church government called by the same name.

As a form of church government, power rests in the hands of the congregation. Each local assembly is autonomous and accountable solely to its own members rather than an exterior hierarchy of leadership. Congregationalists seek to follow what is deemed the New Testament example of church organization, and hold in high regard the scriptural doctrines that (1) Christ is the head of the church (Colossians 1:18), (2) all believers are equals in Christ (Galatians 3:28), and (3) all believers are priests of God (1 Peter 2:9).

As a denomination, Congregationalism began in the sixteenth century in England while Elizabeth I was in power. The first Congregationalists concluded that reforming the Church of England was an impossible task, so they separated from the state-sponsored church. These individuals were also called *independents* and *dissenters*. This group especially found traction in England, France, and the Netherlands. They believed that the state had no right to appoint religious leaders. The ideals of this movement were articulated in the writings of Robert Browne in 1582. He maintained that any group of committed followers of Christ could be a self-governing church. While years later, and after many imprisonments, Browne would retract his earlier teachings, many others did not. Those who did not were often imprisoned, killed, driven underground, or forced to flee to other countries to attain religious freedom.

Congregationalism had a big influence upon the New World. Many on the Mayflower and subsequent ships included Congregationalists who sought religious freedom. From 1646 to 1648, many religious leaders in America met on several occasions to discuss doctrine and practice. They accepted the Westminster Confession as their doctrinal basis of agreement. They also put in writing *A Platforme of Church-discipline* (1648), which articulated the way congregations should govern themselves.

Jonathan Edwards (1703–1758) was one of the more famous and influential theologians of the Congregationalists. Although each congregation maintained individual autonomy, they did emphasize the importance of having a fellowship of congregations for mutual encouragement and missionary efforts. In 1795, the London Missionary Society was established largely by Congregationalists. In 1810, Congregationalists from Massachusetts formed the first foreign mission society (American Board of Commissioners of Foreign Missions). Because the Congregationalists maintained a strong emphasis on missions and evangelism, the movement grew to become a global association.

The Congregational churches, which historically were Calvinistic and theologically conservative, slowly became more Arminian and liberal in their theology. After 1805, many followed the influence of Harvard University into Unitarianism. In 1931, the Congregational churches merged with some Christian Churches to form the Congregational Christian Churches. In 1957, the Evangelical and Reformed Church (which resulted from a merger of two other denominations in 1934) also joined with the Congregational Christian Churches to form a denomination now called the United Church of Christ (UCC).

Despite these mergers, there were some Congregational assemblies that chose to remain independent and form other associations (Conservative Congregational Christian Conference, National Association of Congregational Christian Churches). In 1972, the UCC ordained its first openly gay minister, and in 2005, the General Synod overwhelmingly passed a resolution supporting same-gender marriages. Congregationalists have also been instrumental in uniting other fellowships and associations around the world.

Paul Weaver

Bibliography

Mead, Frank S., Samuel S. Hill, and Craig D. Atwood. "The United Church of Christ." *Handbook of Denominations in the United States.*13th ed. Nashville, TN: Abingdon, 2010.

Rohr, John Von. *The Shaping of American Congregationalism, 1620–1957.* Cleveland, OH: Pilgrim Press, 1992.

Routley, Erik. *The Story of Congregationalism Briefly Told.* London: Independent Press Ltd., 1961.

CONSTANTINE THE GREAT (CA. 275–337)

Roman emperor Constantine was the son of Constantius Chlorus and Helena. The political and military history of how Constantine became sole ruler of the Roman Empire is complex but fascinating.

When Constantine replaced his father as leader of the Roman armies in Gaul and Britain, he moved eastward against one rival at a time, often allowing them to fight one another first. This gave him time to strengthen his holdings before moving farther. In 312, Constantine marched his armies against Rome, where his rival, Maxentius, was waiting for Constantine on the Milvian Bridge north of Rome. Immediately prior to this battle, Constantine claimed to see a vision from God, in which he heard (or saw)

C

in hoc signo vince ("in this sign conquer"), which resulted in Constantine's ordering his commanders to put on their shields the Greek letters *chi* and *rho* (the first two letters in the Greek name for *Christ*). Constantine looked back on his epic victory that day as a gift from God, and from that time forward sought to please the God who gave him victory for his own sake as well as for the sake of the empire.

Constantine's "conversion" has been the subject of much debate among Christian historians. Those who question the genuineness of his conversion point to the fact that he saw himself as a high priest of Roman religions in general, including paganism. He did not become baptized until he was on his deathbed or submit himself to the teaching of Christian leaders, as was the practice of all Christians during that era. On the other hand, those who consider him to be a genuine Christian point to the fact that it was not merely a matter of political expediency for him to convert to Christianity, for Christians were neither wealthy nor powerful but a persecuted minority. When Constantine stopped the empire-sanctioned persecution of Christians with his Edict of Milan in 313, many Christians hailed him as their hero and gift from God. By 322, Constantine's eastward military campaigns resulted in his becoming the sole ruler of the empire. Many Christians hailed him as a spiritual *pontifex maximus*, a title that would later be ascribed to Roman Popes.

Constantine made Byzantium (i.e., modern Istanbul) his new Eastern headquarters. He greatly fortified the city by extending its borders and erecting large walls. He also brought in all sorts of art and precious items from around the empire, and built new buildings, including large churches. He renamed the city *Constantinople* ("City of Constantine"). His work on this city was intended to decrease the power of the old Roman aristocracy and to fortify the Eastern portion of the empire against the growing ambitions of the Germanic tribes to the north.

Also, to solidify the unity of the newly sanctioned churches across the empire, Constantine called the first-ever ecumenical council in Nicæa (325), where he presided over the discussion that resulted in the church's firmly affirming Jesus' deity and rejecting Arianism as heresy (although Constantine would later waver on his anti-Arian stance). He would forever be known in history as Constantine the Great because he officially ended the Roman persecution of Christians, and he promoted the growth and unity of the church in general across the Roman Empire.

Kenneth Cleaver

Bibliography

Bruce, F.F. *The Spreading Flame*. Grand Rapids: Eerdmans, 1958.

Eadie, John W. *The Conversion of Constantine*. Huntington, NY: Krieger, 1977.

Eusebius. *Life of Constantine the Great*. New York: Oxford, 1999.

Odahl, Charles M. *Constantine and the Christian Empire*. New York: Routledge, 2004.

Smith, M.H. From *Christ to Constantine*. London: IVP, 1971.

Stephenson, Paul. *Constantine: Roman Emperor, Christian Victor*. New York: Overlook, 2010.

C

COPTIC CHURCH

Formally known as the Christian Coptic Orthodox Church of Egypt, the phrase *Coptic Church* refers to the branch of Christianity in Egypt that traces its lineage to Mark, the author of the Gospel that bears his name. Evidence of early Christianity in Egypt dates to copies of the Bible translated into the Coptic language in the second century and the Catechetical School of Alexandria founded around 190. The leadership of the Coptic Church is referred to as *Pope* or *Patriarch* and lives in Alexandria. Coptic Christians number more than 15 million.

Along with the Catechetical School, another early contribution of the Egyptian church was monasticism, which began developing in the third century. It included Anthony and Pachomius, and quickly grew in prominence in the fourth century. Many Bibles and theological works were written in the Coptic language. One of the Popes (as defined by Coptics today) was Athanasius, who helped defeat the Arians at the Council of Nicea and who wrote a letter containing the first list of the 27 books of the New Testament.

The Coptic Church broke from the Roman and Byzantine Churches at the Fourth Ecumenical Council in Chalcedon in 451. Alternative explanations as to this occurrence range from a difference in Christological understandings to the recalcitrance of the Coptic Pope. The church has been persecuted since its inception. Their patron Mark was believed to have been martyred by the Romans, numerous Egyptian Christians were persecuted by the Romans, and then again by other Christians after 451.

Muslim armies conquered Egypt in the mid-seventh century. The invaders allowed the Coptic Christians to continue in their faith, but with restrictions. They also increased taxation on the Coptics. For 400 years the Coptics enjoyed relative peace under Muslim rule until the early 1000s, when the Caliph Hakim turned against Christians and Jews and severely persecuted many Coptics.

After Hakim, peace returned for a short time until the Crusades. During the Crusades, the Coptic Christians were caught between the Muslims, who developed a new hatred for Christianity, and the Roman Catholics, who disdained the Coptic Christians. The Muslim hatred became especially acute during the last four Crusades, in which the Crusaders attempted to land in and attack the Holy Land through Egypt. Since that time through the reign of the Ottoman Turks and to the present, the Coptics in Egypt have been constrained to a struggling minority in a largely Muslim land. Today they number around 10 percent of the Egyptian population.

The Coptic Church today is considered to be a part of the Oriental Orthodox Churches. These churches acknowledge the validity of only the first three ecumenical councils, and they are also known as non-Chalcedonian Churches and are in communion with each other.

Mark Nickens

Bibliography

Atiya, Aziz Sourial, ed. *The Coptic Encyclopedia*. New York: Macmillian, 1989.

Meinardus, Otto F. A. *Two Thousand Years of Coptic Christianity*. Cairo, Egypt: The American University in Cairo Press, 2012.

Patrick, Theodore, H. *Traditional Egyptian Christianity: A History of the Coptic Orthodox Church*. Greensboro, NC: Fisher Park Press, 1996.

CRUSADES

The term *Crusades* derives from the Latin word that translates to "cross," and the Crusades refer broadly to military campaigns undertaken by the medieval church of Western Europe to reclaim Palestine, especially the Holy City of Jerusalem, from Muslim rule. Overall, these efforts spanning nearly 200 years were a failure both militarily and morally. By the time of Muhammad's death in 632, Islam had become the dominant faith in the Arabian Peninsula. In 638, Arabian Muslims conquered Jerusalem, which they claimed, along with the Jews and Christians, as their holy city. By 691, Muslims had completed construction of the Dome of the Rock on Jerusalem's temple site as a strong and enduring symbol that Islam was there to stay. For the most part, Islamic leaders were tolerant of the other two Abrahamic faiths in Jerusalem, Judaism and Christianity, and they allowed Christian pilgrims to continue, as they had for centuries, to come visit sacred Christian sites. For a period of about 500 years, Judaism, Christianity, and Islam coexisted in Jerusalem, though with some tensions.

This came to an end when the Seljuk Turks took over Asia Minor and Palestine in 1071. By 1073, they had shut down Jerusalem, making it impossible for Christians to visit or leave. They harassed and killed would-be pilgrims. This Islamic overthrow of the Holy Land upset the Byzantine emperor, situated in Constantinople, and he called for assistance from the Christian West. From the time of the Great Schism between Eastern and Western Christendom in 1054, relations between the two major factions of the church, Roman Catholicism and Eastern Orthodoxy, had been anything but peaceful. The call was, nevertheless, answered, and under the leadership of French Pope Urban II, the First Crusade was underway by 1095.

Pope Urban II recruited crusaders by preaching a highly motivational sermon calling for a crusade to rescue the Holy Land. His exact sermon is not known, but several versions, which have quite similar content, are preserved from eyewitnesses who heard it and wrote it down. The common theme was that this crusade was necessary as a holy and just war to reclaim the Holy Land, especially the Holy Sepulcher of Christ, from the enemies of God and the cross. The religious fervor was great. The crowd began shouting "*Deus Vult*" (God wills it!) and Urban II made this the rallying battle cry for the First Crusade and had every warrior wear the sign of the cross. To elicit commitments he assured that those who participated would gain great wealth in the Holy Land, that they would face no property taxes, and that their sins would be forgiven and they would end up in heaven should they die.

The First Crusade occurred in two waves. The first was a peasants' crusade in which numerous ill-equipped, yet highly motivated, nonmilitary Europeans marched straight into a slaughterhouse when the highly skilled Turkish Muslim warriors met and defeated them before they ever reached their destination. The second wave, and what may be called the official First Crusade (1096–1099), involved European noblemen and trained armies who were able to defeat the Turks and regain Jerusalem by the year 1099. Sadly, this involved a bloodbath in which the Crusaders behaved no better than their enemies as they massacred noncombatants, women, and children, including the Jewish population. Upon achieving their objective, the crusaders set up four crusader states along a thin strip of land extending along the Mediterranean seacoast—the Kingdom of Jerusalem, the County of Tripoli, the Principality of Antioch, and the County of Edessa.

By 1144, Muslims had regrouped enough to take the County of Edessa in the north. The response to this was the Second Crusade (1147–1149), in which the goal was to reclaim Edessa. Bernard of Clairvaux, a fiery preacher, made appeals for support, and an alliance of France and Germany rose to the challenge in 1147. They met with defeat, however in 1149, and the Second Crusade had failed. By 1187, Islamic warriors had rallied their military forces under the leadership of the powerful sultan Saladin, and they sacked Jerusalem and reclaimed most of the land that made up the four crusader states.

The Third Crusade (1189–1192) was led by an alliance of the kings of England,

C

France, and Germany, who set out, once again, to try to reclaim the Holy City. The campaign was ill-fated. Frederick I Barbarossa of Germany drowned along the way, and most of his men returned home. King Philip of France, along with his men, abandoned the mission after a small victory and an unresolved dispute with England's King Richard the Lionheart. This left Richard and his army alone. King Richard eventually negotiated a truce with Muslim leaders, who agreed to grant safe passage for Christian pilgrims to Jerusalem once more. Then Richard was taken captive by the Duke of Austria while journeying through Europe, and the Third Crusade came to a halt, although he eventually was able to return to England.

The Fourth Crusade (1202–1204) set out to attack Egypt, but instead got sidetracked and did great damage to Constantinople, which was thought to have reneged on promised support to the Crusades. The overthrow of this mighty Eastern city by the warriors from the West served only to deepen the animosity and division between the Eastern and Western churches. At the same time, Islam's grip in the Holy Land only tightened, and every attempt to wrest it from Muslim rule failed miserably. The Holy Land Crusades ceased when the final crusader state fell to Muslims in 1291.

The motivations and methods of the Crusades can and should be questioned on the basis of biblical teaching. In Matthew 26:52, Christ was explicit that his kingdom would not be defended with the sword, and throughout the New Testament the apostles repeatedly declared that salvation and the forgiveness of sins are received through faith in Christ alone, and not through any actions that might be done in attempts to earn God's favor.

THE CRUSADES AND KEY FIGURES

First Crusade	1096–1099	Pope Urban II
Second Crusade	1147–1149	Bernard of Clairvaux
Fall of Jerusalem	1187	Saladin
Third Crusade	1189–1192	Richard the Lionheart
Fourth Crusade	1202–1204	Baldwin of Flanders
Fall of last Crusader State	1291	Edward I

Will Honeycutt

Bibliography

Cahill, Thomas. *Mysteries of the Middle Ages: And the Beginning of the Modern World.* New York: Random House, 2006.

Riley-Smith, Jonathan. *The Crusades: A History.* 2d ed. New Haven, CT: Yale University Press, 2005.

Runciman, Steven. *The First Crusade.* Cambridge: Cambridge University Press, 1980.

Tyerman, Christopher. *The Crusades: A Very Short Introduction.* New York: Oxford University Press, 2004.

Williams, Hywel. *A History of the Middle Ages: Power and Pageantry; 950 to 1450.* New York: Metro Books, 2011.

C

CYRIL (826–869) AND METHODIUS (CA. 815–885)

Around 860, Ratislav of Moravia petitioned the Eastern Roman emperor and the church at Constantinople for missionaries to teach his people the Christian faith. In response, the church set apart two brothers from Thessalonica, Cyril (also known as Constantine) and Methodius, to become missionaries to the Slavic peoples of Moravia. Cyril had previously served among Muslims, while both men had experience ministering to Jewish people.

These Catholic missionaries to the Slavs were convinced that the most important step in this ministry effort was to translate the Scriptures and liturgical (worship) manuals into the language of the Slavs. That is, for the gospel to take root among the Slavs, it must be understood and expressed in their language. Sadly, during the ninth century, the church had come to recognize only two possible languages for worship: Latin and Greek. While there were some who attempted to justify this, their explanations were unsatisfying. Ultimately it was the dominance of the Greco-Roman world that determined the languages of worship for the church.

Cyril and Methodius were successful in translating both Scripture and the Byzantine liturgy into Slavic. During their ministry they translated the Psalms, Gospels, Acts, Paul's letters, and the general epistles into Slavic. It should be noted that prior to their mission, the Slavic peoples had no alphabet; so the work of Bible translation required the development of a written language. A later form of this alphabet is what we know as Cyrillic.

Despite this breakthrough, Cyril and Methodius's efforts were resisted by the Roman Catholic leadership. In their defense, the brothers appealed to the example of the Armenian and Syriac churches, which had the Scriptures and worship materials available in their languages. In 867, Cyril and Methodius visited Pope Hadrian II in Rome, shared their mission story, and even led a worship service in Slavic in the basilica at Rome. As a result, the Pope gave his blessing to their efforts of developing an indigenous liturgy. Sadly, following Hadrian's death, subsequent church leaders resisted this approach to ministry and insisted that Latin be the global language of worship.

Cyril and Methodius are important for two reasons: First, they modeled what one scholar has called *the vernacular principle*—that is, the message of the gospel and the Scriptures were meant to be received in people's own languages. Second, in the case of the Slavic peoples, they helped provide them with a written language, a key element of civilization that facilitated other forms of Slavic literature and expression. Indeed, when one travels to Russia or Eastern Europe today, they will find statues and memorials to these two ninth-century missionaries who gave them the gospel and a written language.

Edward Smither

Bibliography

Neill, Stephen. *A History of Christian Missions.* London: Penguin, 1991.

Sanneh, Lamin. *Translating the Message: The Missionary Impact on Culture.* Maryknoll, NY: Orbis, 2009.

Tachiaos, Anthony-Emil N. *Cyril and Methodius of Thessalonica: The Acculturation of the Slavs.* Crestwood, NY: St. Vladimir's Seminary Press, 2001.

Tucker, Ruth A. *From Jerusalem to Irian Jaya: A Biographical History of Christian Missions.* Grand Rapids: Zondervan, 1983, 2004.

CYRIL OF JERUSALEM (CA. 310–386)

Cyril was known for his orthodox beliefs and teachings, and was ordained a deacon in the Jerusalem church around 335 and appointed a presbyter around 345. He specialized in preparing lessons for catechumens in preparation for baptism. In 350, Cyril was elected bishop of the Jerusalem church (during the Byzantine era). He vigorously opposed the idea of rebuilding the Jewish temple, which was put forth by Julian the Apostate. Often banished, Cyril fellowshipped with the bishops of Syria and Asia Minor, led by Melitius of Antioch, to restore the Nicene faith, which he clearly represented at the Second Council of Constantinople in 381. Cyril's 24 Catecheses are his major surviving work. Other biographical details, including criticisms, come from Jerome's Chronicle. Greatly beloved by the people of Jerusalem, Cyril often sold church property in order to help feed the poor.

Ed Hindson

Bibliography

Moyer, Elgin. "Cyril of Jerusalem." *Who Was Who in Church History.* Chicago: Moody, 1962. Toon, Peter. "Cyril of Jerusalem." *The New International Dictionary of the Christian Church.* Edited by J.D. Douglas. Zondervan, 1978.

DA VINCI, LEONARDO (1452–1519)

Born in 1452 near Florence, Italy, Leonardo da Vinci was a multitalented artist, sculptor, and architect. Despite the unflattering nature of his birth—he was the illegitimate son of a notary and a servant girl—da Vinci became known not only for his genius as an artist but also for his contributions to engineering, military science, anatomy, geology, aerodynamics, and botany.

Leonardo's father recognized his son's artistic talent and apprenticed him at the age of 13 to the well-known Florentine artist and sculptor Andrea del Verrocchio (1435–1488). While Leonardo was still an apprentice, Verrocchio allowed him to complete one of his commissioned paintings (*Baptism of Christ by St. John*, 1474–1475). According to legend, the master Verrocchio was embarrassed that a young apprentice demonstrated greater talent such that he eventually ceased painting.

Biblical subjects often served as the themes for da Vinci's artistic executions. For example, among the first paintings fully done by da Vinci, *The Annunciation* (ca. 1474) depicts the visit of the angel Gabriel to the Virgin Mary, and reveals the talents of a budding genius. In a garden setting the faces of Mary and the angel Gabriel glow as if from an unearthly illumination. This work and Leonardo's subsequent paintings reveal mastery of both the intricate and detailed portrayal of nature and landscapes as well as the use of chiaroscuro, or the ability to contrast light and dark to display human emotions and movement. His work served as a model for many subsequent renaissance artists.

At the age of 30, da Vinci suddenly moved to Milan and offered his talents and skill as a military engineer to the court of Ludovico il Moro. During his stay in Milan, da Vinci executed several well-known commissioned works, including the *Virgin of the Rocks* (1483) and the famous *Last Supper* (1498) for the Dominican monks of the convent of Santa Maria delle Grazie. In *The Last Supper*, da Vinci masterfully captured the two central facets of this event as told by the apostle Matthew (26:17-29)—the betrayal of Judas, and Christ's institution of the Lord's Supper.

Following his return to Florence in 1499, da Vinci executed perhaps his best-known work, *Mona Lisa* or *La Gioconda* (1503–1505). Departing from traditional portraits of women, Leonardo depicted a bold and assertive young woman looking directly at the viewer. The mystery and beauty of this painting continues to draw large numbers of viewers to the Louvre in Paris each year.

Leonardo da Vinci died in 1519 at the age of 67. His paintings reveal the work of great genius, and his notebooks with drawings of helicopters, airplanes, canal locks, and many other inventions anticipated the modern world.

Douglas Mann

D

Bibliography

Bramly, Serge. *Leonardo: The Artist and the Man*. New York: Penguin, 1988.

Osborn, Harold, ed. *The Oxford Companion to Art*. New York: Oxford University Press, 1978.

Vasari, Georgio, *The Lives of the Artists*. Translated by Julia Bondanella and Peter Bondanella. New York: Oxford University Press, 1998.

DANTE (1265–1321)

Dante Alighieri's masterpiece, *The Divine Comedy* (ca. 1307–1321), is among Christendom's greatest contributions to literature. Born in Florence, Italy, amidst ongoing religious and political turmoil, Dante held several political offices and fought in support of the papacy, but was exiled from Florence in 1302 after siding with a faction seeking to limit Rome's expanding powers. This political background was one of the greatest influences on Dante's work.

The other great influence was Beatrice Protinari, whom Dante met when they were both children. Although their paths crossed only rarely before Beatrice's death at age 24, Dante's love for her shaped his life and work intellectually, artistically, and spiritually. His passion for Beatrice exemplified the medieval ideal of courtly love, a concept rooted in the adoration of Mary, which extolled a love erotic but virtuous, unattainable but ennobling. Dante eventually married Gemma Donati, to whom he was promised at age 12 by his family, a customary practice of the time. They had several children.

Although chiefly a poet, Dante was also a significant contributor to medieval philosophy. According to his *Convivio* (1304–1307), he studied in various religious orders where he was schooled in scholasticism and the works of Aristotle, Plato, Cicero, Boethius, and many lesser-known ancient and contemporary philosophers. The learning he amassed as a layman was remarkable, as was his successful effort to transmit that learning to the general population by writing in the vernacular rather than Latin.

Dante's *The Divine Comedy*, nearly 15,000 lines composed of three parts—*Inferno* (hell), *Purgatorio* (purgatory), and *Paradiso* (heaven)—is a "comedy" according to the classical sense, ending in happiness rather than tragedy. The work is a dream vision and an allegory, reflecting a medieval worldview both concentric and hierarchical. Dante cast himself as a pilgrim on a journey, both literal and figurative, both physical and spiritual, traveling through the depths of hell, the stages of purgatory, and the heights of heaven. He was guided to the threshold of paradise by the Latin poet Virgil (philosophy), suggesting the ability of secular works to point to divine truth, but in the end it is Beatrice (theology) who leads him to the heights of heaven.

The poem presents a compendium of historical and contemporary figures, all caught in eternity in ways reflective of their actions in life. The most famous section of the poem, *Inferno,* ranks sinners in a hierarchy often startling but instructive to modern-day readers, with sins ordered according to their deviation from *agape* love. The innermost ninth circle of hell thus houses traitors such as Cain and Judas Iscariot for their sins of betrayal. Dante's poems were so powerful that they influenced popular medieval thinking regarding heaven and hell.

Love is the central theme of *The Divine Comedy*. Literally and allegorically, love leads the pilgrim into heaven as Beatrice becomes Dante's guide into heaven because the pagan Virgil is unable to enter. After rising through the ten heavens into the Empyrean, the pilgrim beholds the Beatific Vision, re-entering earth in harmony with divine love.

While visiting Rome as one of the priors of Florence, the city of Florence fell to his political enemies, and Dante was exiled from there and never saw his wife or beloved city again. His Latin treatise, *De Monarchia*, set forth his political views on the conflict between the Catholic Church and the Holy Roman Empire.

Dante continued his political and diplomatic activities until his death at the age of 56, shortly after he had completed *The Divine Comedy*.

Karen Swallow Prior

Bibliography

Auerbach, Erich. *Poet of the Secular World*. Chicago: University of Chicago Press, 1961.

Ciardi, John. *Dante: The Divine Comedy*. New York: Norton, 1977.

Jacoff, Rachel, ed. *The Cambridge Companion to Dante*. Cambridge: Cambridge University Press, 1993.

DARBY, JOHN NELSON (1800–1882)

Darby was the most prominent early leader of the Plymouth Brethren movement and formulator of modern dispensationalism and pretribulationism. Born in London of Irish parents who gave him his middle name in honor of Admiral Lord Nelson, Darby graduated from Trinity College in Dublin in 1819 as a winner of the gold medal in classics. Upon finishing law school, he was converted to Christ and became a clergyman in the Church of Ireland.

It is estimated that about 600 to 800 people a week were coming to Christ in 1826–1827 during Darby's ministry in a rural parish in County Wicklow, south of Dublin. However, this ingathering came to a sudden halt when his bishop required an oath of allegiance to the British crown. Shortly after this great disappointment Darby had a riding accident that required him to rest for a number of months. It was during this time, between December 1827 and January 1828, that he came to believe in the heavenly nature of the church and its vital relationship with her head, Christ in heaven. This thought became the fountainhead for Darby's teachings on dispensationalism and pretribulationism. From then onward, Darby never returned to the Church of Ireland.

Darby is most remembered for his eschatology; however, central to his theology was his view of the church, which he saw as totally distinct from national Israel. He saw the Bible as teaching that God was not finished with Israel; thus, after the church fulfills her earthly mission, she will be taken up to heaven at the rapture. Then the Lord will turn his attention to Israel during what is known as the seventieth week of Daniel's prophecy of the 70 weeks, during which time he will redeem the remnant of Israel and judge the nations, all of which will culminate in the second coming of Christ.

The church will then enter the millennium as the bride of Christ, reigning and ruling with him, while Israel will aid Christ in ruling over the nations during his thousand-year kingdom on earth. Darby held to a consistent application of the grammatical-historical hermeneutic throughout the entire Bible, and he saw history progressing through God's management of successive dispensations until reaching a climax during the millennial reign of Jesus Christ.

Darby is thought to have been one of the five most voluminous writers in the history of the church, including his translation of the entire Bible into three languages (German, French, and English) and the New Testament into six different languages (adding Dutch, Swedish, and Italian). He founded about 1500 churches throughout the world, and his theological influence continues to remain strong in our own day within conservative branches of Christianity. He has been described as the most influential Christian leader many have never heard about.

Thomas Ice

Bibliography

Huebner, R.A. *John Nelson Darby: Precious Truths Revived and Defended, vol. 1: Revival of Truth 1826–1845*. 2d ed., augmented. Jackson, NJ: Present Truth, 2004.

Turner, W.G. *John Nelson Darby: A Biography*. London: C.A. Hammond, 1926.

Weremchuk, Max S. *John Nelson Darby: A Biography*. Neptune, NJ: Loizeaux Brothers, 1992.

Wilkinson, Paul Richard. *For Zion's Sake: Christian Zionism and the Role of John Nelson Darby*. Milton Keynes, England: Paternoster, 2007.

D

DISCIPLES OF CHRIST

Also known as the Christian Church, this mainline Protestant denomination grew out of two independent groups (followers of Barton Stone [1772–1844] and Thomas Campbell [1763–1854]) in the early 1800s. It has no creed and allows for a variety of theological opinions among its members. It was part of the Restorationist movement, which taught that Christianity had moved from its historical roots and so needed to be "restored." Today the Disciples of Christ number nearly 650,000 members in more than 3600 churches in 46 states and in Canada. The denomination has 20 colleges and seminaries throughout the United States.

Barton Stone initially served as a Presbyterian minister. Through his personal studies, he became disillusioned with some Presbyterian beliefs as well as certain beliefs of other denominations. He believed, for example, that the word *Trinity* was not biblical. He began writing and speaking on his belief to "restore" Christianity and subsequently attracted followers. He withdrew from his position as a Presbyterian minister and came to referring to himself and his small movement as "Christian."

Thomas Campbell also served as a Presbyterian minister. He too became disillusioned with then-current Christian beliefs, and in 1809 published his ideas in the *Declaration and Address of the Christian Association of Washington*. In 1811, Campbell and his followers formed Brush Run Church. Soon afterward the members decided to begin baptism by immersion (as opposed to the paedobaptism of the Presbyterians). They accepted the invitation of a nearby Baptist association to join that group in 1815. By 1824, the Baptist association realized that many of Campbell's restorationist beliefs ran counter to their own, and so Campbell moved his church to the Mahoning Baptist Association in 1824. Doctrinal differences continued to ensue, and in 1830, the Mahoning Baptist Association disbanded.

Both Stone and Campbell's groups decided to come together in 1832 with a handshake between Barton Stone and John Stone, who represented Campbell. Stone wanted to continue using the *Christian* moniker for the group, while the Campbellites wanted to use *Disciples of Christ*. An impasse was reached and this led to both names being used to refer to the same denomination. The official name is Christian Church (Disciples of Christ).

D

The denomination split in 1906, with some churches leaving and forming the Churches of Christ. The split occurred mainly due to a difference in opinion over how to incorporate new understandings and practices. For example, the Churches of Christ did not agree with using musical instruments, such as organs, while the Disciples of Christ allowed for their use.

Disciples of Christ churches are autonomous and congregational; therefore, all decisions concerning a church are made within the local church. Members within a church agree, or "covenant," with the denominational teachings and ministries and are included in a regional ministry. A general assembly consisting of all 33 regional ministries meets to conduct denominational business and meets biennially.

Most of the Churches of Christ and Christian Churches (Disciples) are Arminian in theology and teach baptism by immersion unto repentance for salvation. Most evangelicals are concerned that they mix faith and works as both necessary for salvation in relation to their view of baptismal regeneration.

Mark Nickens

Bibliography

Cartwright, Colbert. *People of the Chalice: Disciples of Christ in Faith and Practice*. St. Louis, MO: Chalice Press, 1987.

Davis, M.M. *How the Disciples Began and Grew: A Short History of the Christian Church*. Cincinnati, OH: Standard Publishing Company, 1915.

Garrison, Winfred, and Alfred DeGroot. *The Disciples of Christ: A History*. St. Louis, MO: The Bethany Press, 1948.

DISPENSATIONALISM

Dispensationalism is a system of theology and hermeneutics that believes the Bible teaches God's single plan for history is accomplished through Israel and the church for the purpose of his glorification. This theology arises from a consistent use of the grammatical-historical hermeneutic in understanding Scripture, also known as literal interpretation. While the salvation of mankind is of extreme importance, it is accomplished within the broader purpose of the glorification of God, which is demonstrated through the various administrations of dispensational arrangements of history and also encompasses the angelic realm. Jesus Christ is the hero of history because he left heaven and humbled himself by coming to earth as a man, winning the victory at the cross, rising from the dead, and ascending to heaven. At some point in the future he will take his bride at the rapture, return triumphantly at the second coming, and reign over the earth for 1000 years from Jerusalem. Traditional dispensationalism attempts to systematize biblical teaching for the purpose of glorifying God through Jesus Christ.

While Bible interpreters have divided God's plan for history into various ages or dispensations from the earliest times of church history and throughout the centuries, it was not until the late 1700s and the early 1800s that some interpreters of Scripture in Great Britain began to see a distinction between God's plan for Israel and his plan for the church. Thus, modern dispensational theology (ca. 1825 to present) usually includes a future for national Israel, the pretribulation rapture, premillennialism, and the Israel/church distinction within the single plan of God.

Friend and foe alike trace the systemization of dispensationalism to John Nelson Darby and his Brethren colleagues during the first half of the nineteenth century in Great Britain. Darby's developments were preceded by the beginning of a movement in the late 1700s and early 1800s to return to the futurist views of eschatology taught by the early church. Darby first began to develop his dispensational thinking while convalescing from a riding accident during December 1827 to January 1828 while studying only the biblical text. Darby's developments appear to be the climax of about 250 years of post Reformational development of biblical studies that increasingly saw a future for literal Israel. The more constantly literal interpreters became in developing their Israelology, the more it led to contrasting national Israel and the church.

Finally, in an effort to take both Israel and the church literally within the plan of God, students like Darby realized that there must be a distinction between God's plan for Israel and his plan for the church. Such an understanding then made sense of the rapture of the church, which now had the purpose of removing the completed church at a future time in history so that the Lord could return and deal with Israel during the seven-year Tribulation, or the seventieth week of Daniel's 70-week prophecy.

Dispensationalism began to become influential in Great Britain through the expansion of the Plymouth Brethren movement in the last half of the nineteenth century. Darby and other Brethren brought dispensational theology to North America before the Civil War, and it spread and became popular, especially within Presbyterian circles.

Before the 1900s, Presbyterians were the primary proponents of dispensationalism because it was seen as an answer to the rise of liberalism, and dispensationalism appeared to many conservative evangelicals to make sense of the direction that Christendom and the world was headed. At the same time, dispensationalist thought was spreading to all points of the globe through the missionary work of the Plymouth Brethren and other evangelical missionaries.

As liberalism began to arise after the Civil War throughout the American mainline denominations, a reaction by conservative evangelicals produced a transdenominational fellowship of Bible teachers, most of whom were dispensational in their theology. The Bible conference movement and publications such as *The Truth* and *Our Hope* were the major means of spreading dispensationalism in the late 1800s and early 1900s. C.I. Scofield's study Bible (1909) also became a major conduit for the spread of dispensationalism throughout the English-speaking world, and dozens of Bible institutes and colleges founded throughout North America in the first half of the twentieth century were dispensational in their theology. A great number of seminaries taught dispensationalism as well, with the first one to do so being Dallas Theological Seminary (1924). It is safe to say that by World War II, the overwhelming majority of evangelical educational institutions were dispensational. And after World War II, academics played a leading role in developing a more rigorous formulation of dispensational theology. Led by Charles C. Ryrie and his classic book *Dispensationalism Today* (1965), others made contributions, such as Lewis Sperry Chafer, Alva J. McClain, John Walvoord, and J. Dwight Pentecost.

In the 1980s, an academic movement known as progressive dispensationalism began to result in a departure from classic dispensational theology. Progressive dispensationalists teach that the current church age is a spiritual form of the Davidic kingdom while still holding to a pretribulational rapture view and the premillennial return of Christ. Despite these differences, millions of Bible students still hold that dispensationalism is the best explanation for understanding the biblical teachings of God's plan for history.

Thomas Ice

Bibliography

Blaising, Craig A., and Darrell L. Bock. *Progressive Dispensationalism*. Wheaton, IL: Victor, 1993.

Fruchtenbaum, Arnold G. *Israelology: The Missing Link in Systematic Theology*. Tustin, CA: Ariel Ministries, 1994.

Ryrie, Charles C. *Dispensationalism: Revised and Expanded*. Chicago: Moody Press, 2007.

Showers, Renald E. *There Really Is a Difference! A Comparison of Covenant and Dispensational Theology*. Bellmawr, NJ: Friends of Israel Gospel Ministry, 1990.

Vlach, Michael J. *Dispensationalism: Essential Beliefs and Common Myths*. Los Angeles: Theological Studies Press, 2008.

D

DOCETISM

Docetism, from the Greek *dokesis* ("appearance"), is the early Christian heresy that held that Jesus did not possess an actual human body, but that he appeared as a type of phantom. Some argued that the eternal Christ entered into the man Jesus at his baptism and left after his crucifixion. Proponents of this view have argued that this is how Jesus was depicted by John in his Gospel.

This heresy was first challenged by Ignatius of Antioch (d. 110) through a number of letters that he wrote in the early second century while he was en route to Rome to face martyrdom. In his letter to the Trallians, Ignatius argued, "But if some atheists (that is unbelievers) say he only suffered in appearance only (while they exist in appearance only!), why am I in chains? And why do I want to fight with wild beasts? If that is the case, I die for no reason; what is more, I am telling lies about the Lord" (*Trallians*, 10). That is, Ignatius used the occasion of his own physical suffering to argue that Jesus truly suffered because he had a body. Later in the second century, Polycarp of Smyrna (d. ca. 156) also condemned this teaching in his letter to the Philippians.

Later, another form of docetic teaching was advanced by Gnostic sects who argued that Jesus' existence emanated from a divine realm of light. The fact that Jesus had a body and was crucified ran contrary to the Gnostic view that the spiritual was good and matter was evil. Such teaching was challenged by a number of second- and third-century church fathers, including Irenaeus of Lyons *(Against All Heresies)*, Hyppolytus of Rome *(Refutation of All Heresies)*, and Tertullian of Carthage *(On the Flesh of Christ)*.

Edward Smither

Bibliography

Holmes, Michael W. *The Apostolic Fathers in English*. Grand Rapids: Baker Academic, 2006.

Kelly, J.N.D. *Early Christian Doctrines*. Edinburgh: Continuum, 2000.

Quash, Ben, and Michael Ward. *Heresies and How to Avoid Them: Why It Matters What Christians Believe*. Grand Rapids: Baker Academic, 2007.

DOMINICANS

The Dominicans (also known as Black Friars) are a Roman Catholic order of preachers founded by Dominic (1170–1221). They take vows of poverty, chastity, and obedience, and generally refrain from eating meat. Dominic himself often went barefoot and practiced abstinence, but the greatest emphasis of his ministry was on preaching. Thus, the Dominicans are often symbolized with images of a pregnant St. Mary (pregnant with the Word).

A vigorous opponent of heresy, Dominic supported the longtime crusade against the Albigensians launched by Pope Innocent III in 1209. He eventually established a mendicant order in 1216 of educated friars dedicated to preaching and the conversion of heretics. In the process, he traveled extensively throughout Italy, France, and Spain. He died in Bologna in 1221, and was canonized in 1234.

Individual Dominican houses are ruled by a prior chosen by its members and bound by strict allegiance to the Pope. The order is known for championing Catholic orthodoxy, education, apologetics, and preaching rather than manual labor. The Dominicans produced several leading Catholic scholars during the Middle Ages, including Thomas Aquinas and Albert Magnus. They specialized in teaching apologetics and ancient languages such as Greek, Hebrew, and Arabic. Their missionary zeal was aided by Spanish and Portuguese explorations in the sixteenth and seventeenth centuries. And because of their opposition to heresy, many Dominicans were involved in the Catholic Inquisitions which prosecuted, punished, and executed unrepentant heretics.

Ed Hindson

Bibliography

Hinnebusch, W.A. *History of the Dominican Order*. Staten Island, NY: Alba House, 1966.

Vicaire, M.H. *Saint Dominic and His Times*. Translated by Kathleen Pond. Green Bay, WI: ALT Publishing, 1964.

DORT, SYNOD OF

From November 13, 1618, to May 9, 1619, a synod of the Dutch Reformed Church officially convened by the States of Holland met in the city of Dort to resolve the controversy raised by the teachings of Jacobus Arminius (1559–1609) and the Remonstrance put forth by his followers, the Remonstrants, in 1610. Though also addressing ecclesiastical matters, the synod is principally known for its rejection of the Remonstrance and its explanation of Calvinist theology. The Synod consisted of approximately 100 members, among which were Dutch Reformed pastors, elders, and professors of theology, as well as approximately 25 international delegates. Its president was the Leeuwarden minister Johannes Bogermannus, and he presided over 180 sessions in 128 days.

From its beginning the Synod's purpose was not to consider Arminian doctrine as a legitimate alternative, but to reaffirm traditional Reformed theology and to decide what to do with the Remonstrants within the Dutch Reformed Church. The Synod summoned 13 Remonstrants, and called them as defendants of their views instead of as equal participants in the discussion. Their discussions with the Synod were so heated they were present for only five weeks. After the Remonstrants were dismissed, the Synod wrote the Canons of Dort, ratifying them on April 23, 1619. These five articles condemned the teachings of the Remonstrance and set forth the following tenets: Election to salvation is unconditional (not based on the foreseen faith of believers) and completely a gift of God; the death of Jesus Christ is completely sufficient to expiate the sins of the whole world, but only actually expiates the sins of the elect; all people are so corrupted by sin that they cannot choose salvation apart from a work of the Holy Spirit; the Holy Spirit effectually calls and regenerates a person so that he can become a believer; and those who are saved will certainly persevere to the end, which means they can be assured of their salvation. At the beginning of the twentieth century these five doctrines were given the popular acronym of TULIP, which stands for total depravity, unconditional election, limited atonement, irresistible grace, and perseverance of the saints.

At the final session on May 9, 1619, the Synod confirmed the authority of the Belgic Confession and the Heidelberg Catechism for the Dutch Reformed Church. The Canons of Dort would soon gain confessional authority on par with those two documents. The Synod made it clear that the church was Calvinist, and Arminian theology would not be tolerated. More than 200 Remonstrant pastors were expelled from their pulpits, Arminian theologian Hugo Grotius was sentenced to life in prison, and Arminian leader Johan van Oldenbarnevelt was sentenced to death. Persecution of the Remonstrants in Holland did not end until 1630, and they were not officially tolerated until 1795. The Synod of Dort had an immense influence on the development of Calvinistic theology, set the course for the Dutch Reformed Church for centuries, and intensified the international unity of Calvinism.

Gary L. Shultz Jr.

D

Bibliography

de Yong, Peter Y, ed. *Crisis in the Reformed Churches: Essays in Commemoration of the Great Synod of Dort, 1618–1619.* Grand Rapids: Reformed Fellowship, 1968.

Harrison, Archibald Walter. *The Beginnings of Arminianism to the Synod of Dort.* London: University of London Press, 1926.

Hoekema, Anthony A. "A New Translation of the Canons of Dort." *Calvin Theological Journal* 3 (1968): 133-61.

DWIGHT, TIMOTHY (1752–1817)

American minister and educator Timothy Dwight, an important figure in American Christianity, was the eighth president of Yale University and grandson of Jonathan Edwards. From early on he was destined for spiritual and intellectual life. He could read the Bible by the time he was four, and entered Yale College at age 13, where he distinguished himself as a scholar, studying 14 hours a day. He earned both BA and MA degrees and was later awarded honorary doctorates (STD, LLD) by Harvard and Princeton. After a period as a tutor at Yale, he served as a chaplain during the Revolutionary War and as a pastor before returning to Yale in 1795 as college president. There he was known for holding regular sessions with the entire student body, during which he would toss out a topic for discussion and debate. He usually bested any student who challenged him.

Dwight was a key figure in two of the major cultural influences on modern evangelical Christianity, American exceptionalism, and revivalism. A prolific writer, his works ranged from sermons to poetry, including the long poem "Greenfield Hill." This poem describes an idealized version of Connecticut, but it is essentially a poem about American virtue contrasted with Europe's corruption. Europe, "weak, doting, fallen," has no future. "In dust, thy temples towers and towns decay," he says. By contrast, on these shores, "some land, scarce glimmering in the light of fame…In all thy pomp, shall then majestic shine."

Dwight's vision of America in contrast to Europe was not new. The earliest settlers had seen America as a new and pure country that had escaped from the corruptions of Europe's state churches and aristocratic governments. America's destiny as a shining example to the world of virtuous and free people, of right religion and just government was a central theme in America's earliest days. Dwight encouraged and promoted this popular concept in his writings, adding his voice to the idea of American exceptionalism, which drives much of the conservative religio-political thought of today.

Dwight's other legacy is even more important: His regular debates with the entire student body led him into the role of an apologist. In the late 1700s, the United States had entered a period of moral and spiritual decline, and many Yale students were delighting in the Enlightenment philosophies popular in Europe and rejecting the existence of God and of morality (Cunningham, 304-5). Dwight used the weekly debates to demonstrate the foolishness of this, and to show the truthfulness of the Bible on matters such as the Genesis flood, the creation (Cunningham, 306-10), and the reliability of the New Testament. The resulting revival on campus, during which one-third of the students were converted, fueled the Second Great Awakening in 1802 and following. Yale sent graduates out across the country preaching in the revivalist style that continues to influence worship and church life to this day.

Dwight's theological lectures were posthumously published as *Theology; Explained and Defended* (5 vols., 1818–1819), popularly known as "Dwight's Theology." These volumes express a moderate Edwardsian Calvinism.

C. Fred Smith

Bibliography

Cairns, William. *Early American Writers.* New York: Macmillan, 1912.

Cunningham, Gerald E. *Timothy Dwight 1752–1837: A Biography.* New York: AMS Press, 1942.

Dwight, Timothy. *Theology; Explained and Defended.* 5 vols. New Haven, CT: T. Dwight & Sons, 1843.

Fitzmeier, John R. *New England's Moral Legislator: Timothy Dwight 1752–1817.* Bloomington, IN: Indiana University Press, 1998.

Freundt, A.B. "Dwight, Timothy." *The New International Dictionary of the Christian Church.* Edited by J.D. Douglas. Grand Rapids: Zondervan, 1978.

Murray, Iain H. *Revival & Revivalism: The Making and Marring of American Evangelicalism 1750–1858.* Carlisle, PA: Banner of Truth, 2009.

Smith, H. Shelton, Robert T. Handy, and Lefferts A. Loetscher. *American Christianity*, vol. 1. New York: Scribners, 1960.

✛

JONATHAN EDWARDS
Puritan Pastor
1703–1758

EASTERN ORTHODOXY

Eastern Orthodoxy refers to the family of churches, predominant in Europe and parts of Asia, that share a common faith and commitment to the honorary primacy of the Patriarch of Constantinople. The Patriarch does not function as supreme authority on earth as the Pope does in the West. To Orthodox Christians, orthodoxy refers not only to right belief but also to right worship (Greek, *doxa*). The Orthodox believe their faith is in continuity with that of the earliest Christians, and like Catholics, they believe their current leadership can be traced back to the apostles through the apostolic succession of the episcopacy. With ties to early Christianity, a distinct Orthodox Church emerged from the Byzantine Empire and continues to have strong cultural ties to Greece.

Tensions between the Roman Catholic Church and the Eastern Orthodox Church can be traced back to centuries before they parted ways. Controversies over the preparation of the bread for the Eucharist and theological differences over the relationship between the members of the Trinity, along with tensions over the scope of the Bishop of Rome's ecclesial authority, culminated in a final break between the Roman Church and Orthodox Christians in the Great Schism of 1054. This resulted in the mutual excommunication of both the Western Pope and the Eastern Patriarch.

The Trinitarian controversy between East and West is often called the *filioque* controversy. Eastern Christians rejected the sixth-century addition of the word *filioque* (Latin "and the Son") to the Nicene Creed, an addition that suggested that the Spirit of God proceeds not only from the Father but also from the Son. Hopes of reconciliation seemed to be crushed during the Fourth Crusade (1200–1204) when crusaders attacked Constantinople, but in recent years the two groups have shown willingness to dialogue. While in 1965 Pope Paul VI and Patriarch Athenagoras overturned the two-way excommunication of 1054, Catholic and Orthodox believers nevertheless continue to hold clearly divergent beliefs.

Orthodox Christianity in America has a number of diverse sources, including the influence of Russian missionaries in Alaska and more significantly the influence of Orthodox immigrants throughout the twentieth century. By the 1860s, Orthodoxy had a strong presence in Alaska, but almost no impact in the mainland. Increasing immigration over the last century from Eastern Europe, the Balkans, and the Middle East is responsible for the quick expansion of Orthodox faith in the mainland of the United States. In recent years, the number of Orthodox worldwide has approached 300 million.

Brian Goard

Bibliography

Clenendin, Daniel B. *Eastern Orthodox Christianity, a Western Perspective*. Grand Rapids: Baker, 1994.

Schmemann, Alexander. *The Historical Road of Eastern Orthodoxy*. Crestwood, NY: St. Vladimir's Seminary Press, 1997.

Stamoolis, James, gen. ed. *Three Views on Eastern Orthodoxy and Evangelicalism*. Grand Rapids: Zondervan, 2004.

Ware, Kallistos. *The Orthodox Way*. Rev. ed. Crestwood, NY: St. Vladimir's Seminary Press, 1995.

Ware, Timothy. *The Orthodox Church*. Rev. ed. New York: Penguin, 1997.

ECUMENICAL COUNCILS

In early church history, an ecumenical council was a meeting of the bishops of the churches from across the known world. The bishops were convened in response to controversies and heresies that threatened to divide Christianity and dilute its message. Whereas many of the councils are recognized by the Roman Catholic Church, only the first seven councils are generally accepted by most magisterial branches of Christianity (such as Anglicans and Lutherans) as being valid ecumenical councils.

The seven generally accepted ecumenical councils and their decisions are as follows:

1. First Council of Nicaea (325): Affirmed that Jesus is truly God and equal to the Father, rejected Arianism, and adopted the Nicene Creed.

2. First Council of Constantinople (381): Affirmed the humanity of Christ against the Apollinarians, revised the Nicene Creed into its present form, and prohibited any alteration of the Nicene Creed without the assent of an ecumenical council.

3. Council of Ephesus (431): Affirmed against Nestorianism that Jesus is one person, proclaimed the Virgin Mary as the mother of God, and condemned Pelagianism.

4. Council of Chalcedon (451): Affirmed that in Jesus there are two distinct natures in one person that are hypostatically united "without confusion, change, division or separation," condemned Eutychianism and Monophysitism, and adopted the Chalcedonian Creed.

5. Second Council of Constantinople (553): Reaffirmed decisions and doctrines set forth by previous councils; condemned new Arian, Nestorian, and Monophysite writings and Origenism.

6. Third Council of Constantinople (680–681): Emphasized that Jesus had both a divine and human will, and condemned Monothelitism.

7. Second Council of Nicaea (787): Renewal of the veneration of icons and ended first iconoclasm. The Nicean Council is rejected by some Protestant denominations, preferring the Council of Hieria (754), which had also described itself as the seventh ecumenical council and had condemned the veneration of icons.

The Roman Catholic Church numbers the ecumenical councils at 21, including church councils at Constantinople IV (869–870), Lateran I (1123), Lateran II (1139), Lateran III (1179), Lateran IV (1215), Lyons I (1245), Lyons II (1274), Vienne (1311–1312), Constance (1414–1418), Florence (1431–1445), Lateran V (1512–1517), Trent (1545–1549), Vatican I (1869–1870), and Vatican II (1962–1965). The last 14 councils dealt with various issues, including the condemnation of individuals (such as Photius—Patriarch of Constantinople, John Wycliffe, Jan Hus, and Martin Luther), transubstatiation, and the infallibility of the Pope. Vatican II was called by Pope John XXIII and convened as the twenty-first ecumenical council. While the council addressed contemporary issues of the twentieth century, it also reaffirmed the major doctrines of the Council of Trent and Vatican I. The *De Ecclesia* decree on the Church stated, "The Church exists in Christ as a sacrament…for the whole human race." The priesthood of the Catholic Church was defined as an extension of the Levitical priesthood and "given the power of Sacred Order to offer sacrifice [in the Mass] and to forgive sin…through the sacrament of penance."

George Bannister

Bibliography

Chidester, David. *Christianity: A Global History*. San Francisco: HarperSanFrancisco. 2000.

Flannery, A. *Vatican Council II: The Conciliar and Post Conciliar Documents*. Northport, NY: Costello, 1988.

Murphy, Fr. John L. *The General Councils of the Church.* Milwaukee, WI: Bruce Publishing Company, 1960.

Shelley, Bruce L. *Church History in Plain Language.* 3d ed. Nashville, TN: Thomas Nelson. 2008.

E

ECUMENICAL MOVEMENT

The ecumenical movement has been defined as the quest of Roman Catholic, Orthodox, Anglican, Old Catholic, and some Protestant churches for reconciliation and restoration of their visible unity in faith, in sacramental life, and in witness to the world. The ultimate vision of the ecumenical movement is the transformation and the unification of all people.

The ecumenical movement had its beginnings in 1857 with the formation of the Association for the Promotion of the Unity of Christendom, which advocated praying for the unity of all churches. Most historians credit the 1910 World Missionary Conference with launching the ecumenical movement. The movement gained in momentum in the early decades of the twentieth century with the formation of the Faith and Order movement, the International Missionary Council, and the Life and Work movement. Ultimately, the Faith and Order movement and the Life and Work movement contributed to the formation of the World Council of Churches in 1948. In 1960, the Roman Catholic Church formally entered the ecumenical movement, thereby substantially increasing the movement's influence.

The ecumenical movement's zeal for Christian unity led to over 30 denominational mergers and international confessional alliances. During the decades between 1900 and 1970, denominational mergers in the United States of America resulted in the formation of such major denominations as the United Methodists and the United Presbyterians. Outside of the United States in 1947, the Anglican Church of India, Burma, and Ceylon merged with the South India Province of the Methodist Church and the South India United Church to form the Church of South India. International confessional alliances inspired by the ecumenical movement include the International Congregational Council, the Mennonite World Conference, the World Methodist Conference, the Baptist World Alliance, the Lutheran World Federation, and the World Alliance of Reformed and Presbyterian Churches.

Conservative evangelicals have generally resisted and criticized conciliar ecumenism. The reasons for their resistance include a strong commitment to the authority of the Bible and evangelism, which is not emphasized in the movement, and the apparent doctrinal compromise required of participation in its objectives. Conservative evangelicals chose instead to become involved with groups supporting orthodox Christian theology and advancing world evangelization, such as the National Association of Evangelicals and the International Congress on World Evangelization (Lausanne '74; Lausanne '89, Manila, Cape Town 2010).

George Bannister

E

Bibliography

Cairns, Earle E. *Christianity Through the Centuries: A History of the Christian Church*. Grand Rapids: Zondervan, 1996.

Collins, Michael, and Matthew A. Price. *The Story of Christianity*. New York: Dorling Kindersley, 1999.

Fitzgerald, Thomas. *The Ecumenical Movement: An Introductory History*. Westport, CT: Greenwood, 2004.

Gonzales, Justo. *Church History: An Essential Guide*. Nashville, TN: Abingdon, 1996.

Shelley, Bruce L. *Church History in Plain Language*. Nashville, TN: Thomas Nelson, 2008.

EDDY, MARY BAKER (1821–1910)

Mary Baker Eddy was the founder of Church of Christ, Scientist. She is the self-proclaimed discoverer of Christian Science—a spiritual worldview that denies all matter, sin, sickness, and death.

Mary A. Morse Baker was born on July 16, 1821, in New Hampshire to Mark and Abigail Baker. From her infancy through adulthood she battled serious physical and mental illnesses as she was continually subjected to convulsive attacks and hysterical episodes. As a youth, she was admitted to a Christian Congregational church, but utterly despised the doctrine of predestination and the idea that the unregenerate would be damned to hell.

Mary married George W. Glover in 1843; then in 1853, she married M. Patterson. She also eventually married Asa G. Eddy in 1877. Glover died within months of their marriage, Patterson was divorced by Eddy for desertion, and Asa Eddy died in 1882 from a severe heart condition. In fact, during Mary's lifetime, she violated Christian Science teachings by relying on morphine for her semi-invalid condition and contesting the autopsy report for the death of her last husband.

E

Later in her life, Mary supposedly acquired clairvoyant abilities and delved into spiritualism and mediumship. During these occurrences as a medium, she would fall into deep trances and dispense otherwise unknown information. She also claimed to be able to see the spirits of departed people standing by her bedside, whose messages she allegedly transcribed.

The pivotal moment in Eddy's life came when she met Phineas Parkhurst Quimby, whose work in metaphysics, mental healing, and New Thought formed much of the foundation of Christian Science. In 1862, after suffering "spinal inflammation," she sought Quimby's mental treatment. After claiming to be healed (though the pain returned), she soon became a proponent of Quimby's principles. Eddy "discovered" Christian Science for herself in 1866 when she claimed to miraculously recover three days after falling on icy pavement.

In 1875, Eddy published *Science and Health with Key to the Scriptures*, a major work that embodied the movement's teachings. Four years later, in 1879, she and her followers officially founded The Church of Christ, Scientist (which became the official name) in Boston, Massachusetts. In 1881, at the age of 61, she established the Massachusetts Metaphysical College, where she taught over 4000 students until its closing in 1889. Some of her teachings included the concept of God as a "Divine Principle," mental healing through prayer, and the denial of everything physical, including death. Besides *Science and Health*, she published many other writings. Some of the most notable include *The First Church of Christ Scientist and Miscellany*, *Miscellaneous Writings*, and *Manual of the Mother Church*.

On December 3, 1910, Eddy died at her home in Newton, Massachusetts. Her influence is evident to this day in the fact there are many thousands of adherents to Christian Science teachings, which depart from teachings of evangelical Christianity.

Daryl Rodriguez

Bibliography

Cather, Willa, and Georgine Milmine. *The Life of Mary Baker G. Eddy and the History of Christian Science*. Lincoln, NE: University of Nebraska Press, 1993.

Ehrenborg, Todd. *Mind Sciences*. Grand Rapids: Zondervan, 1995.

Martin, Walter. *The Kingdom of the Cults*. Rev. ed. Edited by Hank Hanegraaff. Minneapolis: Bethany House, 1999.

Nenneman, Richard A. *Persistent Pilgrim: The Life of Mary Baker Eddy*. Etna, NH: Nebbadon Press, 1997.

Rhodes, Ron. *The Challenge of the Cults and New Religions*. Grand Rapids: Zondervan, 2001.

EDWARDS, JONATHAN (1703–1758)

Congregational minister Jonathan Edwards was born in East Windsor, Connecticut, to Timothy, a Puritan pastor and tutor, and Esther Stoddard, granddaughter of Solomon Stoddard. At 13 years of age, Edwards entered the fledgling Collegiate School, later known as Yale University. He obtained his bachelor's and master's degrees there, interacting with the ideas of leading theologians and philosophers of his day and throughout history.

It was during Edwards's years at Yale that he became aware of a "new sense of things" regarding his faith—an understanding and agreement with the central truths of Christianity, but also a profound wonder and enjoyment of those truths. From that point forward, Edwards consistently promoted a Christian faith that provoked the mind and the affections.

After a short stint as an interim preacher in New York and a tutor back at Yale, Edwards accepted a call to assist his maternal grandfather, Solomon Stoddard, at a large and influential church in Northampton, Massachusetts, at which Stoddard had been pastor for more than 50 years. That same year he married Sarah Pierpont, a good friend from his youth. Jonathan and Sarah went on to have 11 children together. Stoddard died two years after Edwards's arrival, leaving Edwards to pastor the prestigious church for more than 20 years.

The church in Northampton and other churches in the area began experiencing spiritual revivals during that time. With the observations of a scientist, the organization of a philosopher, and the biblically rooted explanations of a theologian, Edwards wrote about personal and regional spiritual growth. Writings such as *A Faithful Narrative, Distinguishing Marks of the Spirit of God,* and *Religious Affections* were circulated widely throughout New England and Britain. In *Religious Affections,* Edwards argued that both the mind and the affections play vital roles in genuine Christian faith. As a pastor-theologian, Edwards took a different view on the Lord's Supper than his grandfather had. Stoddard had taken the open communion view, seeing the Lord's Supper as a means by which God might teach non-Christians about the gospel. Edwards, however, took the closed communion view, seeing the Lord's Supper as an ordinance to be kept exclusively by Christians.

A majority of the people in the congregation at Northampton dismissed Edwards over this disagreement, so in 1750, he took on a smaller pastorate on the frontier in Stockbridge, Massachusetts, ministering to a small English congregation and some Native American families there. It was there that Edwards found a relaxing setting in which to write some of his most profound theological and philosophical works, including *Freedom of the Will* and *On the Nature of True Virtue*. In 1758, months after accepting a position as the first president of New Jersey College, later named Princeton University, Edwards died of smallpox from an inoculation he had received to deter it.

Though Edwards will likely be best known for his sermon "Sinners in the Hands of an Angry God," the legacy he left to American churches and Christian schools is that of a deep and genuine faith that ignored neither the mind nor the heart in one's pursuit of God and the truth.

Kenneth Cleaver

Bibliography

Marsden, George M. *Jonathan Edwards: A Life*. New Haven, CT: Yale, 2003.

Murray, Iain H. *Jonathan Edwards: A New Biography*. Carlisle, PA: Banner of Truth, 1987.

The Works of Jonathan Edwards. 26 vols. New Haven, CT: Yale, 2009.

EMERGENT CHURCH

The distinctives of the emergent church include a twenty-first-century approach to evangelism and church ministry marked by flexible theology, a holistic approach to the role of the church in society, a culturally sensitive approach to Scripture, an environmental activism, and concern for the poor and marginalized. Initially, the phrase *emergent* church was a generic term used to describe the innovation, cutting edge technology, and new methods being used by newer and younger churches to do ministry. Later, the term *emergent church* took on a more technical meaning, one associated with the Emergent Village, a website connected with, among others, Brian McLaren, Tony Jones, and Doug Pagitt. *Emergent* thus signifies more than a grassroots church ministry that's innovative, but includes new theology as well as new methodology. Thus a distinction is made between "emergent" and "emerging" churches and ministries.

Emergent churches consider the traditional Christian church to be out of date and seek to contextualize the message of Christianity to postmodernism. The emergent church has adapted itself intentionally to the postmodern age, and since postmodernism rejects universal absolutes, emergent churches have changed their attitudes toward beliefs and behaviors that the traditional evangelical church rejects as questionable or sinful—i.e., the use of alcohol, tobacco, profanity, loosening of sexual standards, homosexuality, and abortion. The more conservative "emerging churches," on the other hand, have a great desire to reach the younger generation without compromising the message. They turn to new methods, using many expressions of contemporary music, art, and electronic communication to reach people. Yet they are also often characterized by a return to expository preaching and to a doctrinal (often creedal) form of ministry.

Emergent churches emphasize grace and consider many of the traditional standards of separation to be vestigial remains of the American culture and historical Christianity, but not New Testament Christianity. Uncomfortable with the "exclusiveness" of Christianity, they are tolerant of other religions, cults, and even other ways to heaven. Salvation may be available to those who have never heard the name Christ, or an opportunity for salvation may exist after death. Some embrace naturalistic explanations for the miracles in the Bible, as well as modern interpretations of verbal inspiration and biblical inerrancy.

The emergent church has been criticized by evangelicals for its abandonment of basic Bible doctrine and theology. There are many who are concerned that the emergent church's so-called "generous orthodoxy" (McLaren) is merely a repackaging of incipient liberalism. In its rush to relevance, good intentions often lead to bad theology. Critics of the emergent church have raised serious concerns about the movement's abandonment of the essential biblical truths that form the heart and core of the gospel.

Elmer Towns

Bibliography

Carson, D.A. *Becoming Conversant with the Emergent Church*. Grand Rapids: Zondervan, 2005.

Gibbs, Eddie. *Emergent Churches*. Ada, MI: Baker Academic, 2005.

Kimball, Dan. *The Emergent Church*. Grand Rapids: Zondervan/Youth Specialties, 2003.

McLaren, Brian D. *A Generous Orthodoxy*. Grand Rapids: Zondervan/Youth Specialties, 2004.

ENGLAND, CHURCH OF

The Church of England represents the various bodies within the Episcopal churches of the worldwide Anglican Communion. The archbishop of Canterbury is the designated spiritual head of the Church of England, and has residences at both Canterbury and Lambeth Palace in London.

E   Christianity was introduced into England very early in the Christian era. The presence of British bishops at the Council of Arles in France in 314 gives evidence of an organized church in England at least as early as the second or third centuries. However, it declined during the time of the Teutonic invasions and was reignited by Roman and Celtic Christians under Augustine and Aidan, with Augustine serving as the first archbishop of Canterbury in the late sixth century.

Catholic English Christianity later conformed more to the European continental model after the Norman conquest of England in 1066. Papal influence reached its peak in England in 1213 with King John's recognition of England as a papal fief. However, by the sixteenth century, Protestant sentiments were being strongly expressed throughout England by various Puritans, allowing King Henry VIII to break from the Roman Catholic Church on the grounds of his divorce from Catherine of Aragon. Ironically, Henry had earlier been designated a defender of the faith by the Pope for a book he had written criticizing Martin Luther in 1521. Nevertheless, the English parliament of 1532–1536 designated Henry as "the only supreme head on Earth of the Church of England," severing all formal ties with the Roman Catholic Church, although the Church of England retained major elements of Catholic theology that later became issues of debate within the English Protestant churches.

Under the reigns of Elizabeth I (1558–1603) and James I (1603–1625), the Church of England saw a growing division between Puritans and High Church Laudians. After the restoration of 1660, the Clarendon Code established the authority of the Anglican Church and required people's conformity to the national church.

In the eighteenth century, revival under the preaching of John and Charles Wesley and George Whitefield produced some outstanding laymen, including William Wilberforce, who vigorously opposed slavery in the British Empire. However, the nineteenth century saw a resurgence of the High Church tradition through the Oxford Movement, which sought to restore the sacramental traditions of the Catholic Church within the Church of England. Since the early twentieth century, the worldwide Anglican Communion has become more and more strained by numerous debates over liturgical experimentation, the ordination of women, and more recently, the ordination of homosexuals.

The theology of the Church of England is generally formulated by the Thirty-Nine Articles, the *Book of Common Prayer*, the Ordinal, and the two Books of Homilies. Whereas the American Episcopal churches have often expressed liberal theological and social views, the African Episcopal churches have generally expressed more conservative views. At the same time, the British wing of the Church has been influenced by evangelicals such as John R.W. Stott and J.I. Packer.

Mal Couch

E

Bibliography

Douglas, J.D., ed. *The New International Dictionary of the Christian Church*. Grand Rapids: Zondervan, 1978.

Dowley, Tim, ed. *Introduction to the History of Christianity*. Minneapolis: Fortress, 2002.

Kurian, George T., ed. *Nelson's Dictionary of Christianity*. Nashville, TN: Thomas Nelson, 2005.

Moorman, J.R.H. *A History of the Church of England*. New York: Morehouse, 1980.

Rhodes. Ron. *The Complete Guide to Christian Denominations*. Eugene, OR: Harvest House, 2005.

EPHREM THE SYRIAN (CA. 306–373)

Ephrem was the greatest theologian of the fourth-century Syriac-speaking church of the East. He was born in Nisibis (modern Nusaybin, Turkey) into a Christian family around 306. When Nisibis came under Persian control, Ephrem moved to Edessa, which had been a part of the Roman Empire since the third century, where he began a theological school. Though he evidently resisted ordination to the office of bishop, Ephrem did serve as a deacon. He died in 373 while caring for people affected by a plague.

Given the nickname "the Harp of the Spirit," Ephrem's key contribution to the church was through the writing of hymns. While these were certainly sung in worship gatherings, they were also the key vehicle through which Ephrem delivered his theology. In the fifth century, his hymns were grouped into categories to facilitate their use in worship. Some of the themes included hymns on faith, the Nativity, the church, the crucifixion, and Paradise.

While Ephrem's theological approach and forms vary greatly from those of historic

Western theology and certainly modern systematic theologies, his approach is noteworthy for two reasons. First, he did theology in the context of the Syriac-speaking East, where poetry and song were more valued than prose when it came to communicating important ideas. Also, these forms were a strategic memory aid for oral learners who wanted to retain the teachings of Scripture and even theology. Second, as Ephrem taught the church in a context in which heresies (Gnosticism, Arianism), rival religions (Zoroastrianism), and political challenges (pressure from the pagan Emperor Julian) abounded, he exegeted the Scriptures with these worldview challenges in mind.

Edward Smither

Bibliography

Ancient Christian Commentary on Scripture. 30 vols. Edited by Thomas C. Oden. Downers Grove, IL: InterVarsity, 2000–2010.

Brock, Sebastian. *The Luminous Eye: The Spiritual World of Saint Ephrem*. Collegeville, MN: Liturgical, 1992.

Ephrem. *Ephrem the Syrian: Hymns*. Translated by Kathleen E. McVey and John Meyendorff. Mahwah, NJ: Paulist, 1989.

EPISCOPAL CHURCH

The term *Episcopalian* was at one time a status within the Church of England that described an area as being under the supervision of a bishop, or an *episkopos*, the New Testament Greek term for bishop. Church of England parishes in areas without a bishop could not use this term to describe themselves. The American branch of the Church of England, however, did not have a bishop until after the Revolutionary War. To differentiate itself from the Church of England after the war, the Anglican congregations in America adopted the official title Protestant Episcopal Church to reflect the fact that in 1785, the first American bishops were consecrated without having to take a vow of obedience to the king of England and to the English Parliament.

The Episcopal Church enjoyed tax support in colonial Virginia and other states; however, it was disestablished as an official state church shortly after the Revolution. The church, despite various difficulties, has had a major presence in American life. Many of the founding fathers of America were members of the church, and it has maintained a presence in most of America's larger communities and cities up through today.

In the nineteenth and twentieth centuries, the Episcopal Church's leadership came to embrace the social gospel, and in the late twentieth century, they began to ordain women. Particularly controversial in recent years has been the matter of ordaining homosexual individuals. This has caused challenges both within, as dioceses who object to such appointments seek to leave the church or find an alternate Anglican church to oversee them; and without, as other Anglican church members have sent missionary bishops to America to establish Anglican parishes in the United States that are not part of the Protestant Episcopal Church.

E

Laverne Smith

Bibliography

Albright, Raymond W. *A History of the Protestant Episcopal Church.* New York: Macmillan, 1964.

Gaustad, Edwin, and Leigh Schmidt. *The Religious History of America.* New York: HarperOne, 2004.

Hein, David, and Gardiner H. Shattucks. *The Episcopalians.* Westport, CT: Praeger, 2004.

ERASMUS, DESIDERIUS (CA. 1466–1536)

Often referred to as the prince of humanists, Desiderius Erasmus was the most respected and sought-after scholar of the northern Renaissance. Born circa 1466–1469 in Rotterdam in the Netherlands, Erasmus was schooled under the Brethren of the Common Life in Deventer, Netherlands. He later entered the Augustinian community at Steyn, though he came to dislike the monastic life and sought a papal dispensation, which was granted, freeing him from his monastic vows.

Erasmus, through his study of ancient languages and texts, sought to bring moral and practical reform to the Roman Catholic Church. In 1500, he published the immensely popular *Adagia,* a collection of over 800 classical proverbs with commentary, which made his wit and wisdom available to Renaissance Europe. In 1505, Erasmus turned to biblical and theological writings with an edition of Lorenzo Valla's *Annotations on the New Testament* (1505). His *Novum Instrumentum* (1516), the first published Greek New Testament, remains a monumental accomplishment in the history of textual criticism. Other major works during this period include *In Praise of Folly* (1509) and the anonymously published *Julius Exclusis* (1514). Both are examples of his superb skill as a writer and his biting criticism of the Roman Catholic Church.

By 1517, Erasmus was the most acclaimed scholar in Europe. Though his work in the classical authors and ancient languages sought reform of the Roman Catholic Church, Erasmus's peaceful and noncombative spirit was that of a pacifistic scholar with little stomach for the combative and revolutionary Martin Luther. At first Erasmus sought to remain above the fray, but eventually he was pulled into the controversy. Luther and Erasmus famously sparred in what both saw as a crucial aspect of the Reforming movement, the freedom of the will (Erasmus, *On the Freedom of the Will*, 1524; Luther, *The Bondage of the Will*, 1525). Both men agreed that reform was needed; however, they disagreed on its form. Erasmus sought a return to right morality in the Roman Catholic Church, while Luther vigorously argued for a return to right doctrine.

Douglas Mann

Bibliography

Bainton, Roland. *Erasmus of Christendom*. New York: Scribner's Sons, 1969.

Huizinga, J. *Erasmus of Rotterdam*. London: Phaidon, 1952.

McConica, J.K. *Erasmus*. New York: Oxford University Press, 1991.

EUSEBIUS OF CAESAREA (CA. 260–339)

Eusebius, often called the father of church history, was the bishop of Caesarea in Palestine. As a young man, he studied under a Christian teacher named Pamphilius. Both men were influenced by Origen of Alexandria who had spent the last two decades of his life in Palestine. For the first 40 years of his life, Eusebius lived in a peaceful Roman Empire and enjoyed the luxury of being able to study. During the Great Persecution under Diocletian (AD 303–311), Eusebius suffered along with many Christians throughout the empire. His work *The Martyrs of Palestine* offers a vivid picture of a persecuted church in the early fourth century. Around 313, Eusebius was set apart as bishop of Caesarea, a position he occupied until his death around 339.

Eusebius's key contributions to the church were many. First, he was a biblical exegete and published commentaries on Psalms and Isaiah. Though he was influenced by Origen, he broke with the Alexandrian father on hermeneutics and interpreted Scripture in a more historical and grammatical manner. Second, he was influential in addressing the Arian heresy. Though Eusebius was initially sympathetic to Arius's views on the Father's supremacy to the Son, and was even condemned for his stance at a local church council in Antioch in 324, he is remembered by the church for proposing the idea of formulating a creed at the Council of Nicaea in 325. Though he signed the Nicene Creed, Eusebius maintained a moderate Arian view of the Godhead.

Finally, Eusebius's greatest contribution to the church was as a historian. He published *Chronicon*, a history of the world until 303 (later revised to 328). As a preserver and compiler of church documents and thought, through his *Church History* (Latin, *Historia Ecclesiastica*) and *Life of Constantine,* he endeavored to interpret history as a fulfillment of biblical prophecy. This was most apparent in how he regarded fourth-century Christianity and Rome's first Christian emperor, Constantine. He served as a spiritual advisor to Constantine and helped develop the political and theological basis of the Byzantine Empire. He also wrote several works of apologetics attempting to affirm Christianity using Old Testament texts.

Eusebius's *Church History* (325) is the major source of information about the history of Christianity in its first three centuries. It is divided into ten books, the last three of which present vivid details of his own era. It survives in Greek, Latin, Syriac, and Armenian versions and has been translated into numerous languages. He especially focused on the challenge of martyrdom so often faced by the early Christians.

Edward Smither

Biography

Eusebius. *Eusebius: The Church History.* Translated by Paul Maier. Grand Rapids: Kregel, 2007.

Grant, Robert M. *Eusebius as Church Historian.* Eugene, OR: Wipf & Stock, 2006.

Noll, Mark A. *Turning Points: Decisive Moments in the History of Christianity.* Grand Rapids: Baker Academic, 2000.

EVANGELICAL ALLIANCE

Formed in London in 1846, the *Evangelical Alliance* sought to promote interdenominational fellowship on the basis of the great evangelical doctrines of the Christian faith, the defense of biblical Christianity, and the promotion of missionary work. During the nineteenth century the Alliance sponsored conferences in most of the major cities of Europe and America. In the twentieth century it also sponsored the evangelistic meetings held by Billy Graham in London in 1954–1955 and 1966–1967. The organization also formed the Evangelical Missionary Alliance in 1948 and was one of the founding members of the World Evangelical Fellowship in 1951. The Alliance has consistently adopted the policy of fellowship with all professing evangelical bodies despite their theological differences and denominational affiliation.

Ed Hindson

Bibliography

Kessler, J.B.A. *A Study of the Evangelical Alliance in Great Britain.* Netherlands: Oosterbaan & Le Cointre, 1968.Kirby, Gilbert. "Evangelical Alliance." *The New International Dictionary of the Christian Church.* Edited by J.D. Douglas. Grand Rapids: Zondervan, 1978.

EVANGELICALISM

Evangelicalism has to do with conservative Protestant theology that emphasizes the proclamation of the gospel (Greek, *evangel* = "good news"). Shelly (14-15) defines evangelicals as all Christians "who emphasize salvation by faith in the atoning death of Jesus Christ through personal conversion." He adds, "Evangelicalism, then, begins its explanation of true religion where Jesus began, with 'repent and believe the gospel' (Mark 1:15). It emphasizes man's need for spiritual rebirth in the experience of conversion." Such conversion is generally viewed by evangelicals as a definite, decisive, and profoundly life-changing experience of being "born again" by the power of the Holy Spirit.

American evangelicalism in particular views itself as the legitimate heir of apostolic biblical Christianity, the Protestant Reformation, Puritanism, Pietism, and the revivals of the Great Awakening. The spiritual fruit of the preaching of Jonathan Edwards, George Whitefield, Charles Finney, the rural camp meeting revivals, and the urban campaigns of D.L. Moody and Billy Sunday all combined to shape the evangelical movement in America. To this foundation has been added the influence of twentieth-century Fundamentalism and Pentecostalism, resulting in a diverse and dynamic religious movement with a generally conservative theological tradition.

Historically, evangelicals have held to a high view of the inspiration and authority of the Bible. Adherence to biblical inerrancy was the foundational tenet of the Evangelical Theological Society, which was formed in 1949. Evangelicals have traditionally held to orthodox Christian views of the Trinity, the deity of Christ, his substitutionary atonement, his bodily resurrection, and the promise of his second coming. However, within evangelicalism there is a wide divergence of opinion on matters of divine sovereignty, free will, church polity, spiritual gifts, and eschatology.

While theological liberalism radically transformed American Protestant Christianity in the nineteenth century, the evangelical movement countered liberalism with its own radical transformation brought about by its emphasis on evangelism, church planting, and the establishment of new educational institutions such as Biola University (1908), Dallas Theological Seminary (1924), Westminster Theological Seminary (1929), and Liberty University (1971). The growth of evangelical churches in America over the past 100 years has been astronomical, outpacing mainline liberal churches, which have been in serious decline during the same period. And despite the rich heritage of British evangelicalism—both in the Anglican Church (e.g., J.C. Ryle), and the nonconformist churches (e.g., C.H. Spurgeon), the evangelical movement in England has been in serious decline since the nineteenth century. In the meantime, British evangelicalism, though represented by outstanding thinkers such as J.I. Packer and John Stott, has remained a small minority within British religious circles.

Despite the obvious success of American evangelicalism, many have raised concerns about the future of the movement in light of the development of emergent church trends, open theism, and attempts to redefine biblical inerrancy. Theologian Francis Schaeffer raised similar concerns about the future of the evangelical movement in *The Great Evangelical Disaster* (1984), observing even then that evangelical accommodation has constantly been in one direction—that is, to accommodate whatever is in vogue with the current dominant form of the world spirit, saying, "It is this same world spirit which is destroying both church and society" (150).

The future of American evangelicalism will likely be determined by how it responds to the spiritual, moral, and intellectual challenges of the twenty-first century.

Ed Hindson

Bibliography

Davis, J.J. *Foundations of Evangelical Theology*. Grand Rapids: Baker, 1984.

Noll, Mark. *The Scandal of the Evangelical Mind*. Grand Rapids: Eerdmans, 1994.

Schaeffer, Francis. *The Great Evangelical Disaster*. Westchester, IL: Crossway, 1984.

Shelly, Bruce. *Evangelicalism in America*. Grand Rapids: Eerdmans, 1967.

Wells, David, and J.D. Woodbridge. *The Evangelicals*. Grand Rapids: Baker, 1980.

☩

JERRY FALWELL
Baptist Pastor and Educator
1933–2007

FALWELL, JERRY (1933–2007)

Baptist pastor, educator, and political activist Jerry Falwell founded Liberty University in Virginia (1971), as well as the Moral Majority (1979). Falwell was converted on January 20, 1952, at Park Avenue Baptist Church in Lynchburg, Virginia, when he was 19 years old. He later graduated from the Baptist Bible College in Springfield, Missouri, and returned to Lynchburg, where he planted the Thomas Road Baptist Church in 1956, which eventually grew to 22,000 members. He founded the Lynchburg (now Liberty) Christian Academy (K–12) in 1967, and Liberty University (originally Lynchburg Baptist College) in 1971, which by 2012 had an enrollment of 100,000 students, making it the largest Christian university in the world.

Falwell's evangelistic preaching articulated his philosophy of saturation evangelism, which was highlighted in his books *Church Aflame* (1971) and *Capturing a Town for Christ* (1973), both coauthored with Elmer Towns. Concerned about America's drift into secularism and political and social liberalism, Falwell founded the Moral Majority along with Tim LaHaye, Charles Stanley, and D. James Kennedy, holding "I love America" rallies on 45 state capitol steps and attracting national attention, including being voted "Man of the Year" in *Good Housekeeping* magazine in 1979. He authored *Listen America!* (1980) and edited *The Fundamentalist Phenomenon* (1981), both published by Doubleday. A strong supporter of the State of Israel, Falwell was awarded the Jabontinsky Award by Israeli prime minister Menachem Begin in 1984.

In 1987, Falwell closed the Moral Majority organization and made a renewed commitment to continue building Liberty University into a world-class institution for evangelical education. At the same time he aligned the Thomas Road Baptist Church with the Southern Baptist Convention (SBC) and played an active role in the conservative resurgence within the SBC during the 1990s and early twenty-first century. He died of a heart attack while at work in his office on May 15, 2007, leaving a legacy of bold faith and unswerving commitment to his Savior, family, ministry, and nation.

Ed Hindson

Bibliography

D'Souza, Dinesh. *Falwell: Before the Millennium*. Chicago: Regnery Gateway, 1984.

Falwell, Jerry. *Building Dynamic Faith*. Nashville, TN: Thomas Nelson, 2005.

———. *Listen America!* Garden City, NY: Doubleday, 1980.

———. *Strength for the Journey: An Autobiography*. New York: Simon & Schuster, 1987.

Falwell, Jerry, and Elmer Towns. *Church Aflame*. Nashville, TN: Impact Books, 1971.

F

FINNEY, CHARLES GRANDISON (1792–1875)

American evangelist and revivalist Charles G. Finney was born in Warren, Connecticut, but grew up in New York. He entered the practice of law and was not saved until the age of 29, when he had a remarkable conversion experience alone in the woods. He wrote that he "received a mighty baptism of the Holy Ghost," which he described as "a wave of electricity going through and through me...in waves of liquid love." He then immediately forsook the legal profession, telling a client the next day that "I have a retainer from the Lord Jesus Christ to plead his cause and I cannot plead yours," and became an evangelist. He was ordained into the Presbyterian Church in 1824.

Finney's preaching expeditions were primarily in the state of New York from 1822–1831. He brought the emotionalism of the Second Great Awakening's camp meetings into the church. He is best known for his "new measures," which included long services, extended prayer meetings, calling the names of notorious sinners from the pulpit, and the use of women to testify and to pray publicly. Many of these measures were controversial, but none more than the "anxious bench" at the front of the church, where sinners were invited to come seeking spiritual victory. He emphasized the altar call, during which the lost were challenged to accept the offer of salvation.

In 1832, Finney accepted a call to become the pastor of the Second Presbyterian Church in New York City. However, in 1835, he became a Congregationalist and a professor of theology in Oberlin College in Oberlin, Ohio. His book *Lectures on Revivals of Religion* (1835) was widely read. He also wrote two large volumes of systematic theology. From 1851–1866 he served as president of Oberlin, where he expressed antislavery sentiments and taught postmillennialism. He felt that revivalism did not prosper in the South because of its practice of slavery. He was a postmillennialist, believing that Christ would return *after* the millennium. He thought that the millennium was likely to arrive in the near future, which some say explains his strong interest in social reform.

Finney's ministry was, in many respects, a result of the Second Great Awakening (1787–1805). His revival methods were influenced more by that movement than by his Presbyterian connections, and caused a rift in that denomination. Even his critics admit he was one of the most influential preachers of the nineteenth century.

Carl Deimer

Bibliography

Cross, Whitney R. *The Burned-over District: The Social and Intellectual History of Enthusiastic Religion in Western New York, 1800–1850*. New York: Cornell University Press, 1981.

Drummond, Lewis A. *Charles G. Finney and the Birth of Modern Evangelism*. London: Hodder & Stoughton, 1983.

Hardman, Keith J. *Charles Grandison Finney, 1792–1875*. Grand Rapids: Baker, 1987.

McLoughlin, William. *Revivals, Awakenings, and Reform*. Chicago: University of Chicago Press, 1978.

F

FOX, GEORGE (1624–1691)

Quaker leader George Fox was born in England to a humble, middle-class family of Puritan leanings. He was apprenticed as a shoemaker, a profession that later provided his living as he preached through parts of England. At age 19 Fox walked away from all he had known after becoming disillusioned with those in the church. A few years later, in 1646, he experienced a mystical salvation experience, and came to realize who he was without Christ. "Christianity then became a way of life to him" (Cairns, 379), and in 1647, he began to travel and preach. The people in his movement were first known as "Children of the Light," but gradually became known as "Friends of the Truth" in connection with what is stated in John 1:9.

Fox refused to follow the teachings of the priests of his time and was very outspoken against them; he was jailed on different occasions as a result. It was during one of his legal trials that the movement received the name *Quaker* (1652), after Fox urged a judge to "quake" before the Lord. The movement began to grow quickly and he married one of his new converts, Margaret Fell, who became the chief organizer of what became known as the Society of Friends.

The rapid growth of the Friends in England brought on persecution of the group and its leader. The years 1655–1675 saw a series of imprisonments with charges ranging from blasphemy to troublemaking. It was during his last imprisonment that Fox wrote his journals (1673–1675).

Fox traveled through the American colonies, the West Indies, Germany, and Holland. He believed that every person had Christ within, an inner light, and taught that Christianity was solely a relationship between man and God. Such beliefs led to the abolishment of all ceremonies in their worship, and worship became a silent quiet time of waiting for the Holy Spirit of God to move on their hearts.

Fox was a pacifist, and he spoke against slavery and for women in ministry. His teachings continue to influence the practices of Quaker churches worldwide.

Barbara Hubbard

Bibliography

Cairns, Earle E. *Christianity Through the Centuries: A History of the Christian Church*. Grand Rapids: Zondervan, 1981.

Hodgkin, Thomas. *George Fox*. London: Adamant Media Corporation, 2006.

Jones, Rufus. *George Fox: Seeker and Friend*. New York: Harper, 1930.

Marsh, Josiah. *A Popular Life of George Fox: The First of the Quakers*. London: C. Gilpin, 1847.

FOXE, JOHN (1516–1587)

The Protestant historian and martyrologist John Foxe was educated at Oxford and became a fellow of Magdalen College in 1539. In 1548, he hosted John Bale in his home and developed a great interest in his views on the apocalypse. He fled to the Continent upon Mary Tudor's accession in 1554. At Strasbourg he published a history of the Reformation entitled *Commentarii Rerum in Ecclesia Gestarum*. He met with Edmund Grindal at Frankfort, who was recording stories of Protestant martyrs. Foxe translated these into Latin and published them in 1559. Upon his return to England, Foxe joined forces with Jon Day, a printer, and published the first English edition of *Actes and Monuments* (popularly known as *Foxe's Book of Martyrs*) in 1563.

Foxe became crucial in the development of English apocalyptic thinking because of the immense popularity of *Actes and Monuments,* which became second only to the Geneva Bible as the favorite book of English Christians of the sixteenth century. Christianson notes that the book became a "folk tradition in Foxe's own lifetime" (30-45).

Accepting Bale's chronological framework for the apocalypse, Foxe brought that framework to life in his massive case studies. He related the martyr stories with an apocalyptic framework based upon the book of Revelation. He interpreted the binding of Satan as beginning with Constantine (ca. 325), and ending a thousand years later around 1325. From that point onward, Satan was on the rampage again. Foxe fixed Bale's chronology and carried it to a higher level of popularity. The two witnesses of Revelation 11 were viewed as Protestants, and their three-and-a-half day demise was paralleled to the three-and-a-half years in which the Council of Constance met, which condemned Jan Huss.

Foxe's book fully depicted Roman Catholic bishops, monks, and friars as the agents of Babylon, whereas the persecuted and simple Protestant preachers were representative of the true church. There is no doubt that the overwhelming popularity of Foxe's book "sold" the apocalyptic schemata to the general public of Elizabethan England even more effectively than mere technical studies had done previously. Rejecting the reserve of Bishop Jewel and others, Foxe virtually convinced the entire Church of England that the Pope was the Antichrist. Contemporary events, such as the excommunication of Elizabeth by the Pope, and the invasion of England by the Catholic Spanish Armada, only further played into the perception of general apocalyptic expectation.

Ed Hindson

Bibliography

Christianson, Paul. *Reformers and Babylon*. Toronto: University of Toronto Press, 1978.

Haller, W. *Foxe's "Book of Martyrs" and the Elect Nation*. New York: Harper & Row, 1963.

Mozley, J.F. *John Foxe and His Book*. London: James Clarke, 1940.

Olsen, V.N. *John Foxe and the Elizabethan Church*. Berkeley, CA: University of California, 1973.

FRANCIS OF ASSISI (1182–1226)

Born Francesco Bernardone at Assisi, Italy, in 1182, Francis of Assisi came from a wealthy family but gave it all up, including his inheritance, and settled outside of the town in which he was born and raised. He lived in poverty and gave himself to a life of prayer. He developed a following and wandered the hills of Tuscany, teaching and giving himself to helping the extremely needy. Insisting that his followers cared for others with joy to God, his work was approved in 1210 by Pope Innocent III for his simple Rule devoted to apostolic poverty. His followers, who went barefoot, were called the Minor Friars. Because they wore dark gray clothes, they were often called the Gray Friars.

In time, Assisi's fellow teachers were called *Franciscans*, or the Fraticelli. Sometimes they refused to obey the orders of the Pope and altered his rules, and thus they were associated with other persecuted groups and suppressed movements. The Franciscans were accused of being anti-intellectual even though they established colleges and seminaries. They produced leading medieval theologians such as Albert Magnus and Thomas Aquinas.

To encourage missionary activities, Francis tried to go to Syria (1212) and to Morocco (1213–1214) but was stopped by much opposition. In 1219, he traveled to the Middle East, where he tried unsuccessfully to convert the sultan of Egypt. While Assisi was absent from Italy troubles broke out between some of his followers, which he had to deal with upon returning. Several cardinals were appointed to oversee his work during his travels, which changed the nature of his movement. Because his order had became so different from what he had originally intended, Francis retired from its leadership to a hermitage on Monte Alvernia, where he supposedly received the miracle of a stigmata (the breaking out of bodily sores or wounds that correspond to the wounds Jesus endured at his crucifixion).

In latter years and in spite of illnesses, pains, and even blindness, Francis composed what he called his "Canticle of the Sun," his *Admonitions,* and his *Testament,* before giving in to "Sister Death" in 1226 at age 44. Known for his love of nature, Francis saw in created objects love that pointed to its Creator. Thus he enjoyed his solitude and it is reported that even the animal world enjoyed his sermons given before God.

Some have said that Francis was one of the most noble and Christlike figures who ever lived. He was canonized by the Roman Catholic Church in 1228. Many consider him the greatest of medieval saints, and he is especially known for the following prayer:

> Lord, make me an instrument of thy peace.
> Where there is hatred, let me sow love;
> Where there is injury, pardon;

Where there is doubt, faith;
Where there is despair, hope;
Where there is darkness, light;
Where there is sadness, joy.

Francis also produced 12 points described as the Rule of Francis. He closed the Rule with the statement, "Always being submissive and lying at the feet of that same holy church, steadfast in the Catholic faith, we may observe poverty and humility, and the holy gospel of our Lord Jesus Christ, as we have firmly promised."

Francis was canonized as a saint by Pope Gregory IX two years after his death. Respected by Catholics and Protestants alike, Francis remains a spiritual ideal of the simple Christian life of a sincere man who renounced the material things of this world, saw the glory of God in nature, and lived with his eyes on heaven while helping the poor on earth.

Upon the retirement of Pope Benedict XVI in 2013, Argentine cardinal Jorge Mario Bergoglio became the 266th pontiff of the Roman Catholic Church, taking the name Francis I because of St. Francis's appeal to the simple life and concern for the poor.

Mal Couch

Bibliography

Clouse, Robert. "Francis of Assisi." *The International Dictionary of the Christian Church*. Edited by J.D. Douglas. Grand Rapids: Zondervan, 1978.

Dowley, Tim, ed. *Introduction to the History of Christianity*. Minneapolis: Fortress, 2002.

Englebert, O. *St. Francis of Assisi*. Cincinnati, OH: St. Anthony Messenger Press, 1966.

Habig, M., ed. *St. Francis of Assisi: Writings and Early Biographies*. Quincy, IL: Franciscan Press, 1973.

FRANCISCANS

The Franciscans were a Roman Catholic Order founded by Francis of Assisi in 1209, emphasizing apostolic poverty, preaching, and penance. Originally designated as the Order of Friars Minor by Pope Innocent III, the Franciscans were reorganized by Pope Honorius III by the document known as *Regula Bullata*. Francis himself later expressed regret over the loss of his original ideals in his *Testament* (1226), reaffirming his commitment to apostolic poverty and the imitation of Christ.

Strict followers of Francis's *Testament* were eventually designated as *Zelanti* or Spirituals, and many later formed the schismatic Fraticelli. More moderate Franciscans were designated Conventuals, Observants, and Capuchins. After several centuries of divisions within the various branches of the order, they were united under a uniform constitution in 1897 by the decree of Leo XIII.

Over the centuries, the Franciscans have produced five Popes and such scholars as Bonaventure, Duns Scotus, Roger Bacon, and William of Ockham. They also instituted numerous devotions, such as the Stations of the Cross. They are known especially for their missionary endeavors and commitment to social work.

Ed Hindson

Bibliography

Clouse, Robert. "Franciscans." *The International Dictionary of the Christian Church*. Edited by J.D. Douglas. Grand Rapids: Zondervan, 1978.

Huber, R.M. *A Documented History of the Franciscan Order*. Milwaukee, WI: Nowiny Publishing Apostolate, 1944.

Kurian, George. *Nelson's Dictionary of Christianity*. Nashville, TN: Thomas Nelson, 2005.

FUNDAMENTALISM

At the beginning of the twentieth century, a movement of conservative orthodox Christians began to grow in reaction to the doctrinal liberalism that was becoming widespread in mainline Protestant churches. The word *fundamentalism* was coined to describe the set of theological beliefs that were articulated by these concerned Christians—beliefs that became a unifying influence within Protestant communities, especially in the United States. In many cases, fundamentalism promoted separation from worldly lifestyles as well as from liberal denominations. Fundamentalists expressed unwavering allegiance to their irreducible beliefs and convictions. With time, the term *fundamentalism* took on a pejorative meaning among those who disagreed with, or rejected, the essence of fundamentalist beliefs.

The term *fundamentalism* gained popular support in 1901 when Lyman Stewart, president of the Union Oil Company in California, began printing, mailing, and distributing widely a collection of 12 books called *The Fundamentals*. These were a collection of articles by conservative authors emphasizing...

* the inspiration and authority of the Bible
* the virgin birth and deity of Christ
* the vicarious substitutionary death of Jesus Christ to atone for sins
* the bodily resurrection of Jesus Christ from the dead
* the historic reality of Christ's miracles
* the literal second coming of Christ in the future

In its early days, the movement had broad denominational support and included such figures as J. Gresham Machen (Presbyterian), William B. Reily (Baptist), C.I. Scofield (Independent), Bob Jones Sr. (Methodist), and J. Frank Norris (Baptist). Those who held to these beliefs became known as *Fundamentalists,* and Frank Norris called his newspaper *The Fundamentalist.* Jerry Falwell later published a magazine called *The Fundamentalist Journal.*

Fundamentalism had a resurgence in the United States in the 1950s and 1960s as the world faced turbulent political upheaval: the setback of wars in Korea and Vietnam, the challenge of the Cold War against Russia, the youth revolt of the 1960s, the constant barrage of evolutionary teaching in public schools; and setbacks by the Supreme Court's decisions limiting the use of the Bible and prayer in the public schools of America. Fundamentalism began to take definite organizational steps, creating alternate schools, denominations, and organizations that stood against the growing liberalism in mainline denominations. Among the new organizations that arose were the Independent Fundamental Churches of America (IFCA), Independent Fundamental Mission (Board) of America (IFMA), the National Association of Evangelicals (NAE), the Orthodox Presbyterian and Bible Presbyterian churches, the General Association of Regular Baptist Churches, and the Baptist Bible Fellowship. Some of the later leaders were John R. Rice, Lee Roberson, Carl McIntire, Bob Jones Jr., and Jerry Falwell.

Many who were called fundamentalists began to change their identification after the 1942 conference that founded the NAE. *Evangelical* became the term generally identified with those who adhered to the theological tenets of fundamentalism but took a more moderate approach to issues of Christian separatism. Carl F.H. Henry and others observed that Fundamentalism had come to represent a social disposition that was often viewed as anticultural and therefore opted for referring to themselves as evangelicals. In time, the split between evangelicals and fundamentalists grew wider, and the NAE loosened its theological requirements so that Pentecostals and denominations with broader theological statements of faith could become members.

Fundamentalist influence in American culture reached its apex with the election of Ronald Reagan (1980, and again in 1984), in which fundamentalists played a major role through the efforts of Jerry Falwell and the Moral Majority organization. Internal differences within the movement tended to divide moderate and militant fundamentalists, especially on issues of associational separation. The unfortunate labeling of all religious conservatives (Christian, Muslim, Jewish) as *fundamentalist extremists* (M. Marty) has caused many conservative Christians to prefer calling themselves *evangelicals*. However, the basic issues that divide conservative and liberal Protestants still remain matters of keen theological debate.

American fundamentalism in the twentieth century was marked by fervent evangelism, church planting, and the establishment of conservative seminaries, colleges, and Christian day schools. As fundamentalists grew in numbers, their separation from liberal theological institutions and the secular culture in general left an ever-widening gap between them and secular society, which many fundamentalists see as continually drifting toward apostasy. How the fundamentalists will continue to engage the culture and reignite its original passion for evangelism is one of the great challenges of the twenty-first century.

Ed Hindson and Elmer Towns

Bibliography

Dollar, George. *A History of Fundamentalism in America*. Greenville, SC: Bob Jones University Press, 1973.

Falwell, Jerry, ed., with Ed Dobson, and Ed Hindson. *The Fundamentalist Phenomenon*. Garden City, NY: Doubleday, 1981.

Marsden, George M. *Fundamentalism and American Culture*. Oxford: Oxford University Press, 1980.

Marty, Martin E. *The Fundamentalism Project*, vols. 1-5. Chicago: University of Chicago Press, 1994–2004.

Russell, C. Allyn. *Voices of American Fundamentalism*. Philadelphia: Westminster, 1976.

GENEVA BIBLE

The Geneva Bible was an English translation of Scripture produced by English exiles and published at Geneva, Switzerland, in 1560. Led by William Whittingham, Anthony Gilby, William Cole, and possibly John Knox, the translators produced what became the first English translations of the Bible based strictly upon Hebrew and Greek texts. It was the most popular Bible of its day, outselling and outliving the Great Bible (1539) and the Bishops' Bible (1568). It was the first Bible printed in Scotland and was the favorite Bible of the Pilgrims, arriving in America on the Mayflower in 1620. It was also the version used by Shakespeare, Bunyan, and Milton. It outsold the King James Version (1611) for nearly 100 years.

The popularity of the Geneva Bible was due to its use of Roman type, 6500 cross references, 700 literal renderings for difficult words, book introductions, maps, and charts and illustrations of Noah's ark, the tabernacle, Solomon's temple, Ezekiel's temple, the tribes of Israel, and Paul's journeys. The most unique feature of the Geneva Bible was its annotations, especially those of apocalyptic passages, which viewed the Roman Catholic Church as the beast, the Pope as the Antichrist, and the bishops and others as locusts from the abyss. The notes also criticized "wicked Anabaptists" and "Mohammedan Turks." The annotations also foresaw the future conversion of the Jews to Christianity. In these ways the Geneva Bible served as the first "study Bible" for the English people and introduced them to the theology of Calvin and the Geneva reformers, who viewed the Reformation as a "cosmic conflict between the forces of Christ and those of Antichrist" (Christianson, 36).

Ed Hindson

Bibliography

Christianson, Paul. *Reformers and Babylon: English Apocalyptic Visions.* Toronto: University of Toronto Press, 1978.

Firth, K.R. *The Apocalyptic Tradition in Reformation Britain 1530–1645.* Oxford: Oxford University Press, 1979.

Hindson, E. *The Puritan's Use of Scripture in the Development of an Apocalyptic Hermeneutic.* Pretoria, University of South Africa, 1984.

Lupton, L. *The History of the Geneva Bible.* 12 vols. London: The Olive Tree, nd.

GIDEONS INTERNATIONAL

In 1898, John Nicholson and Samuel E. Hill met while staying in a hotel in Wisconsin. They conversed about their faith, read the Bible together, and discussed the need to encourage other Christian men who traveled regularly. In 1899, they met again, along with William J. Knights, and began an association for Christian traveling salesmen. After reading Judges 6–7 and praying together, they chose the name *Gideons* because Gideon was a man who was willing to do exactly what God wanted him to do and exhibited humility, faith, and obedience. The organization adopted the symbol of the two-handled pitcher and torch mentioned in recalling Gideon's victory over the Midianites (Judges 7:20).

Gideons International is the oldest association of Christian business and professional men in the United States of America. It is a Protestant/evangelical, parachurch, nonprofit organization whose members come from many denominations, live all over the world, and are dedicated to bringing the lost to Christ through personal witnessing and the distribution of God's Word. Because "faith comes by hearing and hearing by the Word of God" (Romans 10:17), Gideons believe that making God's Word available can and does lead people to faith in Christ.

Members consist of business and professional men (except clergymen) who hold that the Bible is the inspired, infallible, inerrant Word of God, and that the Lord Jesus Christ is the eternal Son of God. Members must know Jesus as their personal Savior, strive to follow Him in their daily lives, be in good standing in their Protestant/evangelical churches, and have the recommendation of their pastors. Today there are more than 287,000 Gideons and auxiliary members (wives of Gideons).

In 1908, during the Gideon convention in Louisville, Kentucky, a recommendation to place Bibles in hotel rooms was approved. The first placement of Scriptures consisted of 25 Bibles. Today, Gideons are organized in over 190 countries, print Bibles and New Testaments in over 90 languages, and have placed over 1.7 billion copies of them in hotels, hospitals, medical offices, and jails. Bibles are also distributed at schools to students in fifth grade and above, to prisoners, police officers, medical and military personnel, and any individual to whom a Gideon might witness. Their Life-Book movement aims to reach high school students with God's Word by having Christian students give Bibles or New Testaments to classmates at school. On average, more than two copies of God's Word are distributed per second, and more than one million are distributed every 4.5 days.

David Roberts

Bibliography

"Gideons International." *Nelson's Dictionary of Christianity*. Edited by George Thomas Kurian. Nashville, TN: Thomas Nelson, 2005.

The Gideons International 100 Years: Sharing God's Word. Nashville, TN: The Gideons International, 2008.

GILL, JOHN (1697–1771)

G

Baptist pastor, writer, and theologian John Gill countered the latitudinarianism, Deism, and Socinianism that swept through the Christian churches of his day by writing many books, including *The Cause of God and Truth*, a *Body of Doctrinal and Practical Divinity*, and expositional commentaries on every book of the Bible. Sometimes referred to as Dr. Voluminous due to the amount of content he penned, the pastor-theologian was either lauded or lambasted by his peers. In 1745, he was recognized and given an honorary doctorate by Marischal College, Aberdeen University, for scholarship in biblical literature, the oriental languages, and Jewish antiquities.

Born in 1697 at Kettering in Northamptonshire into a Particular Baptist family, Gill had a desire to learn. By age 12, he had mastered the Latin classics and had become proficient in Greek. He also taught himself Hebrew, theology, and philosophy. Just before his nineteenth birthday, he became a Christian and made a public profession of faith and was baptized. That same night, some church members invited him to their home and asked him to give an exposition of Isaiah 53. The next Sunday evening, he was requested to preach his first sermon in church. His text was 1 Corinthians 2:2.

In 1718, Gill married Elizabeth Negus, a member of his church. They were married for 20 years until her death in 1738. In 1719, Gill temporarily supplied the pulpit at Goat Yard Church, Horsleydown, in Southwark, London. However, in March 1720, a group separated from that church and called and ordained Gill as their pastor. He served them for more than 51 years until his death in 1771.

Gill was a Calvinist and has been accused of being a hyper-Calvinist as well as an antinomian because of his beliefs in eternal justification, the adoption of the elect, and an eternal covenant of grace. While Gill was uncomfortable with the concept of the free offer of the gospel, he believed (unlike his contemporaries John Brine and Joseph Hussey) that sinners should be sincerely urged to come to Christ and find relief in him from their sin-burdened consciences.

Gill's other writings included *The Doctrine of the Trinity* (1731), *Exposition of the*

Old and New Testaments (9 volumes, 1746–1763), *A Body of Doctrinal Divinity* (1767), and *A Body of Practical Divinity* (1770).

David Roberts

Bibliography

Freundt Jr., A.H. "John Gill." *Evangelical Dictionary of Theology.* Edited by Walter A. Elwell. Grand Rapids: Baker, 1989.

Nettles, Thomas J. *The Baptists: Key People Involved in Forming a Baptist Identity,* vol. 1. Ross-shire, Scotland: Mentor, 2005.

———. *By His Grace and for His Glory.* Cape Coral, FL: Founders Press, 2006.

GNOSTICISM

Gnosticism is rooted in neo-Platonism and in the mystery religions of the Greco-Roman world. It developed independently of Christianity until the second century, when it incorporated Christian elements, becoming a Christian heresy. Neo-Platonism said reality is an emanation from "the One," the source of all being. Emanations from the One generate lower levels of reality, each level generating the level below it. The One is said to generate the *nous*, an exact duplicate of the One. Being one step removed, the nous is the perfect form of everything else, yet it separates that existence from the One. This nous or "demiurge" generates the world-soul, which stands between the nous and visible reality. We are said to live several steps removed from the One and have no contact with it. Each level is less perfect than the level above, and has less of its being, except for the nous, a perfect mirror of the One.

Gnosticism adopts this idea that the visible world has no contact with ultimate reality. It also incorporates ideas from the Mystery Religions, first century mythologies that were supposedly fresh manifestations of Egyptian or Persian religions. One of these, the Cult of Isis, a pseudo-Egyptian religion, offered the hope of immortality. It and similar religions initiated followers to a secret knowledge, known only to members of the cult. This secret knowledge was considered the key to release from the visible world.

The Persian influence came from Zoroastrianism, which taught that the forces of good and evil, light and darkness, were in constant battle with each other. Gnosticism modified this, saying that light, upon penetrating the darkness, had been captured by it. Light was now trapped in the human body. Light and darkness spawned a series of subdeities who were in constant battle with one another, humanity being caught in the fray. Ideally, humans would be released from this world as a result of this battle and enter the realm of light.

Valentinius (AD 100–160/161) created the most widespread form of Christian Gnosticism. In his cosmology, the higher god—now called the *pleroma* (fullness)—struggled with the lower god, the demi-urge, resulting in the lower having been deceived into giving to humanity the breath of life. Lured into eating from the Tree of Life, the human race then discovered that the demi-urge was in fact not the ultimate Being, not the higher God. The demi-urge then caused mankind to forget this fact. This is the Gnostic version of the fall. The *pleroma* eventually sent a messenger (Christ) to recall the human race to true spiritual knowledge. That is why this religion is called Gnosticism—it is a religion of salvation based on knowledge, not faith.

This version of Gnosticism said that the *pleroma* abandoned Jesus before he was crucified. The "risen Christ"—no longer restricted to a human body—now has the power to call human beings back to true spiritual knowledge. In Gnosticism, Jesus is not the eternal Son; he is adopted by the Father. He does not die for sins; he communicates secret knowledge. The goal of Gnosticism is to attain release from this visible world, not the resurrection of the body.

Before Christian forms of Gnosticism emerged in the second century, earlier versions of it had some influence on Christianity. Paul exhorted the Colossians to avoid empty philosophies, the mortification of the body, and worshipping angels rather than Jesus Christ directly. In fact, Paul called Christ "the *pleroma*," saying further that "in Him all the fullness [Greek, *pleroma*] of Deity dwells in bodily form" (Colossians 2:9 NASB). This appears to be a direct challenge to Gnostic understandings of *pleroma* as a being separate from this world, and a separate being from Jesus Christ in his bodily state.

Similarly, in 1 John 1 the apostle John emphasized "that which...our hands have handled, of the Word of life" (verse 1)—he taught clearly the physical nature of Christ, apparently over against the idea of Christ as a spiritual being only. John also exhorted his readers to avoid sin, and yet to avoid claiming that they have no sin (1 John 1:7-9). This appears to counter the Gnostic idea that the spiritual side of our being is sinless no matter what happens to the physical side.

Gnostic ideas are found today in Christian Science and in New Age religions, some of which emphasize the goal of spiritual release from the chains of this world, and use the word *light* in ways more Gnostic than biblical. Some New Agers believe that we are about to enter a new age of consciousness, where spiritual and mystical knowledge will be widely dispersed and various mysteries revealed.

Early Christian apologists such as Tertullian, Irenaeus, and Hippolytus offered serious refutations of Gnosticism, and Gnosticism largely disappeared in the ancient world under the relentless witness of those who offered the true gospel. Christians today who seek to reach New Age adherents with the gospel would do well to read the ancient texts of the Christian apologists.

Fred Smith

Bibliography

Borchert, G.L. "Gnosticism." *The Evangelical Dictionary of Theology*. Edited by Walter Elwell. Grand Rapids: Baker: 2001.

Grant, R.M. *Gnosticism and Early Christianity*. New York: Columbia University Press, 1967.

Yamauchi, Edwin. *Pre-Christian Gnosticism*. Eugene, OR: Wipf & Stock, 2003.

G

GRAHAM, BILLY (1918–)

The American evangelist Billy Graham came from humble beginnings. He was born November 7, 1918, on a farm outside of Charlotte, North Carolina. Named after his father, William Franklin Graham Jr. grew up through the Great Depression and had to work hard. Although he was raised in a Christian family, Graham did not ask Jesus to be his Savior until the age of 15, when he attended the revival services of Mordecai Ham near his home. He tried to avoid the pointing finger of the evangelist, but when the invitation was given, Graham could no longer resist the conviction of the Holy Spirit. On the last verse of the song "Just as I Am," he walked up to the platform and made a decision to follow Christ.

In college, Graham preached when asked, but he wrestled with the idea of making it his life's work. Then in 1938, during a soul-searching walk, he knelt down at the eighteenth hole of a golf course across from the Florida Bible Institute (later Trinity College) and surrendered his life to God. He went on to receive his BA degree from Wheaton College, graduating in 1943. That same year his ministry began in a significant way when he became Youth for Christ's first full-time evangelist. In 1948, while president of Northwestern College in Minneapolis, Minnesota, he gained national attention through his crusades held in Los Angeles. In 1950, he formed the Billy Graham Evangelistic Association to be a parent organization for his evangelistic work.

In 1943, Graham married Ruth Bell, and they had five children together. Each of their children has served in ministry. In fact, their son Franklin Graham is president of the Billy Graham Evangelistic Association, and their grandson Will leads crusades for the organization. In 2007, Ruth Graham died at the age of 87, and she was buried at the site of the Billy Graham Library in Charlotte, North Carolina.

Early in his ministry, Graham realized that many evangelists' reputations were being ruined by various kinds of scandals. So in a hotel room in California, he and his ministry team drew up a set of rules (later called the Modesto Manifesto) to avoid these kinds of problems. In the area of money, Graham would receive an agreed-upon annual salary no matter how large his offerings were. To guard against immorality, Graham and other men were never alone with other women. To prevent against exaggerated crusade attendance figures, Graham used the numbers determined by the managers at the facilities he visited. He and his associates also agreed not to publicly criticize other pastors or churches.

Graham's impact has been global. He has reached and taught people through crusades, books, films, websites, newspaper columns, radio programs, magazines, television broadcasts, training schools, and congresses on world evangelism. The number of people to whom Graham has preached is measured in the hundreds of millions. He cofounded *Christianity Today* magazine and edited his own *Decision* magazine for several decades. His book *Peace with God* (1952) has been distributed by the millions of copies in dozens of languages. Graham has often been voted the most respected man in America.

Dan Russell

Bibliography

Aikman, David. *Billy Graham: His Life and Influence*. Nashville, TN: Thomas Nelson, 2007.

Billy Graham Evangelistic Association. "Biographies." http://www.billygraham.org/biographies_index.asp

Graham, Billy. *Just As I Am: The Autobiography of Billy Graham*. New York: HarperCollins, 1997.

Martin, William. "The Riptide of Revival." *Christian History and Biography*, Fall 2006.

———. *A Prophet with Honor: The Billy Graham Story*. New York: William Morrow, 1991.

GREAT AWAKENING

The Protestant religious revival movement in the American colonies between 1725 and 1760 is popularly known as the Great Awakening. During the years of colonial expansion there came a growing dissent with the established churches, and the awakening spread across denominational lines. As a result, a renewed spiritual fervor encouraged by clear gospel preaching, calls to repentance, and fervent prayer formed the basis of a new evangelical consensus throughout the American colonies and still characterizes much of American evangelicalism today.

The earliest indications of revival occurred among the Dutch Reformed churches in New Jersey through the fervent preaching of T.J. Frelinghuysen and among the Presbyterian churches through the preaching of Gilbert Tennent and in New Brunswick and Nova Scotia (later Canada) through the preaching of Henry Alline. Characterized by a call to repentance, personal conversion, and heartfelt religion, the revival spread to Enfield, Connecticut, and Northampton, Massachusetts, through the preaching of Jonathan Edwards's famous sermon "Sinners in the Hands of an Angry God." In the South, the revival spread through the preaching of Englishman George Whitefield, who traveled to the American colonies seven times to conduct extensive itinerant preaching campaigns. Revivals took place among the Methodists through the preaching of Devereux Jarratt, and among the Baptists revivals through the preaching of Daniel Marshall and Shubal Stearns.

The fervency of the revival movements stood in stark contrast to the established churches and was eventually opposed by Harvard College and the established clergy led by Charles Chauncy, who expressed antirevivalist views in his *Seasonable Thoughts on the State of Religion in New England* (1743). Critics charged the revivalist preachers with excessive enthusiasm and antinomianism. Jonathan Edwards, considered the most brilliant theological and philosophical mind in colonial America, responded with his *Thoughts Concerning the Revival* (1743) and *Treatise Concerning Religious Affections* (1746), which followed his earlier writings, *Narrative of the Surprising Works of God* (1737) and *Justification by Faith Alone* (1738). Edwards defended the revival as an expression of divine sovereignty, combining what many scholars have called an intellectual and speculative personal devotion that resulted in an evangelical Calvinism.

Continued resistance from the established churches eventually led to several theological divisions. Among the Congregationalists, Edwards's followers were known as New Lights as opposed to Old Lights. The Presbyterians split into New Side and Old Side groups, and the Baptists into Separate and Regular Baptists. On the positive side, the Great Awakening brought to many people a new biblical focus and spiritual intensity, and an increased fervor for evangelizing to the general public and increased missionary activity among the Native Americans, calls to abolish slavery, and the establishment of new educational institutions such as Princeton, Rutgers, Brown, and Dartmouth. Shelly also notes that the Great Awakening provided a "mood of tolerance that cut across denominational lines...that contributed to a national spirit of religious tolerance" (426) and paved the way to the freedom of religion later expressed in the US Constitution.

The Second Great Awakening (1787–1825) led to another national revival. It began among students in Virginia at Hampton-Sydney College and Washington College and later spread to Yale College under the preaching of Timothy Dwight, a grandson of Jonathan Edwards. In the Western states, revival movements of the early nineteenth century took on a more emotional flavor in the camp meetings in Kentucky, which were attended by thousands and later spread among Methodists, Baptists, and Presbyterians.

Ed Hindson

Bibliography

Kidd, Thomas. *The Great Awakening: The Roots of Evangelical Christianity in Colonial America*. New Haven, CT: Yale University Press, 2009.

Orr, J. Edwin. *The Second Evangelical Awakening*. Fort Washington, PA: Christian Literature Crusade, 1964.

Pollock, John. *George Whitefield and the Great Awakening*. Garden City, NY: Doubleday, 1972.

Shelly, Bruce. "Great Awakening." *The International Dictionary of the Christian Church*. Edited by J.D. Douglas. Grand Rapids: Zondervan, 1978.

Wood, A. Skevington. *The Inextinguishable Blaze*. Grand Rapids: Eerdmans, 1980.

GREAT SCHISM

The Great Schism of 1054 marked the split between the Eastern Orthodox Church (Greek) and the Catholic Church (Latin). Though it occurred in 1054, relations between the Eastern and Western churches had for centuries been in decline. The differences leading to the split were multiple, involving theological, political, cultural, and ecclesiastical disputes, and disagreement over the extent of papal authority.

The event that many consider to have made the schism official was a meeting in 1054 between the representatives of Pope Leo IX of the Catholic Church and Patriarch of Constantinople Michael Cerularius. Pope Leo IX sent legates to Constantinople to demand, among other things, that Cerularius recognize Rome's claim to be the head of all the churches, and to desist from proclaiming himself the Ecumenical Patriarch. When Cerularius refused to comply, Cardinal Humbert excommunicated him from the Church. Likewise, Cerularius excommunicated Cardinal Humbert and his fellow legates.

The separation has continued down through the modern day, though in 1965, Pope Paul VI and the Ecumenical Patriarch of Constantinople Athenagoras I agreed to nullify the anathemas of 1054. This was more of a goodwill gesture and did not lead to any sort of official reconciliation. While today there are visits between key leaders of the two sides, they still retain many distinctives that keep them divided.

A second schism occurred in the Roman Catholic West in 1378–1417. It began when Pope Clement V moved the Holy See to Avignon (France) in 1309 for security purposes. However, this soon led to rival Popes in Rome and Avignon both claiming to be the rightful Pope at the same time. This Western schism came to be called the "Babylonian Captivity of the Papacy." The issue was eventually resolved when a third Pope, Martin V, was elected in 1417 and moved back to Rome in 1420.

Ed Hindson

Bibliography

Chadwick, Henry. *East and West: The Making of a Rift in the Church.* Oxford: Oxford University Press, 2003.

Pelikan, Jaroslav. *The Christian Tradition: A History of the Development of Doctrine, Volume 2: The Spirit of Eastern Christendom (600–1700).* Chicago: University of Chicago Press, 1977.

GREGORY OF NAZIANZUS (CA. 330–390)

Fourth-century theologian Gregory of Nazianzus is one of a trio of early church theologians known as the Cappodocian (East Asia Minor) fathers (Basil, Gregory of Nazianzus, and Gregory of Nyssa, Basil's younger brother). His father was bishop of Nazianzus. He later studied rhetoric at Athens with Basil, who would go on to become bishop of Caesarea. After returning home, Gregory entered monastic life at the invitation of Basil. There he collaborated with Basil on a book of selected writings of Origen, and a book of monastic rules. Against his will, Gregory was ordained a priest, and for 12 years he assisted his father at Nazianzus (until his father's death).

While variously called upon thereafter to use his rhetorical and theological skills in various bishoprics, the reticent Gregory avoided such until, in the midst of the ongoing theological and political debates in the church with the resurgent Arianism, Apollinarianism, and other crucial doctrinal concerns that sought to undermine the strong Nicene faith (Nicene Creed, 325) to which he was committed, he gave himself actively to responding and contributing answers to those who would attack the faith. In 379, shortly before the great Council of Constantinople (381), Gregory accepted the invitation to lead a small Nicene (orthodox) church in Constantinople. His eloquent, deep, insightful, and constructive doctrinal sermons there led to his being given the title "the Theologian." These sermons advanced and clarified the christological and trinitarian teaching of his "hero," Athanasius of Alexandria.

Five of these messages, known as the theological orations (27-31), laid the theological groundwork for the anticipated Council at Constantinople and were instrumental in answering and overcoming Arianism, thus firmly establishing the earlier Nicene Creed (325). These sermons were preached in 380, and strongly defended the deity of the Son and the Holy Spirit. In oration 31 in particular, Gregory gave clear and potent arguments for the non-Sabellian (nonmodalist) nature of the Nicene *homoousion* (same essence) doctrine, thereby solidifying and defending the church's teaching on the divine equality of the three persons of the Trinity. He argued that the Father is "unbegotten," the Son is "eternally begotten" of the Father, the Holy Spirit "eternally proceeds from the father *through* the Son."

Against the Apollinarian heresy, which denied the complete humanity of Christ, Gregory rightly pointed out the dependence of our human salvation on Christ's complete humanity. Putting it in pithy fashion, it was Gregory who declared of Jesus Christ, "What was not assumed (by Christ of our human nature) cannot be healed (saved/restored to God); it is only what (of our complete human nature) is united with God that is saved." Like most of the Eastern Church, Gregory viewed salvation as deification—i.e., that our redeemed human nature fully participates in God (2 Peter 1:4). Shortly after the Council, Gregory returned home to the monastic life.

John Douglas Morrison

Bibliography

Gonzalez, J. *A History of Christian Thought*. New York: Harper & Row, 1984.

Grillmeier, A. *Christ in Christian Tradition*. Louisville, KY: Westminster John Knox, 1988.

Kelly, J.N.D. *Early Christian Doctrines*. Harrisburg, PA: Continuum, 2000.

Nazianzus, Gregory. *Theological Orations*, 27-31.

✠

BILLY GRAHAM
American Evangelist
1918–

HANDEL, GEORGE FRIDERIC (1685–1759)

Considered one of the greatest composers of all time, Handel was born in Germany but resided in England for the majority of his life. Along with Johann Sebastian Bach, Antonio Vivaldi, Domenico Scarlatti, and Georg Philipp Telemann, Handel is regarded as one of the important composers of the Baroque era. He composed music for virtually every genre of his time. His most famous works include the orchestral works *Water Music, Music for the Royal Fireworks,* and the oratorio (a genre Handel created) *Messiah* (1741).

When Handel was a boy, his father forbade him from playing music, preferring that his son study law. Despite his father's restriction, he practiced secretly and later the Duke of Saxe-Weissenfels overheard him playing the organ. He was so impressed he convinced Handel's father to allow him to obtain musical training. Then at age 12, after his father died, he became the organist at the Calvinist Domkirche.

Subsequent to a handful of successful compositions, including several operas in the Italian style, Handel was appointed Kapellmeister to the electoral court in Hanover. After spending several years between Hamburg, Hanover, Rome, and Venice, Handel finally settled in London in 1712, where he would live the rest of his life. There he received a salary from Queen Anne, which allowed him greater autonomy to compose as he desired without the constraints of a patron. The Royal Academy of Music was founded by Handel in 1719 for the express purpose of bringing Italian-style opera to London. It was there that one of his most important operas, *Giulio Cesare,* premiered.

In 1723, Handel became composer of music for His Majesty's Chapel Royal. For the coronation of King George II in 1727, Handel composed four new anthems, including *Zadok the Priest,* which has been performed at every British coronation since. After leaving the Royal Academy of Music, Handel wrote several very successful operas for a new theater, Covent Garden. There, *Ariodante* and *Alcina,* two of his outstanding operas, made their debut, along with revivals of *Acis and Galatea* and *Esther.* In addition, Handel performed his own organ concertos, a new genre.

When public interest in opera began to wane, Handel turned to oratorio. From the 1740s until the end of his life, oratorio dominated his musical output. The majority of his oratorios were based on biblical themes: *Saul, Samson, Israel in Egypt, Esther,*

Jeptha, and of course, *Messiah.* He also used the Apocrypha for oratorios such as *Judas Maccabaeus* and *Alexander Balus.*

Handel's compositional style was a synthesis of the musical cosmopolitan practices in contemporary Europe. He wrote Italian operas, songs, and trios; German Lutheran church music; English songs and anthems; and overtures in the French style. Handel's output consists of operas, oratorios, organ works, songs, concerti grossi, orchestral, solo and trio sonatas, suites, overtures, and cantatas.

Michael Brennan

Bibliography

Burrows, Donald. *Handel.* Oxford: Oxford University Press, 1994.

Hogwood, Christopher. *Handel.* London: Thames & Hudson, 1985.

Kavanaugh, Patrick. *Spiritual Lives of the Great Composers.* Grand Rapids: Zondervan, 1996.

Keates, Jonathan. *Handel: the Man and His Music.* London: Victor Gollancz, 1985.

Robbins Landon, H.C. *Handel and His World.* London: Weidenfeld & Nicolson, 1984.

HARVARD, JOHN (1607–1638)

John Harvard was a Congregationalist clergyman, pastor of the Massachusetts colony, and a benefactor and namesake of Harvard College (now Harvard University). He was born in Southwark, England, and his early life was marked by tragedy. In 1625, most of his family died of the plague; leaving only himself, his younger brother Thomas, and their mother, Katherine. She married twice more and died ten years later in 1635.

John attended Emmanuel College, Cambridge, a college known for its Puritan leanings. There he earned a BA degree in 1632 and MA degree in 1635. He was probably ordained a dissenting minister in 1636, and the same year married Ann Sadler. Before leaving England, he sold several inherited properties and with the proceeds purchased a significant scholar's library of classical and theological texts.

In 1637, Harvard emigrated with his wife and a group of Puritans to New England, where he was appointed a teaching elder and assistant preacher of the First Congregational Church in Charlestown under the Reverend Zechariah Symmes. By this time he was the sole survivor of his family and heir to a fairly sizable estate. By standards of the day, he was a wealthy citizen. He was made a freeman shortly after his arrival, giving him political privilege and responsibility, evidenced by the fact that he was placed on a committee to formulate a body of laws (Shaff-Herzog V 162). He was deeded a large tract of land near the church, built a fairly sumptuous home, and prepared to settle down in his adopted country. He died, however, in little over a year on September 14, 1638.

As early as 1633, John Eliot, a missionary to the Indians in the colony, had appealed unsuccessfully to Sir Simonds D'Ewes in England for a sizeable donation to establish a school to train ministers and professionals in the New World (Eliot, 130). In 1636, the General Court appropriated £400 toward establishing the school in New Towne. Harvard seems to have taken a special interest in this project. Near his death, he bequeathed an additional £400 (half of his monetary estate) and his entire scholar's library of 320 volumes to the project, which as yet had no buildings, students, library, or instructors. This was sufficient to begin classes the following year. In gratitude, the founders renamed the institution Harvard College. They also renamed the community of New Towne *Cambridge*, using the name of the school from which Harvard had graduated (Winthrop, 301). His story is a reminder of the godly heritage of this venerable institution, which was originally founded to produce ministers of the gospel.

Today, Harvard University, which still maintains an active divinity school, is recognized as among America's most prestigious educational institutions. However, it is also known for its liberal and progressive ideologies, which seem to be far removed from what John Harvard might have envisioned for the school so many years ago. Still, John Harvard's example of supporting Christian education as foundational to the spiritual experience in Colonial America continues to speak to us today.

Daniel R. Mitchell

Bibliography

Eliot, John. "A College Proposed for Massachusetts Bay." *The Annals of America*. Edited by Mortimer J. Adler. 18 vols. Chicago: Encyclopedia Britannica, 1976.

"Harvard, John." *The New Schaff-Herzog Religious Encyclopedia*. Edited by S.M. Jackson. Grand Rapids: Baker, 1952.

"John Harvard." *The Columbia Encyclopedia*, 6th ed. New York: Columbia University Press, 2000.

Winthrop, Robert. *The Life and Letters of John Winthrop*, 2d ed. Boston: Little, Brown and Co., 1869.

HAYSTACK REVIVAL

One major point that emerges from a survey of church history is that the task of world evangelization is rife with seemingly impossible hurdles. Many Christians have balked at the notion of endeavoring to convert people from every tribe and nation, considering some to be too resistant to persuade. However, in 1806, five students at Williams College in northwestern Massachusetts determined, "We can do this, if we will!" Their fervor sparked a prayer movement for international missions. The five men were Samuel Mills, James Richards, Francis Robbins, Byram Green, and Harvey Loomis.

The five met regularly on the college campus to pray. One day in August a severe thunderstorm came along and they were forced to seek the protective shelter offered by a haystack. While there, one of them, Mills, explained that he'd been reading William Carey's pamphlet *An Enquiry into the Obligations of Christians* (1792). Mills had caught Carey's missionary enthusiasm and agreed with Carey that the Great Commission (Matthew 28:19-20) is a mandate for all Christians—not just for the apostles.

These men believed that if they had sufficient determination, God would enable their generation to evangelize the world. They committed to praying for all the nations and getting involved in world missions. Thus began the first student mission movement in North America, formally called the Society of Brethren at Williams College and Andover College (Shaw, 481). Subsequently, many other college campuses in North America came to adopt this same spirit of prayer for the nations.

Today, historians trace the existence of a number of mission agencies back to the Haystack Prayer Meeting. The Student Volunteer Movement (SVM) is an example of a student-led association that was born out of the Haystack Prayer Meeting. In 1910, SVM president John Mott chaired the worldwide missionary conference at Edinburgh, Scotland. Missions leaders from all over the world gathered to strategize for "world evangelization in this generation" partly due to the missionary fervor that began with these five men taking shelter in a storm more than 100 years earlier.

Interestingly, the roots of the Haystack Prayer Meeting can be traced further back to another giant of Christian history—Jonathan Edwards, who mentored a pastor named Edward Griffin, who preached a missionary message titled "The Kingdom of Christ." Later at Andover Seminary, Griffin led Adoniram Judson to Christ. Judson was the first North American to serve overseas as a missionary. The young college student at Williams College, Samuel Mills, eventually acquired a copy of Griffin's missionary sermon and began distributing the message on the campus of Williams College.

What makes the Haystack Prayer Meeting so significant from a missiological perspective is that its impetus for missions came from young people rather than from denominational leaders. It was not a directive issued by a missions board; rather, it was a grassroots movement. This movement is an example of missionary efforts that have arisen from ordinary laypeople like students and cobblers, and not leaders and clergy.

Kenneth Nehrbass

Bibliography

Kurian, George T. "Haystack Prayer Meeting." *Nelson's Dictionary of Christianity.* Nashville, TN: Thomas Nelson, 2005.

Shaw, Ryan. "A Haystack that Changed the World." *Evangelical Missions Quarterly* (October 2006): 480-86.

H

HEIDELBERG CATECHISM

The Heidelberg Catechism (1563) is a classic formulation of Reformed Protestant theology. While the Reformation inspired many catechisms, the Heidelberg Catechism was particularly influential because of its irenic spirit and gospel focus. A beloved standard, it is one of the most widely translated and distributed works in the world. The Heidelberg Catechism originated in Heidelberg, in the Palatinate, a state in southern Germany. In that era, the region witnessed frequent religious struggles between Roman Catholics, Lutherans, and Reformed Christians. The Heidelberg Catechism largely avoided religious polemics, seeking a middle ground between Lutheran and Reformed teachings.

The father of the Heidelberg Catechism was Frederick III (1515–1576), the Elector of the Palatinate. A devout Christian, Frederick III had a sincere but cautious Reformed agenda. His threefold vision for the Heidelberg Catechism was for catechizing (teaching children gospel precepts), preaching (providing a standard in the churches), and theological unity (for doctrinal consistency in the Palatine). The creation of the Heidelberg Catechism was entrusted to a learned committee from Heidelberg. The primary author was Zacharias Ursinus (1534–1583), a Heidelberg professor who had already composed two catechisms. Another key contributor was Caspar Olevianus (1536–1587), the court preacher in Heidelberg. That the Heidelberg Catechism was drafted by such young men is remarkable.

The Heidelberg Catechism is composed of 129 theological questions and answers.

Frederick III insisted on biblical faithfulness, and the Heidelberg Catechism includes 700 scriptural proof texts. The questions are organized in three great themes: man's misery, man's redemption, and man's gratitude for salvation.

The Heidelberg Catechism became a theological foundation for continental Reformed churches in Germany and the Netherlands. Catechism questions were clustered in 52 weekly units, corresponding to Lord's days, to encourage catechetical preaching. In Dutch Reformed Churches, Sunday evening sermons were systematically tied to the Catechism's doctrinal themes. An abridged version of the Catechism, published in 1611 as *The Compendium*, encouraged memorization. Along with the Belgic Confession (1561) and the Canons of the Synod of Dort (1618–1619), the Heidelberg Catechism comprised the Three Forms of Unity, an enduring Reformed confessional standard.

The Heidelberg Catechism is highly regarded for its warm, evangelical piety. Its use of the first person encouraged personal commitment. It emphasizes spiritual consolation in Christ. The Heidelberg Catechism's famous first question reveals its pervasive tone: "What is thy only comfort in life and death?" Answer: "That I with body and soul, both in life and death, am not my own, but belong unto my faithful Savior Jesus Christ; who, with his precious blood, has fully satisfied for all my sins, and delivered me from all the power of the devil..."

Roger Schultz

Bibliography

Beeke, Joel, ed. *Doctrinal Standards, Liturgy, and Church Order*. Grand Rapids: Reformation Heritage Books, 1999.

Beirma, Lyle, et al. *An Introduction to the Heidelberg Catechism: Sources, History, and Theology*. Grand Rapids: Baker, 2005.

Dennison Jr., James. *Reformed Confessions of the 16th and 17th Centuries in English Translation*, vol. 2. Grand Rapids: Reformed Heritage Books, 2010.

Ursinus, Zacharias. *Commentary on the Heidelberg Catechism*. Grand Rapids: Baker, 1992.

HENRY, CARL F.H. (1913–2000)

American evangelical theologian Carl F.H. Henry has been called "the most prominent evangelical theologian of the second half of the twentieth century," and stands as one of "the few individuals who can claim to have shaped a major theological movement" (Grenz and Olson, 288; Mohler, 279). That is high praise for a descendant of German immigrants who settled on Long Island, New York, and, due to the tensions during World War I, quit speaking German as a household language. He was raised in a nominally religious home and accepted Christ as his Savior while working for a local newspaper. It was his conversion experience and the desire to prepare for full-time Christian service that changed the direction of his life.

Henry had already displayed his literary skills while working as a newspaper editor. At Wheaton College, he developed the sharp and penetrating mind that would see him earn two doctorate degrees (ThD, Northern Baptist Seminary; PhD, Boston University), join the founding faculty of Fuller Seminary, and become the founding editor of *Christianity Today*. He also positioned himself at the crossroads of neo-evangelicalism as it separated itself from Fundamentalism. He chaired the Berlin Congress on Evangelism, issued a cry for evangelical cooperation that resulted in Key '73 (a project that united many in the work of evangelism), was elected as president of the Evangelical Theological Society and the Association of Theological Schools, participated in the International Council on Biblical Inerrancy, and served as a lecturer-at-large for World Vision. The combination of his writing and keen intellect had a tremendous influence on the theological landscape of the United States in the second half of the twentieth century.

Of all Henry's accomplishments, his writings left perhaps the largest imprint. He is well-known for his magnum opus, a six-volume work entitled *God, Revelation and Authority* (1976–1979). In this magisterial treatise, Henry lays out a credible, critically engaged defense of biblical authority and inerrancy. While *GRA* comes as a type of capstone of robust theological writings, Henry had foreshadowed his theological passion that called for cultural engagement with the gospel. *The Uneasy Conscience of Modern Fundamentalism* (1948) served as his call to engage culture with social ministries and renewed commitment to academic excellence. Two other books from the earlier period of Henry's writing forecasted the type of deep philosophical analysis that he possessed. In *Remaking the Modern Mind* (1946) and *The Protestant Dilemma* (1948), Henry laid out the basic theological method that he would follow throughout his career.

Henry left evangelicalism a remarkable legacy. He also edited *Revelation and the*

Bible (1958), *Basic Christianity* (1962), and *Christian Faith and Modern Theology* (1964). Through his prodigious literary output in his books and innumerable articles he wrote as editor of *Christianity Today*, his tireless efforts to mobilize evangelicals in obeying the Great Commission, and his modeling of a critically informed and intellectually robust faith, Henry's contributions to the kingdom of God are as monumental in their breadth and scope as the King he served.

Kevin L. King Sr.

Bibliography

Grenz, Stanley, and Roger E. Olson. *20th Century Theology*. Downers Grove, IL: IVP Academic, 1992.

Henry, Carl. F.H. *Confessions of a Theologian*. Waco, TX: Word, 1986.

———. *God, Revelation and Authority*, 6 vols. Waco, TX: Word, 1976–1979.

House, Paul R. "Remaking the Modern Mind: Revisiting Carl Henry's Theological Vision." *SBJT* 8, no. 4 (Winter 2004): 4-24.

Mohler Jr., R. Albert. "Carl F. H. Henry." *Theologians of the Baptist Tradition*. Edited by Timothy George and David S. Dockery. Nashville, TN: Broadman & Holman, 2001.

HENRY, MATTHEW (1662–1714)

Nonconformist clergyman Matthew Henry was born October 18, 1662, the same year the parliament of England passed the Act of Uniformity, an act that prescribed a single form of worship, based on the *Book of Common Prayer*, in all English churches. This act resulted in the ejection of nearly 2000 nonconformist ministers from their parishes. One of the ejected ministers was Henry's father, John Henry (1631–1696), who was forced out of his parish and home shortly before the birth of young Matthew. It is well documented that young Matthew grew up in a Welsh home marked by the Puritan tradition of gathering together for morning and evening family prayer, Bible study, and catechizing. He was said to be able to read the Bible at three years of age.

When Henry was ten, he heard a sermon preached by his father on Psalm 51:7, and three years later, he formally recognized that his quest for Christ had started with that sermon. By age 14, Henry had a sound assurance that through repentance and belief he had found the pardon of God.

Henry's father served as his primary tutor until he was 18, and then in July of 1680, he was sent off to London to study under Thomas Doolittle (1630–1707), who ran a nonconformist academy that was sympathetic to Puritan theology and objections to the liturgy of the Church of England. He studied Latin, Greek, Hebrew, and French. While in London, Henry became very ill with a "fever" that had left hundreds dead in the city. He returned home in September 1680, ending his studies at Doolittle's academy. After Henry recovered, he returned to London to attend law school. While studying law, he continued his private religious education, attending various dissenters meetings and theological discussion groups.

Henry left London in 1686, still very interested in the ministry, and returned to his parents' home, where opportunities to preach began to present themselves. While on a trip to Chester, Henry laid the groundwork that would result in dissenters in the area calling him to be their pastor. He was ordained to gospel ministry by six Presbyterian ministers on May 9, 1687. Henry would go on to minister in Chester for nearly 26 years (turning down a series of calls to other churches) before moving to Hackney, just outside London, for the last two years of his ministry and life.

The move to London was partly motivated by Henry's rigorous writing commitments and the resources that London would afford him, but the move was not easy and Henry was plagued by diabetes and kidney stones up until his death in June 1714. Henry's best-known work, *Exposition of the Old and New Testaments*, begun in November 1704, was left incomplete at his death, and other ministers took up where he left off in the book of Acts and completed the task. Now known as Matthew Henry's Commentary, the set's quality and personality continues to warrant widespread publication and use to this day.

Matthew Henry remains to this day one of the most widely read commentators on the English Bible despite the fact that his biblical and theological education was basically self-taught. He also remains a prime example of what one person can accomplish in a lifetime of total commitment to the study of the Word of God. Married twice, he was the father of nine daughters and one son, and he is most remembered as one of the more outstanding Bible expositors of his time.

Brian Goard

Bibliography

Harman, Allan M. *Matthew Henry: His Life and Influence*. Fearn, UK: Christian Focus, 2012.

Roberts, Henry David. *Matthew Henry and His Chapel 1662–1900*. Liverpool: Liverpool Booksellers, 1900.

Tong, William. *An Account of the Life and Death of Mr. Matthew Henry*. London: n.p., 1716.

HOLINESS MOVEMENT

The Holiness movement arose in America during the mid-nineteenth century out of the teachings of John Wesley (1703–1791), who revived and developed a doctrine of Christian perfectionism. Wesley and most figures in the offshoot holiness movement did not teach that Christians could be sinless, but rather, that they could be perfect in love. Wesley himself believed that entire sanctification from intentional, known sin was possible in this life. He believed all Christians could live free from willful or deliberate sin, perfect in their conscious intentions and love toward others. Common to Wesley and holiness teachers is the belief in a two-stage process of salvation—the first being justification, and the second an experience of cleansing—wherein one is freed from the fallen propensity to sin. This second experience is commonly called *entire sanctification* and the results of the experience are often called the Christian higher life, full salvation, or perfect love.

The Wesleyan view rejects the doctrine of progressive sanctification, the idea that Christians progress toward final sanctification over a lifetime and the process is incomplete until one sees the Lord face-to-face. The primary catalyst of the Holiness movement was a concern over the erosion of holiness and Christian consecration to the Lord in the church.

Early perfectionists were found predominantly in the Methodist Church, but the Holiness movement eventually spread far beyond Methodist circles. Lay evangelist and Methodist Phoebe Palmer (1807–1874) was perhaps the most predominant early figure in the movement. Charles Finney also dispersed a form of perfectionism from Oberlin College, where he served as the school's second president and as a professor of systematic theology (1835–1858) and of pastoral theology (1835–1875). Asa Mahan, the college's first president, also taught and published works on Christian perfectionism. Mahan and Finney are thus largely responsible for the perfectionist strain of thought known as Oberlin theology. Methodist preacher Timothy Merritt, who edited an important work on Christian perfectionism in 1824 and later founded the first periodical completely dedicated to holiness teachings, exercised notable influence at the beginning of the Holiness movement as well.

A less prominent influence in the early movement was a commune of perfectionists residing in Oneida, New York. Their significance largely rests in the teachings of their founder John Humphrey Noyes (b. 1811), who believed that the millennium had begun in AD 70 and that Christians therefore could expect to form sinless communities here on earth. The Holiness movement began experiencing strong growth immediately following the American Civil War, and in 1867, the National Camp Meeting Association for the Promotion of Holiness was formed, an institution that experienced steady—and sometimes remarkable—growth, and which endured through several name changes up through the late twentieth century, with the most recent being the Christian Holiness Partnership.

In the early twentieth century Pentecostalism emerged with its own distinctives as an offshoot of the Holiness movement. A number of Holiness denominations and sects—including most notably the Church of the Nazarene, the Salvation Army, and the Wesleyan Church—remain distinct from Pentecostalism and continue to spread the holiness faith.

Brian Goard

H

Bibliography

Jones, Charles Edwin. *Perfectionist Persuasion: The Holiness Movement and American Methodism, 1867–1936*. Metuchen, NJ: Scarecrow, 1974.

Kostlevy, William, ed. *Historical Dictionary of the Holiness Movement*. Lanham, MA: Scarecrow, 2009.

Peters, John Leland. *Christian Perfection and American Methodism*. New York: Abingdon, 1956.

Warfield, B.B. *Perfectionism*. 2 vols. Edited by E.D. Warfield. New York: Oxford University Press, 1931.

HUBMAIER, BALTHASAR (CA. 1480–1528)

Controversy is nothing new in the history of the church, but few persons were more controversial than Anabaptist reformer Balthasar Hubmaier. Even in the midst of the turbulent times of the Reformation, Hubmaier was a divisive figure. A staunch advocate of *sola scriptura*, Hubmaier's study of God's Word led him further along the path of reform than most of his contemporaries.

Hubmaier's date of birth is unknown; he was born in Freidburg, Bavaria, and likely reared in a religious home. He entered the University of Freidburg in 1503 and received his bachelor's degree within a year. Continuing his studies under John Eck, Hubmaier received his master of arts, and then he obtained his doctorate of theology at the University of Ingolstadt. With education in hand, he was appointed a preacher, and soon became vice rector of the university.

Hubmaier's speaking abilities soon landed him a call to the new cathedral of Regensburg, which became a turning point in his life. A conflict between Christians and Jews, miraculous happenings, and an epidemic of an unknown disease became the catalysts that pushed him toward the much smaller town of Waldshut. Here, Hubmaier's popularity increased, along with his zeal for evangelical convictions. Driven by a belief that Scripture should be interpreted literally, Hubmaier's transformation led him increasingly toward his famous dictum "truth is immortal." This conviction brought him to the forefront of Swiss reform, but for Hubmaier, theological change had not gone far enough.

Publishing *The Eighteen Theses Concerning the Christian Life* in 1524, Hubmaier began both an oratorical and literary campaign. Resistance increased, however, from the Catholic King Ferdinand as Hubmaier's services were rendered in the vernacular German language, images were removed, the meaning of the mass was changed, and priests were allowed to marry. Following his own convictions, Hubmaier went on to marry Elizabeth Hugeline.

In September 1524, Hubmaier fled to Schaffhausen, where he wrote *Concerning Heretics and Those Who Burn Them*, in which he outlined a defense for religious liberty. Returning to Waldshut in October, he continued work that led to his acceptance of believer's baptism. This created further conflict between him and Reformation leader Ulrich Zwingli. When Hubmaier published *The Christian Baptism of Believers* in 1525, the wedge between him and other reformers became still deeper. With hostilities from local authorities increasing, Hubmaier sought refuge in Zurich, but he and his wife were arrested by Zwingli for their Anabaptist beliefs. Imprisoned and tortured, the conflicted reformer eventually recanted.

Ashamed and broken, Hubmaier fled to Nikolsburg, Moravia, where he became a leading pastor in the Anabaptist movement. Here the Anabaptists experienced their most significant growth and for more than a year Hubmaier enjoyed the fruits of his labor. Yet his work was not to continue, for King Ferdinand finally gained political control of Moravia and had Hubmaier arrested. During his imprisonment in Vienna Hubmaier was tortured, and finally delivered over to be burned at the stake on March 10, 1528. Three days later, his wife followed him in martyrdom when she drowned in the Danube River.

Hubmaier is most remembered for his fervent commitment to the doctrines that laid the foundation for Baptist theology.

Keith Church

Bibliography

Bergsten, Torsten. *Balthasar Hubmaier: Anabaptist Theologian and Martyr*. Edited by William R. Estep. Valley Forge, PA: Judson Press, 1978.

Caner, Emir Fethi. *Truth Is Unkillable: The Life and Writings of Balthasar Hubmaier, Theologian of Anabaptism*. Dissertation: The University of Texas at Arlington, 1999.

Estep, William R. *The Anabaptist Story*. Grand Rapids: Eerdmans, 1963.

Pipkin, H. Wayne, and John H. Yoder, eds. *Balthasar Hubmaier: Theologian of Anabaptism*. Classics of the Radical Reformation, vol. 5. Scottdale, PA: Herald Press, 1989.

Vedder, Henry C. *Balthasar Hubmaier: The Leader of the Anabaptists*. New York: The Knickerbocker Press, 1905.

H

HUGUENOTS

The story of the Huguenots, who were French Protestants, is one birthed out of the climate of the humanism that accompanied the Calvinist reformers' struggle for religious freedom in what was predominantly Roman Catholic France around the middle of the sixteenth century. Upon gaining concessions with the Edict of Nantes in 1598, the Huguenots enjoyed a reasonable period of peace and prosperity until the edict was revoked in 1685, ultimately resulting in renewed persecutions and subsequent flights of thousands of French Protestants into more tolerant lands such as England, Holland, Ireland, and the English colonies in America.

The Huguenot movement in France steadily grew out of appreciable tensions associated with the general consensus of the major Protestant reformers—Lutherans, Zwinglians, and Calvinists—that private citizens had no religious right to actively resist governing authorities hostile to the newly emerging movement. An oppressive government was viewed as one that was comprised of legitimate if not tyrannical rulers, intentionally placed on earth by God to serve his purposes. Finding their impetus in the Magdeburg Confession of 1550–1551, Huguenot pamphleteers, most notably Theodore Beza (1519–1605) and Philippe du Plessis Mornay (1549–1623), argued for the right of ordinary people to take a public stance against tyrants through their chosen representatives in government, slightly raising the bar on a more passive resistance that characterized some of the earlier attempts by the Anabaptists to secure Protestantism in their homelands.

The Protestant appeal to the mostly Roman Catholic nobility of France, though considered to be providentially placed in their stations as agents of justice, resulted in no permanent victory for the reformers, who looked to Beza and Calvin for their theology and to Gaspard de Coligny, the Huguenot leader and French admiral. However, the

Huguenots had already experienced serious reprisals by the French monarchy in both the massacre of the Waldensians of Mérindol in 1545 and the St. Bartholomew's Day Massacre in 1572, in which Coligny was murdered along with several thousand Huguenots.

Ironically, the assassination of Henry III by a fanatic Catholic made Henry of Navarre, a Huguenot leader, heir to the throne. To pacify the civil strife he turned Catholic for purely political reasons, ended the civil conflict, and issued the Edict of Nantes in 1598, granting full toleration of and civil rights to the Huguenots, leaving them for all practical purposes as a state within a state.

Regrettably for the Huguenots, these reprieves did not last. And because no major Protestant writer encouraged popular political resistance by the common people, either collectively or individually, in circumstances where lower magistrates were not successful, Huguenot defenders of the constitutional rights of a nation's citizenry were left with little recourse other than either waiting out the shifting tides of sentiment or making the pilgrimage to friendlier places.

Louis XIV (reigned 1643–1715) was determined to make France the most powerful nation in Europe. For this reason he was committed to unifying all of France under the Catholic Church. Repressive measures were instituted, persecution followed, and the Edict of Nantes was revoked in 1685. As a result, any Huguenots were sentenced to the galleys and some to public hangings.

Thousands of Huguenots fled France in the years that followed, many settling in North Carolina in America. Religious toleration of the Huguenots was finally granted once again during the French Revolution, and today, the Reformed Church of France unites most of the Protestant Calvinist groups in France, although they remain a relatively small minority.

Thomas Provenzola

Bibliography

Diefendorf, Barbara B. *Beneath the Cross: Catholics and Huguenots in Sixteenth-Century Paris*. New York: Oxford University Press, 1991.

Kamil, Neil. *Fortress of the Soul: Violence, Metaphysics, and Material Life in the Huguenots' New World, 1517–1751*. Baltimore, MD: Johns Hopkins University Press, 2005.

Mentzer, Raymond A., and Andrew Spicer. *Society and Culture in the Huguenot World, 1559–1685*. Cambridge: Cambridge University Press, 2007.

Smiles, Samuel. *The Huguenots in France*. Hamburg, Germany: Tredition Classics, 2012.

Soman, Alfred, ed. *The Massacre of St. Bartholomew: Reappraisals and Documents*. The Hague, Netherlands: Martinus Nijhoff Publishers, 1975.

HUSS, JAN (CA. 1373–1415)

Czech reformer Jan Huss (also Hus) was born in southern Bohemia and studied at the University of Prague. He later taught at the University of Prague and served as the university's rector (ca. 1403 for six months and 1409 for one year). In addition to teaching, Huss served as the pastor of Bethlehem Chapel in Prague. He was influenced by the Czech reformer Matthew of Janov and also the writings of John Wycliffe. Seeking to reform the Roman Catholic Church from within, Huss utilized his influence from the pulpit and the classroom to advance his ideas. His teachings combined traditional Roman Catholic doctrines with an emphasis on salvation only being offered through belief in Jesus Christ. He especially targeted clergy as he spoke against the sale of indulgences for the crusade against Naples that the Pisan Antipope John XXIII sought to finance. Huss advocated the authority of the Scriptures as primary over the authority of the church. His influential positions and teachings led to his popularity throughout Bohemia and the rest of Europe.

The Roman Catholic Church, however, condemned Huss's teachings and he was excommunicated. Huss left Prague (1412), but continued writing on the need for reform. Two years later, Huss was promised safe conduct to the Council of Constance, which had gathered primarily to address the so-called Western Schism. Upon arriving at the council, Huss was imprisoned. Refusing to recant his beliefs before his accusers, Huss was condemned as a heretic by the council and was burned at the stake on July 6, 1415.

Even after his death, Huss's teachings continued to influence reform. His ideas were advanced through his written works, such as De Ecclesia (1413) and many letters (see The Letters of John Huss). His followers include the Taborites, some of whom later formed the Bohemian Brethren, from which the Moravian Church was formed, and also the Hussites. A century after Huss's death, reformer Martin Luther was also influenced by the writings of Jan Huss. Huss's focus on the authority of Scripture, the need for reform within the church, and the accountability each individual believer has before God influenced Christian thought for centuries after his death.

Gabriel Etzel

Bibliography

Huss, John. *The Church*. Translated by David S. Schaff. Westport, CT: Greenwood, 1976.

Spinka, Matthew. *John Hus and the Czech Reform*. Hamden, CT: Archon, 1966.

———. *John Hus at the Council of Constance*. New York: Columbia University Press, 1965.

Spinka, Matthew, trans. *The Letters of John Huss*. Manchester: Manchester University Press, 1972.

✠

JAN HUSS
Czech Reformer
1373–1415

IGNATIUS OF LOYOLA (1491–1556)

Ignatius of Loyola is known primarily as the founder of the Jesuits and the author of *Spiritual Exercises*. Throughout his life, Ignatius remained steadfastly devoted to the papacy and the traditions of the Roman Church. In 1521, at the age of 30, he was severely wounded in battle while defending the Spanish city of Pamplona from French invaders. His recovery took several weeks and required several agonizing procedures. Although he survived the battle, his legs were badly injured and he lived the rest of his life with a severe limp. During the weeks of his recovery, Ignatius spent much time reading of the lives of several notable saints and was inspired to commit the remaining years of his life in devotion to the church. Once he was well enough to travel, Ignatius set out for Jerusalem to begin his new life.

Prior to his arrival in Jerusalem, Ignatius spent nearly a year in the Spanish town of Manresa, where he devoted an abundant amount of time to private prayer and meditation and composed much of his influential work, *Spiritual Exercises*. In addition, he visited the Santa Maria de Montserrat abbey in Catalonia, where he claimed to have experienced a vision that played a significant role in the development of his theological outlook.

Shortly after arriving in Jerusalem, Ignatius was ordered by the Franciscans to leave the city because conflicts with the Muslims rendered it unsafe to live there. Following his short stay in Jerusalem, Ignatius returned to Spain to study for the priesthood. After periods of study in the cities of Barcelona, Alcala, and Salamanca, Ignatius left Spain to study at the University of Paris. It was there that he met a group of young men who agreed to travel with him to Jerusalem to live in complete devotion to Christ.

Because of the Muslim presence in the Holy Land, travel to Jerusalem remained impossible. So Ignatius and his companions traveled to Rome instead, where they established a community. In 1540, Pope Paul III formally recognized this community, thus forming the order known as the Society of Friends (Jesuits), a Roman Catholic order that has been responsible for a significant amount of missionary work and the establishment of many educational institutions throughout the world.

In the summer of 1556, Ignatius died as a result of severe stomach complications that had afflicted him throughout much of his adulthood. In addition to the pivotal role he played in the establishment of the Jesuits, Ignatius's work was composed primarily in Manresa and includes a collection of prayers and devotional material intended to lead readers to greater devotion to Christ and separation from worldly influence. The writing is designed to be read in roughly four weeks and has been regarded as one of the foundational texts of the Jesuit order.

Benjamin Laird

Bibliography

Caraman, Philip. *Ignatius Loyola*. New York: Harper & Row, 1990.

De Dalmases, Candido. *Ignatius of Loyola, Founder of the Jesuits*. St. Louis, MO: Institute of Jesuit Sources, 1985.

Idígoras, José. *Ignatius of Loyola: The Pilgrim Saint*. Translated by Cornelius Michael Buckley. Chicago: Loyola Press, 1994.

Meissner, W.W. *Ignatius of Loyola: The Psychology of a Saint*. New Haven, CT: Yale University Press, 1994.

Ravier, Andre. *Ignatius Loyola and the Founding of the Society of Jesus*. San Francisco: Ignatius Press, 1987.

INQUISITION

The term *inquisition* derives from the words *inquire* and *inquest*. Historically, the Inquisition refers to a tribunal established by the Roman Catholic Church to investigate charges of heresy and to punish heretics. During the twelfth century, the Roman Catholic Church became concerned over the growing number of heretics in various places, and church officials sought to squelch their voices through investigations and punishments. These heretics, broadly defined, were people whose doctrines were not consistent with those of the Roman Catholic Church.

By the year 1233, Pope Gregory IX instituted the Papal Inquisition, composed mostly of Dominican clergymen, whose mission was to investigate charges of heresy as well as seek out and try heretics. While the intention of the Inquisition was not to kill people, but rather to place pressure on those the inquisitors deemed heretics to confess and recant their heresy, they were fully prepared to try, judge, torture, and execute the accused.

When the inquisitors, or agents of the Inquisition, came to a town, they generally offered a month-long grace period to allow people to come forth to issue charges of heresy or to renounce their own heresy. The process invited injustice and abuse on two counts. The accused were not allowed to face or dispute their accusers, and the accused were considered guilty until they were proven innocent (which rarely happened because they had no legal representation). People accused of heresy against the church would then variously have their property confiscated, be imprisoned for years (which might include severe torture), or if they continued in their defiance, they were turned over to the local secular authorities to be burned at the stake. The same fate awaited those who relapsed into heresy.

The Spanish Inquisition of the late fifteenth to sixteenth centuries was more draconian in its approach. In 1469, Spain was reunited with the marriage of Isabella of Castile and Ferdinand of Aragon. This created a new world superpower. The monarchs were intensely devoted to their faith and equally dedicated to bringing Spain under the rule of the Roman Catholic Church. This led to an effort to purify the land of "anti-Christian forces," represented primarily in the Jewish and Muslim communities. By royal decree, these minorities had the choice either to convert or to depart Spain altogether, leaving all their property behind. When the Spanish Inquisition was established in 1478, the initial purpose was to investigate Jews and Muslims who claimed to have converted to Christianity but still were suspected of practicing their non-Christian faith secretly. Tomas Torquemada, a Dominican monk, was appointed to preside over the effort as the Grand Inquisitor, and his brutal torture methods are infamous. Estimates are that there were some 5000 to 10,000 executions under Torquemada's direction.

In the sixteenth century, the Roman Inquisition became one of the major arms of the Counter-Reformation. Decreed by Pope Paul III in 1542, its chief mission was to detect and ultimately destroy Protestantism. Clearly a continuation of the thirteenth-century Inquisition, and modeled after both earlier inquisitions, it used similar methods of torture and terror to elicit confessions. In addition, when Protestants started spreading their influence after the invention of the printing press, the Roman Church established an index of forbidden books. These methods were used with effectiveness to curb the spread of Protestantism in Europe in the late Middle Ages.

But not all Roman Catholic countries countenanced the methods of the inquisitors, thus its force was limited to only a few countries, most notably Italy and Spain. Eventually, after a lengthy struggle between Catholics and Protestants, called the Thirty Years' War (1618–1648), the Peace of Westphalia recognized whole countries as Protestant states. Subsequent inquisitions were continuations of and modeled after the three (or two) initial ones discussed above and were carried out through the 1800s. Thus for a total of nearly 600 years, they were used as a method of eliminating and controlling heresy.

Will Honeycutt

Bibliography

Cairns, Earl E. *Christianity Through the Centuries: A History of the Christian Church.* Grand Rapids: Zondervan, 1981.

Cantor, Norman F. *The Civilization of the Middle Ages.* New York: Harper, 1994.

Dowley, Tim. *Introduction to the History of Christianity.* Minneapolis: Fortress, 1995.

Manchester, William. *A World Lit Only by Fire: The Medieval Mind and the Renaissance.* New York: Little, Brown, 1993.

IRENAEUS OF LYONS (CA. 120–202)

Early church father Irenaeus was born in Smyrna (modern Izmir, Turkey) in the province of Asia. There, he was mentored in the Christian faith by the yet-to-be-martyred bishop Polycarp, who had been a disciple of John the Evangelist. Around 150, Irenaeus answered the call to pastor a congregation of Greek-speaking immigrants in the city of Lyons (modern France) in Gaul. For much of Irenaeus's time as pastor, the church at Lyons was persecuted by the broader pagan populace and also at the hands of the Roman government. In 177, the church suffered one of the most traumatic accounts of persecution in the early church—a campaign led by the stoic emperor Marcus Aurelius. Though Irenaeus escaped the 177 persecution—he was away tending to church business in Rome—he was nevertheless killed in a similar attack against the church in 202.

Irenaeus is remembered by the church for a number of outstanding qualities. First, he was the leading apologist against the Gnostic heresy that was plaguing the second-century church in Gaul and other places. Before writing his anti-Gnostic work *Against All Heresies,* Irenaeus spent about 20 years studying the heresy firsthand from Gnostic teachers. After carefully articulating Gnostic thought in the first three books of *Against All Heresies,* his apologetic was threefold: first, he showed the baseless, mythological foundation of the heresy; second, he argued that the Gnostics had no connection to the historical Jesus; and third, he demonstrated how the Gnostic interpretation of Scripture was flawed.

Irenaeus's theology, a second contribution for which he is remembered, was clearly developed in the crucible of his battle with the Gnostics. For instance, in response to the Gnostic's baseless historical claims, he emphasized the basis for authority in the Christian faith, which came through the Scriptures and the rule of faith. Also, in contrast to the Gnostic view of creation, Irenaeus showed that the God of the Old Testament and the God of the New Testament are one and the same and that Jesus is both creator and redeemer.

Finally, Irenaeus was significant because he was a missionary bishop. Though it has been noted that he left Smyrna to pastor an immigrant church in Gaul, Irenaeus went further and began to minister to the Gaelic-speaking peoples in the villages around Lyons. In order to do this, he spent time learning the Gaelic dialect. In fact, while writing *Against All Heresies,* he complained somewhat that his command of his mother tongue of Greek was slipping because he had spent so much time communicating in other languages.

Irenaeus remains today an excellent role model of the qualities that are desirable in a pastor, theologian, apologist, and missionary.

Edward Smither

Bibliography

Irenaeus. *Against All Heresies. Ante-Nicene Fathers,* vol. 1. Edited by A. Roberts, and J. Donaldson. Peabody, MA: Hendrickson, 2004.

Mins, Denis. *Irenaeus: An Introduction.* Edinburgh: T&T Clark, 2010.

Osborn, Eric. *Irenaeus of Lyons.* Cambridge: Cambridge University Press, 2005.

ISIDORE OF SEVILLE (CA. 560–636)

Isidore, the archbishop of Seville (Spain) and a Christian encyclopedist, was born and educated in Seville and eventually became archbishop about the year 600. His *Sententiarum,* in two volumes, was the first manual of Christian doctrine in Latin, and his *Etymologiarum* was a 20-volume encyclopedia of knowledge covering numerous topics such as grammar, rhetoric, theology, mathematics, and jurisprudence. Toon (519) observes, "He died at Seville and became a national hero of the Spanish Church." He was canonized in 1598 and made a "Doctor of the Church" in 1722.

Ed Hindson

Bibliography

Brehaut, Ernest. *An Encyclopedist of the Dark Ages, Isidore of Seville.* Charleston, SC: Nabu Press (reprint), 2011.

Toon, Peter. "Isidore of Seville." *The New International Dictionary of the Christian Church.* Edited by J.D. Douglas. Grand Rapids: Zondervan, 1978.

✠

JEROME
Latin Church Scholar
ca. 340–420

JEHOVAH'S WITNESSES

The Jehovah's Witnesses were founded by Charles Taze Russell, who saw himself as one of the angels of the seven churches mentioned in Revelation chapters 2 and 3 (along with Arius and Martin Luther). Though he never attended college, nor studied theology, he challenged the deity of Christ, the Trinity, salvation by faith, and the reality of eternal punishment in hell. A shameless self-promoter who claimed to know the classical and biblical languages (a claim proven false), Russell's publicity stunts, including a "world tour," led many to succumb to and follow his teachings. He established what became the Watchtower Bible and Tract Society in the late nineteenth century to sell his publications. These were eventually gathered into *Studies in the Scriptures*, which Russell claimed were more important to know than even reading the Bible. With the great success he enjoyed from the widespread sales of his writings, Russell died a wealthy man.

Russell was succeeded by Judge J.F. Rutherford, who ran the Watchtower organization even more ruthlessly than Russell had, and he too ran it for his personal profit as Russell had. The Watchtower has grown over the years and now has workers in more than 200 countries and publishes in more than 500 languages. The Jehovah's Witnesses continue to carry on Russell's teachings that Jesus is not God but is a created being, and that the Holy Spirit is a force rather than a person.

The Jehovah's Witnesses have their own version of the Bible, *The New World Translation*, which is very different from standard translations of God's Word. The New Testament, for example, has no foundation in any ancient Greek manuscript. Some teachings have, of necessity, been modified, such as the one that stated the literal second coming of Christ would happen in 1914. He is now said to have come as a spiritual being in that year, awaiting his full manifestation as a result of the ministry of the 144,000 "witnesses."

Fred Smith

Bibliography

Hoekema, Anthony. *The Four Major Cults*. Grand Rapids: Eerdmans, 1984.

Martin, Walter, and Ravi Zacharias. *Kingdom of the Cults*. Minneapolis: Bethany House, 2003.

Rhodes, Ron. *The Challenge of the Cults*. Grand Rapids: Zondervan, 2001.

Russell, Charles Taze. *Studies in the Scriptures*. Np: Ulan Press, 2012.

JEROME (CA. 340–420)

Biblical scholar and translator Jerome was a Latin church father who is most well known for producing the Vulgate translation of the Bible. Roman Catholicism honors him as a "doctor of the church."

Named Eusebius Hieronymous, he was born in Dalmatia of aristocratic Christian parents, Jerome was sent to Rome and educated in the classics. While there, he engaged in some of the sensual activities common to a young man away from home. To assuage his guilt, he would visit the venerable tombs of the apostles and martyrs on the Lord's day, where the pitch darkness would remind him of the judgment of hell. While still a student he ultimately succumbed to the call of Christ and was baptized by Pope Liberius in 365.

Subsequent to his conversion, Jerome focused his attention on the Bible and studied theology in Antioch and elsewhere. During this period of his life, he had a dream that led to a radical break from his veneration of the pagan Roman classics. In his vision before the judgment seat, Jerome heard God pronounce the dire verdict that Jerome was a Ciceronian and not a Christian. Determined to embrace a more severe asceticism, he spent three years in the desert at Chalcis in Syria, during which time he learned Hebrew. Upon his return to Antioch, he was ordained under the condition that he would be free to lead the life of a monk and not serve in the church.

Soon after his ordination Jerome was back in Rome, where his gifts had caught the attention of Pope Damasus. Jerome was made a secretary and tasked with the work of standardizing the corrupt Latin copies of the Bible by using his considerable scholarly training to create a new Latin version. He began in 383 with the Psalms and the New Testament Gospels. And outside of his scholarly pursuits, Jerome became the spiritual confidant of several Christian noblewomen, including a widow named Paula and her two daughters, whom he encouraged in ascetic practices.

After the death of his supporter Pope Damasus (384), Jerome was forced to leave Rome after accusations arose concerning the nature of his relationship with Paula, coupled with charges that his exhortations to extreme fasting had led to the death of Paula's daughter Blesilla (Frend, 717). Accompanied by his patron Paula and other female disciples, he eventually ended up establishing monasteries in Bethlehem, where he completed his work on the Old Testament portion of the Vulgate. His rejection of the Greek Septuagint in favor of the Hebrew text caused him grief even from Augustine, who saw the Septuagint used by the New Testament writers as being divinely inspired. Jerome's prodigious literary output included many commentaries on the Bible. As one example, his work on Daniel answered the criticisms of the pagan Porphyry, who had claimed that Daniel was a second-century BC forgery. Jerome died in 420.

In the process of translating the Vulgate in Bethlehem, Jerome appears to have used Origen's *Hexapla* and consulted with local rabbis while working on Old Testament passages. He also questioned the inclusion of the Apocrypha, although he finally allowed it for devotional reading. Altogether, Jerome's work as a biblical scholar and Bible translator using the original Hebrew and Greek texts set a standard for Christian scholarship for all future generations to come.

Jerome's personal and ecclesiastical renunciation of Rome's classical past and vigorous defense of asceticism helped pave the way for the rise of monasticism in the Christian West. In addition, his translation of the Vulgate provided a standardized version of the Bible for the Latin Church to use in teaching the faithful and engaging in debates with heretics that remained unchallenged for a thousand years until the time of the Reformation. As Roman Catholicism's official version of Scripture, the Vulgate was used as the base text from which the Catholic English translation, the Douay-Rheims Bible, was rendered. Finally, Jerome's text-critical practice of utilizing the original language base text for translation is now axiomatic for the scholarly practice of Bible translation.

David Pettus

Bibliography

Frend, W.H.C. *The Rise of Christianity.* Philadelphia: Fortress, 1984.

Jerome's Commentary on Daniel. Translated by Gleason Archer. Grand Rapids: Baker, 1977.

Kelly, J.N.D. *Jerome: His Life, Writings, and Controversies.* New York: Harper & Row, 1976.

Schaff, Philip, ed. *A Select Library of the Nicene and Post-Nicene Fathers of the Christian Church.* 2d Series, vol. 6. Grand Rapids: Eerdmans, 1979.

JESUITS

The Society of Jesus, or Jesuits, is the powerful and controversial Catholic order founded in the sixteenth century by the Spaniard Ignatius of Loyola (1491–1556). Organized along military principles, these soldiers for Catholicism in many ways personified the Roman Catholic Church's response to the Protestant Reformation. They are unique among religious orders in their vow of obedience to the Pope, strongly supporting him at the Council of Trent and becoming the foremost of Catholic apologists.

Ignatius was a man of noble birth given to pleasure and desirous of military glory. In his convalescence from battle wounds received in 1521, Ignatius experienced a "conversion" fueled by visions allegedly from God, extreme austerity, and suicidal thoughts. During this time he fashioned the *Spiritual Exercises*, which became an undergirding document of the order.

In 1534, outside of the University of Paris, Ignatius formed a society among six friends, including Francis Xavier, who prepared to offer themselves in the service of the Pope. In 1540, Pope Paul III approved the order's formation and appointed Ignatius as the first Superior General.

Ignatius envisioned the society as men ready to be dispatched for any task anywhere. Key to their success was their discipline and willingness to endure any hardship. Also key was the submission of their wills to church authority in general, and papal authority in particular. As Ignatius noted in the *Spiritual Exercises*, "We ought always to hold that the white which I see, is black, if the Hierarchical Church so decides it…" The term *Jesuit* often came to be associated with the idea that "the end justifies the means."

In time the order grew in wealth and power, focusing on missions and education to spread Catholic control and influence. The members also participated in the Inquisition and considered Protestants to be heretics. Often mistrusted by other orders within Catholicism, their power exceeded the proportion of their numbers. Their influence over the papacy is generally acknowledged, so much so that the term *Black Pope* has been colloquially assigned to the Superior General of the Jesuit order.

Often cloaked in secrecy and political intrigue, Jesuits have been implicated in numerous conspiracies and assassinations throughout history. Often the confessors of kings and officials, they were accused of abusing the confessional and keeping Europe in political turmoil. In the eighteenth century, Jesuits suffered expulsions from various countries as a reaction to their activities. Eventually, Pope Clement XIV (who later was poisoned) disbanded them in 1773. Pope Pius VII reinstated the order in the post-Napoleonic era in 1814. As an aside, the word *Jesuitism*, meaning craftiness, duplicity, or intrigue, has become a part of our language.

Today, Jesuits dedicate themselves to Catholic spirituality and the willingness to serve wherever they may lead in the mission of their church. As one example, they currently operate the Gregorian University in Rome as well as 28 colleges and universities in the United States, often named for Loyola and Xavier. Jesuits uphold Catholic tradition and oppose Protestant beliefs, such as justification by grace through faith in Christ alone.

Terry Barnes

Bibliography

Boettner, Loraine. *Roman Catholicism*. Phillipsburg, NJ: P&R Publishing, 1962.

Martin, Malachi. *The Jesuits*. New York: Simon & Schuster, 1988.

Mulan, Elder, trans. *The Spiritual Exercises of St. Ignatius of Loyola*. New York: P.J. Kennedy & Sons, 1914. http://www.jesuit.org/jesuits/wp-content/uploads/The-Spiritual-Exercises-.pdf. Accessed July 17, 2012.

O'Malley, John W. *The First Jesuits*. Cambridge, MA: Harvard University Press, 1993.

J

JOACHIM OF FIORE (1135–1202)

Joachim of Fiore was a medieval mystic, historian, and apocalyptist. Born in Calabria, Italy, he became a Cistercian monk and later abbot of Curazzo. In 1192, he founded the order of San Giovanni in Fiore. While on an earlier pilgrimage to the Holy Land, he claimed mystical experiences on Mount Tabor, which he believed gave him the gift of interpreting history and prophecy. He is generally recognized as the most influential medieval thinker in the area of apocalyptic eschatology. His views were expressed in three major works: *Exposition of the Apocalypse*, *Psalterium of Ten Strings*, and *Concordance of the Old and New Testaments*.

Joachim held to a literal expectation of the fulfillment of prophecy throughout the ages of church history. He viewed the seven seals of the apocalypse as predictions of seven ages of church history, with the last stage as the "Age of the Spirit," which he viewed as a time of peace and prosperity prior to the final cataclysm. He also held a Trinitarian view of history, with the first age associated with the Father (law), the second age the Son (grace), and the third age the Spirit (liberty). His ideas were later taken to extreme by the Fraticelli, who attempted to bring in the third age by revolution.

Joachim's views were augmented by his adaptation of an old third-century Jewish Midrash indicating the length of human history would be 6000 years: 2000 years from creation to Moses, 2000 years for the age of the Messiah, after which Joachim said would come the age of the Spirit. Thus, Joachim's ideas spread the concept of dividing the eras of human history based upon his interpretations of biblical prophecy. Many of his ideas later influenced Protestant reformers such as Philip Melanchthon, who developed a similar chronology in *Carion's Chronicle* (1532). In general, many of Joachim's ideas influenced later concepts of seven ages of dispensations of God's activity in human history and a coming millennium of peace and worldwide prosperity associated with the return of Christ.

Ed Hindson

Bibliography

Clouse, Robert. "Joachim of Fiore." *The New International Dictionary of the Christian Church*. Edited by J.D. Douglas. Grand Rapids: Zondervan, 1978.

Reeves, M. *The Influence of Prophecy in the Later Middle Ages: A Study of Joachimism*. Oxford: Clarendon Press, 1969.

———. *Joachim of Fiore and the Prophetic Future*. London: SPCK, 1976.

Walker, G.S.M. *The Growing Storm*. Grand Rapids: Eerdmans, 1961.

JOAN OF ARC (1412–1431)

This French mystic and patriot was known in her lifetime as the Maid of Orléans or simply La Pucelle. Joan of Arc entered French history at a critical moment during the Hundred Years' War. The right to the throne of France was in dispute and Joan, a poor peasant girl from the town of Domrémy, became a catalyst for ensuring the succession of the Valois heir, Charles VII.

Joan's childhood was ordinary in every way except one. As a young girl, she exhibited unusual piety and, at the age of 13, she began to have mystical experiences during which certain "voices" spoke to her. By 1428, she came to believe she had been ordered to assist the dauphin Charles against his Burgundian opponents and to claim the French throne. She only reluctantly accepted the mission, recognizing that as a young peasant girl she was an unlikely aide to the would-be king.

Joan's persistence resulted in an audience with Charles in March 1429, and she appeared at his court with cropped hair and dressed in men's clothes. She won the confidence of the king by giving him a sign, something neither of them ever revealed, after which she was subjected to intense examination by church authorities to ensure that her motives were pure and that she was free from the taint of heresy. After three weeks of questioning, she was finally released to lead the French army in lifting the siege at Orléans, a turning point that led to the coronation of Charles at Reims in July of that year. That Joan had predicted the successful end to the siege and the coronation of the dauphin seemed to affirm the legitimacy of her claims to divine appointment.

Joan continued to press for a complete victory over the English, but was captured in battle in May 1430. She was turned over to English authorities, who, in an attempt to discredit her mission and embarrass the French, ordered her tried as a heretic by the bishop of Beauvais at Rouen. Subjected to weeks of questioning by a panel of churchmen, Joan's replies were simple and straightforward. When it seemed that they were attempting to trap her, she either refused to answer or replied in ways that confounded her examiners. Nevertheless, Joan was found guilty of heresy on May 29, 1431, and executed by burning the next day.

Twenty-four years after her death, a rehabilitation trial was opened at Paris and a parade of men and women who knew Joan personally testified to her piety, virtue, and great deeds. The original verdict was overturned and her sentence annulled. The English persisted in regarding her as a heretic or a witch, whereas she was viewed more favorably by her countrymen. She was ultimately canonized by the Roman Catholic Church in 1910. A national heroine of France, Joan of Arc is often cited as a decisive force in the formation of a French national consciousness.

Donna Davis Donald

Bibliography

Margolis, Nadia. *Joan of Arc in History, Literature, and Film: A Select, Annotated Bibliography*. New York: Garland Publishers, 1990.

Pernoud, Régine, and Marie-Véronique Clin. *Joan of Arc: Her Story*. Edited by Bonnie Wheeler. Translated by Jeremy duQuesnay Adams. New York: St. Martin's Press, 1999.

Taylor, Craig, ed. and trans. *Joan of Arc: La Pucelle*. Manchester: Manchester University Press, 2006.

Taylor, Larissa. *The Virgin Warrior: The Life and Death of Joan of Arc*. New Haven, CT: Yale University Press, 2009.

Wheeler, Bonnie, and Charles T. Wood, eds. *Fresh Verdicts on Joan of Arc*. New York: Garland Publishers, 1996.

JOSEPHUS, FLAVIUS (CA. 37–100)

A first-century Jewish-Roman historian, Josephus wrote treatises on Jewish history and his people's war with Rome that provide information of inestimable value for understanding that time period. Of no less import is Josephus's controversial reference to the historical existence of Jesus Christ in the first century.

Josephus was a prominent, well-educated Jewish aristocrat of priestly descent born and raised in Jerusalem. When the Jewish rebellion against the Roman occupiers in Israel began (AD 66), he was made governor of Galilee and commanded the Galilean defense forces. On the verge of defeat by the Romans and trapped in a cave, Josephus reneged on a suicide pact made with his troops and convinced the sole surviving soldier under his command to surrender with him to the conquering army. To add to the ignominy of the circumstances of his surrender, Josephus ingratiated himself to the Roman general Vespasian by supposedly predicting Vespasian would become the Roman emperor and offering to record a history of Rome's war with the Jews. This helped to gain his freedom. Later, when Vespasian's son marched against Jerusalem, Josephus accompanied him and attempted to negotiate with the besieged Jews, though without success, and witnessed the city's fall to the Roman occupiers in AD 70.

After the fall of the Jewish capital city, Josephus returned to Rome, where he served both the emperor Vespasian and his son, Titus, who succeeded his father as ruler of Rome, even taking their household patronymic (name), Flavius. Josephus remained in Rome until his death (ca. 100), where under the patronage of his earlier masters, he lived quite well and was free to write his major treatises. Josephus penned *The Wars of the Jews*, *Antiquities of the Jews*, an apologetic work titled *Against Apion*, and his autobiography, *The Life*. The first covers the history of the Jewish wars from the Maccabean period till the fall of Jerusalem to Rome in 70. The work *Antiquities* encompasses Jewish history from the time of creation until 66, and *Against Apion* defends the Jewish faith against pagan criticisms, presenting Judaism as a respectable and ancient religion and philosophy.

Perhaps the most controversial item in Josephus's volumes is his reference to Jesus as a messianic figure existing in a first-century context *(Antiquities of the Jews*, Book 18:3,3). Like the New Testament, the account states that Jesus was a miracle worker crucified under Pontius Pilate. Josephus further identified Jesus as the superhuman Jewish Messiah who rose from the dead. Josephus's matter-of-fact identification of Jesus as one who possesses supernatural power has been enough for some to reject the *Testimonium Flavianum* (testimony of Flavius [Josephus]) altogether and suggest that it is all spurious and reflects a later Christian interpolation by the church father Eusebius writing in the fourth century.

While some have defended the authenticity of the entire passage dealing with Jesus, the current scholarly consensus holds that the original passage referred to Jesus as a historical figure who was reputed to be a prophet and miracle worker and was finally crucified by the Roman governor of Judea. The statements that Jesus was the resurrected superhuman Messiah are generally seen as later Christian additions to Josephus's text. The fact Josephus mentions John the Baptist and James the brother of Jesus, who is "the one called the messiah," supports the view that Josephus at the least recognized Jesus as an important historical figure (*Antiquities*, 15:2; 20:9).

Despite the much-debated biases in his writings, Josephus endeavored to show how true Judaism need not be identified with the actions of Jewish messianic rebels. The Jewish War placed the blame for the fall of Jerusalem on tyrannical Jewish leaders and incompetent local Roman officials. Josephus's work on Jewish history presents the story of his people at times interpreted in the light of Greek philosophy to impress a cultured Roman audience and provides testimony outside the New Testament of the influence of Jesus Christ and the sect known as Christians on first-century Judaism and Rome.

David Pettus

Bibliography

Feldman, Louis H. *Josephus and Modern Scholarship*. New York: deGruyter, 1984.

Goldberg Gary J. "The Coincidences of the Emmaus Narrative of Luke and the Testimonium of Josephus." *The Journal for the Study of the Pseudipigrapha* 13 (1995): 59-77.

Thackeray, H. St. J., Ralph Marcus, et al., translators. *Josephus*. 10 vols. Cambridge: Harvard University Press, 1926–1965.

Whealey, Alice. *Josephus on Jesus: The Testimonium Flavianum Controversy from Late Antiquity to Modern Times*. Bern: Peter Lang, 2003.

William, Whiston. *The Works of Josephus: Complete and Unabridged*. Updated ed. Peabody, MA: Hendrickson, 1980 (1737).

JUDSON, ADONIRAM (1788–1850)

Born in Malden, Massachusetts, Adoniram Judson was the son of a Congregationalist minister. However, he "lost his faith" while a student at Brown University and, after graduating, began to live a degenerate life. During travels in the West, he became a Christian in 1808. Returning home, he enrolled in Andover Seminary (Congregationalist). There, he read about Burma and responded to God's call to missions in 1810. Missions fervor was high in Massachusetts at that time due to the influence of some students from nearby Williams College, who were promoting the cause of missions everywhere they went. In 1812, Adoniram was commissioned by the American Board of Commissioners for Foreign Missions (Congregationalist) for Burma. Luther Rice (1783–1836) was commissioned at the same time.

In that same year Adoniram married Ann Hasseltine, who became a great asset to him in the missions work. During the four-month trip from America to Calcutta, India, where he anticipated meeting with William Carey, the British Baptist missionary, Adoniram studied the issue of baptism in his Greek New Testament. Before meeting Carey, Adoniram became convinced that the Bible taught believer's baptism (rather than infant baptism). Judson and Carey then convinced Rice of believer's baptism as well. Adoniram and Rice were baptized in Calcutta, and subsequently resigned from the Congregationalist mission board.

Without Congregationalist support, the three men decided that Rice, being single, was the obvious choice to return to America to secure support from Baptists for their mission. Rice ultimately was successful when American Baptists founded the Triennial Convention in 1814 to support them. As it turned out, Rice's work in America in raising funds for the work was so crucial that he never returned to assist Judson in Burma, much to Judson's disappointment.

Judson's pioneering work in Burma included many victories and numerous challenges. He is still remembered today as one of America's greatest missionaries. It took six years of work before he had his first convert, Moung Nau, but by 1837 he had baptized 1144 souls. His greatest work was the Burmese Bible. In 1824, he was imprisoned for 17 months during a war between Britain and Burma. Tragically, his wife, Ann, who had been an able assistant, especially with her encouragement during his imprisonment, died in 1826. The couple also lost all three of their sons, each dying before the age of three. Judson later married Sarah Boardman, the widow of another missionary in 1834. They had eight children, five of whom survived to adulthood. Sarah died in 1845. The next year Judson married Emily Chubback, and they had one daughter.

In 1849, Adoniram caught pneumonia and died the next year while seeking a restoration of his health at sea. He was buried at sea in the Bay of Bengal in the Indian Ocean.

Carl Deimer

Bibliography

Anderson, Courtney. *To the Golden Shore: The Life of Adoniram Judson.* Valley Forge, PA: Judson, 1987.

Deusing, Jason, ed. *Adoniram Judson: A Bicentennial Appreciation of the Pioneer American Missionary.* Nashville, TN: B&H, 2012.

Hambrick, Sharon. *Adoniram Judson: God's Man in Burma.* Greenville, SC: JourneyForth, 2001.

Hunt, Rosalee Hall. *Bless God and Take Courage: The Judson History and Legacy.* Valley Forge, PA: Judson, 2005.

James, Sharon. *My Heart in His Hands: Ann Judson of Burma.* Durham, UK: Evangelical Press, 1999.

JUSTIN MARTYR (CA. 100–165)

J

A Christian apologist born of pagan parents in Flavius Neapolis (formerly Shechem, today Nablus) in Samaria, Justin Martyr studied the philosophies of Aristotle, Plato, Pythagoras, and the Stoics. After years of intellectual searching, he was converted through a conversation with an old man and concluded that Christianity was the "one sure worthy philosophy."

From the time of his conversion (ca. 132), Justin began teaching, proclaiming, and defending the Christian faith, serving as one of the church's earliest Christian apologists. His *First Apology,* addressed to Emperor Antonius Pius, argued that Christianity was not a new religion but the supreme and full revelation of the eternal *Logos.* In *First Apology,* Justin emphasized salvation through Christ alone and explained the sacraments of baptism and communion (Eucharist) for pagan readers.

Justin's *Second Apology* defended Christians from unjust persecution and his *Dialogue with Trypho* narrated his conversation with a learned Jew and his friends, showing his desire to see the Jews converted to "the Christ of Almighty God."

Ed Hindson

Bibliography

L.W. Barnard. *Justin Martyr: His Life and Thought.* Cambridge, UK: Cambridge University Press, 1967.

☩

JOHN KNOX
SCOTTISH REFORMER
ca. 1514–1572

KEMPIS, THOMAS À (CA. 1380–1471)

German mystic Thomas à Kempis, born Thomas Haemerken to poor German parents, was educated as a young boy in Deventer at the school of the Brethren of the Common Life. The school had been started earlier by Gerard Groote, and introduced Thomas to the life he would live until his death at the age of 91. Thomas's brother, John, preceded him in the monastic life, being prior of the monastery of Mount St. Agnes at Agnietenberg near Zwolle (the Netherlands). When Thomas was 19, special permission was granted for the brothers to occupy the same monastery. Thomas took his vows and was later ordained as a priest in 1413. In 1425, he became subprior of the monastery and occupied various administrative posts, yet he much preferred the life of training novices, writing, copying manuscripts, preaching, and functioning as a trusted spiritual advisor.

Thomas's commitment was to the simple life, to exist quietly and as close to the life of Christ as possible. His desire, along with those of his order, was to be solely devoted to the Lord. A true and deep love for God was the driving motive expressed by consistent work, healthy living, and sound learning. Simplicity is not always simple, however, and the religious order to which Thomas belonged experienced some of the political and social issues present in the Catholic Church of the late Middle Ages. Thomas also lost his beloved brother John, 15 years his senior, in 1432.

Thomas's most famous work, *The Imitation of Christ*, was written around 1427 and is one of the widest-read and most beloved religious books outside of the Bible. It has been translated, reprinted, and distributed throughout the world and remains a popular Christian classic. Interestingly, since no ancient manuscript bears the name of its author, its writing has been attributed to as many as 25 other authors beyond Thomas. Evidence for Thomas's authorship is, however, very strong.

The Imitation of Christ is composed of four books and covers many aspects related to nourishment of the soul. It is an unpretentious work that focuses on a deeper love for God. From the inward life to outward acts of devotion, Thomas speaks of those attitudes and acts necessary to draw one closer to Christ. Although inclusive of many Catholic practices of his day later called into question by the reformers, *Imitation* remains a venerable classic of devotional literature. In addition, Thomas wrote sermons, biographies, homilies, and hymns, all of which were reflective of his abiding passion for the Lord.

Keith Church

Bibliography

Bigg, C. *The Imitation of Christ: also called The Ecclesiastical Music*. Revised and translated. London: Metheun & Co., 1898; reprint 1954.

Kettlewell, S. *Thomas à Kempis and the Brothers of the Common Life*, vol. 2. New York: Putnam's Sons, 1882.

Scully, Vincent. *Life of the Venerable Thomas à Kempis*. London: R.&T. Washbourne, 1901.

Thomas à Kempis. *The Imitation of Christ*. Translated by Richard Whitford. Edited with introduction by Harold C. Gardner. New York: Image Books, 1955 (1530).

K

KENNEDY, D. JAMES (1930–2007)

Presbyterian pastor Dennis James Kennedy was the founding pastor of the Coral Ridge Presbyterian Church in Ft. Lauderdale, Florida, from which he also founded Evangelism Explosion, a training program that taught Christians how to share their faith with others. Kennedy earned his BA degree from the University of Tampa, his MDiv from Columbia Theological Seminary, and his PhD from New York University. He was the speaker on the *Coral Ridge Hour* telecast, founder of Knox Theological Seminary, and one of the cofounders with Jerry Falwell, Tim LaHaye, and Charles Stanley of the Moral Majority. A conservative in both theology and politics, Kennedy was a political activist, calling for the preservation and restoration of America's religious heritage. To further this concern he founded the Center for Reclaiming America.

Kennedy's many publications included *Evangelism Explosion* (1996), *The Gates of Hell Shall Not Prevail* (1997), *The Presence of a Hidden God* (2008), *What Happened to American Education?* (1988), and *What If Jesus Had Never Been Born?* (1994). Ever passionate about evangelism and Christian education, Kennedy became one of America's leading evangelical voices in the late twentieth century. He combined Calvinistic theology with an evangelistic passion, pastoral ministry, cultural confrontation, and an international outreach through his television ministries.

Ed Hindson

Bibliography

Balmer, Randall. "Kennedy, D[ennis] James." In *Encyclopedia of Evangelicalism*. Louisville, KY: Westminster John Knox, 2002.

Kurian, G.T., ed. "Kennedy, Dennis James." *Nelson's Dictionary of Christianity*. Nashville, TN: Thomas Nelson, 2005.

Williams, Herbert Lee. *D. James Kennedy: The Man and His Ministry*. Nashville, TN: Thomas Nelson, 1990.

KESWICK MOVEMENT

The Keswick Convention began in 1875 as a summer holiday gathering at Keswick, England, to bring speakers together who would teach on the deeper Christian life. Originally called the "higher Christian life," the phrase "deeper Christian life" came to characterize the movement's emphasis on practical holiness. The first Keswick Convention was held in a tent on the lawn of St. John's vicarage, Keswick, and had over 400 in attendance. They met under the banner "All One in Christ Jesus," which remains the convention's motto today.

The Keswick message has been represented by many well-known Bible speakers/ teachers over the years—some held fervently to its tenets, others hold loosely. Early speakers included Hudson Taylor, Hannah Whitall Smith, A.T. Pierson, Andrew Murray, H.C.G. Moule, H.W. Griffith Thomas, and F.B. Meyer. Later speakers included A.W. Tozer, Stephen Olford, Major Ian Thomas, and L.E. Maxwell.

The catalyst and focal point of Keswick are often identified with the book *The Higher Christian Life* by William E. Boardman, published in 1858. The book sold over 100,000 copies and argued that Christ could give sanctification at a time after justification. Boardman traveled widely throughout England and his higher-life conferences did much to set the foundation for the Keswick movement.

The Keswick message is that victory can be obtained through a "crisis of surrender," after which one may live life on a "higher plane." This "secondness" message is not the same claimed by some Pentecostals, who teach on the eradication of the old nature, or entire sanctification, which is said to often be accompanied by speaking in tongues. Keswick theology, rather, emphasizes sanctification by means of a constant exercise of faith, and avoiding "the energy of the flesh" by focusing on prayer and "union with Christ." Its progressive view of sanctification has at times been criticized as devotional mysticism. Proponents, however, view it as a positive form of spiritual revival.

Elmer Towns

Bibliography

McQuilkin, J. Robertson. "The Keswick Perspective." *Five Views on Sanctification.* Grand Rapids: Academie, 1987.

Packer, J.I. *Keep in Step with the Spirit.* Old Tappan, NJ: Fleming H. Revell, 1984.

Pollock, J.C. *The Keswick Story.* Chicago: Moody, 1964.

Towns, Elmer L. *Understanding the Deeper Life.* Old Tappan, NJ: Fleming H. Revell, 1988.

KIERKEGAARD, SØREN (1813–1855)

Danish philosopher and religious thinker Søren Kierkegaard is often regarded as the father of existentialism. Born and raised in Copenhagen, Denmark, he was brought up in a strict Pietist family. He initially pursued theological studies with the intention of entering the Lutheran ministry. Instead, he shifted his focus to philosophy, primarily under Hans Martensen, the leading Danish Hegelian. Kierkegaard earned his master's degree in 1840 and wrote a lengthy thesis on Socrates, *The Concept of Irony*, attacking the Hegelian idealism that he viewed as having such a devastating effect on Danish Christianity.

Kierkegaard's early works were anti-Hegelian treatises or works on Christian discipleship, in which he called for a passionate *imitation Christi* (imitation of Christ). His writings included *Either/Or* (1843), *Fear and Trembling* (1843), *The Concept of Anxiety* (1844), *Philosophical Fragments* (1844), *Concluding Unscientific Postscript to Philosophical Fragments* (1846), *Works of Love* (1847), *Christian Discourses* (1848), and *Training in Christianity* (1850). His religious works emphasize the need for incarnational truth ("the god in time"). Thus, he attempted to "re-invent" Christianity, thereby opposing Hegelianism, "the system," as the false culmination of the Socratic-idealist tradition. Thus, he emphasized the need for passionate decision and commitment. In this way, he opposed the cold Enlightenment scientism of his day.

John D. Morrison

Bibliography

Carnell, E.J. *The Burden of Søren Kierkegaard.* Grand Rapids: Eerdmans, 1965.

Collins, James. *The Mind of Kierkegaard.* London: Wartburg, 1969.

Eller, Vernard. *Kierkegaard and Radical Discipleship.* Grand Rapids: Eerdmans, 1972.

KING JR., MARTIN LUTHER (1929–1968)

African-American pastor and civil rights leader Martin Luther King Jr. is a beloved individual in American history as a central figure in the civil rights movement of the 1950s and 1960s. King was the son of a minister in the Deep South in a racially segregated time in US history. Born in Atlanta, Georgia, King's ethnic background, religion, education, upbringing, and providential setting in Montgomery, Alabama, as a pastor set the stage for his odyssey, triumph, and death by an assassin's bullet, all of which stamped his impact and legacy upon American cultural history.

Martin Luther King Jr. observed his father's ministerial approach in the 1930s and 1940s as pastor of Ebenezer Baptist Church in Atlanta and came to embrace a socially pragmatic approach to the gospel, believing his vital ministry was to improve the lot and lifestyles of black people wherever that might be or whatever that might entail. King attended Morehouse College (BA), Crozer Seminary (BD), and Boston University (PhD). It was his attendance at these institutions that gave King the theological, philosophical, and intellectual structures that would substantiate his forthcoming crusade for the civil rights of African-Americans.

In 1954, King became the pastor of the Dexter Avenue Baptist Church of Montgomery, Alabama, and also served as copastor with his father of the Ebenezer Baptist Church in Atlanta. King's preaching came to be equated not only with the salvation of the souls of individuals, but the historical redemption of people in social settings as well.

In 1956, King became the galvanizing leader of a bus boycott in Montgomery, Alabama, after civil rights pioneer Rosa Parks refused to give up her bus seat to a white patron. Subsequent to this event, King would come to employ nonviolent means of protest in confronting racism in the United States. From 1957 to 1968, with the aid of the Southern Christian Leadership Conference (SCLC) organization, King and Rev. Ralph Abernathy engaged in sit-ins, peaceful civil marches, and arrests in the South to protest the issue of racial segregation. These activities were covered by the international press and media.

The momentum in the civil rights struggle continued to grow, and in 1963, King spearheaded the March on Washington, where he delivered his famous "I Have a Dream" speech. In 1964, because of his increased commitment to advocating civil rights, he became the youngest person to ever win the Nobel Peace Prize. He also inspired the passage of the Civil Rights Act of 1964–1965.

In the course of his work, which often placed him in unusually hostile situations, King exhibited tremendous courage and resilience. He was stabbed in 1958, jailed in several cities through the years, most notably in Birmingham and Atlanta, in 1963, stoned in Harlem, New York, in 1964 and finally, assassinated by a white racist in Memphis, Tennessee, on April 4, 1968.

In 1986, King was honored with a national holiday celebrating his birthday and extraordinary life.

Dennis McDonald

Bibliography

Carson, Clayborne, ed. "Between Contending Forces: Martin Luther King, Jr., and the African American Freedom Struggle." *OAH Magazine of History* 19 (January 2005): 17-21.

Carson, Clayborne, ed. *The Autobiography of Martin Luther King, Jr.* New York: Warner Books, 1998.

Elders, Ann. "Martin Luther King, Jr." *School Library Journal* 50.8 (August 2004): 72-73.

Haskins, Jim. "Martin Luther King, Jr." *Cobblestone* 31 (January 2010): 28-29.

Sandidge, O'Neal C. "The Uniqueness of Black Preaching." *Journal of Religious Thought* 49 (October 1992): 91-97.

Sturm, Douglas. "Martin Luther King, Jr., as Democratic Socialist." *The Journal of Religious Ethics,* 18 (Fall 1990): 79-105.

K

KITTLE, GERHARD (1888–1948)

This German biblical scholar is best known as the editor of a multivolume theological dictionary of the New Testament. He served as professor of New Testament at Greifswald (1921–1926) and Tübingen (1926–1945). He was also the author of several works on the Jewish-Hebrew background of the New Testament. His extensive word studies combined the secular use of classical Greek and background information on the Old Testament Hebrew and Septuagint Greek texts to help determine the meaning of New Testament words.

Ed Hindson

Bibliography

Moyer, Elgin, ed. "Kittle, Gerhard." *Who Was Who in Church History*. Chicago: Moody Press, 1962.

KNIGHTS TEMPLAR

Originally known as The Poor Fellow-Soldiers of Christ and the Temple of Solomon, the Knights Templar were one of 26 military orders formed during the Crusades (1095–1291). They were formed in 1118, received official recognition from the Catholic Church in 1129, and were disbanded in 1312.

The Crusaders had captured Jerusalem and substantial surrounding areas by 1099. Yet Christian pilgrims were often mistreated and killed by hostile forces as they traveled to the Holy Land. In 1118, French knight Hugues de Payens presented the king of Jerusalem, Baldwin II, with a proposal for the creation of a monastic order that would provide safe travel for the pilgrims. Baldwin agreed and provided space for its headquarters in the captured mosque located beside the Dome of the Rock; the pilgrims believed that Solomon's temple had previously existed where the Dome of the Rock stood. At this time, the order consisted of less than a dozen knights and had limited funding. Therefore, the name chosen for the new order was The Poor Fellow-Soldiers of Christ and the Temple of Solomon.

Bernard of Clairvaux, a major figure in twelfth-century Catholicism, embraced this young order and sought to raise funds for it. The order received many contributions and offers for service. Pope Innocent II wrote a papal bull in 1139 that established the order and granted to the Templars all spoils they received from battle, plus exemption from tithes and taxes. Bulls by later Popes encouraged Catholics to contribute to the Knights Templar, allowing the Templars to collect taxes on property they owned, and gave them increased freedom from local church authority. This, in essence, allowed the Templars to have complete local control over all the lands they owned.

As Muslim forces continued to gain ground, however, and especially with the fall of Jerusalem to Saladin in 1187, the fortunes of the Templars began to change. First, they moved their headquarters to Acre. Then they began fighting Muslims as well as defending pilgrims. Yet the Muslim advances continued, and slowly the Catholics lost ground. In 1291, Acre was taken, and the Templars had to relocate their headquarters to the tiny island of Arwad, just off the present-day coast of Syria. The Templars lost this as well in 1302 when Egyptian forces laid siege to the island and the Templars surrendered.

Still, the Templars continued to run a massive organization in Europe, which included much property (not taxable), businesses, farms, as well as great wealth. Eventually the Templars were wrongly accused of heresy, idolatry, and other wrong doing, and many were arrested. In 1307, Pope Clement V issued a bull that ordered the arrest of all Templars. Many Templars were tortured and coerced into signing false statements of guilt. Later, many of the Templars who had done this recanted of what they had done.

Eventually the situation moved into the arena of public opinion and began causing collateral damage to the Catholic Church. Pope Clement V issued another bull in 1312, and this time he disbanded the Templars. He also directed that most of the Templars' lands and wealth be handed over to another military order, the Hospitallers.

Mark Nickens

Bibliography

Haag, Michael. *The Templars: History and Myth*. London: Profile Books, 2008.

Martin, Sean. *The Knights Templar: The History and Myths of the Legendary Military Order*. New York: Thunder's Mouth Press, 2004.

Smart, George. *The Knights Templar Chronology*. Bloomington, IN: AuthorHouse, 2005.

K

KNOX, JOHN (CA. 1514–1572)

Scottish Reformer John Knox was born at Haddington, east of Edinburgh in Scotland, and educated at University of St. Andrews. Knox's encounters with Protestant reformers in England, Scotland, and Geneva ultimately played a crucial role in his becoming one of the principle architects of the Reformed Church of Scotland. Unlike his Huguenot counterparts in Protestant France, Knox emerged as a strong proponent of active resistance by private citizens against tyrannical political powers, being convinced that the ordinary Christian had a primary duty to overthrow rulers who did not permit its citizens the freedom to practice what the Protestants saw as true religion. Knox called for the violent overthrow of the Catholic monarchies in Scotland and England in his day.

Knox was among a number of discontented Catholic clergy who eventually came under the influence of a popular Protestant preacher named George Wishart (ca. 1513–1546), and as a result of taking part in a Protestant revolt in St. Andrews Castle, Knox was imprisoned for 19 months as a galley slave before he was allowed to take exile in England in 1549. After pastoring an English congregation near the Scottish border (1549–1554), he was forced to flee to Geneva when the Catholic Mary Tudor became queen and initiated repeals that would once again make England a Catholic land.

While on the continent, Knox met with John Calvin at Geneva and Heinrich

Bullinger at Zurich. He became actively associated with the English exiles at Geneva in the production of the Geneva Bible (1560) with its anti-Catholic apocalyptic annotations. Ultimately, the combined Catholic monarchies of Mary Tudor's England and that of Mary, Queen of Scots, came under the harsh blow of one of Knox's most radical and infamous writings, his *First Blast of the Trumpet Against the Monstrous Regiment of Women* (1558). In 1559, Knox returned to Scotland and helped draft the *Scots Confession* and the *Book of Discipline,* which laid the foundation for the Presbyterian Church of Scotland. He competently defended the central principles of early Protestantism, most notably, *sola Scriptura* (Scripture alone) and *sola fide* (faith alone) in his *History of the Reformation in Scotland* (1559). He also demanded the execution of Mary Stuart, and after her abdication, he preached at the coronation of her son James I.

Thomas Provenzola

Bibliography

Greaves, R.L. *Theology and Revolution in the Scottish Reformation: Studies in the Thought of John Knox*. Grand Rapids: Christian University Press, 1980.

Kyle, Richard G., and Dale W. Johnson. *John Knox: An Introduction to His Life and Works*. Eugene, OR: Wipf & Stock, 2009.

Reid, W. Stanford. *Trumpeter of God*. Grand Rapids: Baker, 1974.

Ridley, Jasper Godwin. *John Knox*. Oxford: Clarendon Press, 1968.

Wilson, Douglas. *For Kirk and Covenant: The Stalwart Courage of John Knox*. Nashville, TN: Cumberland House, 2000.

K

✠

MARTIN LUTHER
German Reformer
1483–1546

LAHAYE, TIM (1926–   )

Baptist pastor, best-selling author, and moral and political activist Tim LaHaye was born in Detroit, Michigan, in 1926 and received Christ as his personal Savior at a young age. His father died when he was only nine, and young LaHaye was deeply impressed by the funeral sermon given by his uncle, who made reference to the biblical promise of the rapture. Educated at Bob Jones University (BA, DD), where he met his wife, Beverly, he later received the DMin from Western Baptist Theological Seminary and the honorary DLitt from Liberty University.

LaHaye pastored Baptist churches in Minneapolis, Minnesota (1950–1956), and San Diego, California (1956–1981), and was one of the original founders of the Moral Majority organization, along with Jerry Falwell, Charles Stanley, and D. James Kennedy. At the same time, Beverly LaHaye founded Concerned Women for America (CWA) to challenge women to confront the culture and defend traditional Christian values.

Tim LaHaye is best known for his 16-volume fiction series of Left Behind™ novels. Coauthored with Jerry Jenkins and selling over 65 million copies, the series became the all-time sales leader of Christian books ever written. In the series, LaHaye and Jenkins developed characters, plots, and subplots that took their readers into the eschatological future from the rapture, through the Tribulation, and into the millennium. Based upon a pretribulational view of the rapture, the books found popular acceptance among many American evangelicals.

Altogether, LaHaye has authored or coauthored more than 50 titles, including nonfiction best-sellers such as *Spirit-Controlled Temperament*, *The Act of Marriage*, *Battle for the Mind*, and numerous books based on biblical eschatology. He is also the founder of Christian Heritage College (now San Diego Christian College) and the Pre-Trib Research Center (1992). Tim and Beverly LaHaye also serve as board members of Liberty University in Lynchburg, Virginia.

Ed Hindson

Bibliography

LaHaye, Tim, and Ed Hindson, eds. *The Popular Encyclopedia of Bible Prophecy.* Eugene, OR: Harvest House, 2004.

LaHaye, Tim, and Ed Hindson, eds. *The Popular Handbook on the Rapture.* Eugene, OR: Harvest House, 2012.

LaHaye, Tim, and Jerry Jenkins. Left Behind™ series. 16 vols. Carol Stream, IL: Tyndale House, 1995–2007.

LATIMER, HUGH (1485–1555)

English bishop, Reformer, and martyr Hugh Latimer was born in Leicestershire and educated at Christ's College, Cambridge, where he received BA, MA, and BD degrees. At one time an opponent of the Reformation, he later became a champion of the cause. At one point his antipathy toward the Roman Catholic Church caused him to be examined by Cardinal Thomas Wolsey, who gave him a warning yet permitted him to continue preaching. In 1530, Latimer was appointed royal chaplain and given a pastorate at West Kingston, Wiltshire. Soon thereafter, Latimer began preaching the doctrines of grace and justification by faith, which he had learned from Thomas Bilney and the group of theologians who met at the White Horse Inn in Cambridge. Quoting Romans 5:1, Latimer confessed, "If I see the blood of Christ with the eye of my soul, that is true faith that his blood was shed for me" (Pollard, 581).

In 1535, Latimer was made bishop of Worchester, but resigned in 1539, refusing to sign King Henry VIII's Six Articles, which represented a return to a Roman Catholic position. A fiery and popular preacher, Latimer continued preaching and wrote *A Faithful Exhortation to the Reading and Knowledge of Holy Scripture*. He was especially critical of clerical abuses and, in consequence, was imprisoned in the Tower of London for a time. Released by Edward VI in 1547, he preached a series of messages at St. Paul's Cross, "Sermon on the Plough," calling for reform of the clergy, observing that "since lording and loitering hath come up, preaching hath come down." His powerful preaching was filled with lively narrative and compelling anecdotes. He was twice imprisoned during the latter years of the reign of Henry VIII, and upon the accession of Bloody Mary Tudor, who favored Catholicism, he was confined to the Tower of London in 1553.

In 1555, Latimer was burned at the stake along with Nichols Ridley in front of Balliol College at Oxford. His last words were, "Be of good cheer Master Ridley, and play the man; we shall this day light a candle by God's grace in England as I trust shall never be put out." Their deaths, along with that of Thomas Cranmer a year later, marked the height of the Marian persecutions and today they remain among the most famous martyrs of the Protestant Reformation.

Ed Hindson

Bibliography

Darby, H.S. *Hugh Latimer*. London: Epworth Press, 1953.

Moyer, Elgin. "Latimer, Hugh." *Who's Who in Church History*. Chicago: Moody Press, 1968.

Pollard, Arthur. "Latimer, Hugh." *The New International Dictionary of the Christian Church*. Edited by J.D. Douglas. Grand Rapids: Zondervan, 1978.

LEWIS, CLIVE STAPLES (1898–1963)

Christian apologist and author Clive Staples Lewis (popularly known as C.S. Lewis), was born in Belfast, Northern Ireland, and died November 22, 1963, at the Kilns, his Oxford home. Arguably the most important and recognized twentieth-century Christian apologist, Lewis wore several hats: apologist (books like *Mere Christianity, The Screwtape Letters, The Problem of Pain, Miracles*), critical theorist and expert in Medieval and Renaissance literature (contributing a volume to the prodigious series *Oxford History of English Literature*), author of poetry, science fiction, and beloved children's stories. He lost his mother at age nine to cancer, a very traumatic life event for Lewis and his older brother, Warren. He chose to be an atheist by age 13. Lewis's father eventually hired retired headmaster William Kirkpatrick, fondly called "The Great Knock," whose rigorous tutelage played a pivotal role in Lewis's intellectual development. Kirkpatrick demanded careful attention to clear utterance and vivid expression, to give relentless chase to truth.

Kirkpatrick prepared Lewis for a successful entry to Oxford (April 1917), though Lewis's studies were interrupted by World War I and a battle injury in 1917. Lewis graduated with Firsts in Greek and Latin literature, philosophy and ancient history, and English, and went on to teach philosophy at Oxford in 1924 before securing a permanent post there in 1925, where he would remain until 1954, taking a chairmanship in Medieval and Renaissance Literature at Cambridge.

While in his twenties, Lewis continued relentlessly to pursue truth, beauty, and goodness (those three leading virtues in Plato's pantheon of virtues) in his field, pursuing it in myth, story, narrative, mythology, and poetry. In the process, Lewis's atheism was eroding. Lewis's reading of G.K. Chesterton and George MacDonald, and his discussions on myth, history, and Christianity with Hugo Dyson and J.R.R. Tolkien, made Lewis realize that truth, now understood as personified in God, had been patiently pursuing him. Lewis's eventual conversion to theism (1929), then Christian theism (1931), is recounted in *Surprised by Joy*. Lewis's conversion in midlife from atheism to theism doubtlessly forms strong reason for his popularity as a Christian apologist. Nevertheless, he is best known to many as the author of the children's classic series The Chronicles of Narnia.

Lewis's apologetic contributions came in written and other formats. Chief among the written are his moral argument (in *Mere Christianity* et al) and his argument from desire (in *Pilgrim's Regress, Surprised by Joy*, et al.). The first states that the moral law of conduct is known by all—because it's objectively real, and personal in nature, and thus a morally perfect moral agent must explain this law. Similarities to Kant's argument abound, but Lewis's is suitably Christianized with unique expressions throughout. The second says that there is a feeling or state of desire which, upon reflection, no earthly state of affairs can satisfy. Thus, this desire can be satisfied only in God's presence.

Lewis's most important nonwritten contribution came as faculty representative of the Socratic Club, a theistic-atheistic dialogue group at Oxford, where he interacted with many noteworthy thinkers (including a famous encounter with well-versed Catholic philosopher Elizabeth Anscombe in 1948). Lewis scholarship continues unabated in the new century, and he remains one of the most widely read apologists of our time.

Edward Martin

Bibliography

Duriez, Colin. *The C.S. Lewis Handbook*. Eastbourne, England: Monarch, 1990.

Kilby, Clyde S., and Marjorie Lamp Mead, eds. *Brothers & Friends: An Intimate Portrait of C.S. Lewis, the Diaries of Major Warren Hamilton Lewis*. San Francisco: Harper & Row, 1982.

Lewis, C.S. *Mere Christianity*. New York: Macmillan, 1943, 1945, 1952, 1960.

Lewis, C.S. *Surprised by Joy*. New York: Harcourt Brace, 1955.

Ward, Michael. *Planet Narnia*. Oxford: Oxford University Press, 2008.

LIVINGSTONE, DAVID (1813–1873)

Scottish missionary to Africa David Livingstone was born into poverty in Scotland in 1813, and he studied medicine and later went to southern Africa as a missionary in 1841 with the London Missionary Society. For the first ten years of service, he engaged in typical missionary work (that is, evangelism and teaching) and helped to start three mission stations. In 1845, Livingstone married Mary Moffat, the daughter of Robert Moffat, who served as a missionary for a half century in southern Africa.

Livingstone's work took a different turn in 1852 when he began to explore the previously uncharted regions of Africa. Beginning in Angola, he traveled through the heart of Africa to the east coast of Mozambique. During his explorations, of which he kept meticulous scientific and geographic records, he discovered Victoria Falls. In 1857, Livingstone returned to England to a hero's welcome and went on a one-year speaking tour relating the experiences that he documented in his book *Missionary Travels and Researches in South Africa.*

Livingstone resigned from the London Missionary Society and accepted a position with the British government that would allow him to focus on exploration. In 1858, he returned to Africa to navigate the Zambezi River. Later, in 1865, he went on an unsuccessful mission to find the source of the Nile. It was in 1871 that the American journalist Henry Stanley found the aged and emaciated Livingstone in the African bush, prompting the famous statement, "Dr. Livingstone I presume." Interestingly, Stanley was converted to Christ and eventually became a missionary. He wrote about his own work in *How I Found Livingstone.* Livingstone died in 1873 and was given a state funeral in Westminster Abbey. Though his body and papers were returned to England, his African friends buried his heart in Africa.

Livingstone made several key contributions to church and missions history. First, Livingstone's exploration work and desire to open up Africa was to facilitate evangelization. He spoke of going to "one thousand villages where no missionary had ever been." Second, he was an advocate of transformation in Africa. While his statements about opening Africa for "Christianity and commerce" have often been misunderstood, he believed that if Europe would trade with Africa, then Africans would stop selling other Africans in the global slave market. Hence, he was very deliberate about putting an end to slavery. As a result, he is still dearly loved by the African people. Finally, though Livingstone was not a gifted mission organizer, he was a great visionary and he succeeded in using his speaking and writing platform to mobilize many in England to missions in Africa. He is buried in a prominent place in Westminster Abbey in London.

Edward Smither

Bibliography

Livingstone, David. *Missionary Travels and Researches in South Africa*. London: John Murray, 1857.

Neill, Stephen. *A History of Christian Missions*. London: Penguin, 1991.

Stanley, Henry. *How I Found Livingstone*. New York: Scribner, Armstrong, 1872.

Tucker, Ruth A. *From Jerusalem to Irian Jaya: A Biographical History of Christian Missions*. Grand Rapids: Zondervan, 1983, 2004.

LOLLARDS

The term *Lollards* was applied to the followers of John Wycliffe, who were English lay preachers. The original group was comprised of Oxford scholars led by Nicholas of Hereford and John Purvey, Wycliffe's secretary. The movement spread among the English laity in the fourteenth century through various preaching missions in the town of England. Lollard beliefs were summarized in the Twelve Conclusions presented to the English Parliament in 1395. They specifically rejected traditional Roman Catholic beliefs such as transubstantiation, clerical celibacy, prayers for the dead, pilgrimmages to shrines, and icons in the churches. They were condemned by Parliament in 1401 by the statute *De heretico comburendo* ("Regarding the burning of heretics"). Despite governmental suppression, Lollard beliefs and sympathies spread through the general public, finally merging with the Protestant movement of the sixteenth century.

Ed Hindson

Bibliography

Clouse, Robert. "Lollards." *The New International Dictionary of the Christian Church*. Edited by J.D. Douglas. Grand Rapids: Zondervan, 1978.

Dickens, A.G. *Lollards and Protestants in the Diocese of York, 1509–1558*. Oxford: Oxford University Press, 1959.

LOMBARD, PETER (CA. 1100–1160)

Medieval scholastic theologian Peter Lombard was born in Lombardy, Italy. Having studied at the Cathedral school of Notre Dame in Paris, he followed in a succession of highly influential thinkers of Western theological knowledge prior to the twelfth and thirteenth centuries whose writings came to be identified with the scholastic method. While the full range of Aristotle's writings was not recovered until the thirteen century, other medieval theologians before him, such as Anselm of Canterbury (1033–1109) and Peter Abelard (1079–1142), had benefitted enormously from what was at that time known of Aristotle's corpus on logic, the *Categories* and *On Interpretation*, that Boethius (ca. 480–525) had earlier translated from Greek into Latin. It was within this newly emerging intellectual discipline that Lombard ultimately produced his famous textbook, *Four Books of Sentences*, which went on to become one of the central discussion pieces in the Western canon of theological education among teachers and students at European universities (including Thomas Aquinas, Duns Scotus, William of Ockham, and Martin Luther) for some 500 years subsequent to its publication.

Although Lombard was clearly influenced by Abelard's use of the scholastic logical method, he managed to avoid the more controversial aspects of the methodology that tended to draw attention to Abelard's work from church authorities suspicious of what came to be known as the dialectic approach. Departing somewhat from his more famous mentor, Lombard's qualities in *Sentences* are found in his ability to use the logical method to arrive at an orthodox understanding of doctrine. From the Latin *sententia* (maxims, opinions, or statements), the *Sentences* bring together in one unified source a compilation of authoritative citations ranging from the church fathers down to several medieval theologians such as Anselm of Laon, and including Lombard's own contemporaries such as Hugh of Saint Victor and the notable Abelard. Divided into four sections covering God, the creation, the Trinity, and the sacraments, Lombard's objective in the work was to teach advanced students of theology how to use reason and logic to arbitrate between the often conflicting and contradictory views of the received authorities on Christian doctrine. Lombard showcases the dialectic method in his book by raising various tensions on conflicting theological positions, citing a number of authorities on both sides of the issue, noting and addressing specific objections on the matter at hand, and then going on to suggest a tentative summary of the problem without necessarily resolving its more controversial features.

Completed only one year before his appointment as bishop of Paris (1159), *Sentences* is a comprehensive and innovative writing, giving evidence not only of Lombard's extensive knowledge of the field and its major players, but also providing him with a venue in which to apply the dialectic method to his view that there are only seven primary sacraments of the church. The *Sentences* were ruled orthodox at the Fourth Lateran Council (1215) despite accusations from critics that Lombard, possibly following Abelard, had less than orthodox views on the humanity of Christ and on his conceptions of the Trinity.

Thomas Provenzola

Bibliography

Aquinas, Thomas. *On Love and Charity: Readings from the Commentary on the Sentences of Peter Lombard.* Translated by Peter A. Kwasniewski, Thomas Bolin, and Joseph Bolin. Washington, DC: Catholic University Press of America, 2008.

Evans, G.R. *Mediaeval Commentaries on the Sentences of Peter Lombard: Current Research.* Leiden, Netherlands: Brill Academic, 2002.

Fairweather, E.R. *A Scholastic Miscellany: Anselm to Ockham.* London: SCM, 1956.

Rogers, Elizabeth Francis. *Peter Lombard and the Sacramental System.* New York: np, 1917.

Rosemann, Philipp W. *The Story of a Great Medieval Book: Peter Lombard's Sentences.* Toronto: University of Toronto Press, 2007.

LUTHER, MARTIN (1483–1546)

German Reformer Luther is generally credited with launching the Protestant Reformation when he posted his *95 Theses* on the church door at Wittenberg on October 31, 1517. He received his BA in 1502 and MA in 1505 from the University of Erfurt. Later, in 1505, he entered the Hermits of St. Augustine house in Erfurt and was ordained a Catholic priest in 1507. In 1508, he transferred to the new University of Wittenberg, earning a BD in 1509 and a doctor of theology in 1512, thereafter becoming a lecturer at Wittenberg.

By 1518, Luther had developed strong convictions regarding biblical authority (*sola scriptura*) as the basis of his theology and became a champion of *sola fide* (faith alone). During this time, he lectured on Psalms and Hebrews, debated Johann Eck at Leipzig, and was interviewed by Cardinal Cajetan at Augsburg in 1519. His most controversial works appeared in 1520, including *Sermon on the Mass* (dealing with the priesthood of the believer), *Treatise on Good Works* (focusing on salvation by faith) and *On the Papacy at Rome* (in which he called the pope the Antichrist).

In April 1521, Luther was summoned by the youthful Emperor Charles V of the

Holy Roman Empire (which included Germany) to answer charges of heresy at the Diet of Worms, where he declined to recant, boldly stating, "Here I stand, I can do no other." Luther spent most of the next year in the Wartburg Castle, where he translated the New Testament from Greek into German in 1522. In 1534, he completed translating the Old Testament from Hebrew, setting the literary standard for the German language.

In 1525, Luther wrote *The Bondage of the Will* in contradiction to Erasmus's view of free will. In 1526, he wrote *The Sacrament of the Body and Blood of Christ Against the Fanatics,* in which he disagreed with Zwingli's view of the Lord's Supper, arguing for the literal meaning of Jesus' words "this is my body…this is my blood." The resulting Colloquy of Marburg in 1529 failed to resolve the issue, with Luther standing firm in his position. He wrote both a *Large Catechism* and *Small Catechism* in 1529. Luther's other practical works included *Table Talk,* recorded by his students between 1531 and 1544, and he is most remembered for his *Lectures on Galatians* (1535), which clearly express the theological conclusions that influenced the entire Protestant Reformation.

Luther married Katherine von Bora, a former nun, in 1525. Together they set a standard for married clergy in the Protestant churches with their exemplary family life. Luther was known as a gracious host, powerful preacher, and practical leader. However, his critics note his vitriolic outbursts against the Jews, the Anabaptists, the Radical Reformers, and his general unwillingness to compromise with other Protestants with whom he disagreed. At the same time, many of his biographers point out that it took such a determined personality to risk his life to stand up against the domination of the Roman Catholic Church in sixteenth-century Europe.

Ed Hindson

Bibliography

Bainton, Roland. *Here I Stand: A Life of Martin Luther*. Nashville, TN: Abingdon, 1960.

D'Aubigne, J.H.M. *The Life and Times of Martin Luther*. Chicago: Moody Press, 1968.

Kleeberg, M.A., and G. Lemme. *In the Footsteps of Martin Luther*. St. Louis, MO: Concordia, 1968.

Meyer, Carl. "Luther, Martin." *The International Dictionary of the Christian Church*. Edited by J.D. Douglas. Grand Rapids: Zondervan, 1978.

Nestingen, J.A. *Martin Luther: His Life and Teachings*. Philadelphia: Fortress, 1982.

LUTHERANISM

Lutheranism has to do with Protestant religious beliefs originally influenced by Martin Luther and resulting in a Lutheran confession and ecclesiastical communion embodied in *The Book of Concord* (1580). Lutheran beliefs are based upon the Augsburg Confession (1530), Luther's small and large catechisms (1529) and the Schmalkaldic Articles (1537). Carl Myer (613) notes: "Justification by grace alone through faith alone in Jesus Christ is the primary doctrine accented by Lutheranism."

Lutheran theology is strongly Christocentric (*solus christus*), emphasizing the redemptive power of Christ's death and resurrection. Good works are viewed as the fruit of faith and the Spirit and not the cause or means of salvation. Nevertheless, Lutherans believe that baptism and the Lord's Supper are means of grace (thus, sacraments). Therefore, baptism is viewed as "the water of regeneration" and the bread and wine of communion are the "real presence" of the body and blood of Christ.

The Lutheran World Federation was formed at Lund, Sweden, in 1947 to serve as an ecumenical voice for Lutherans worldwide. The Lutheran churches of Scandinavia (Norway, Sweden, Denmark, and Finland) virtually serve as national churches with combined memberships of about 20 million. German Lutherans number over 12 million, and American Lutherans number about 8 million and are mainly divided into the Evangelical Lutheran Church of America and the Lutheran Church–Missouri Synod. H.M. Muhlenberg organized the first Lutheran Church in America in Pennsylvania in 1742. American Lutherans emphasize preaching, music, and the Eucharist. Some may have been influenced by pietism, others by rationalism.

Lutheran educational institutions in America include Augustana College, Capital University, Gettysburg College, Wartburg College, Wittenberg University, Valparaiso University, and several schools named Concordia College or University. Prominent Lutheran scholars include Philip Melanchthon (d. 1560), Philipp Spener (d. 1705), Søren Kierkegaard (d. 1855), E.W. Hengstenberg (d. 1869), Johann Keil (d.1888), and Franz Delitzsch (d. 1890). More recent Lutheran scholars include Jaroslav Pelikan (d.2006), Martin Marty, Frederick W. Danker (d.2012), and John Warwick Montgomery.

Ed Hindson

Bibliography

Bodensieck, J. *The Encyclopedia of the Lutheran Church*. 3 vols. Minneapolis: Augsburg Fortress, 1965.

Danker, Frederick W. *No Room in the Brotherhood*. St. Louis, MO: Clayton, 1977.

Myer, Carl. "Lutheranism." *The International Dictionary of the Christian Church.* Edited by J.D. Douglas. Grand Rapids: Zondervan, 1978.

Nelson, E. Clifford. *The Lutherans in North America*. Revised edition. Philadelphia: Fortress, 1980.

MACHEN, JOHN GRESHAM (1881–1937)

American Presbyterian scholar and theologian John Gresham Machen was a seminary professor, churchman, and leader of conservative Presbyterians during the great controversy over modernism during the early twentieth century. Machen was the last great champion of orthodoxy at Princeton, and his departure demonstrated the theological decline of mainline Presbyterianism.

Machen studied at Johns Hopkins University and Princeton Theological Seminary, where he was greatly influenced by B. B. Warfield. He also studied in Europe, where he encountered liberal theology. Machen's academic career was spent at Princeton Theological Seminary (1906–1929) and Westminster Theological Seminary (1929–1937), the conservative institution he founded.

Machen was a leading defender of biblical Christianity. *The Origin of Paul's Religion* (1921) showed the continuity between the teachings of Jesus and the theology of Paul, something modernists contested. *The Virgin Birth of Christ* (1930) showed the reliability of New Testament documents and their consistent witness to this fundamental doctrine. His radio addresses gave straightforward explanations of biblical doctrines for popular audiences.

Machen's highly influential and polemical *Christianity and Liberalism* (1923) emphasized the presuppositional differences between orthodox Christianity and theological liberalism. Liberalism was not an outgrowth of Christian teaching, he argued, but a radically new, naturalistic philosophy. Liberals rhetorically employed scriptural language, but twisted its meaning into something alien. True Christianity, Machen showed, was tied to the doctrines of the historic faith as set forth in Scripture.

Machen had conservative and libertarian commitments and was engaged with political and cultural issues. He criticized socialism, statism, and secularism. He opposed the Prohibition, which disappointed some Christian colleagues. With other conservatives, he warned about the secular trajectory of public education, the unconstitutional and collectivist nature of FDR's legislation, and fascist and communist tyrannies abroad.

Above all, Machen was the central figure in the Presbyterian controversy of the 1920s and 1930s. He warned against the creeping liberalism in Presbyterian circles, even before the modernist Auburn Affirmation of 1924. When Princeton was reorganized by liberal forces in 1929, he founded Westminster Seminary. When theological liberalism became tolerated in the official Presbyterian mission board, Machen established the Independent Board for Presbyterian Foreign Missions (IBPFM). When the Presbyterian Church (USA) compelled ministers to abandon the IBPFM, Machen stood his ground. Put on trial and suspended from the ministry for not leaving the IBPFM, Machen organized a new denomination, the Orthodox Presbyterian Church. The new denomination split within a year of its founding, with fundamentalist Presbyterians establishing the Bible Presbyterian Church.

Machen's untimely death in 1937 robbed conservative Presbyterians of their most effective voice. He stood in the line of Old Princeton and was a stalwart defender of the faith for his generation.

Roger Schultz

Bibliography

Hart, D.G. *Defending the Faith: J. Gresham Machen and the Crisis of Conservative-Protestantism in Modern America*. Baltimore, MD: Johns Hopkins University Press, 1994.

Longfield, Bradley. *The Presbyterian Controversy: Fundamentalists, Modernists, and Moderates*. New York: Oxford University Press, 1993.

Rian, Edwin. *The Presbyterian Controversy*. Grand Rapids: Eerdmans, 1940.

Stonehouse, Ned B. *J. Gresham Machen*. Grand Rapids: Eerdmans, 1954.

Wells, David, ed. *Reformed Theology in America: A History of Its Modern Development*. Grand Rapids: Baker, 1997.

MAGNUS, ALBERTUS (1193–1280)

Dominican theologian and philosopher Albertus Magnus was born in Bavaria of noble parents and entered the Dominican Order and taught at Dominican schools in Germany (1228–1245), and later in Paris, Cologne, and Strasbourg (1245–1255). His most famous student was Thomas Aquinas. He also served as a papal emissary and arbitrator in ecclesiastical disputes and later as bishop of Regensburg until 1262. He was the first medieval scholar to master the works of Aristotle and wrote 21 volumes on religion, science, and philosophy. His Neoplatonism became popular among Dominican scholars. He was canonized and declared a doctor of the church in 1931. Albertus is most remembered for his emphasis on the right of scholars to investigate all human knowledge to explain divine revelation.

Ed Hindson

Bibliography

Clouse, R.G. "Albertus Magnus." *The International Dictionary of the Christian Church*. Edited by J.D. Douglas. Grand Rapids: Zondervan, 1978.

Kurian, G.T. "Albertus Magnus, St." *Nelson's Dictionary of Christianity*. Nashville, TN: Thomas Nelson, 2005.

MANICHAEISM

Manichaeism was a gnostic religion founded in the third century by the prophet Mani (ca. AD 216–276) in Persia. Although his writings were largely lost over time, many ancient translations and fragmentary texts have recently been recovered in China, Turkistan, and Egypt. In contemporary usage, the term *Manichean* is used to describe a philosophical worldview which, often simplistically, views reality as a moral dualism between good and evil.

Mani was raised in a Ebionite Jewish-Christian sect, the Elkesaites, a "strange mixture of Judaism, Christianity, and paganism" (Runia, 51). Emphasizing the Mosaic Law and circumcision, they rejected sacrifice. They were especially known for their asceticism and frequent ablutions (baptisms) that were scheduled according to the position of the stars (Runia, 51). They were also influenced by Mandaeanism and Jewish apocalyptic writings similar to those found at Qumran (such as the book of Enoch). Many of these influences would be later observed in the Manichean teachings.

It was said that Mani received revelations when he was 12 and again when he was 24 (Reeves, 6-9). His "annunciation" at age 24 marked the beginning of his public declaration of himself, at which time he began to preach the doctrines that would become the core teachings of the new religion. Emerging in the waning centuries of the Roman Empire particularly in the Aramaic-Syriac speaking regions, Manichaeism competed with established Christianity against regional paganisms (BeDuhn and Mirecki, 6-7). From the outset there was a geopolitical objective to convert the world to the new religion. Mani quickly had his writings translated into other languages and organized extensive mission initiatives into the Roman Empire and across North Africa (influencing Augustine prior to his conversion to Christianity).

Despite Mani's death in the latter part of the third century, the fourth century marked the apex of Manichaean expansion in the West as far as southern Gaul and Spain. Within 200 years, however, it would be virtually eliminated from these regions, though its influence would continue in some measure. Groups such as the Paulicians (Armenia, seventh century), the Bogomilists (Bulgaria, tenth century), and the Cathari or Albigensians (southern France, twelfth century) betrayed Manichaean influence.

Manichaeism was a syncretistic Gnosticism; a dualistic religion that offered salvation through special knowledge (*gnosis*) of spiritual truth. The Coptic texts recovered from Medinet Madi in Egypt, probably dating from the fourth century, identify Adam, Seth, Enosh, Enoch, Noah, and Shem as "apostles" who preceded Mani in proclaiming the message of the "Realm of Light." Zoroaster, Buddha, Jesus, and Paul are also listed. Manichaeism had the character of an ecumenical and universal religion, integrating elements of Zoroastrianism, Buddhism, Judaism, and Christianity in its belief system.

Manichaeism spread as far as China and became the state religion of the Turkic Uyghurs. Various Manichean texts have survived in Coptic, Uyghur, Chinese, Greek, and Persian. The religion taught salvation by being reunited with the Divine Light.

Daniel R. Mitchell

M

Bibliography

BeDuhn, Jason, and Paul Allan Mirecki, eds. *Frontiers of Faith: The Christian Encounter with Manichaeism in the Acts of Archelaus*. Nag Hammadi and Manichean Studies, vol. 61. Leiden: Brill Academic, 2007.

Reeves, John C. *Heralds of that Good Realm: Syro-Mesopotamian Gnosis and Jewish Traditions*. Nag Hammadi and Manichean Studies, vol. 41. Leiden: Brill Academic, 1996.

Runia, Klaas. "Elkesaites." *The Encyclopedia of Christianity*, vol. 4. Edited by Philip E. Hughes. Marshallton, DE: The National Foundation for Christian Education, 1972.

Welburn, Andrew. *Mani, the Angel and the Column of Glory: An Anthology of Manichaean Texts*. Edinburgh: Floris Books, 1998.

MAR THOMA CHURCH

Also known as the Malankara Mar Thoma Syrian Church or the Mar Thoma Syrian Church, *Mar Thoma* is Aramaic and means "Saint Thomas." The Mar Thoma Church believes that they were founded by the apostle Thomas in AD 52. The inclusion of *Syrian* in the name refers to the Eastern nature of the worship and not to any control by Syria, although the Mar Thoma Church's theology is more Protestant. The head of the denomination is known as the Metropolitan, and the Mar Thoma Church has approximately 500,000 members with 1075 parishes and congregations. Mar Thoma Theological Seminary (est. 1926) is the main seminary, and the denomination has a number of other religious higher-education institutions in India.

Mar Thoma tradition holds that Christianity was brought to India by the apostle Thomas in the year 52. Thomas founded seven churches, with most being located close to the coastline of India. The Portuguese arrived in 1498 and established colonies in the area. With them came Catholicism, and the Roman pontiff wanted to bring the Mar Thoma churches under his authority. Many Thomist (Mar Thoma) churches joined under pressure. As the Portuguese empire waned, some of the churches declared their independence in 1653, with the Oath of Coonen Cross. The archdeacon of these churches, whose name was Thomas, was consecrated Mar Thoma I in 1665 by Mar Gregorius of Jerusalem. At this point, the Mar Thoma churches became aligned with the Western Syrian liturgy.

Through the influence of the Western powers that controlled India, Portugal, Netherlands, and particularly England, the Thomist Christians were introduced to Protestant thought. A Reformation occurred within the Mar Thoma Church during the mid and late 1800s, with the church leaders reevaluating many of their beliefs. Many Catholic beliefs and practices were discarded and communion was to be conducted in the mother tongue of Malayalam. In early 1911, the church adopted the name Mar Thoma Church. Mar Thomists have traveled and settled in various locations over the past century, and so Mar Thomist churches are now located throughout Europe, in America (which has 86 parishes/churches), New Zealand, Australia, and Singapore.

Mark Nickens

Bibliography

Cheriyan, C.V. *Orthodox Christianity in India*. Kottayam, India: Academic Publishers, 2003.

Mathew, K.V. *The Faith and Practice of the Mar Thoma Church*. Kottayam, India: Mar Thoma Theological Seminary, 1985.

Varghese, Zac, and Matthew A. Kallumpram. *Glimpses of Mar Thoma Church History*. London: Society of St. Thomas and St. Augustine, 2003.

MARCION OF SINOPE (D. AD 160)

Marcion of Sinope was the leader of an unorthodox Christian sect that came to bear his name. At some time during the first half of the second century, Marcion relocated to Rome, where his teachings eventually led him into disagreement with the Roman bishop. Based on the accounts of Tertullian and other patristic sources, a break with the Roman Church took place around AD 144. So heated was this conflict that the Roman Church returned a large sum of money that Marcion had donated some time earlier. Despite significant opposition to his teachings, Marcion continued his efforts to form new communities which were in line with his thinking.

Among other things, Marcion was well-known for espousing the viewpoint that the God described in the Old Testament was a deity responsible for creating an evil world and that this God should not be confused with the Jesus revealed in the New Testament or Jesus' heavenly Father. According to Marcion, Jesus' role was to redeem the evil world from its fallen state, thus placing his eschatological role at direct odds with the God recorded in the Hebrew Bible. In addition to these aberrant beliefs, Marcionite communities observed strict ascetic practices which, among other things, included a prohibition of marriage, wine, and all meat except fish.

What might be known of Marcion is of special significance to our understanding of the New Testament canon in the second century. Marcion devised a version of the New Testament that was limited to an edited Gospel similar to that of Luke—the *Evangelikon*—as well as an altered edition of Paul's letters—the *Apostolikon*. It seems that his selection of writings was driven largely by theological considerations and that he edited only those books that he considered to be generally free from what he perceived to be "corrupt" Jewish influence and editing.

Marcion is often considered to be the first known figure to define the extent of the biblical canon. Adolf von Harnack was especially influential in advancing the theory that Marcion's creation of a biblical canon placed the Orthodox Church in the awkward position of having a heretical teacher as the first to define the extent and scope of the biblical canon and that this unfortunate circumstance prompted the Orthodox Church to respond with its own list of what it considered to be authoritative Scripture.

Benjamin Laird

Bibliography

Barton, John. "Marcion Revisited." *The Canon Debate*. Edited by Lee Martin McDonald and James A. Sanders. Peabody, MA: Hendrickson, 2002.

Blackman, E.C. *Marcion and His Influence*. London: SPCK, 1948.

Clabeaux, John James. *The Lost Edition of the Letters of Paul: A Reassessment of the Text of Pauline Corpus Attested by Marcion*. Catholic Biblical Quarterly Monograph Series no. 21. Washington, DC: Catholic Biblical Association of America, 1989.

Knox, John. *Marcion and the New Testament: An Essay in the Early History of the Canon*. Chicago: University of Chicago Press, 1942.

Von Harnack, Adolf. *Marcion: The Gospel of the Alien God*. Translated by John E. Steely and Lyle D. Bierma. Durham, NC: Labyrinth Press, 1990.

MELANCHTHON, PHILIPP (1497–1560)

The German Lutheran Reformer Philipp Melanchthon was born Philip Schwarzerdt in 1497 near Frankfurt, Germany. He distinguished himself in high school, and when he entered the University of Heidelberg at age 13, he took the Greek version of his name, Melanchthon, which was the custom of humanist scholars in his day. He finished his BA studies in two years and when he finished his MA studies in 1512, the degree was not conferred because he was too young. He went on to teach at Tübingen University and they conferred the MA degree. He had a classical education, and as a humanist, was interested in all areas of education including mathematics, natural sciences, philosophy, astrology, ancient classical languages, literature, dialectics, rhetoric (particularly the works of Aristotle), and theology.

Melanchthon became a professor of Greek at Wittenberg University in August 1518, and quickly identified with Martin Luther, 14 years his elder. Luther had posted his 95 theses on the door of the Wittenberg Church, October 31, 1517, and the two men worked to further the Reformation cause. Melanchthon championed *sola Scriptura* (Scripture alone) in his BD thesis at Wittenberg in 1519. He accompanied Luther to the Leipzig Disputation and published his commentary on Galatians and the Psalms. When John Eck called Melanchthon a grammarian and not a theologian, Melanchthon responded in an attack on Eck and the Roman Catholic Church, stating his famous words, "I believe the [church] fathers because I believe the Scriptures."

Luther confessed to being a theological hothead, saying, "My books are very stormy and warlike," whereas Melanchthon was more diplomatic in his presentation and answered with academic reserve. Melanchthon did not pursue a doctor's degree, was never ordained into ministry, and never preached a sermon. Rather, he worked as an educator who assisted Luther, the preacher.

During Luther's stay at the Wartburg Castle, Melanchthon led the Lutheran movement in Germany. Melanchthon's *Loci Communes* (1521) became the first systematic treatment of Lutheran theology. Melanchthon was the primary author of the Augsburg Confession, which became the unifying instrument for Lutherans for the next 400 years. He is recognized as the veiled thinker of the Lutheran Reformation, and because of his brilliance, the Reformation was not merely a revolt against the Roman Catholic Church, it also worked to replace Catholic doctrine with a Protestant body of theology and beliefs that became foundational to the continued spread of the Reformation around the world.

Melanchthon, like Luther, recognized the biblical mandate of civil government; thus the two men cooperated with civil authorities in the establishment of schools and universities. Melanchthon prepared school plans for Eisleben (1525), Nürnberg (1526), Saxony (1528), Herzeberg (1538), Cologne (1543), Wittenberg (1545), Mecklenberg (1552), and the Palatinate (1556). He also wrote extensive catechetical works in Latin that were translated into German, covering topics such as law, gospel, justification, preservation of faith, the sacraments, baptism, confession, and the Lord's Supper. These works provided clear statements of what Lutherans believed about life in society, politics, and the church. However, Melanchthon's catechisms were overshadowed by Luther's *Small Catechism* and *Large Catechism,* published in 1529.

Melanchthon died in 1560 and was buried next to Luther, and is recognized as one of the greatest Christian teachers in German history.

Elmer Towns

Bibliography

Eby, F., ed. *Early Protestant Educators.* New York: McGraw-Hill, 1931.

Green, L.C. "Melanchthon." *The Encyclopedia of the Lutheran Church,* vol. 2. Minneapolis: Augsburg, 1965.

Manschreck, C.L. *Melanchthon, the Quiet Reformer.* Nashville, TN: Abingdon, 1958.

Tillman, W.G. *The World and Men Around Martin Luther.* Minneapolis: Augsburg, 1959.

MENNONITES

The Mennonites are a Christian denomination whose roots can be traced to the Anabaptist movement of the sixteenth century. The Anabaptists were so called because of their practice of rebaptizing adults who had been baptized as infants. The Mennonites take their name from Menno Simons, a Dutch priest who was converted to the Anabaptist movement and helped take it to Holland. Like all Anabaptists of the sixteenth century, the Mennonites faced severe persecution, which was still ongoing as late as 1710 in parts of Switzerland. Mennonites hold to the historic tenets of Orthodox Christianity, emphasizing the authority of the Scripture, especially the New Testament, in matters of faith and practice. They also practice believer's baptism by immersion and emphasize strong spiritual disciplines as the outward sign of an inward change. Mennonites are also known for the practice of separation from worldly groups and amusements, which forms the basis for their practice of shunning those who refuse to repent of such practices.

Today, the 12 major Mennonite groups represent over one million members worldwide, and the Mennonite World Conference represents Mennonite churches in 51 countries from around the world. During the Colonial period and for some time after, Mennonites in America were represented by two major groups. The first group was the followers of Jacob Ammon, who were later called the Amish and known for their refusal to embrace modern fashions and appliances. The second group, sometimes called the Old Mennonites, later broke into groups such as the Mennonite Brethren Church, the Mennonite Church USA, and the General Conference Mennonites. Strongly pacifist, the Mennonites uphold the virtues of spiritual simplicity. Their schools include Goshen College (Indiana), Hesston College (Kansas), and Eastern Mennonite University (Virginia).

Joseph Buchanan

Bibliography

Dyck, Cornelius J. *An Introduction to Mennonite History: A Popular History of the Anabaptists and the Mennonites.* 3d ed. Scottdale, PA: Herald, 1993.

Estep, William. *The Anabaptist Story: An Introduction to Sixteenth-Century Anabaptism.* Grand Rapids: Eerdmans, 1996.

Roth, John. *Beliefs: Mennonite Faith and Practice.* Scottdale, PA: Herald, 2005.

Smith, C. Henry. *The Story of the Mennonites.* Newton, KS: Mennonite Publication Office, 1950.

Wenger, John Christian. *Glimpses of Mennonite History and Doctrine.* Scottdale, PA: Herald Press, 1947.

METHODISM

Methodism arose in early eighteenth-century England from a small group of Anglican clergy at Oxford, including John and Charles Wesley and George Whitefield. At times derisively called the Holy Club, the group's members focused on methodically cultivating personal piety through Scripture reading, study of the church fathers and devotional classics, and charity work among the poor. Upon returning to England in 1738 after a failed trip to Georgia, John Wesley came under the influence of the Moravians and doubted his salvation. Both he and his brother experienced conversion in May of 1738.

Methodism emerged as an organized reform movement within the Anglican Church in the 1740s and was part of a transatlantic religious awakening called the Evangelical Revival in Great Britain and the Great Awakening in the United States. Following the Wesleys' original small-group plan, and owing in part to Moravian influences, groups called "bands" formed to encourage followers to live a holy and disciplined life. Members would pray, read Scripture, and confess sins. Soon, larger, less-exclusive groups called "classes" formed, designed to win new converts and train new believers. Both still exist today and are used in various ways in Methodist denominations throughout the world.

Methodists generally hold to an Arminian soteriology. Both original sin and universal atonement are affirmed, with predestination and the perseverance of the saints being rejected. Prevenient grace convicts the individual of sin, at which point he or she can either accept or reject salvation. At salvation, Christ's righteousness is imputed, but the new believer also begins the process of becoming actually holy. Falling away, however, is possible. Wesley's emphasis on holy living caused him to see salvation as the sum total of God's work in a person, far more than just going to heaven. Thus, the goal after justification is the pursuit of entire sanctification. Christian perfection means loving both God with the entirety of one's being and loving the neighbor as oneself (Heitzenrater, 107, 220).

A key component of holy living is social responsibility. In Wesleyan theology, there is no distinction between personal and social holiness. Wesley admonished his followers to earn all they could, save all they could, and give all they could. This combination of hard work and generosity resonated well with the working- and lower-middle-class people among whom Methodism thrived in both England and the United States in the eighteenth and early nineteenth centuries. It also inspired English and American Methodists to take leadership roles in various reform movements in the nineteenth and early twentieth centuries, including antislavery, temperance, and suffrage movements.

In the United States, Methodism split into several branches before the Civil War along racial, geographical, political, and theological lines. The two largest branches, the Methodist Episcopal Church and the Methodist Episcopal Church, South reunited in 1939, and were joined in 1968 by the Evangelical United Brethren to form the United Methodist Church. This is the third largest denomination in the United States, although its membership is in decline. On the other hand, Methodism worldwide continues to grow, with Methodist churches existing in more than 130 countries.

Joseph Super

Bibliography

Cracknell, Kenneth, and Susan J. White. *An Introduction to World Methodism.* Cambridge: Cambridge University Press, 2005.

Heitzenrater, Richard P. *Wesley and the People Called Methodists.* Nashville, TN: Abingdon, 1995.

Hempton, David. *Methodism: Empire of the Spirit.* New Haven, CT: Yale University Press, 1995.

Norwood, Frederick A. *The Story of American Methodism.* Nashville, TN: Abingdon, 1974.

Tucker, Karen B. Westerfield. *American Methodist Worship.* New York: Oxford University Press, 2001.

M

MICHELANGELO (1475–1564)

Michelangelo di Lodovico Buonarroti Simoni, better known as Michelangelo, remains among the most celebrated and famous architects, sculptors, and painters of the Renaissance. His works, on display in Florence, Italy, and the Vatican basilicas in Rome, draw millions of admirers each year who remain entranced by the intricate detail and depth of emotion Michelangelo was able to capture.

Michelangelo was born in the small town of Caprese in the territory of Florence. Though the young artist displayed genius at drawing, his father sought a career as a civic officer for his son. Finally, for lack of better financial options, his father apprenticed the young Michelangelo to the noted Florentine frescoist Dominico Ghirlandaio (1448–1494). Michelangelo's drawings soon eclipsed those of his fellow pupils and eventually even his master, and he moved into the court of Lorenzo the Magnificent, where he honed his sculpturing skills. Following the death of Lorenzo, Michelangelo traveled through Italy and eventually to Rome, where he executed his first masterpiece, the famous *Pieta* (1498–1499). The *Pieta,* or Pity, was a common theme in northern Europe but was a relatively new subject for Italians. Many in Rome were unsettled by the sculpted image of the dead Christ in the arms of his mother. Despite the unfamiliarity of the subject, the Romans came to appreciate the brilliance in the sculpting skill possessed by the young Michelangelo, and he quickly became the foremost sculptor in all of Italy. Florence sought the return of its native son, and in 1501, he returned and executed his famous sculpture of the young David (1501–1504) now on display in the Gallerie dell'Accademia, Florence.

Michelangelo's skill and fame continued to grow and he was eventually called back to Rome by *il Papa Terrible,* Pope Julius II, for two commissioned projects that would dominate his life. Julius II sought Michelangelo's skill in sculpturing the largest and most elaborate tomb in Rome. Realizing that the proposed tomb would not fit within St. Peter's, Julius II began drawings for a new Basilica of St. Peter's. This new project, as well as the many wars he fought, drained the papal treasury and eventually forced the Pope to set aside his grand tomb. Michelangelo constantly sought to return to sculpting the various pieces of Julius II's tomb but was only able to execute one full statute, the horned *Moses* (1513–1515), which is now on display in the Roman basilica San Pietro in Vincoli (St. Peter in Chains).

In 1508, Julius II commissioned a reluctant Michelangelo to paint frescoes on the ceiling of the Sistine Chapel. Taking nearly four years to complete, this work remains one of the singular masterpieces of art in the world. Michelangelo's skill in portraying the human form and emotion, as well as the nearly three-dimensional quality of the frescoed ceiling, is unsurpassed in the history of art.

In 1536, Pope Paul III brought Michelangelo back to the Sistine Chapel to fresco the Altar Wall with the *Last Judgment* (1536–1541). Later in life, Michelangelo moved from sculpture and fresco to architecture. He served as the chief architect (1546–1564) for the new St. Peter's. The dome of this structure, though completed after his death in 1564, is Michelangelo's design and serves as a visible testament to his artistic genius.

Douglas Mann

Bibliography

Bull, George. *Michelangelo: A Biography.* New York: St. Martin's Griffin, 1997.

Hibbard, Howard. *Michelangelo.* 2d ed. New York: Harper & Row, 1985.

Osborn, Harold, ed. *The Oxford Companion to Art.* New York: Oxford University Press, 1978.

Vasari, Georgio, *The Lives of the Artists.* Translated by Julia Bondanella and Peter Bondanella. New York: Oxford University Press, 1998.

MILTON, JOHN (1608–1674)

John Milton, an English poet, is best known as the author of *Paradise Lost*. He was educated at St. Paul's Grammar School and Christ's College, Cambridge, where he wrote *On the Morning of Christ's Nativity* in 1629. Always a deep and serious thinker, Milton's poetry explored themes dealing with the meaning and purpose of life. For example, the poetic masque *Comus* represents the conflict between chastity and vice (*luxuria*).

Vehemently opposed to the episcopacy, Milton began as an Anglican with moderate Puritan leanings. Then he turned Presbyterian, then independent with antitrinitarian Arian leanings. During the English civil wars he became the author of numerous pamphlets supporting the parliamentary cause and individual liberty. He later served as secretary of Latin correspondence under the Commonwealth. His pamphlets included *Of Reformation of Church Discipline in England* (1641), in which he advocated divorce on the grounds of incompatibility as well as adultery; *Of Education* (1644); and *Aeropagitica* (1644), which appealed for freedom of the press.

Milton was widowed twice and married three times. He went blind around 1652 and lived his last years in retirement using a secretary to transcribe his greatest works. *Paradise Lost* appeared in 1667 and represents the finest quality of English epic poetry. In it, Milton "ranges through heaven, hell, and earth in his examination of motive, conflict and responsibility…in his extensive treatment of the fall" (Pollard, 661). Milton next wrote *Paradise Regained* and *Samson Agonistes* in 1671. Milton's poems were often an expression of his own theological challenges as he wrestled with issues of divine sovereignty and human free will, and in time, he came to reject the Calvinist doctrine of predestination.

Milton died peacefully in 1674 and was buried in the chancel of St. Giles Church at Cripplegate, London. Milton is still remembered as a champion of liberty and one of England's greatest poets.

Ed Hindson

Bibliography

Hughes, Merritt Yerkes, ed. *John Milton: Complete Poems and Major Prose*. Indianapolis, IN: Hackett Publishing, 1957.

Pollard, Arthur. "Milton, John." *The New International Dictionary of the Christian Church*. Edited by J.D. Douglas. Grand Rapids: Zondervan, 1978.

MODERNISM

Modernism, or the philosophy of scientific realism, began with the writings of René Descartes (1506–1650). His *Meditations on First Philosophy* laid a new foundation for knowledge. The medievals had founded knowledge on authority—Greek philosophers, especially Aristotle, along with certain Roman authors, the Bible, and early church theologians were said to be the final authorities on matters of truth in almost every field. Descartes noticed that these authorities often contradicted each other, and he sought a way to achieve absolute certainty on every topic.

Descartes determined to begin with doubt. He even doubted that the room around him existed, that he was warmed by a fire, even that he was sitting at his desk. Finally, Descartes realized that one thing he could not doubt was that he was doing the doubting. Because he was obviously doubting everything else, he could not doubt his own existence as "a thing that thinks," and that doubt believes, hopes, and reasons.

Descartes reasoned from the fact of his own existence as a thinking being to the existence of God, and then to the existence of the external world. He doubted everything he saw in the world until the truth of it was presented "clearly and distinctly" to his own mind. Until that level of certainty and clarity was attained, he determined to remain in a state of doubt. Thus, only truths of reason (logic and mathematics) and things presented clearly to his senses (science) could be trusted as true.

In the next century, philosophers of the Age of Reason took Descartes's method and secularized it, basing all accepted truth on reason and the senses. These thinkers were the first to divide history into three eras—ancient, medieval, and modern. The ancient world had been subject to superstition and religion. Reason had flourished for a short while in Greece, but had been swept away by the rise of Christianity. The fall of Greco-Roman civilization ushered in the Middle Ages, the time between the ancient world and the modern world. The modern world, using Descartes's method, would, they believed, finally rid humanity of superstition and religion, as the triumph of reason would bring utopia.

Descartes's method, beginning with doubt, has led to apologetic challenges. Julius Wellhausen (1844–1918) used Descartes's method on the Old Testament. He began by doubting that Moses had written any of the books of Genesis through Deuteronomy (the Pentateuch), which are traditionally ascribed to him. He studied these books carefully, seeking to find the "real" author. His theory of multiple authorship was based on the different names for God that were used in different sections of these books. He concluded that the books were the work of four different authors, whose various accounts were woven together centuries later by editors and redactors.

Also, Wellhausen and his followers believed the Bible could not have been inspired by God. They said the supernatural elements in it were a product of religious superstition, now superceded by reason and science.

The New Testament has suffered a similar fate, with many scholars doubting that Paul wrote all of the letters attributed to him. Even more so, the authorship of John has come under scrutiny over the past couple of centuries. Scholars have proposed various authors, including a committee of John's followers, and even an "elder John" who lived in the same town, but who was a different John, and not the apostle John.

Modernism in the twentieth century came to refer to everything from philosophy to architecture. In theological circles, modernism reflected an antisupernatural, critical approach to Christianity, both Catholic and Protestant. Many trace the roots of theological modernism to the German theologians Friedrich Schleiermacher and Albrecht Ritschl and popularized by Harry Emerson Fosdick. In reaction, theological conservatives, led by J. Gresham Machen (*Christianity and Liberalism*) and the publication of *The Fundamentals* (1905–1915) responded with a strong antimodernist defense of the fundamental beliefs of the traditional Christian faith.

By wedding itself too closely to the modernist method, the liberal church accepted liberal teaching on the Bible, and even modernism's antisupernatural mind-set, and has been at some pains to extricate itself ever since. As the world moves into the postmodern era, those eager to embrace "postmodern Christianity" would do well to look at what close ties to modernism did to the church, and learn from past experience to beware of the influence of secular philosophy. The church's posture today, as in the first century, the sixteenth century, and any century, must be to challenge the prevailing worldview and call the world to repentance and faith, rather than to accept the spirit of the age and then wonder why the world ignores its message.

Fred Smith

Bibliography

Descartes, René. *Meditations on First Philosophy*. Indianapolis, IN: Hackett, 1993.

Helin, Paul. "Modernism." *The New International Dictionary of the Christian Church*. Edited by J.D. Douglas. Grand Rapids: Zondervan, 688.

Machen, J.G. *Christianity and Liberalism*. Grand Rapids: Eerdmans, 2009.

Marsden, G., ed. *Evangelicalism and Modern America*. Grand Rapids: Eerdmans, 1984.

MONTANISM

Montanism, a second-century charismatic apocalyptic movement, was founded by Montanus, who had been a pagan priest before he converted to Christianity (ca. 155). Sometime later he began prophesying, claiming he was possessed by the Holy Spirit. Montanus was soon joined by two prophetesses, Priscilla and Maximilla. These three and their followers, known thereafter as Montanists, believed that the final era in human history was just then being ushered in by a fresh outpouring of the Spirit of God in anticipation of the second coming. Some in the church were repulsed by the emphasis of the Spirit over the Son, but others, like Tertullian, were attracted to this renewed emphasis of the Spirit and his active work in the lives of Christians. The Montanists claimed that the Spirit was giving new revelation that was subsequent to what appeared in the New Testament. Montanus himself proclaimed that many of the leaders of the churches had chased the Holy Spirit into a book rather than to let him continue his revelatory work.

With this renewed emphasis on the revelation of the Spirit, there was also a call for personal holiness in light of what was believed to be the end of the age. Montanists were ascetics. They deprived themselves of things that would give them physical pleasure, especially things associated with food, clothing, and shelter. They abhorred the tendency of many church leaders to forgive sin so quickly and completely. Montanists claimed this easy forgiveness decreased Christians' fear of sinning and therefore increased their likelihood that they would continue to live in sin. Montanists also forbade their followers to remarry, and they refused to accept into fellowship anyone who fled in the face of persecution.

Montanists referred to their followers as the *pneumatici* ("sprit-filled") and their Catholic counterparts as the *psychici* ("animal-men"). A significant reason for their emphasis on personal holiness was their disgust with the rationalist tendencies of the Gnostics of their era, who seemed to be luring the church into an academic set of propositions rather than a living faith. And yet another reason for their emphasis on personal holiness was the Montanists' belief that Christ's second coming was imminent. Montanus prophesied that Christ would return to Pepuza, Phrygia (located in what is now modern Turkey), which Montanus referred to as the "New Jerusalem" (see Revelation 21). When the event did not occur as prophesied, the movement lost its original zeal and many of its followers.

In reaction to the Montanists' theological claims and their criticisms of the church as a whole, the earliest recorded synods in church history met in Asia at the end of the second century to agree in their condemnation of the Montanist movement. Formally banned by their neighboring churches, the organized movement spread into northern Africa, which probably accounts for the early ascetic tendencies of desert monks in the following century. Montanism was the earliest of many major reform movements in the history of the Christian church which would claim divine revelation among their prophets, advocate personal holiness, predict the imminent return of Christ, and question certain tendencies of the established church leaders.

Kenneth Cleaver

Bibliography

Tabbernee, William. *Fake Prophecy and Polluted Sacraments: Ecclesiastical and Imperial Reactions to Montanism.* Leiden: Brill Academic, 2007.

———. *Prophets and Gravestones: An Imaginative History of Montanists and Other Early Christians.* Peabody, MA: Hendrickson, 2009.

Trevett, C. *Montanism: Gender, Authority and the New Prophecy.* Cambridge: Cambridge University Press, 2002.

MOODY, DWIGHT LYMAN (1837–1899)

Dwight Lyman Moody (popularly known as D.L. Moody) is recognized as one of the most significant evangelists of the nineteenth century. One of nine children, Moody was born to a growing Unitarian family in Northfield, Massachusetts. His alcoholic father died when Moody was only four years of age, leaving the family destitute. After a difficult childhood, Moody moved to Boston at the age of 18 to live with his uncle and work in his shoe store. One of the requirements mandated by his uncle was church attendance at the local Congregational church. This requirement ultimately resulted in his conversion experience. Edward Kimball, a devoted Sunday school teacher, visited Moody while he was at work and shared the gospel of Christ with him. At the back of this shoe store, Moody accepted Christ.

In 1856, Moody moved to Chicago and established himself as a successful shoe salesman. In time, however, he began to apply his primary energies and talents to the winning of souls for Christ. This resulted in his decision to commit his life to full-time Christian service in 1861. Shortly thereafter, he began a Sunday school in an abandoned saloon. As the class grew in size, he found it necessary to move it to North Market Hall. Eventually this Sunday school attained a membership of 1500 people, comprised mostly of indigent and homeless people. This, in turn, resulted in the formation of the Illinois Street Church in 1863. In addition, Moody was significantly involved in the work of the Chicago Young Men's Christian Association (YMCA).

Sydney Ahlstrom noted that, between 1867 and 1872, Moody experienced four significant events in his life: (1) The preaching of a Plymouth Brethren preacher, Harry Moorehouse, taught Moody of the great love God had for sinful man. (2) Moody solicited the assistance of the song leader, Ira Sankey, in 1870, and they continued to work together in ministry for a long time thereafter. (3) In 1871, while Moody was visiting New York, he had a spiritual encounter with God that renewed his zeal for the lostness of humanity. (4) His first international preaching engagement was in London in the spring of 1872, where more than 400 people responded to the gospel invitation. For Moody, this event confirmed God's call for him to engage in full-time revival evangelism.

The positive response to the gospel message in the London church encouraged Moody to extend his visit. Between 1873 and 1875, an estimated three to four million people attended the numerous meetings Moody held in England, Scotland, and Ireland. The reports regarding the British evangelistic campaigns preceded the return of Moody and Sankey to America. They were in great demand by denominational and civic leaders and held revival campaigns from New York to the Pacific coast. Ahlstrom provided this description: "With listeners in the millions, converts in the thousands, their hymns on every lip, their names a household word, Moody and Sankey rejuvenated the revival" (744).

Moody was also responsible for establishing the following institutions that would aid in the training of future missionaries and evangelists: Northfield School for Girls (1879), Mount Hermon School for Boys (1881), and the Chicago Evangelization Society (1886), later named the Moody Bible Institute. Moody's influence on American evangelism lives on today, more than a century after his death in 1899.

John Durden

Bibliography

Ahlstrom, Sydney E. *A Religious History of the American People*. 2d ed. Foreword by David D. Hall. New Haven, CT: Yale University Press, 2004.

Dorsett, Lyle W. *A Passion for Souls: The Life of D.L. Moody*. Chicago: Moody Press, 2003.

Noll, Mark A. *A History of Christianity in the United States and Canada*. Grand Rapids: Eerdmanns, 1992.

Tucker, Ruth A. *Parade of Faith: A Biographical History of the Christian Church*. Grand Rapids: Zondervan, 2011.

MORE, SIR THOMAS (1478–1535)

English lawyer, statesman, scholar, and author Sir Thomas More served as a councilor to King Henry VIII, and later as the Lord Chancellor of England for three years. Born in London, the son of a lawyer, he attended the finest schools. At the age of 12, More was sent to live with and be mentored by John Morton, the archbishop of Canterbury and the Lord Chancellor of England. More proved to be a fine student, and Morton consequently sent him to Canterbury College, Oxford, where he studied law.

In 1504, More married Jane Colt. The couple had three daughters and a son before Jane died in 1511. More then quickly married Alice of Middleton, a widowed woman. Lady Alice was a beloved wife and a wonderful mother to Thomas's children.

Sir Thomas More's accomplishments and personal influence were extensive. In fact, the renowned Dutch humanist Desiderius Erasmus, a close friend of More, considered him to be England's only genius (Watson). He excelled as an orator, educator, and lawyer. The most noted aspect of his legacy would come from his powerful polemical poems, letters, papers, and books. Among More's most prominent works are the *History of King Richard III* (1512–1519) and the classic book entitled *Utopia* (1516). Because of his literary prowess, More was responsible for writing a letter of rebuttal to Martin Luther (on behalf of King Henry VIII, 1523). In addition, he utilized his prolific pen to address what he saw as the troubling Reformation theologies being propagated by a growing number of English Protestants.

More shared the angst of King Henry with regard to the Lutheran Reformation, but was also opposed to King Henry's political posturing and policies, which were designed to usurp the Pope as the head of the Church in England. Ultimately, King Henry's desire was to make accommodations to facilitate an end to his marriage with Catherine of Aragon, thus allowing him to marry Anne Boleyn. The day after the clergy gave their submission to the king's Act of Succession in 1532, More resigned as Lord Chancellor, citing health reasons. On April 12, 1534, More was given his final opportunity to swear to King Henry's Act of Succession and to take the Oath of Supremacy, which would make the monarch the supreme governor of the Church of England. More was willing to swear to the Act, but not to the Oath. His refusal made him guilty of high treason, and More was then beheaded in London on July 6, 1535. It is reported that his final words were that he died "the king's good servant, and God's first" (*About Thomas More—Famous Quotes*, 2010).

Contemporary Catholicism continues to give great honor to Thomas More. He was beatified by Pope Leo XIII in 1886, canonized in 1935, and on October 31, 2000, he was proclaimed by Pope John Paul II to be the patron saint of statesmen and politicians (Sylvester, 2010).

Troy Matthews

Bibliography

About Thomas More—Famous Quotes (2010). The Center for Thomas More Studies. http://www.thomasmorestudies.org/quotes_1.html. Accessed September 1, 2012.

Barron, Caroline M. *The Making of a London Citizen.* The Cambridge Companion to Thomas More. Edited by George M. Logan. Cambridge: Cambridge University Press, 2011. Cambridge Collections Online. Assessed 09 August 2012.

Sylvester, R.S. "More, Sir Thomas, ST." *New Catholic Encyclopedia Supplement*, vol. 2. Farmington Hills, MI: Gale Cengage Learning, 2010.

Watson, K. "Sir Thomas More." *Prospects: The Quarterly Review of Comparative Education* (1994): 185-202.

MÜLLER, GEORGE (1805–1898)

British philanthropist George Müller was born in Prussia on September 27, 1805, and is well known for his outstanding orphanage work in Bristol, England, where he cared for 10,024 boys and girls over the course of his ministry. Particularly notable is that he never made public requests for finances, but only asked God for provisions in prayer, trusting by faith that the needs of the children would be met. He also established 117 schools for Christian education to over 120,000 children. He was one of the founders of what is known as the Plymouth Brethren movement, and later became the leading representative of the Independent Brethren. His example in fund-raising has influenced the founding of many faith-based independent mission boards, Bible colleges, and ministries.

Müller studied divinity at the University of Halle. Up till that time, he wasn't a Christian, and it showed in his behavior. While at the university he attended a prayer meeting and was convicted when he saw a man on his knees praying. He went home, repented of all his sins, begged God for forgiveness, and immediately began preaching and meeting with Christians.

Müller moved to England to work with the London Missionary Society for Promoting Christianity Amongst the Jews. Later he left the organization and became pastor of Ebenezer Chapel, Teignmouth. He was paid £55 per year but gave it up to live by faith. He moved to Bristol, England, in May of 1832, and preached at Bethesda Chapel with his friend Henry Craik and stayed in that ministry position until his death. Müller founded The Scriptural Knowledge Institution for Home and Abroad to aid missionaries and Christian schools as well as to distribute Christian literature.

Müller opened his home to orphans, and from there, he went on to have several buildings built to house the orphans under his care. At times funds were tight, but Müller never solicited money, and there were many occasions where food arrived just in time for the meal. Müller kept scrupulous records of all the donations and always printed and distributed receipts for all to examine, and these included many stories of God's miraculous supply at just the right time. The George Müller Charitable Trust still exists to this day to dispense funds to Christian ministries.

Elmer Towns

Bibliography

Ellis, James J. *George Müller: The Man Who Trusted God.* London: Pickering & Inglis, 1912.

Müller, George. *Autobiography of George Müller: The Life of Trust.* Edited by H. Lincoln Wayland. Grand Rapids: Baker, 1984.

Pierson, A.T. *George Müller of Bristol.* London: James Nisbet, 1912.

M

✠

D.L. Moody
American Evangelist
1837–1899

NATIONAL COUNCIL OF CHURCHES

The National Council of Churches (NCC) is a cooperative ecumenical agency of American Protestant and Orthodox churches, which was founded in 1950 as the successor to the Federal Council of Churches (founded in 1908). The NCC includes most mainline Protestant denominations and very few evangelical groups. Churches that remain outside the NCC include the Roman Catholic Church, Southern Baptists, Lutheran Church–Missouri Synod, and virtually all Pentecostal, Holiness, evangelical, and Fundamentalist churches (Kurian, 485).

The NCC describes itself as "a community of Christian communions which... confess Jesus Christ...as Savior and Lord." However, its principle areas of concern seem to be social justice, ecumenical unity, international peace efforts, racism, and civil rights, as opposed to evangelism and theological integrity. The NCC was instrumental in the translation and publication of the Revised Standard Version (RSV) of the Bible in 1952. It is viewed by most evangelicals as being sympathetic to liberal theological and social concerns.

Mal Couch

Bibliography

Anderson, Gordon L. "The Evolution of the Concept of Peace in the Work of the National Council of Churches." *Journal of Ecumenical Studies* 21, no. 4 (September 1, 1984): 730-54.

Kurian, G.T. "National Council of Churches." *Nelson's Dictionary of Christianity*. Nashville, TN: Thomas Nelson, 2005.

NESTORIANISM

Nestorianism promotes the heretical teaching that "the second person of the Trinity was two persons: the man Jesus who was born, suffered and died, and the divine Logos, eternal and unbegotten" (Harvey, 645). It is also the popular but inaccurate name for the "Church of the East" that emerged from the Christological controversies of the fifth century. It takes its name from Nestorius (AD 386–451), bishop of Constantinople (428–431), who was alleged to have compromised the integrity of the unity of the two natures (human and divine) in the one person of Jesus Christ. While the heresy is real, the charge that it was explicitly taught by Nestorius and supported as such by the Church of the East has been challenged in recent scholarship. It nevertheless is a charge from which neither Nestorius nor the Persian Christians who embraced his teachings could extricate themselves, and this led eventually to a major schism, separating the Assyrian Church of the East from the Byzantine Church.

The issue was sparked by a sermon (supported by Nestorius) that Mary was not *Theotokos* (the "bearer of God") but *Christotokos* ("bearer of Christ"). In supporting this language change, Nestorius made two mistakes. He defended his position with the suggestion that Mary bore the human person Jesus, but not the divine Logos. This indeed divided the natures in a way that led to heretical conclusions. His second mistake was to take on the ecclesiastical establishment on the matter of the veneration of Mary; a cult that Nestorius rightly considered dangerous because it viewed Mary as only slightly less than a goddess. This brought him into conflict most notably with a rival bishop, Cyril of Alexandria, who accused him of heresy. While it is likely that Cyril sincerely considered Nestorius to have "denied the Alexandrine principle of the unity of the Savior," it was also an opportunity he could not resist "to reaffirm the authority of the Alexandrian see over that of Constantinople" (Gonzalez, 354).

The First Council of Ephesus (431) anathematized Nestorius for his teachings concerning the two natures of Christ, and his rejection of the term *Theotokos* for Mary (Braaten, 84). Nestorius was banished to his former monastery in Antioch, then to the Libyan desert, and finally to Egypt, where he lived to 451. He was still living when his last defender, Theodoret of Cyrrhus, finally agreed at the Council of Chalcedon (451) to anathematize him. The Church of the East, in eastern Mesopotamia and Persia, never accepted his condemnation, and for this reason it was called the Nestorian Church.

In addition to its failure to properly understand the person of Christ as the God-man, Nestorianism is theologically problematic for the doctrine of salvation. If only the human Jesus died on the cross, how is his death of infinite value? In the Eastern churches, with Gregory of Nazianzus, "that which was not assumed is not healed." The Western churches and Protestantism stress that it is only as the God-man that Christ could truly be the mediator between God and man.

Daniel R. Mitchell

Bibliography

Braaten, Carl E. *Mary, Mother of God*. Grand Rapids: Eerdmans, 2004.

Gonzalez, Justo L. *A History of Christian Thought*, vol 1. Rev. ed. Nashville, TN: Abingdon, 1992.

Harvey, S.A. "Nestorianism." *Encyclopedia of Early Christianity*. Edited by Everett Ferguson. New York: Garland, 1990.

NEWMAN, JOHN HENRY (1801–1890)

English theologian, academic, Tractarian, and controversialist John Newman was one of the most illustrious of English converts to the Catholic Church. He began his career as an Anglican priest and scholar and ended as a Roman Catholic cardinal. He had a conversion experience at age 15 in response to the evangelical preaching in a strict evangelical Calvinist wing of Anglicanism. In the same year he matriculated at Trinity College, graduating in 1821 with a BA degree. He had wanted to go on with his studies, but the stress of the academic regimen had resulted in his graduating with third-class honors. Subsequently he acquired a fellowship at Oriel College (1822), a center of intellectualism at Oxford. E.B. Pusey joined him there the following year. Newman was said to be shy to a fault, and this character trait would follow him throughout his career. However, it did not diminish the courage of his convictions or his influence among young Oxford academics.

In 1827, Newman was appointed vicar of University Church of St. Mary the Virgin in Oxford. It was during this time that his association with low-church Anglicans began to abate. He was still associated with the Church Missionary Society as secretary when he circulated a letter suggesting how to wrest power in the society from the nonconformists. This led to his ouster from the post and shortly thereafter his association with the evangelical wing of the Church of England.

After a trip abroad with R.H. Froude, which included a visit to Rome, Newman returned to Oxford in 1833. Inspired by a sermon preached by John Keble, he seems to have taken it on himself to begin writing the *Tracts for the Times*, which launched the Catholic Anglican Tractarian movement at Oxford. Pusey joined this effort in 1835. What became the Oxford Movement would continue for nearly a decade, creating a large following among the students. A turning point for Newman was the publication in 1841 of *Tract 90*, which was a detailed examination of the *Thirty-Nine Articles*, in which he alleged that the *Articles* assumed a misrepresentation of true Catholic teaching. His bishop, Archibald Tait (later archbishop of Canterbury) along with other Anglican Church leaders, responded with severe indignation. *Tract 90* would be the last published. It was only a matter of time before Newman completed his journey back to Rome.

In 1845, Newman entered the Roman Catholic Church. In 1846, he was ordained a priest at Rome and was given an honorary DD degree by the Pope. He returned to England and established the Birmingham Oratory in 1848. He also participated in founding the Catholic University of Ireland. In 1877, he was the first person to be elected to an honorary fellowship of Trinity College, and in 1879, he was appointed a cardinal by Pope Leo XIII. From about 1886 onward Newman's health declined, and in August 1890, he died of pneumonia.

Newman was officially beatified by Pope Benedict XVI in 2010. Some of his major writings include his autobiography, *Apologia Pro Vita Sua* (1865–1866), the *Grammar of Assent* (1870), the poem *The Dream of Gerontius* (1865), and the popular hymns "Lead, Kindly Light" and "Praise to the Holiest in the Height."

Daniel R. Mitchell

Bibliography

Bowden, John. "Newman, John Henry, 1801–90." *Encyclopedia of Christianity*. New York: Oxford University Press, 2005.

Ker, Ian. *John Henry Newman: A Biography*. Oxford: Oxford University Press, 1990

Rennie, L.S. "Newman, John Henry." *Evangelical Dictionary of Theology*. Edited by Walter Elwell. Grand Rapids: Baker, 1984.

NEWTON, JOHN (1725–1807)

Born in Wapping, London, to John and Elizabeth Newton, John Newton emerged from a turbulent and violent life to become a well-known author, pastor, political activist, and writer of the most famous hymn in history, "Amazing Grace."

Newton was born into a seafaring family and, at the age of 17, was forced into service in the British Navy. While in the service Newton displayed an astonishing appetite for violence, rebellion, and recklessness. For attempted desertion, he was publicly flogged by his ship captain and demoted. Later, he was transferred to a slave ship bound for West Africa. His appetite for violence and troublemaking only increased until, following his rescue from a remote West African port, he began to read *The*

Imitation of Christ by Thomas à Kempis. On March 21, 1748, in the midst of a raging storm at sea, he was dramatically converted to Christianity. Newton later wrote of this date, "I began to know there is a God who answers prayer."

Though this was a "great turning day" for Newton, he continued to serve in the slave trade and became captain for several slave-trading ventures in the early 1750s. Over time he became convinced of the inhumanity of the trade and by 1754 left the trade for good. His final voyage as a slave ship captain was a remarkable humanitarian effort for the fact that no sailor or slave perished during the voyage. Slave mortality rates during the Middle Passage generally ranged from 15 to 20 percent as a consequence of the inhumane conditions and maltreatment of their captors. The inhumanity and brutality of the slave trade would continue to haunt Newton and spur him on toward advocating for an end to the transatlantic slave trade.

In 1750, Newton had married Polly Catlett, and in 1755, after he left the slave trade, he went to work as the surveyor of tides for the city of Liverpool. He was mentored in his Christian faith by George Whitefield and John Wesley, who came to Liverpool to preach. By the close of the 1750s, Newton sensed a call from God to serve as an ordained minister, and received his first parish in 1764 at Olney. In that same year Newton published his first book, *An Authentic Narrative*, which became an instant national and international best-seller and dramatically increased Newton's fame. Newton's literary career is also tied to that of the great English poet William Cowper, with whom he collaborated on several volumes of hymns.

In 1780, Newton moved to the St. Mary Woolnoth parish in the heart of London's financial district. It was during this time that he met and advised a young member of Parliament for Hull, William Wilberforce, to remain in Parliament and serve God as a Christian statesman. Newton's testimony in the House of Commons (1788) and his pamphlet *Thoughts upon the African Slave Trade* (1788) made him a highly visible and forceful ally to Wilberforce's efforts to end the transatlantic slave trade. Newton lived just long enough to see these efforts bear fruit when the House of Commons passed legislation to end British involvement in the transatlantic slave trade in 1807.

John Newton served as an influential pastor and writer; he mentored many young ministers and led efforts to place men such as Richard Johnson and William Carey as missionaries in Australia and India. When asked, near the end of his life, to reflect on his life and ministry, the former slave trader and unbeliever replied, "I am a great sinner, but Christ is a great savior" (Aiken, 347).

Douglas Mann

Bibliography

Aiken, Jonathan. *John Newton: From Disgrace to Amazing Grace*. Wheaton, IL: Crossway, 2007.

Metaxas, Eric. *Amazing Grace: William Wilberforce and the Heroic Campaign to End Slavery*. New York: HarperCollins, 2007.

Newton, John. *An Authentic Narrative*. Edited by Bruce Hindmarsh. Vancouver, Canada: Regent College Publishing, 1998.

Newton, John, and William Cowper. *Olney Hymns*. Charleston, SC: Nabu, 2012.

NICENE COUNCILS

In the late second and early third centuries, the theologian Origen of Alexandria was working out his views of God (the Father) and the relation of Father to the incarnate Son, and to the world. He did so by reflecting on Scripture via the Platonic philosophical influences that then dominated the Eastern Roman Empire, especially at Alexandria. Two aspects of Origen's thought that had a lasting influence on the Eastern Church—especially the two opposing sides of what would later be called the Arian Crisis, leading to the first great Nicene Council—were first his view that the Son was "eternally begotten" or "generated" from the Father (not created) and is of one being/essence substance (Greek, *homoousios*) with the Father; and second, his "subordinationism," or that the Son and Spirit are by nature significantly subordinate to and "lesser" in glory than the Father. In the fourth-century Arian Crisis, the Orthodox party would emphasize the first of the two elements, the Arians the latter.

About 318, at Alexandria, the Arian dispute first ignited when a church presbyter, Arius, worked out a view of Christ that radicalized the subordinationist strain from Origen and took it to its logical end. Emphasizing the Father's transcendence, Arius and his followers concluded that the Son, Christ, was only a creature created first out of nothing, that as a creature he had a beginning (a favorite Arian slogan: "There was [a time] when he [the Son] was not"), that the inferior Son had no communication with or direct knowledge of the utterly transcendent Father, and thus that the Son is liable (as a creature) to change and even sin. Being very capable political, literary, and logical tacticians, the Arians strategically called Jesus "god," but only functionally and as a title of honor—that is, he functioned on the Father's behalf. At the same time, the Arians accused the Orthodox position of the heresy of Sabellianism for claiming that the Son is truly God, not a creature. Given the unresolved tensions in Origen's influential theology in the Eastern Church, Arius's views drew numerous supporters. In order to achieve church unity, the Emperor Constantine called the first ecumenical (universal) church council at Nicaea (modern Isnik, Turkey).

The Nicene Council opened June 325, with the emperor present. At the beginning, the Arian leaders presented a formula of faith that so clearly broke away from the church's traditional understanding of the apostolic testimony to the true deity of Christ and his eternal relation to God the Father that the council as a whole erupted in strong disapproval. The basic content of what became the first Nicene Creed probably started as a local church baptismal creed which, under the guidance of bishop Ossius of Cordoba, Constantine's theological advisor, was then modified by the council point by point in order to meet the Arian theological issues in question, especially inclusion of the crucial theological term *homoousios*—i.e., that the Son is of the same divine essence or nature/substance as the Father. As the Nicene Creed states, the Son is "true God of true God," "begotten from the Father, not made," "from the being essence of the Father." Then a list of Arian phrases, reflecting their heretical view of Christ, were condemned. The first Nicene Creed, while essentially espousing the Trinity, only confesses about the Holy Spirit our faith in him. This lack of clarity would change over the next 50 years.

By the latter half of the fourth century, a revitalized Arianism had again asserted itself, even becoming a dominant position in the Eastern Church. At the same time, several other prominent heresies had arisen to shake the faith of the church. Nicene orthodoxy became, for a time, a minority view, but under the leadership of Athanasius (who had been a young deacon under Alexander in 325) and later the Cappadocian fathers (Basil and the two Gregorys), among others, orthodoxy was reaffirmed and clarified at the Council of Constantinople, called by Emperor Theodosius I in 381.

At Constantinople, several heresies were anathematized: that of the Pneumatomachians, who denied the Spirit was *homoousios* with Father and Son; that of the Arians (or Eunomians); that of the neo-Sabellians, who did not see the personal distinctions in God as eternal; and that of Apollinarianism, which denied the true and complete humanity of Christ (that the divine Word replaced Christ's human mind and soul at the incarnation).

Positively, the council affirmed and restored the earlier Nicene Creed (325), but with clarifications regarding the Holy Spirit. Following Basil, the creed states very biblically that the Spirit is "Lord," "Life-giver," "who with the Father and Son is worshiped and together glorified." Though stated in the council's (lost) *tomas*, the official statement of the creed itself does not explicitly state that the Spirit is *homoousios* with Father and Son (as known via a synodal letter of 382). All this and a full trinitarian doctrine for the East (and whole church) were herein major council contributions. It is noteworthy that what has come to be called the Nicene Creed as regularly recited in many churches is not the statement of 325, but this second statement from Constantinople in 381. Hence, it is best called the Niceno-Constantinopolitan Creed.

There was later a second major church council at Nicaea (787), called the Second Council of Nicaea (seventh ecumenical council), intended to bring conclusion to the iconoclastic controversy—that is, the question of the propriety of the use of icons (for example, of Christ, Mary, angels, saints). Despite strong opposition to the practice, which had been growing for three centuries, the Second Council of Nicaea authorized the veneration of such images in the churches.

John Douglas Morrison

Bibliography

Anatolios, Khaled. *Retrieving Nicaea.* Grand Rapids: Baker, 2011.

Athanasius. *The Orations of St. Athanasius Against the Arians.* Edited by William Bright. Oxford: Oxford University Press, 1884.

Gonzalez, Justo L. *A History of Christian Thought.* New York: Harper & Row, 1984.

Grillmeier, Aloys. *Christ in Christian Tradition.* Louisville, KY: Westminster John Knox, 1988.

Kelly, J.N.D. *Early Christian Doctrines.* Harrisburg, PA: Continuum, 2000.

N

NORRIS, JOHN FRANKLYN (1877–1952)

Fundamentalist Baptist pastor John Franklyn Norris was born in 1877 in Dadeville, Alabama, and he was popularly known as J. Frank Norris. He grew up in Texas, where he became a Christian in a Baptist revival meeting in the early 1890s as a teenage boy. He began pastoring at Mount Antioch Baptist Church in 1897 when he was 20 years old. He was a scholar, seminary president, publisher, and most of all, a preacher. He addressed several state legislatures, was a friend of presidents, and even though he was a fierce opponent of Catholicism, he spent time with the Pope at his private villa outside Rome, Italy.

Norris graduated as valedictorian from Baylor University and graduated from Southern Baptist Theological Seminary in Louisville, Kentucky. He was ordained a Southern Baptist minister in 1899 and soon became editor of the the Southern Baptist Convention's state paper, *The Baptist Standard.* Norris also aided Dr. B.H. Carroll with founding Southwestern Baptist Theological Seminary in Fort Worth, Texas, and became the pastor of First Baptist Church in Fort Worth in 1909. He remained in that position until his death in 1952.

In 1935, Norris also accepted the pastorate of the Temple Baptist Church in Detroit, Michigan, and he held joint pastorates for 15 years, flying between the cities to carry on the work of both churches. Weekly Sunday school attendance at both churches reached 5000, making them among the largest churches in America.

Critical of the growing influence of the teaching of evolution at Baylor University, Norris left the Southern Baptist Convention and organized World Baptist Fellowship (originally called the Premillennial Missionary Baptist Fellowship) and founded Baptist Bible Seminary (later Arlington Baptist College). He was a major influence in the independent Fundamentalist movement until his death in 1952.

Norris also indirectly influenced the Baptist Bible Fellowship (BBF), which split from the World Baptist Fellowship in 1950. The BBF established Baptist Bible College at Springfield, Missouri. The latter group was led by G.B. Vick, who took over as the pastor of the Temple Baptist Church in Detroit, and John Rawlings, pastor of Landmark Baptist Temple in Cincinnati, Ohio. During the 1970s, the BBF included many of America's largest churches and followed methods that had been adopted from Norris's earlier influence.

Elmer Towns

N

Bibliography

Dollar, George. *A History of Fundamentalism in America.* Greenville, SC: Bob Jones University Press, 1973.

Hankins, Barry. *God's Rascal: J. Frank Norris and the Beginnings of Southern Fundamentalism.* Lexington, KY: The University Press of Kentucky, 1996.

Morris, C. Gwin. *He Changed Things: The Life and Thought of J. Frank Norris.* Lubbock, TX: Ph.D. dissertation, Texas Tech University, 1973.

Russell, C. Allyn. *Voices of American Fundamentalism.* Philadelphia: Westminster Press, 1976.

✠

JOHN NEWTON
English Minister and Hymn Writer
1725–1807

ORIGEN (CA. 185–254)

Origen, a third-century Christian exegete and the father of the allegorical method of interpretation, was the protégé of Clement of Alexandria and one of the giants of early Greek Christianity. He is best remembered as an exegete who fused Greek thought and biblical exposition by the use of allegorical principles of interpretation.

Origen was reared in the home of Christian parents in the prominent city of Alexandria. As a teenager, he sought to join his father in martyrdom when the latter was imprisoned for the faith. His mother famously hid his clothes to prevent her son from rushing out to declare himself a Christian as well. By all accounts, Origen lived the life of a disciplined ascetic. Eusebius reports that he practiced self-castration in his attempt to win victory over sexual temptation, though he adds that he would later regret this immature act of enthusiasm. Rather late in life, during the infamous Decian persecution, Origen was imprisoned and brutally tortured. He steadfastly refused to recant, thus earning the esteemed title of "Confessor."

Origen's many works were produced under the sponsorship of a wealthy patron, Ambrose. A veritable team of copyists and scribes worked together to make Origen one of the most prolific and influential writers of early Christianity. Sadly, most of his work is lost or extant only in fragments. Three of his best-known works help serve to highlight his role in the early church.

As an apologist, Origen produced *Against Celsus*, which became the definitive reply to pagan objections toward Christianity. His greatest passion, however, was as an expositor and exegete. Though most of his commentaries have been lost, his devotion to the exegetical task can be gauged from *Hexapla*, a work designed as a tool for exegetes. It consists of a six-columned layout of the Old Testament that featured the Hebrew text, a Greek transliteration, and four different available Greek translations. His *On First Principles* can be seen as one of the earliest attempts to produce a systematic theology.

Some of Origen's works would later be condemned as heretical at the Fifth Ecumenical Council. While it is true that at points his works strayed from orthodox doctrines of Christ as found in Scripture, it should be remembered that he worked and wrote in an era before there were such clarifying events as the Council of Nicaea.

Origen's errors seem to stem more from his creativity and originality in exploring difficult doctrinal questions than from any aversion to truth.

Origen's most lasting negative influence on the church is to be found in his almost incalculable influence in the area of hermeneutics. While he is to be warmly remembered for his elevation of the authority of Scripture and the need for careful exposition of the text, his embrace of allegorical methods of interpretation provided a model that would increasingly lead the church further and further away from hearing God accurately through the Bible. The eventual triumph of Alexandrian exegesis over the more literal approach favored by the rival school at Antioch would become a major stumbling block to the pursuit of truth in the years of Roman Catholic uniformity.

Paul Brewster

Bibliography

Crouzel, Henri. *Origen: The Life and Thought of the First Great Theologian*. Translated by A.S. Worrall. San Francisco: HarperCollins, 1989.

Eusebius. *Ecclesiastical History*. Complete and Unabridged. Updated ed. Translated by Christian Frederick Cruse. Peabody, MA: Hendrickson, 2006.

Heine, Ronald E. *Origen: Scholarship in Service of the Church*. Oxford: Oxford University Press, 2010.

Roberts, Alexander, and James Donaldson, eds. *The Ante-Nicene Fathers*, vol. 4, 223-669. Revised by A.C. Coxe. Peabody, MA: Hendrickson, 2004.

O

OWEN, JOHN (1616–1683)

Puritan theologian John Owen was a leading figure and perhaps the greatest theological mind among the Puritan divines. Theologically, he was in agreement with the view of salvation held by the Particular Baptists, Presbyterians, and Congregationalists of his day. He was a major figure in drafting the Savoy Declaration written in 1658, a modification of the Westminster Confession of Faith. Born in Stadhampton near Oxford, he was the second son of Henry Owen, a local Puritan pastor. He entered Queens College, Oxford, at the age of 12 and graduated with a BA in 1632 and with an MA in 1635. Owen read widely and was highly familiar with the theology of the patristic, medieval, and early Reformation eras.

During his time as a private tutor and chaplain (1637–1643), Owen began a 41-year span of writing during which he produced more than 80 works. In 1643, he took his first pastorate in Fordham and in 1646, he moved to Coggeshall, where he served as pastor of St. Peter's Church. At this second church, he converted from Presbyterianism to Congregationalism and began to restructure the church on Congregational principles.

That same year, Owen was asked to preach before the House of Commons. He preached there again in 1649 and impressed Oliver Cromwell so much that the next day Cromwell asked Owen to go with him to Ireland to reorganize Trinity College in Dublin along Puritan lines. Owen served as a chaplain to Cromwell's army and in 1650 was appointed as an official preacher to the state. Cromwell called Owen to London many times during the 1650s to help settle a variety of disputes related to the church. In 1651, Owen became dean of Christ Church, Oxford, and 18 months later, he became vice-chancellor of Oxford University. These positions provided him with opportunities to train ministers for the state church set up by Cromwell. Against his own wishes, in 1653 a Doctor of Divinity degree was conferred upon him by Oxford University.

Because Owen opposed efforts to make Cromwell the king, he was eventually ejected from Oxford and Christ Church. Being unable to minister in the national church, he retired to his home in Stadhampton, where he held services for two years, having rejected episcopacy and the idea of a written liturgy. After the Great Plague (1665) and the Great Fire of London (1666), he returned to London to preach. Owen suffered from asthma and gallstones, which often kept him from preaching but not from writing. He died in 1683 and was buried in Bunhill Fields.

Owen's writings are deeply theological and still popular to this day. His works address a variety of topics such as the perseverance of the saints, Christ's satisfaction, the mortification of sin, Arminianism, catechisms for adults and children, the proper behavior of church members, the Trinity, schisms, temptation, indwelling sin, the authority of Scripture, pneumatology, an exposition of Psalm 130, an extensive commentary on Hebrews, and numerous tracts on religious liberty.

David Roberts

Bibliography

Finn, Nathan. "Review of 'John Owen: Reformed Catholic, Renaissance Man, Great Theologians.'" *Founders Journal*, no. 78 (Fall 2009): page nr. http://www.founders.org/journal/fj78/reviews.html#n_finn. Accessed August 24, 2012.

Owen, John. "The Atonement," *Introduction to Puritan Theology*. Edited by Edward Hindson. Grand Rapids: Baker, 1976.

Toon, P. "John Owen." *Evangelical Dictionary of Theology*. Edited by Walter A. Elwell. Grand Rapids: Baker, 1989.

OXFORD MOVEMENT

The Oxford Movement was a short-lived (1833–1845) but enduringly influential nineteenth-century party within the Church of England that promoted traditional, non-evangelical ideas in England's government-sponsored church. The Oxford Movement was led primarily by men associated with Oxford University, including John Henry Newman (vicar of St. Mary's, Oxford) and John Keble (tutor at Oriel College, Oxford).

From the moment when King Henry VIII forced the separation of the Church of England from Roman Catholicism, England's national church was torn between Protestant and Roman Catholic tendencies (in 1521, Henry himself published a pamphlet *against* the teachings of the reformer Martin Luther). Confronting this spiritual divide, the Oxford Movement aimed to steer the Church of England along a middle path between Roman Catholicism and Protestantism in both its evangelical and liberal forms. Thus, the Oxford Movement at first defined itself by what it *opposed* as much as by what it *favored*, a point strikingly made in the title that its leaders gave to a series of their writings: *Tracts for the Times against Popery and Dissent*. As the movement progressed, however, it increasingly veered toward Roman Catholicism.

John Keble's 1833 sermon "National Apostasy," which suggested that England was in danger of becoming a non-Christian nation, marked the beginning of the Oxford Movement. A deep affection for post-New Testament theological developments is already clear in this sermon, but the Oxford Movement's commitment to these ideas grew until in 1841, Newman argued, in the last of the *Tracts for the Times* (Tract 90), that the Church of England's official doctrinal formula, the *Thirty-Nine Articles*, is essentially compatible with Roman Catholicism. Newman thus led the Oxford Movement to the very doorstep of the Roman Catholic Church, leaving its members with little choice between retracing their steps or stepping into the Roman Catholic Church. In 1845, several leaders of the movement, including Newman himself, took the final step into Catholicism; later, Newman became a Roman Catholic cardinal, thus marking the end of the Oxford Movement as a viable religious movement within the Church of England.

The movement spurred strong evangelical opposition. Evangelicals disliked the movement's enthusiasm for medieval beliefs and rituals, seen in its emphasis on celibacy, ecclesiastical robes, fasting, the use of images in worship, and the like. Evangelicals also objected to the Oxford Movement's teaching on such issues as purgatory and transubstantiation, the view that at the communion service bread and wine *become* the literal, physical body and blood of Jesus. Above all, evangelicals reacted against the Oxford Movement's increasingly Pelagian teaching on salvation.

Greg Enos

Bibliography

Darby, John Nelson. "Analysis of Dr. Newman's *Apologia Pro Vita Sua*: With a Glance at the History of Popes, Councils, and the Church." *The Collected Writings of J.N. Darby*. Edited by William Kelly, vol. 18, 145-248. London: G. Morrish, 1879.

Keble, John. *National Apostasy Considered: In a Sermon Preached in St. Mary's, Oxford, Before His Majesty's Judges of Assize, on Sunday, July 14, 1833*. Charleston, SC: BiblioBazaar, 2009 (1833).

Newman, John Henry. *Apologia Pro Vita Sua: Being a History of his Religious Opinions*. Edited by Martin J. Svaglic. Oxford: Oxford University Press, 1967.

———. *Tract Number Ninety: Remarks on Certain Passages in the Thirty-Nine Articles*. Charleston, SC: Nabu Press, 2011 (1841).

O

PACKER, JAMES INNELL (1926–   )

British evangelical theologian and author J.I. Packer is best known for his writings on evangelicalism, lectures on Puritanism, and teaching at Latimer House, Oxford (1961–1970), Trinity College, Bristol (1971–1979), and Regent College, Vancouver, Canada (1979–1996). Converted in 1944 while a student at Corpus Christi College, Oxford, Packer received his BA, MA, and DPhil degrees from Oxford University. He also received an honorary doctorate from Westminster Theological Seminary.

Packer's influence was spread by his books dealing with various issues pertinent to evangelical theology. His most influential works were *Fundamentalism and the Word of God* (1958), *Evangelism and the Sovereignty of God* (1961), *Knowing God* (1973), *Rediscovering Holiness* (1992), and *Concise Theology* (1993). In regard to Packer's influence, McGrath (280) writes: "To study the life of Packer is thus to explore the story of the emergence and consolation of the post war evangelical movement." He further lauds Packer's practical and spiritual emphasis on historical and theological reflection as a counterbalance to anti-intellectual trends in some extreme forms of evangelicalism.

Packer's later years have been marked both by praise and criticism. He received the Gold Medallion Lifetime Achievement Award from the Evangelical Christian Publishers Association in 1996 for his outstanding contribution to evangelical thinking. At the same time, he has been criticized for his collaboration with the Evangelicals and Catholics Together initiative in the 1990s. Nevertheless, he remains a voice within mainstream evangelicalism.

Ed Hindson

Bibliography

McGrath, Alister. *J.I. Packer: A Biography*. Grand Rapids: Baker, 1997.

Packer, J.I. *Evangelism and the Sovereignty of God*. Westmont, IL: InterVarsity, 1961.

———. *Fundamentalism and the Word of God*. Grand Rapids: Eerdmans, 1958.

———. *Knowing God*. Downers Grove, IL: InterVarsity, 1973.

PAPIAS (CA. AD 60–130)

Papias was the bishop of Hierapolis in Phrygia, which today is in Turkey. Papias and Justin Martyr are the two oldest known postapostolic fathers of the church. Papias is said by Irenaeus to have learned Christianity directly from the apostle John and to have been a colleague of Polycarp, and is thought to have died as a martyr. Eusebius and Irenaeus said that Papias wrote his most famous work, the five-volume *Expositions of the Sayings of the Lord,* around 110. While no complete manuscripts of this work are extant today, fragments have been preserved, mainly from the writings of Irenaeus and Eusebius. Jerome indicates that Papias also wrote a work entitled *Second Coming of Our Lord or Millennium.*

Papias is known primarily for two things: First, he is often cited as a source for extrabiblical oral traditions about the apostles and the four Gospels. Second, as the postapostolic father of premillennialism, he is said to have influenced many in the early church to adopt premillennial views.

Papias is said to be the source of oral traditions about Matthew having been originally written in Hebrew and the notion that Mark's Gospel reflects the viewpoint of the apostle Peter. Many other extrabiblical oral traditions concerning the early church and the apostles are alleged to have been recorded by Papias.

Papias is also known as the father of ancient millennialism, according to Eusebius and Irenaeus. After speaking of the fact that Papias was a millennialist (that is, an early premillennialist), Eusebius said, "For he was a man of very little intelligence, as is clear from his books. But he is responsible for the fact that so many Christian writers after him held the same opinion, relying on his antiquity, for instance Irenaeus and whoever else appears to have held the same views" (*Ecclesiastical History*, Book III, Section 39). Irenaeus provided a sample of Papias's millennialism as follows:

> The days will come, in which vines shall grow, each having ten thousand branches, and in each branch ten thousand twigs, and in each true twig ten thousand shoots, and in each one of the shoots ten thousand clusters, and on every one of the clusters ten thousand grapes, and every grape when pressed will give five and twenty metretes of wine. And when any one of the saints shall lay hold of a cluster, another shall cry out, "I am a better cluster, take me; bless the Lord through me" (*Against Heresies*, Book V, Section 33.3).

Thomas Ice

Bibliography

The Apostolic Fathers: Epistle of Barnabas. Papias and Quadratus. Epistle to Diognetus. The Shepherd of Hermas. Loeb Classical Library, vol. 2. Translated and edited by Bart D. Ehrman. Cambridge, MA: Harvard University Press, 2003.

Gregory, Joel Cliff. *The Chiliastic Hermeneutic of Papias of Hierapolis and Justin Martyr Compared with Later Patristic Chiliasts.* Waco, TX: PhD dissertation, Baylor University, 1983.

Monte, Allen Shanks. *Papias and His Witness to the Development of the New Testament.* Fort Worth, TX: PhD dissertation, The Southern Baptist Theological Seminary, 2008.

PARHAM, CHARLES FOX (1873–1929)

Charles Fox Parham is often credited as the father of the modern American Pentecostal movement. His teachings were spread through his evangelistic events and the school which he founded, Bethel Bible College. Parham emphasized the role of the Spirit in the life of the believer, especially as manifested through healings and "missionary tongues," or the impartation of foreign tongues at conversion for the purpose of evangelism. Parham believed these tongues were actual, known, foreign languages (*xenoglossia*) rather than heavenly or spiritual ones (*glossolalia*), and were the evidence of authentic Spirit baptism at conversion. It was believed by Parham that these tongues were a sign of the end times and of the near return of Christ. This return would be preceded by a revival he termed as the Latter Rain, which was identifiable by the presence of *xenoglossia*.

Parham's development of the doctrine of tongues as the sign for Spirit baptism and his emphasis upon its eschatological implications provided the foundation for early Pentecostalism. Parham also held to the annihilation of the wicked after death and the premillenial second coming of Jesus Christ. The movement begun by Parham was concentrated in the midwestern and southwestern portions of the United States, spreading out from Topeka, Kansas, where Parham's ministry was located.

Parham has been criticized for having complicity with racial segregation, his promotion of Anglo-Israelism, and his public support of the Ku Klux Klan in 1927. Parham's interactions with nonwhite races were complex—he was known to preach to crowds of African-Americans, Native Americans, and Hispanics, and he even tutored a young African-American pastor named William Seymour, who went on to lead the Azusa Street Revival in Southern California. Parham was initially in favor of Seymour's

P

work, but eventually he condemned his revival work for its spontaniety and lack of racial segregation. The two movements then separated, with Parham's movement becoming known as the (Old) Apostolic Faith Movement. Parham's separation from Seymour and questions about his moral behavior limited his continued influence in the movement.

A. Chadwick Thornhill

Bibliography

Blumhoffer, Edith L. *Restoring the Faith: The Assemblies of God, Pentecostalism, and American Culture.* Champaign, IL: University of Illinois Press, 1993.

Dayton, Donald W. *Theological Roots of Pentecostalism.* Grand Rapids: Zondervan, 1987.

Goff, James. *Fields White unto Harvest: Charles F. Parham and the Missionary Origins of Pentecostalism.* Fayetteville, AR: University of Arkansas Press, 1988.

Parham, Sarah E. *The Life of Charles F. Parham: Founder of the Apostolic Faith Movement.* New York: Garland, 1930.

Wacker, Grant. *Heaven Below: Early Pentecostals and American Culture.* Cambridge: Harvard University Press, 2001.

PASCAL, BLAISE (1623–1662)

P

Mathematician, physicist, and religious thinker Blaise Pascal was born the middle child of a wealthy magistrate in Clermont-Ferrand, France. His mother died when he was three, prompting his father, Etienne, to homeschool him until they moved to Paris. Pascal showed a prodigious mind for science and math. Blaise rediscovered Euclidean geometry on his own, which allowed him to make great strides in the field of mathematical probability, philosophy, and apologetics. He devised the first calculating machine and discovered the hydraulic principle known as Pascal's law.

Experiences during the 1640s led Pascal to conclude Christianity demanded more than mere biennial ecclesial observance. He favored Jansenism, a reformed Augustinian Catholic position, writing a defense of it in *Provincial Letters* (1657), which, along with *Pensees,* remain classics in French literature. Pascal remained unfulfilled in his Christian walk until he had a very significant personal encounter with Christ on November 23, 1654, concerning which he wrote an account. So precious was this life-changing episode Pascal secretly sewed the account of his "night of fire" into the liner of his favorite jacket (only accidentally discovered by a servant after Pascal's death). His personal theology emphasized grace alone as the basis of salvation.

Pascal's most important Christian contribution was his apologetic treatise for which he collected thoughts (hence *Pensees*) but never completed. He had a frail constitution his whole life, beset often by dyspepsia, and died early at age 39—perhaps from cancer or tuberculosis (*Pensees*, 16).

Begun originally as an *Apology for the Christian Religion,* the work was completed after his death from his extensive notes. The *Pensees* form a trenchant defense of the fundamental truth of Christianity. The "thoughts" show humans set between radical binary opposites: between nothing and infinity, death and life, meaningfulness and vanity, soul and matter, skepticism and dogmatism, etc. In the midst of these *pensees* dwells the famous "wager on God" argument, which is based on expected value, the probabilistic idea of playing the odds based on expected payback if one "wins." Suppose someone is "on the fence" regarding evidence for or against God. For which possibility shall he wager? The outcome "God exists, and one believes in God" holds the most expected value. For if God doesn't exist, there is no infinite good lost in believing or not, but still conducting oneself well in this life will avoid many pains and sorrows, with the slight inelegance of having believed in God falsely. However, if God does exist, and one fails to believe in him, one gains small positives of sinful pleasures, but loses an *infinite* good (trumping *any* finite good).

For Pascal, faith was a matter of the heart and not reason alone. Man's need for God becomes evident when he recognizes his misery apart from God. At the same time, Pascal found evidences to validate Christianity in history, prophecy, and the self-authentication of Scripture (Bechtel, 749).

Edward Martin

Bibliography

Bechtel, Paul M. "Pascal, Blaise." *The New International Dictionary of the Christian Church*. Edited by J.D. Douglas. Grand Rapids: Zondervan, 1978.

Morris, Thomas. V. *Making Sense of It All: Pascal and the Meaning of Life*. Grand Rapids: Eerdmans, 1994.

Pascal, Blaise. *Pensees*. Translated by A.J. Krailsheimer. Harmondswroth, Middlesex, England: Penguin Books, 1966.

PATRICK, SAINT (CA. 373–463)

Patrick was a missionary sent by Pope Celestine to Ireland, and he arrived in 432, following Palladius's arrival. Questions about Patrick's identity and accomplishments surface from (1) the fact there are only two authentic Patrician documents: *Confession* (late in life) and *Epistle to Coroticus the Soldier* (in which Patrick appeals for the release of Christian female captives); and (2) early Irish annals (eighth-ninth century) naming two Patricks, blurring dates of Patrick's arrival, death in Ireland, and his relation to Palladius (also sometimes called Patricius in the annals). However, from these sources and Ireland's conversion, we can conclude that Patrick was born of Calpurnius, son of presbyter Potitus, in Bonavem Taberniae, Britain (location unknown). When he was 16, pirates took him captive with thousands of others to Ireland, where he was held for six years. After that he escaped, probably to Gaul. He then resumed his education, which through *Confession* he recounts his obsequiousness over simplistic Latin and rhetorical knowledge. Patrick's simplicity, transparency, and sweetness were his hallmarks.

Patrick said God often directed him through dreams. His escape from his captor of six years evidently took this form, as did an experience he had while traveling with some sailors. Patrick prayed for their conversion. They sailed for three days, came to land, then traveled by foot for 28 days. At this point they were close to starvation, and the leader exclaimed, "Why is it, Christian? You say your God is great and all-powerful; then why can you not pray for us?" Immediately Patrick said they should all put their faith in the true God, for he was ever present and would provide for them continually. Soon a herd of pigs appeared before them, causing his travel companions to praise God "with utmost thanks," and to favor Patrick. After another short captivity, Patrick escaped and returned to his family in Britain.

In another dream, the Irish beckoned this "holy youth" to live again in Ireland. Repeated dreams and voices concretized Patrick's resolve to become a missionary in his former place of captivity. Back in Ireland, Patrick evangelized to many, and over time, posted priests throughout the land to hear confessions and to baptize new believers.

The Irish, not part of Roman Britain, had a long history of heathen worship, vulgar sexual practices, human sacrifice (often of the firstborn), various divinations ranged from fire walking to consulting gods in wells or rivers, ritualistic cleansings, baptisms expressing Druidical ritualistic beliefs, special powers ascribed to mistletoe and oak, and the belief that right-handedness was a sign of blessing whereas the converse was a sign of cursing, and so on.

Patrick had the unique experience, character, and insights to effectively evangelize a lost Irish civilization. In spite of the Druidic prohibition against written teachings,

Patrick instilled the importance of written language to propagate and preserve texts. Thomas Cahill well expresses the crucial role Irish monks played in the preservation of texts during the Dark Ages through the establishment (through Columba, et al) of 80 to 100 monasteries throughout much of Europe in the sixth and seventh centuries. Blair (752) notes: "There is no doubt that he broke the power of heathenism in Ireland and that his teaching was scriptural and evangelical." Despite the fact Patrick functioned outside the Church of Rome, he was later canonized a saint by the Roman Catholic Church.

Edward Martin

Bibliography

Blair, Hugh J. "Patrick of Ireland." *The New International Dictionary of the Christian Church.* Edited by J.D. Douglas. Grand Rapids: Zondervan, 1978.

Cahill, Thomas. *How the Irish Saved Civilization.* New York: Doubleday Bantam, 1995.

Ellis, Peter Berresford. *The Druids.* Grand Rapids: Eerdmans, 1994.

McNally, Robert E. "St. Patrick: 461-1961." *The Catholic Historical Review,* XLVII (1961), 305-27.

Patrick, Saint. *The Confession of Saint Patrick and Letter to Coroticus.* Translated by John Skinner. New York: Image Books, 1998.

P

PAUL, THE APOSTLE (CA. AD 1–68)

The apostle Paul was born to Jewish parents in the city of Tarsus. Paul had the benefits of receiving a quality Jewish education in a leading Greek city, and of bearing Roman citizenship. This uniquely enabled him to make an impact on all three cultures of his day.

Little is known of Paul's early life, though much is known of his public ministry thanks to the historical accounts of Luke as well as Paul's own records in his epistles. In his early years he was among the most zealous, well-educated persecutors of Christians. He played an official role in Stephen's martyrdom (Acts 7) and went from house to house in Jerusalem to hunt down Christians. He also secured permission from the Jewish Sanhedrin to pursue Christians as they were fleeing to Damascus and were seeking shelter among the Jewish Christians there.

While Paul was on the road to Damascus, the resurrected Jesus personally confronted him about his persecution of Christians (Acts 9). This encounter with Jesus resulted in Paul's conversion and call to apostleship to take the Christian message to the Gentile world. Physically blinded by the light of Jesus' presence, Paul was led to Damascus, where he was healed, baptized, and began to argue from the Scriptures that Jesus is the Son of God. He spent three years in the Arabian desert preparing for ministry, and afterward, the church in Antioch commissioned him to set out on three missionary journeys into Asia Minor, Greece, and eventually to Rome. During the years from AD 47 to 57, Paul planted churches in four provinces of the Roman Empire (Galatia, Macedonia, Achaia, and Asia). From about AD 51 until his death he wrote at least 13 New Testament letters.

As Paul was once the persecutor of Christians, so he found himself being persecuted by other zealous Jews who did not recognize Jesus as their Messiah. Each time he entered a city, he would first talk with the Jews in their synagogues, then eventually to the Gentiles. His habit was to leave behind some of his fellow laborers to continue the work he had started as he himself moved on to the next city.

Marshall notes that Paul regarded himself as an apostolic missionary (Galatians 1:1; Romans 1:1-6), especially to the Gentiles (Galatians 2:7). He writes, "There emerges incidentally a pattern of missionary preaching where he worked long enough to establish a self-propagating church" (757). Paul also exemplified a fatherly and pastoral concern for the churches to which he wrote his letters. Paul's theology was Christ-exalting, emphasizing Jesus' death, resurrection, and second coming. His gospel was a message to be preached empowered by the Holy Spirit, calling men and women to personal salvation that resulted in spiritual union with Christ (Romans 6:1-11; Colossians 2:12). Thus he could face either life or death with the assurance, "For to me, to live is Christ, and to die is gain" (Philippians 1:21).

As Paul left behind new Christians in city after city, he wrote epistles to them, encouraging them, reporting on God's work among the nations, and helping them answer doctrinal questions. These divinely inspired letters laid much of the foundation for Christian theology, which is what Paul is mostly remembered for in church history. Paul especially focused on the views of Judaizers by reminding Christians that they were saved by grace through faith, and not by their adherence to Jewish laws and customs. He taught that salvation was made possible by Jesus the Messiah's death and resurrection, applied by the Holy Spirit, and received by faith alone.

Paul wrote at least nine epistles to churches and four to individuals, and many have suggested that he was also the author of the epistle to the Hebrews. In his final years, he was imprisoned twice and eventually stood trial before Caesar. Though no reliable account of his death exists, it is generally believed that he was beheaded in Rome by the order of Nero in AD 68.

Kenneth Cleaver

Bibliography

Bruce, F.F. *Paul: Apostle of the Heart Set Free*. Grand Rapids: Eerdmans, 1977.

Drane, John. *Paul*. New York: Harper & Row, 1976.

Gorman, Michael J. *Apostle of the Crucified Lord: A Theological Introduction to Paul and His Letters*. Grand Rapids: Eerdmans, 2004.

Marshall, I. Howard. "Paul the Apostle." *The New International Dictionary of the Christian Church*. Edited by J.D. Douglas. Grand Rapids: Zondervan, 1978.

Polhill, John B. *Paul and His Letters*. Nashville, TN: Broadman & Holman, 1999.

PELAGIANISM

Pelagianism, which arose through the teachings of Pelagius, a Roman monk, was denounced by the early church as heretical. The movement of Pelagianism is thought to have originated from within the ascetic monastic movement of the fourth century, of which Pelagius was a participant. Little is known about Pelagius's background, though it is often held that he was of British, or possibly Irish, descent. His theology was largely driven by pragmatic and pastoral concerns as he was troubled by professing believers whose lives showed little evidence of authentic conversion.

Pelagius's writings have survived primarily through excerpts included in the writings of his opponents (primarily Augustine and Jerome), so the precise reconstruction of his own beliefs is somewhat difficult to achieve. Some have argued that his beliefs were mischaracterized, and thus that he was condemned unnecessarily. Pelagius is said to have opposed the doctrines of predestination and infant baptism, held that Adam's sin did not injure the whole of the human race, and believed that Adam would have died whether or not he had sinned.

In a letter to Pope Innocent I, Pelagius denied opposing infant baptism and declared that he believed in the free will of humans to do good works, though for Christians this was accomplished through divine grace. He adamantly denied that he had taught that the grace of God was unnecessary for salvation, but rather that it enabled humanity to receive what they could not through their own initiative. He was accused by his opponents of changing his beliefs in order to avoid condemnation.

P

Pelagius defended his view of the freedom of the will and was not condemned at that time, forcing Augustine to respond more forcefully to the controversy. Pelagius was later condemned by Pope Zosimus in AD 418.

Pelagianism is typically defined in ways that extend beyond the apparent beliefs of Pelagius himself. Rufinus of Syria and Caelestius also contributed to the beliefs of the movement, though Pelagius has been forever dubbed as its figurehead. Pelagianism, like Pelagius, holds to the radical free will of humans. It holds that humanity can acheive salvation through the exercising of one's free will to choose such. God is said to only foresee the salvation of the elect, as they are not predestined by his choosing for salvation. Pelagianism also holds that humans have not inherited a sin nature from Adam, and thus it is possible (though difficult) to live life without sin.

After the condemnation of Pelagianism, a modified form of the doctrine began to spread, which later became known as semi-Pelagianism. Semi-Pelagianism holds that humans, though depraved, are able to initiate salvation through the exercise of faith or the exercise of the will for the performance of good works. This initiation of salvation through human activity is then completed by God through his grace. Semi-Pelagianism is often historically associated with John Cassian, and was likewise condemned as heretical at the Second Council of Orange (529), though forms of Pelagianism and semi-Pelagianism still persist within Christianity today.

A. Chadwick Thornhill

Bibliography

Evans, Robert F. *Pelagius: Inquiries and Reappraisals*. Eugene, OR: Wipf & Stock, 2010.

Herren, Michael W., and Shirley Ann Brown. *Christ in Celtic Christianity: Britain and Ireland from the Fifth to the Tenth Century*. Woodbridge, UK: Boydell Press, 2002.

McGrath, Alister E. *Christian Theology: An Introduction*. West Sussex, UK: Wiley-Blackwell, 2011.

Olson, Roger E. *Arminian Theology: Myths and Realities*. Downers Grove, IL: InterVarsity, 2006.

Rees, B.R. *Pelagius: A Reluctant Heretic*. Suffolk, UK: Boydell & Brewer, 1992.

PENTECOSTALISM

Pentecostalism is a worldwide Christian movement that emphasizes the baptism of the Holy Spirit and the gifts of the Spirit, generally including speaking in tongues, prophecy, and physical healing. Modern Pentecostalism was "born" just past midnight on January 1, 1901, at the Bethel Bible School at Topeka, Kansas. At that time, as a result of the peculiar Holiness emphasis of the school's founder, former Methodist pastor Charles Fox Parham, student Agnes Ozman requested that Parham lay his hands on her head with the purpose of seeking "the baptism of the Holy Ghost," which would be evidenced by *glossolalia*, or involuntary tongues-speaking. It was Parham, long a preacher in the post-Civil War Holiness movement, who first singled out tongues-speaking as the only sure evidence that one had been baptized with the Holy Ghost. As a result of Ozman's request and Parham's petition, it is reported that she began "speaking in the Chinese language" while a "halo seemed to surround her face." Soon Parham and all the Bethel students sought and had similar experiences. Thus, Parham is often referred to as the father of Pentecostalism.

Soon Parham closed the school and went on to lead several revival and healing campaigns. Then he opened a second school in Houston to teach his unique Pentecostal doctrine, emphasizing the "initial evidence" of tongues-speaking for "the baptism," as a *third* work of grace (after conversion and then entire sanctification, as commonly taught in many sectors of the Holiness movement). At Houston, an unofficial student, W.J. Seymour, the African-American "apostle of Azusa Street," received several months of Parham's teaching. He later moved to Los Angeles, California, and began speaking in an abandoned Methodist church on Azusa Street. Seymour reportedly received the baptism experience on April 9, 1906. Then from 1906 to 1909, Seymour "led" the Azusa Street Revival, which became the ground base from which, directly and indirectly, all Pentecostal denominations and missions agencies had their beginning.

The religious, cultural, and environmental processes that led to the Azusa Street Revival are generally traced back to John Wesley (1703–1791) as the ultimate human progenitor of the movement. Wesley's emphasis upon holiness and entire sanctification led many of his followers, such as John Fletcher (1729–1785), to seek a deeper work of the Spirit in their lives.

In the meantime, the democratization of American culture led to a stronger Arminian and Wesleyan shift in theology. Mother Ann Lee, founder of the Shakers (a movement which included *glossolalia*), and the lawyer-turned-revivalist Charles Finney, played potent roles, methodologically and doctrinally, in ways that opened the path to Pentecostalism. Finney's one-volume *Systematic Theology* and his book of

P

lectures titled *Revivals of Religion* remained the basic literature of the Holiness and Pentecostal movements for well over a century.

In the years prior to the Azusa Street Revival, many evangelicals testified to experiences of an outpouring of the Holy Spirit in their lives, including the famous evangelist D.L. Moody and the Yale University and Divinity School trained evangelist, pastor, teacher, and writer, R.A. Torrey (1856–1928). In his books, such as *Baptism with the Holy Spirit* and *What the Bible Teaches*, he encouraged readers to experience the work of the Holy Spirit in their lives. While Torrey did not espouse speaking in tongues, many believe his emphasis on the work of the Spirit set the stage for the later development of the Pentecostal movement. Even more influential was Asa Mahan (1799–1889), a graduate of Andover Seminary and president and professor of theology at Oberlin College from 1835 to 1850. His books *Christian Perfection* and *The Baptism with the Holy Ghost* shifted the post–Civil War Holiness movement from its previous "pneumaticized" Christocentricity to Spirit-centricity, thus conceptually completing the path leading to the Azusa Street Revival.

After Azusa Street, new Pentecostal denominations and foreign missions organizations sprang up almost immediately. Missionaries were dispatched to Chile (1909), Brazil (1910), China (1910), and Africa (1910). Pentecostalism also spread throughout Scandinavia, Russia, and Europe at about the same time. The Pentecostal-Holiness Church, the Assemblies of God, the Apostolic Faith Church, the Open Bible Standard Churches, Church of God (Cleveland, Tennessee), and the Church of God of Prophecy sprang up over the next few years. By 1923, Aimee Semple McPherson pastored the Angelus Temple of the Foursquare Gospel Church in Los Angeles and attracted huge crowds.

Doctrinal differences eventually developed over whether speaking in tongues as evidence of the baptism of the Spirit was a finished work (W.H. Durham) or a repeatable experience (B.H. Irwin). A second early controversy involved the doctrine of the Trinity. Oneness or "Jesus only" Pentecostalism began in 1911 when Glen Cook and Frank Ewart rejected the doctrine of the Trinity, based on the baptism references in Acts ("in the name of Jesus"). Schism occurred in 1916, and the United Pentecostal Church and other groups resulted. While most Pentecostal statements of faith are clearly Trinitarian, those of the Oneness movement claim that Jesus alone is the Father, Son, and Holy Spirit.

In 1960, the Pentecostal experience of post-conversion Spirit-baptism, as evidenced by tongues, spread from classic Pentecostal denominations and entered into mainline Protestant denominations. Dennis Bennett, an Episcopal priest, experienced "the baptism," and soon the experience was spreading through Episcopal,

Lutheran, Presbyterian, and even Roman Catholic churches. While this development was at first called neo-Pentecostalism, it is most generally known as the Charismatic movement. The dynamics of this movement are generally seen as expressive and participatory worship (which now influences most evangelical churches), lay leadership, female as well as male leadership, and openness to a fresh work of God's Spirit. Criticisms of the Pentecostal-Charismatic movement are generally focused on theological issues related to the doctrine of sanctification, the cessation of apostolic gifts, and the excesses of many in the movement with regard to laughing, barking, prophesying, and other profound expressions of alleged Spirit baptism.

John Douglas Morrison

Bibliography

Anderson, R.M. *Vision of the Disinherited: The Making of American Pentecostalism*. New York: Oxford University Press, 1979.

Donald Dayton, *The Theological Roots of Pentecostalism*. Grand Rapids: Baker, 1987.

MacArthur, John. *The Charismatics*. Grand Rapids: Zondervan, 1978.

Synan, Vinson. *The Holiness-Pentecostal Movement in the United States*. Grand Rapids: Eerdmans, 1971.

Williams, John Rodman. *The Gift of the Holy Spirit Today*. Alachua, FL: Bridge-Logos, 1980.

P

PIETISM

Pietism was a historical movement that returned the church to its New Testament roots of a warm personal faith, the new birth, devotional Bible reading, prayer, and evangelism. It began in Europe and spread to America during the seventeenth and eighteenth centuries.

Pietism began with Philip Jacob Spener (1635–1705), a Lutheran pastor in Frankfurt, Germany, who observed that Luther's emphasis on the above traits had been lost during the Thirty Years' War (1618–1648) in favor of doctrinal rigidity. In his attempt to restore them he began prayer, Bible study, and testimony meetings. His ideas were enumerated in his work *Pia desideria* (Pious desires), which gave rise to the term *Pietism*.

August Hermann Francke (1663–1727), a professor of Hebrew at the University of Leipzig, picked up on Spener's ideas and went to the University of Halle in 1692 to make it a center of Pietistic teaching. Franke had experienced a dramatic conversion and felt that one's conversion should be a life-altering experience. Although neither Spener nor Franke intended that their emphasis should divide the Lutheran Church, the opposition of many Lutheran clergy caused many Pietists to leave Lutheran ranks.

Nikolaus Ludwig, Count von Zinzendorf (1700–1760), a Lutheran nobleman in Saxony, was raised by his grandmother, who was a Pietist. Spener was his godfather, and at age ten, Zinzendorf became a student of Franke at Halle. At age 19 he devoted his life to missionary service. Gathering Moravian refugees, descendants of Jan Huss's movement scattered throughout Europe after the Thirty Years War, on his estate, he organized them into the Moravian Church and led them to embrace the worldwide missions task. Added to this group were pietistic Lutherans and Anabaptists. At a communion service in 1727, revival broke out and prayer became fervent for missions. Thus began the "100-year prayer meeting." Zinzendorf became their bishop and traveled to England and America promoting world evangelization.

It was a Moravian, Peter Boehler, who influenced John Wesley (1703–1791) to seek true conversion. When Wesley attended a Moravian meeting on Aldersgate Street in London in 1738, he found this conversion and stated, "I felt my heart strangely warmed. I felt I did trust in Christ, Christ alone for salvation; and an assurance was given me that he had taken away my sins, even mine, and saved me from the law of sin and death." Wesley's ministry was transformed and he became the leader of the Evangelical Revival in England. He was assisted by his brother Charles and by George Whitefield (1714–1770). Together they founded the Methodist Church, which embodied pietistic sentiments, especially the doctrine of sanctification. Whitefield was also a leader of the First Great Awakening in America. The emphases of Pietism came to influence most American Protestant denominations in the areas of personal prayer, Bible reading, practical devotion, evangelism, and missions.

Carl Diemer

Bibliography

Brown, Dale W. *Understanding Pietism*. Napanee, IN: Evangel, 1996.

Spener, Philip Jacob. *Pia desideria*. Translated by Thomas Tappert. Eugene, OR: Wipf & Stock, 2002.

Stoeffler, F.E. *The Rise of Evangelical Pietism*. London: Brill, 1965.

PLYMOUTH BRETHREN

Although not founded by him, the history and influence of the Plymouth Brethren is coterminous with that of John Nelson Darby (1800–1882). Followers of this separatist movement in Plymouth, England, in fact, were often called *Darbyites*. Darby was trained as a lawyer at Trinity College, Dublin, and began his practice there. After his conversion to Christ, he followed the call to ministry into the Episcopal Church. In time, however, he became disenchanted with the spiritual laxity, the concept of apostolic succession, and the lack of conformity to New Testament Christianity in the established church. At length he renounced his association with the Episcopal Church and joined with a group of believers in Dublin who met in private homes for mutual edification and Bible study. In this small gathering he discerned the "true" church. In 1831, he joined with a similar group in Plymouth, where, under his leadership, the gathering grew to over 1000 people, leading to bands in Exeter, London, and several other places (Woeman, VIII, 305).

The group established a newspaper, the *Christian Witness*, wherein Darby published many of his views dealing especially with the nature of the true church and the second coming of Christ. Here they became known as the Plymouth Brethren. By 1838, due to pressure against them from the established church and factions within, the membership fell sharply and Darby left England to respond to an invitation to come to Switzerland to "fight the Methodists" (Woeman, VIII, 305). From there the movement spread to France, Belgium, Holland, and Italy. In time, groups were organized around the world.

The theological influence of the Plymouth Brethren would be far more widespread than the movement itself. They were particularly noted for their insistence that the true church was marked by spiritual unity, fellowship, and obedience to Scripture against the "manmade systems" of established denominations (Hoffecker, 317). This led to the planting of independent churches throughout Europe, New Zealand, Canada, and the United States. Another element that would shape the thinking of evangelical Christians over the next century was the propagation of Darby's views concerning the dispensational interpretation of Scripture and eschatology. Innovations to classic orthodoxy included teachings concerning the church age as a "parenthesis" in God's program for Israel, a two-stage second coming with a unique rapture for the church, and the idea of a Great Tribulation (3½ years) preceding the establishing of the millennium at the second coming.

Pretribulational ideas were popularized at Bible conferences such as the Niagara Bible Conference in New York (Hoffecker, 317), and the Rumney Bible Conference in

New England. Bible institutes and colleges were founded and generated thousands of missionary graduates who spread these teachings around the globe. Darby's eschatological views also figured prominently in the 1920s as dispensationalists and Princeton Calvinists joined forces against liberalism (Hoffecker, 318). Later, these teachings concerning the nature of the church and the details of biblical eschatology would become defining doctrines for fundamental churches throughout the world.

Daniel R. Mitchell

Bibliography

Coad, F.R. *A History of the Brethren Movement*. Vancouver, Canada: Regent College Publishing, 2001.

Hoffecker, W.A. "Darby, John Nelson." *Evangelical Dictionary of Theology*, 2d ed. Edited by W. Elwell. Grand Rapids: Baker, 2012.

Woeman, J.H. "Plymouth Brethren." *Cyclopedia of Biblical, Theological and Ecclesiological Literature*. Edited by J. McClintock and J. Strong. 12 vols. New York: Harper & Brothers, 1891.

POLYCARP OF SMYRNA (D. CA. 156)

Christian bishop and martyr Polycarp was born in the late first century and served as the bishop of the church at Smyrna (modern Izmir, Turkey), in the province of Asia, in the first half of the second century. According to Irenaeus, Polycarp was a disciple of John the evangelist, who probably pastored the church in nearby Ephesus. Irenaeus reported that Polycarp was his spiritual mentor.

Polycarp is not remembered for producing any major treatises or works of theology. Though Irenaeus indicated that Polycarp wrote a number of letters, only one (addressed to the Philippians) has survived. In that letter, Polycarp responded to the church's request for the corpus of Ignatius's letters, which the bishop of Antioch had written on his way to martyrdom in Rome in 110. In addition to writing a cover letter to accompany Ignatius's letters, Polycarp also instructed the Philippian church on how to handle the challenge of one of its leaders, Valens, who was found guilty of mismanaging church funds.

Polycarp is most well known in church history for the way that he died. According to the author of *Martyrdom of Polycarp*, some Christians had already been put to death in Smyrna, including an elderly man named Germanicus, who had refused to recant his faith. Irritated by the "atheist" Christians—those who refused to worship Rome's traditional gods—a pagan mob instigated the search for Polycarp, which resulted in his eventual trial. According to *Martydom,* Polycarp initially went into hiding, but after having a dream about his imminent death, he gave himself up to the authorities. Once arrested, he offered his captors hospitality and requested an hour to pray. When brought before the governor and given the opportunity to renounce his faith, the aging bishop uttered the famous words, "Eighty and six years have I served him, and he has done me no wrong; how then can I blaspheme my king who saved me?" (*Martyrdom,* 9).

According to the same account, Polycarp was initially burned at the stake, but when his body would not be consumed by the flames, he was killed with a sword. As a martyred Christian and bishop, Polycarp followed in the footsteps of Ignatius of Antioch and ultimately served as a model for other Christians to confess their faith in a context of suffering. The author of *Martyrdom* concluded that Polycarp "was not only a great teacher but a conspicuous martyr, whose testimony, following the Gospel of Christ, everyone desires to imitate" *(Martyrdom,* 19).

Edward Smither

Bibliography

Holmes, Michael W. *The Apostolic Fathers in English.* Grand Rapids: Baker Academic, 2006.

Polycarp. *Epistle to the Philippians.* Ante-Nicene Fathers, vol. 1. Edited by A. Roberts, and J. Donaldson. Peabody, MA: Hendrickson, 2004.

Tucker, Ruth A. *From Jerusalem to Irian Jaya: A Biographical History of Christian Missions.* Grand Rapids: Zondervan, 2004.

P

PRESBYTERIANISM

Presbyterianism was the system of Reformed Christianity established in Scotland in the 1560s under the leadership of John Knox (1514–1572). Presbyterianism emphasized reforming the church in doctrine, government, and worship, and it had a broad impact on society.

The term *Presbyterian* comes from the New Testament Greek word translated "elder." Presbyterian churches are elder-governed: In addition to the minister (teaching elder), churches are led by ruling elders. Presbyterians believe that their system of government is prescribed by Scripture, in contrast to episcopal (or bishop-governed) polity. Biblical Presbyterianism is representative (with popular election of officers), has a hierarchy of courts (local sessions, regional presbyteries, national assemblies), and stresses shared authority. Examples of Presbyterian polity are Knox's *First Book of Discipline* (1560), *The Second Book of Discipline* (1578), and *The Form of Presbyterial Church-Government* (1645).

Doctrinally, Presbyterianism is Calvinistic and Reformed. It emphasizes God's sovereignty, man's depravity, predestination, particular redemption, and salvation through faith in Jesus Christ. Early doctrinal standards were Knox's *Scots Confession* (1560), the *King's Confession*, or *Negative Confession,* (1581), and the *Westminster Confession of Faith* (1647). Presbyterians advocated simple, Puritan-style worship. Knox's *Book of Common Order* (1556) was a liturgy standard until surpassed by the Westminster *Directory for Public Worship* (1645). Scottish Presbyterians emphasized Bible-based worship and unadorned psalm-singing. They resented English attempts to impose the use of bishops, ritualistic Anglican practices, and *The Book of Common Prayer*.

Scottish Presbyterians developed national covenanting and pioneered biblical theories of government and resistance. Influenced by John Knox and Old Testament patterns, they covenanted with the Lord for religious and political ends. The *National Covenant* (1638) and the *Solemn League and Covenant* (1643) exemplified this, and the political theories of George Buchanan and Samuel Rutherford limited the power of the monarchy. England subsequently persecuted the Covenanters, and in the 1680s thousands of Scottish Presbyterians were martyred during the "Killing Time."

Presbyterians migrated to British colonies around the world. Scot-Irish Presbyterians had major impact on the North American colonies in the eighteenth century. Presbyterians were involved in the great revivals of American history, and Princeton Seminary was a bastion of orthodox Christianity. Presbyterians were also heavily involved in world missions.

There are many Presbyterian denominations today. In the United States, the largest body is the mainline Presbyterian Church (USA). The Presbyterian Church in America (PCA) is the largest conservative body. There are many other conservative and evangelical Presbyterian denominations, such as the Orthodox, Evangelical, and Associate Reformed Presbyterian Churches. Some of the best-known leaders of twentieth-century American evangelicalism have been Presbyterian ministers, including Francis Schaeffer, D. James Kennedy, R.C. Sproul, and James Montgomery Boice.

Roger Schultz

Bibliography

Fortson, S. Donald. *Colonial Presbyterianism: Old Faith in a New Land.* Eugene, OR: Wipf & Stock, 2007.

Greaves, Richard. *Theology and Revolution in the Scottish Reformation: Studies in the Life of John Knox.* Washington, DC: Christian College Consortium, 1980.

Hall, David, ed. *Paradigms in Polity: Classic Readings in Reformed and Presbyterian Church Government.* Oak Ridge, TN: Covenant Foundation, 1994.

Smith, Frank. *The Presbyterian Church in America: The Continuing Church Movement.* Manassas, VA: R.E.F., 1985.

Thompson, Ernest Trice. *Presbyterians in the South.* 3 vols. Richmond, VA: John Knox Press, 1963–1973.

PROTESTANTISM

Protestantism is a form of Christianity that emerged in sixteenth-century Europe during the Protestant Reformation. The Reformation began in 1517 when Martin Luther wrote his *Ninety-Five Theses*, challenging the doctrines and practices of the Roman Catholic Church. The name *Protestant* comes from the Diet of Speyer (1529), when reform-minded princes "protested" the actions of the Roman Catholic majority. Protestantism, Roman Catholicism, and Eastern Orthodoxy comprise the three great communions of Christendom.

Protestants opposed the doctrines, practices, and government of Roman Catholicism. A key issue was authority, with Protestants rejecting Popes, councils, and traditions. The issue of salvation also concerned the reformers, who disliked the Roman system of works, sacraments, and indulgences. Protestants were critical of the church hierarchy, with its monetary and moral corruption and the ignorance and immorality of priests. In particular, Protestants rejected the Roman Catholic mass and the doctrine of transubstantiation, which teaches that the bread and wine used for communion literally and substantially become the body and blood of Jesus Christ.

Protestantism retained the ecumenical creeds of the ancient church (such as the Nicean and Apostles' Creed), yet also stressed evangelical and biblical themes. Protestants emphasized the final authority of Scripture (*sola scriptura*) and encouraged Bible translations in the vernacular. Luther translated a Bible into German, and Tyndale a Bible into English. Protestant liturgies also made heavy use of Scripture. Protestantism also emphasized salvation by God's free grace (*sola gratia*), the finished redemptive work of Christ, Jesus as the only mediator between God and man (*solus Christus*), justification by faith alone (*sola fide*), and the sovereign purpose and glory of God (*soli deo gloria*). These five *solas* summarized core teachings of Protestantism.

Different reformers represented multiple strands of Protestantism. Luther

(1483–1546) and Philipp Melanchthon (1497–1560) provided leadership for Lutheranism, which flourished in northern Germany and Scandinavia. Ulrich Zwingli (1484–1531) and John Calvin (1509–1564) led Reformed churches in Switzerland. Reformed movements also existed in France, southern Germany, and Hungary, and Reformed Christianity was especially strong in the Netherlands and Scotland. For national and dynastic reasons, Henry VIII (1491–1547) established a moderate Protestantism in England. Menno Simmons (1496–1561) was an Anabaptist leader, the best known "radical Reformer." Protestantism was established mainly by "magisterial reformers" who worked cooperatively with the state, but Anabaptists emphasized the separation of church and state.

Since the Reformation, Protestantism has spread around the world. The British North American colonies were a safe haven for persecuted Protestants, and by the time of the American Revolution, the United States was overwhelmingly Protestant. And today, Pentecostal forms of Protestantism are growing rapidly in the developing world.

Wherever it has gone, Protestantism has had a profound impact on economic, political, and social life. Some Protestant denominations have lost their spiritual vitality, but many remain true to the great biblical and evangelical principles of the Reformation.

Most Protestants hold to the principles of biblical authority, justification by faith, subjective certitude of salvation, and the priesthood of believers. Protestants differ from Catholic and Orthodox beliefs regarding the hierarchy of the church, papal authority, the means of grace, and the relation of the laity to the clergy.

Roger Schultz

Bibliography

George, Timothy. *Theology of the Reformers*. Nashville, TN: Broadman & Holman, 1988.

Grimm, Harold. *The Reformation: 1500–1650*. New York: Macmillan, 1973.

Johnson, Terry. *The Case for Traditional Protestantism: the Solas of the Reformation*. Carlisle, PA: Banner of Truth, 2004.

Weber, Max. *The Protestant Ethic and the Spirit of Capitalism*. New York: Scribner's, 1958.

PURITANISM

The Protestant reform movement within the Anglican Church took place during the sixteenth and seventeenth centuries. The Puritans advocated "purifying" the Church of England of all religious elements of Roman Catholicism that they believed could not be supported by the Bible. They strongly opposed High Church notions and advocated a Calvinistic theology of sovereign grace and biblical infallibility. They preferred the Geneva Bible (1560) with its anti-Catholic and apocalyptic annotations, and they urged personal piety, morality, and family Bible reading in the home.

Peter Toon (815) divides Puritan history into three distinct periods: (1) from the accession of Queen Elizabeth I in 1558 until her rejection of Presbyterianism in 1593; (2) from 1593 until the beginning of the long Parliament in 1640; (3) from 1640 to the restoration of King Charles II in 1660. Puritanism flourished during the years of the English Civil Wars and the Protectorate of Oliver Cromwell, but was unable to effectively reform the national church. The restoration of the monarchy in 1660 eventually led to the Act of Uniformity in 1662, which effectively forced hundreds of Puritan pastors from their pulpits. As a result, a strongly evangelical nonconformist movement with Puritan sentiments developed that included groups as diverse as Presbyterians, Congregationalists, Baptists, and Quakers.

Puritanism in general involved a rediscovery of God's sovereignty and Christ's all-sufficiency. It wed biblical theology, to spiritual piety and called Christian believers to a life of personal discipline and practical holiness. The key to Puritan devotion was discipline, which resulted in what has often been described as the "Protestant work ethic." At the core of Puritan beliefs was confidence in the absolute authority of Scripture, by which standard the Puritans attempted to reform or "purify" church life in England. For the Puritans, true devotion to Christ involved strict obedience to the moral law of God. They viewed the truth of God as the only valid basis for law, justification, education, and philosophy. Otherwise, man was viewed as being left with meaningless options of self-preservation and self-gratification. Thus, the Puritans emphasized the practical use of the law to restrain sin, convict the soul, lead men to Christ, and direct believers' conduct.

The English Puritans were preachers who appealed to the people. The founding of Emmanuel College at Cambridge in 1584 encouraged the training of Puritan preachers whose influence spread by the publication of their sermons and by the example of their personal conduct. Their devotion to Scripture caused them to declare the "words of wisdom" so often heard in the High Church. Their application of biblical truth to practical living caused their preaching to be classified as "practical divinity" (Haller, 19). Haller notes they were "bent on saving the world through religious revival and ecclesiastical reform." They taught people what to believe and how to act in accord with their own theological views.

The Puritans were also quick to express their disdain for those with whom they disagreed, including Arminians, papists, antinomians, Anabaptists, witches, blasphemers, and atheists. Eventually they leveled their criticisms at William Laud, archbishop of Canterbury and an advocate of High Church Anglicanism. Between 1640 and the outbreak of civil war in 1642, many Puritans painted an apocalyptic vision that convinced the Long Parliament of a just cause for war against King Charles I. Preachers like Joseph Caryl, William Sedgwick, and William Bridge announced that Christ would soon return to establish a thousand-year rule of the saints on earth. Satan would be bound, Babylon would fall, and the Antichrist would be forever defeated by the removal of both Charles and Laud. They viewed the Parliament as God's instrument to bring in the millennium and a New Jerusalem in London. By 1643, the Westminster Assembly convened to revise the Thirty-Nine Articles of the Church of England to remove every element considered to be Arminian, Pelagian, or Roman. Even the renowned theologian Jon Owen preached before Parliament the day after the execution of Charles I, quoting Jeremiah 15:19-20 as justification for the king's execution.

Various factions within Puritanism (Fifth Monarchists, Levellers, Diggers) ultimately led to the disintegration of the Puritan consensus and the movement divided and splintered into opposing factions. By the time of Cromwell's death in 1658, the Congregationalists, led by Goodwin, Bridge, Caryl, and Owen, met at Savoy to adopt their own *Declaration of Faith and Order*. Unfortunately for most Puritans, the restoration of the monarchy in 1660 meant the end of their political dominance in England. Thereafter, many Puritans moved to the Massachusetts colony in America in the hopes of pursuing the dream of a "pure church." As a result, American Puritanism reached its zenith in the eighteenth century under the preaching of men like Jonathan Edwards and Cotton Mather. Today, the influence of Puritanism can still be seen in many elements of American evangelicalism.

Ed Hindson

Bibliography

Haller, William. *The Rise of Puritanism*. Philadelphia: University of Pennsylvania Press, 1978.

Hindson, Edward E., ed. *Introduction to Puritan Theology*. Grand Rapids: Baker, 1976.

Ryken, Leland. *Worldly Saints*. Grand Rapids: Zondervan, 1986.

Toon, Peter. "Puritanism." *The New International Dictionary of the Christian Church*. Edited by J.D. Douglas. Grand Rapids: Zondervan, 1978.

Wakefield, G.S. *Puritan Devotion*. London: Epworth Press, 1977.

QUAKERS

Also known as the Society of Friends, the Quaker movement originated in the northern part of England circa 1647. At the time, England was going through a period of religious and political rebellion, and "Quakerism was the embodiment of the Puritan dislike to the 'one man' system, and to set forms of service" (Bickley, 7). Quakerism finds its roots in its early leader and founder George Fox (1624–1691), who began traveling and preaching after his revelation of truth from God via a mystical experience. Fox believed in an "inner light" that was given to all men by the creator God. Such light allowed God to speak directly to any person. Because God could speak directly to his people, Quaker ministers did not need formal training, and Scripture was secondary to the revelations (although they said those revelations should not contradict Scripture).

Quaker distinctives were simple and charitable living; devotion to truth; women as ministers; and equality of sex, class, nation, and race. Quakers were pacifists and instrumental in advocating for the abolition of slavery. Fox's beliefs, and those of the Friends, included living a moral life, listening to the "innver voice" of God speaking, the nonpractice of communion and baptism, and silent meetings, or waiting worship (in which the congretation sits in silence and waits for God to inspire someone to speak). Quakerism spread throughout England, neighboring countries, and overseas; such dispersion was due in part to their strong missionary focus. Many Quakers were persecuted and imprisoned because of their beliefs and teachings.

Quakers began to arrive in America in the 1680s; however, many faced imprisonment and even death because of their refusal to attend services, pay tithes to the established church, and suspicions of witchcraft. The Friends experienced their first schism in 1827, which led to the eventual formation of the Friends General Conference, the most liberal branch of Friends. In 1887, many of the other Friends signed the Richmond Declaration, which lessened the emphasis on the "inner light" for that of biblical authority. Eventually this group of Friends would split into the Friends United Meeting and the Evangelical Friends International. The Evangelical Friends are the closest to mainline Protestant churches in their theology and practice, while those who are part of the Friends United Meeting still hold to Fox's early views.

Among Quakerism's notable followers were Robert Barclay (who became the theologian of the movement), William Penn (founder of Pennsylvania), Mary Dyer, Elizabeth Fry, John Woolman, Rufus M. Jones, Susan B. Anthony, Herbert Hoover (thirty-first president of the United States), and Richard Nixon (thirty-seventh president). The Quakers' lack of interest in doctrine has fostered extreme mysticism and a lack of evangelical theology.

Barbara Hubbard

Bibliography

Bickley, Augustus C. *George Fox and the Early Quakers.* London: Hodder & Stoughton, 1884.

Cairns, Earle E. *Christianity Through the Centuries: A History of the Christian Church.* Grand Rapids: Zondervan, 1981.

Dandelion, Pink. *The Quakers: A Very Short Introduction.* Oxford: Oxford University Press, 2008.

Hamm, Thomas D. *The Quakers in America.* New York: Columbia University Press, 2003.

Q

REFORMATION, THE

While the Reformation of the sixteenth century had numerous social and political aspects, it was essentially a religious revival and renewal. The Reformation took place at a time when the world was in transition, with rising nationalism opposing medieval papal claims to universal power. The Holy Roman Empire was crumbling, and several nations made an attempt to reform the church in their own countries. Germany, Switzerland, Holland, and England had the greatest success in this endeavor. Medieval feudalism was also yielding to a rising merchant middle class. Furthermore, the Renaissance, which brought a revival of learning, provided a printing press, a critical edition of the Greek New Testament that would be used by the reformers to translate the New Testament into the vernacular of their country, and the grammatical-historical method of interpreting the Scriptures all contributed to the Reformation. Previous attempts to reform the church—most notably by John Wycliffe in England, Jan Huss in Bohemia, and the Waldensians—had failed to gain widespread support up to that time.

Three distinct reformation efforts are historically identifiable. The *classical*, or magisterial, reform of Luther, Zwingli, Calvin, Knox, and the Anglicans sought to eliminate the theological and moral abuses of the medieval church without separating church and state. The *radical*, or Anabaptist, reform sought to take the church back to its New Testament roots, including the separation of church and state. Both the classical and radical efforts agreed on three principles: the sole authority of the Scriptures, faith as the only means of salvation, and the priesthood of the believer. The *counter* Reformation of the Roman Catholic Church sought only to correct internal moral problems and clarify Catholic doctrine.

Historians have generally agreed that the Reformation began with the posting of Martin Luther's (1483–1546) *Ninety-Five Theses* to the doors of All Saints' Church in Wittenberg on October 31, 1517. He was an Augustinian monk who found salvation, not through the church or good works, but through the Scriptures, especially Romans 1:17. When the indulgence trade invaded his territory, he objected to this sale of spiritual benefits (time off from purgatory) for money and expressed his dissent in his *Theses*. Between 1517 and 1521, Luther, operating from Wittenberg, spread the

Reformation throughout Germany. After being excommunicated by the Church of Rome in 1520, he was further banned from the empire at the Diet of Worms in 1521. However, his reform movement had taken root, especially in Germany, and served as an example for reformers in other countries. Luther was a prolific writer as well, and the most significant theological document to appear out of the Lutheran Reformation was the Augsburg Confession (1530).

Ulrich Zwingli (1484–1531) was a contemporary of Luther. His reform efforts in Zurich, Switzerland, began the movement that has come to be known as reformed theology. He worked out of the Great Minster, Zurich's cathedral church, and sought to advance his reform through academic disputations. Some of his followers desired to go further with the reform than Zwingli was willing to go and became founders of the Anabaptist movement.

Zwingli saw his reform spread to Strasbourg, Bern, and Basel. However, his early death in battle prevented his movement from reaching its full potential. It was John Calvin (1509–1564) who took up the reformed mantle in Geneva. Calvin adopted a strict system of reformation and, as a result, struggled mightily through two periods of ministry in Geneva, 1536–1538, and 1541–1564. His greatest writing was his systematic theology titled *Institutes of the Christian Religion,* which carried his views into France, Holland, and Scotland. His system of doctrine, posthumously called Calvinism, is considered by many to be his most lasting contribution.

The Anglican reform in England was more political than religious in its origins. King Henry VIII (1491–1547), unhappily married to Catherine of Aragon, and without a male heir, decided to divorce Catherine and marry Anne Boleyn. However, he was unable to gain the Pope's blessing for this divorce and subsequently declared that he, rather than the Pope, was the head of the English (Anglican) Church. He accomplished this change through the Act of Supremacy (1534). Before he was done, Henry had taken six wives (one at a time), but was able to sire only one son. When his son, Edward VI, became king, he continued the emphases of his father, but then when Henry's first daughter, Mary, became queen, she reversed them and made England Roman Catholic again. When her half-sister, Elizabeth, became queen, she restored the Anglican Church, and during a 45-year reign "established" the English Church as Protestant. The major documents of the Anglican Church, the *Book of Common Prayer* and the *Thirty-Nine Articles*, do not distance the Anglican Church as far from the Roman Catholic Church as the other reform movements had.

In Holland, the reformed emphasis of Calvin took root, but the modification of Calvinism, which came to be known as Arminianism, was also spawned there. In Scotland, the work of John Knox's (1514–1572) reform was very successful. Having studied under Calvin, he established a rigorous system of reformed theology. His major opponent was Queen Mary of Scotland, a devout Roman Catholic, but she was forced to abdicate in 1567 and Scotland was won for the Protestant Reformation.

French Protestants (Huguenots), although they strove mightily for reform in France, were severely persecuted and ultimately, were unsuccessful. In Spain, the Protestants achieved even less success.

The radical, or Anabaptist (see article on same), reform went further than the classical reformers in establishing a church patterned after the first-century church described in the New Testament. They are best known for their practice of believer's baptism and the separation of church and state.

Although the Roman Catholic Church disagreed with Protestant theological conclusions, it recognized that immorality within the Catholic Church had become problematic and began what has been called the Counter-Reformation. The Church made significant progress in cleaning up medieval immoral practices. However, it made its commitment to medieval theology even more rigid than before through the Council of Trent (1545–1563), which refuted the sole authority of Scripture, faith as the sole means of salvation, and the priesthood of the believer.

The Thirty Years' War (1618–1648) was an attempt to settle the religious differences between Roman Catholics and Protestants through military means. However, neither side was able to win a clear victory. The Peace of Westphalia (1648) divided Europe into Roman Catholic and Protestant areas and declared that the ruler of an area could dictate the religion of his realm. In the end, the Protestant Reformation changed the course of Western civilization and set the stage for the emergence of what would become the modern European states as well as influencing colonial America.

Carl Diemer

R

Bibliography

Bainton, Roland H. *The Reformation of the Sixteenth Century*. Boston: Beacon Press, 1960.

Dickens, A.G. *Reformation and Society in Sixteenth Century Europe*. London: Thames & Hudson, 1966.

Grimm, Harold J. *The Reformation Era*. New York: Macmillan, 1954.

Hillerbrand, Hans J. *The Protestant Reformation*. New York: Harper Perennial, 2009.

Rops, H. Daniel. *The Protestant Reformation*, New York: Doubleday, 1961.

REMONSTRANCE

Outside of the writings of its founder, Jacobus Arminius, the Remonstrance is the foundational statement of Arminian theology. On January 14, 1610, soon after Arminius's death, approximately 46 members of the Dutch Reformed clergy (the exact number is debated) met in the city of Gouda to sign the *Remonstrantie ende Vertooch* (Remonstrance and Representation). Drawn up by Arminius's close friend Johannes Wtenbogaert, the Remonstrance had three primary purposes. First, it presented five alleged errors of the prevailing Reformed theology of the time, with five corresponding explanations of what the Arminians believed the Bible to teach. Second, the document called for a national synod to revise the Belgic Confession and the Heidelberg Catechism, the standards of doctrine for the Dutch Reformed Church, because it was believed these documents needed to be brought into closer harmony with the Bible. Third, the statement called upon the States of Holland for toleration of Arminianism.

The Remonstrance primarily addressed the issues of predestination and salvation. It affirmed that God has eternally and unchangeably elected for salvation those who believe in Jesus Christ and persevere in that faith until the end; that in accordance with this work of election, Jesus Christ died on the cross for every person in order to obtain reconciliation and forgiveness for every person, though only those who believe in him partake of this forgiveness; that no person can produce saving faith through his own free will because each person is in a state of rebellion before God, and therefore it is necessary that God through the Holy Spirit cause him to be born again so that he can live for Christ; that God's grace is the beginning, progress, and end of salvation and any good a person does, and apart from this grace no good is possible, though this grace is not irresistible; and that those who are truly saved by Christ through faith are enabled to persevere in that faith, though the Scriptures needed to be more thoroughly examined concerning whether or not a believer can apostatize from their faith.

In affirming these five tenets, the Remonstrance rejected both supralapsarian and infralapsarian forms of predestination, that Jesus Christ only died for the elect, and that the Spirit's work of salvation was irresistible. While the Remonstrance is not a complete statement of Arminian theology, it captures its essence.

In August of 1610, the States of Holland responded to the Remonstrance by granting the Remonstrants (their name arose from the name of their document) tolerance. On March 16, 1611, six Remonstrants met with six of their opponents before the States of Holland in the Hauge, where a Counter-Remonstrance was presented. These attempts at dialogue and conciliation were short-lived, however. Over the ensuing decade the conflict between the Remonstrants and the Counter-Remonstrants became more and more polarized, eventually leading to the condemnation of the Remonstrance at the Synod of Dort in 1618–1619 and the expulsion of over 200 Remonstrant pastors. The Remonstrants would not be officially tolerated in Holland again until 1795.

Gary L. Shultz Jr.

Bibliography

Bangs, Carl. *Arminius: A Study in the Dutch Reformation*. Nashville, TN: Abingdon, 1971.

Harrison, Archibald Walter. *The Beginnings of Arminianism to the Synod of Dort*. London: University of London Press, 1926.

Olson, Roger E. *Arminian Theology: Myths and Realities*. Downers Grove, IL: InterVarsity, 2006.

RIDLEY, NICHOLAS (CA. 1500–1555)

English reformer and martyr Nicholas Ridley was born in Northumberland, England, and was educated at Pembroke College, Cambridge, where he became a fellow in 1524. Ridley studied at the Sorbonne in Paris and the University of Louvain in France from 1527–1530, then returned to Pembroke and was made proctor of the University of Cambridge. In 1537, he was appointed chaplain to Thomas Cranmer, archbishop of Canterbury, and in 1541, he became chaplain to King Henry VIII and was instrumental in carrying out Henry's reforms. By 1545, when he became canon of Westminster, he clearly rejected the Catholic doctrine of transubstantiation and convinced Cranmer, who in turn convinced Hugh Latimer.

In 1547, Ridley was named bishop of Rochester and assisted Cranmer in coupling the *Thirty-Nine Articles* and *The Book of Common Prayer* of 1549 and its revision in 1552. In 1550, Ridley was consecrated bishop of London. However, after the death of Edward VI in 1553, he opposed both Mary and Elizabeth as the proper heirs to the English throne in favor of Lady Jane Grey. When Mary Tudor ("Bloody Mary") ascended the throne, he was imprisoned along with Cranmer and Latimer at Oxford in 1554, and burned at the stake with Latimer for heresy against the Roman Catholic Church in 1555. Cranmer was executed the following year. Together, the three became among the most famous English Protestant martyrs of the sixteenth century.

Ed Hindson

Bibliography

Christmas, Henry, ed. *The Works of Nicholas Ridley, D.D.: Sometime Lord Bishop of London, Martyr 1555*. Eugene, OR: Wipf & Stock, 2008.

Ridley, J.G. *Nicholas Ridley*. London: Longman, 1957.

ROBERTS, GRANVILLE ORAL (1918–2009)

Popularly known as Oral Roberts, he was an American Pentecostal evangelist and founder of Oral Roberts University in Tulsa, Oklahoma. Claiming to have been healed from tuberculosis in 1935, Roberts became an evangelist with the Pentecostal Holiness Church in 1936. In 1937, he claimed to receive the gift of healing, and in 1947, launched the Oral Roberts Evangelistic Association with an emphasis on gospel preaching and physical healing. Many of his dramatic healing crusades were captured on film and broadcast on his television network beginning in 1954 and went on to reach a worldwide audience of millions of viewers by the 1970s, making him a major figure in the televangelist movement of the times. Largely uneducated himself, Roberts valued education and was determined to establish an accredited institution of higher learning where every teacher was a "born again, baptized with the Spirit" believer. In 1962, he founded the Oral Roberts University in Tulsa.

Roberts's theological views aligned with orthodox Arminian Pentecostal beliefs, including a strong emphasis on the "latter rain" of the Holy Spirit in the last days, speaking in tongues, and the gift of healing. Harrell (440) observes, "Oral Roberts [was] the greatest popularizer of the central beliefs of the Pentecostal revival of the early twentieth century." Roberts is also remembered for popularizing slogans like "Expect a miracle," "Turn your faith loose," and "Something good is going to happen."

In 1968, to the surprise of many of his fellow Pentecostals, Roberts joined the United Methodist Church. Often criticized by those outside the Pentecostal and Charismatic movements, Roberts nevertheless left his imprint on American evangelicalism in the twentieth century.

Ed Hindson

Bibliography

Harrell, D.E. *Oral Roberts: An American Life*. San Francisco: Harper & Row, 1985.

Potts, R.R. *My Dad, Oral Roberts*. Nobel, OK: Icon, 2011.

Roberts, Oral. *The Call*. Garden City, NY: Doubleday, 1972.

ROBERTSON, MARION "PAT" (1930–   )

American Charismatic televangelist and Christian educator Marion Robertson was ordained in the Southern Baptist ministry shortly after his conversion. In 1959, he purchased a television station in Norfolk, Virginia, which eventually became the Christian Broadcasting Network (CBN), headquartered in Virginia Beach, Virginia. In 1968, he became the host of *The 700 Club*, which became America's premier Charismatic Christian talk show. In 1977, Robertson founded what is now Regent University, including a law school, and Operation Blessing, a worldwide humanitarian relief agency. In 1989, he established the Christian Coalition of America to influence social and political issues. He has authored numerous books including, *Shout It from the Housetops* (1972), *The Secret Kingdom* (1982), and *The New World Order* (1991).

Ed Hindson

Bibliography

Harrell, David Edwin. *Pat Robertson: A Life and Legacy*. Grand Rapids: Eerdmans, 2010.

Marley, David John. *Pat Robertson: An American Life*. Lanham, MD: Rowman & Littlefield, 2007.

ROGERS, ADRIAN (1931–2005)

Southern Baptist pastor Adrian Rogers was known for his golden voice, powerful preaching, and his leadership role in the conservative resurgence in the Southern Baptist Convention (SBC) in the late twentieth century. He earned his BA at Stetson University and MDiv at New Orleans Baptist Seminary, and received six honorary doctorates, including a DTS from Southwest Baptist University and a DD from Liberty University. A native of Florida, Rogers pastored the First Baptist Church, Merritt Island, Florida, before accepting a call to pastor the historic Bellevue Baptist Church in Memphis, Tennessee, from 1972–2005.

Rogers's election as president of the SBC in 1979 effectively began the conservative resurgence in the SBC led by Rogers, Charles Stanley, Jerry Vines, Paige Patterson, and Judge Paul Pressler. Rogers was eventually elected president of the SBC a total of three times (1979–1980, 1986–1987, 1987–1988). Under his leadership and influence, the SBC repudiated incipient liberalism as theological conservatives took back control of the seminaries, Sunday school boards, missions, and publishing arms of the convention. Rogers's radio and television broadcasts of *Love Worth Finding* are still on the air nationwide.

Ed Hindson

Bibliography

Rogers, Adrian, ed. *By His Grace and for His Glory.* Memphis, TN: Bellevue Baptist Church, 2003.

Rogers, Joyce. *Love Worth Finding: Life of Adrian Rogers.* Nashville, TN: Broadman & Holman, 2005.

ROMAN CATHOLICISM

Roman Catholicism is the largest sect of Christianity (approximately 1.1 billion people worldwide). The word *catholic* is derived from the Latin word *catholicus*, meaning "universal." The name *Roman Catholic* emphasizes the church's connection with, and recognition of, the authority of the Pope (the bishop of Rome).

The Roman Catholic Church has developed an ecclesiastical and theological system based upon three authorities: sacred tradition, sacred Scripture, and the magisterium of the church. The ecclesiastical structure and the doctrinal distinctives of Roman Catholicism are a result of a lengthy historical development.

From a historical perspective, the ecclesiastical office of Pope was nonexistent until the sixth century. Prior to this time, there were only three offices that were common to Christianity: bishops (also called elders), presbyters, and deacons. Officers and their organization varied from location to location. The term *Pope* originally referred to important or respected bishops, such as Cyprian and Athanasius.

The title "Pope," in the modern sense, was first used by Leo of Rome (fifth century). Leo believed that Christ granted Peter and his successors (Roman bishops) the authority to rule the church. The traditional arguments for the papacy originated in Leo's writings. For some time after Leo, the churches retained their organization apart from Rome. As late as the mid-sixth century, bishop Gregory of Rome still did not claim universal authority over the church.

In the following centuries, however, the position of bishop changed. Certain bishops became prominent in ecclesiastical and political ways. The bishops of Alexandria, Antioch, Jerusalem, Constantinople, and Rome became the major influencers until the rise of the Muslim empire. With the spread of Islam and the subjugation of the Eastern churches under Muslim control, the bishop of Rome became prominent; and the title "Pope" began to assume its modern significance.

Many doctrines of the Roman Catholic Church developed over the course of multiple centuries. For example, the doctrine of purgatory was introduced by Pope Gregory in the sixth century. Through the centuries, a number of other doctrines were introduced by the Pope and affirmed by the magisterium. Some of these doctrines include the veneration of images and relics, the canonization of dead saints, the celibacy of priests, Maryology, and tradition accorded equal authority with Scripture. For example, in 1870, Vatican I asserted the infallibility and primacy of the Pope. Nearly a century later, Vatican II (1962–1965) expressed a new ecumenical spirit of cooperation with Protestantism, Islam, and Eastern Orthodoxy. The council also affirmed the sacramental value of indulgences that the Church believed contained "the merits of the Blessed mother of God" (Flannery, 70-71).

On October 11, 1992, the thirtieth anniversary of Vatican II, Pope John Paul II endorsed the new *Catechism of the Catholic Church* as the authoritative statement of Catholic faith and doctrine, which includes the affirmation that "baptism is necessary for salvation" (*CCC,* 1257).

Critics of Roman Catholicism in the twenty-first century object to a variety of issues, especially the sexual abuse of children by Catholic priests, for which the church has had to pay large sums in legal settlements. The resignation of Pope Benedict XVI because of ill health in 2013 was the first papal resignation in almost 600 years. He was replaced by Pope Francis, the first Pope to be a Jesuit and the first ever from Latin America.

George Bannister

R

Bibliography

Boettner, Loraine. *Roman Catholicism.* Phillipsburg, NJ: P&R Publishing, 2000.

Catechism of the Catholic Church. Rome: Liberia Vaticana, 1992.

Edwards, David. *Christianity: The First Two Thousand Years.* Maryknoll, NY: Orbis Books, 1997.

Flannery, Austin. *Vatican Council II—The Conciliar and Post-Conciliar Documents.* Northport, NY: Costello, 1988.

Gendren, Mike. "Roman Catholicism." *The Popular Encyclopedia of Apologetics.* Edited by Ed Hindson and Ergun Caner. Eugene, OR: Harvest House, 2008.

Kohmescher, Matthew. *Catholicism Today: A Survey of Catholic Belief and Practice.* 3d ed. New York: Paulist Press, 1999.

C.H. Spurgeon
English Baptist Pastor
1834–1892

SABELLIANISM

Also known as monarchianism, modalism, subordinationism, and patripassianism, sabellianism is a third-century heresy that stressed the unity of the Godhead to such a degree that the Son and the Holy Spirit were deemed modes or aspects of the one heavenly Father rather than coeternal Persons. A modern variant of this teaching is expressed in Oneness Pentecostalism, which views the Trinity in terms of the divine manifestation as Father, Son, or Holy Spirit.

Sabellius was a third-century priest and theologian whose influence upon early Christianity was felt from Rome to Libya in North Africa. The monarchian teachings advanced by Sabellius were known to Justin, Athanasius, Basil, Hilary, Chrysostom, and continued to be known as late as Epiphanius (d. 403), who attested to the great number of followers as late as 375, and later still, Augustine. All these early church figures condemned Sabellius's teachings as misrepresentative of the Trinity.

What is known of Sabellius is known chiefly from his opponents, and it is strongly suspected that his ideas may have been subject to revision in the posturing of his theological opponents. The teachings of Sabellius especially caught the attention and opposition of Hippolytus and Tertullian, from whom he received the eponym *patripassian*, inasmuch as the logical extension of his thought was that the Father suffered on the cross in the "mode" of the Son. "By this Praxeas [Sabellius] did a twofold service for the devil at Rome: he drove away prophecy, and he brought in heresy; he put to flight the Paraclete, and he crucified the Father" (*Adv Prax*, I).

However, whether explicitly taught by Sabellius or not, the early theologians of the church defined the position as heresy at the Council of Nicaea (325) and at later councils. They rightly discerned the danger of attempting to describe the eternal and transcendent relations of the Father, Son, and Spirit in temporal or human terms. For example, Sabellius had used the sun as an analogy of what the Trinity was like. As the sun emits light, warmth, and has circular form, so it is with God. He illuminates through the Son, warms the heart through the Holy Spirit, and has shape according to the Father.

Dating from the time of Nicaea, it would be another 200 years before the early church was able to establish a vocabulary to talk about the unity and diversity of the

Godhead in the Trinity. Thoughtful believers continue to reflect on this mystery, and as they do it is always instructive to review the various theological dead ends such as this one in order to discern false teaching in our time.

Daniel R. Mitchell

Bibliography

Brown, H.O.J. *Heresies: Heresy and Orthodoxy in the History of the Church*. Peabody, MA: Hendrickson, 1998.

Lyman, J.R. "Heresy." *Encyclopedia of Christianity*. Edited by John Bowden. New York: Oxford University Press, 2005.

SALVATION ARMY, THE

In response to what they viewed as *laissez faire* Methodism within nineteenth-century England, William (1829–1912) and Catherine (1829–1890) Booth founded The Christian Mission in 1865 in Whitechapel, London (*Eerdmans' Handbook,* 516). Zealously dedicated to the task of reaching the underprivileged masses with the gospel of Jesus Christ, The Christian Mission quickly gained momentum in the poverty-stricken streets of London and greater England. Whereas this quasidenominational organization counted only ten full-time members in 1867, by 1874 there were nearly 1000 volunteer workers and 42 evangelists in its ranks (*History of the Salvation Army*, 1). Moreover, between the years 1881 and 1885, an astounding 250,000 Englanders accepted salvation as a direct result of The Christian Mission's work (*History of the Salvation Army*, 1). Although the Booths encountered much resistance from their Methodist brethren, there was little stopping this fledgling evangelistic association.

By 1878, however, pangs of discontent had begun to reverberate within the organization. In order to stave off a potential coup, Booth assumed nearly unilateral control of The Christian Mission and declared himself its "General" (*Eerdmans' Handbook*, 517). He then organized the group along paramilitary lines, even changing its name to The Salvation Army (*Encyclopedia of Religious Revivals*, 380). Denominational publications such as *The War Cry* left little doubt as to the founder's fundamental objectives. His was a crusade to rid England of its casual commitment to the Great Commission. In William Booth's mind, it was only through an organized army of Christian soldiers that he could sustain this singularity of purpose and ultimately fulfill the will of God.

Although historians have debated Booth's motives and strategies, few can argue with his successes. After 1878, The Salvation Army began a worldwide migration that has continued to this day. By the beginning of the twenty-first century, The Salvation Army numbered over two million constituents in 109 countries, with an annual income of over $1 billion (*Encyclopedia of Religious Revivals*, 381). In the United States alone, membership has topped some 450,000 people in recent decades (*Encyclopedia of Religious Revivals*, 381).

The Salvation Army is a veritable "force to be reckoned," and its contemporary members have the same "reputation for social service" (*Religious History of America*, 246) as did their nineteenth-century forebears. William and Catherine Booth's legacy is still strong, and The Salvation Army continues to remain active in its work worldwide.

Mark Tinsley

Bibliography

Briggs, J.H.Y. "The Salvation Army." *Eerdmans' Handbook to the History of Christianity*. Edited by Tim Dowley. Grand Rapids: Eerdmans, 1982.

Dieter, Melvin E. *Encyclopedia of Religious Revivals in America*. Westport, CT: Greenwood, 2007. S.v. "Salvation Army."

Gaustad, Edwin, and Leigh Schmidt. *The Religious History of America: The Heart of the American Story from Colonial Times to Today*. San Francisco: Harper, 2002.

Hattersley, Roy. *Blood and Fire: William and Catherine Booth and Their Salvation Army*. New York: Doubleday, 2000.

"History of the Salvation Army." The Salvation Army, www.salvationarmyusa.org/usn/www_usn_2.nsf/vw-dynamic-index/816DE20E46B88B2685257435005070FA? Opendocument. Accessed August 29, 2012.

S

SAVONAROLA, GIROLAMO (1452–1498)

Girolamo Savonarola was an Italian reformer who was concerned about the worldly conditions of the Roman Church and the papal states in Italy in the fifteenth century. Savonarola was a preacher of moral reform who awakened the people of Italy, yet his influence would last but for a short period and would not be revived for generations.

Savonarola was born in Ferrara, Italy, and studied humanism and medicine in the universities though his heart was more concerned with the spiritual darkness of the various Italian states. Therefore he renounced these pursuits and became a Dominican in 1474, hoping to change the religious direction of Catholicism.

Savonarola served in several northern Italian cities, where his sermons on the apocalypse attracted popular attention at Brescia in 1486. By 1491, he was elected prior of San Marco and became a very popular teacher and preacher in Florence. Some claimed he was a premillennialist in that he spoke of a great judgment coming on the city, and all of Italy, followed by a golden age that would come afterward. Florence would unite all of Italy in a just and spiritual commonwealth. This teaching was embraced by many Catholic citizens, but was taken as an offense by Catholic authorities.

Savonarola's words seemed to come to pass in 1494 when Charles VIII, king of France, invaded Italy. The Medici family members who dominated the monarchy fled Florence. Many took Savonarola's words as a biblical prediction that was coming to pass. Under the new government, Savonarola rose to a position of power and authority. He initiated tax reforms, helped the poor of the area, reformed the courts, and advocated a republican form of government. He also denounced Pope Alexander VI and the corrupt papal court. This got a mixed response. Many trusted and followed him, while many others felt he had gone too far.

An uproar followed that resulted in Savonarola's excommunication. Fearing the entire city would be put under papal interdict, the people reacted and became frightened. They took their eyes off of the moral issues at stake, and Savonarola became the target of their fears. He was eventually tried for heresy and sentenced to be hanged and burned. His death was remembered for decades among the people of the city of Florence and became a symbol for later Italian Protestants.

Mal Couch

Bibliography

Clouse, Robert. "Savonarola." *The New International Dictionary of the Christian Church*. Edited by J.D. Douglas. Grand Rapids: Zondervan, 1978.

Dowley, Tim, ed. *Introduction to the History of Christianity*. Minneapolis: Fortress, 2002.

Ross, J.B., and M.M. McLaughlin, eds. *The Renaissance Reader*. New York: Viking Press, 1968.

Weinstein, D. *Savonarola and Florence: Prophecy and Patriotism in the Renaissance*. Princeton, NJ: Princeton University Press, 1970.

S

SCHAEFFER, FRANCIS (1912–1984)

Twentieth-century apologist Francis Schaeffer was born in Philadelphia and attended Hampden-Sydney College in Virginia. After marrying Edith Seville (1914–2013), he attended Westminster Theological Seminary near his hometown, but later went to and graduated from Faith Theological Seminary. He pastored churches, but his life's work as a missionary and apologist came about in Switzerland, where he founded L'Abri in 1955.

At L'Abri, those with serious questions about the Christian faith found equally serious answers. The cultural revolution of the 1960s caused young people to bring serious questions to L'Abri. Schaeffer's writings in the 1960s and 1970s were deeply influenced by these questions, and honest answers were given. Schaeffer insisted that Christianity is true and based his ministry on the Bible's ability to provide answers to every question and face every challenge.

Schaeffer's early books arose out of his ministry at L'Abri. *Escape from Reason* (1968) and *The God Who Is There* (1968) examine the erosion of belief in truth and its causes. Schaeffer issued one of the first warnings of the challenge posed to Christianity by what we now call postmodernism, which replaces universal truth with relativism and reduces significant concepts such as God, truth, and morality to mere words. *He Is There and He Is Not Silent* (1972) expanded upon the fact that the Bible is inerrant, and that God is its author. *Genesis in Space and Time* (1972) defended the reality that Adam and Eve are genuine historical people, and that their moral failure, the fall, happened in real time, at a real place on earth.

Later, Schaeffer turned his attention to moral and practical matters. His book and film series *How Should We Then Live?* (1976) was a warning that a nation founded on secular humanist philosophy will inevitably turn to totalitarianism as the state takes the place of God. *Whatever Happened to the Human Race?* (1979) was a major influence in turning the attention of evangelicals to the issues of abortion and euthanasia. His last work, *The Great Evangelical Disaster* (1984), warned evangelicals of the dangers of religious and theological compromise.

Schaeffer came on the scene at a time when evangelical Christianity was beginning to look for ways to assert its influence in the larger culture. He died in 1984 in Rochester, Minnesota, yet his legacy continues in the ongoing ministry of L'Abri and in his books, which are still in print. Several organizations seek to preserve and extend Schaeffer's work, including the Francis A. Schaeffer Foundation and the Francis A. Schaeffer Institute of Church Leadership Development. His collected papers are archived at Southeastern Baptist Theological Seminary in Wake Forest, North Carolina, and at the PCA Historical Center in St. Louis, Missouri.

Fred Smith

Bibliography

Dennis, Lane. *Francis Schaeffer: Portrait of the Man and His Work*. Westchester, IL: Crossway, 1986.

Schaeffer, Edith. *L'Abri*. Westchester, IL: Crossway, 1992.

Schaeffer, Francis. *The Complete Works of Francis A. Schaeffer*. 5 vols. Westchester, IL: Crossway, 1982.

SCHAFF, PHILIP (1819–1893)

Swiss-American seminary professor, Bible scholar, and church historian Philip Schaff was raised in a Christian pietist environment in Switzerland. Schaff was trained in the principles of the new scholarship in Germany, and emigrated to America as a young man. He spent his academic career primarily at the German Reformed theological seminary in Mercersburg, Pennsylvania (1844–1863), and Union Theological Seminary in New York City (1870–1893). He was also the founding president of the America Society for Church History and is considered the father of church history in America.

Schaff was dedicated to church cooperation and ecumenism. His inaugural message at Mercersburg, published as *The Principle of Protestantism*, deplored the sectarianism and divisiveness of American Protestant bodies. His philosophy of history, influenced by Georg Wilhelm Friedrich Hegel, saw ecclesiastical progress and synthesis as an expected and desirable outcome. He was actively involved in the Evangelical Alliance, and his message to the 1893 World's Parliament of Religions, on the eve of his death, emphasized Christian unity.

Schaff's ecumenism raised concerns among conservatives in his denomination, the German Reformed Church. Heresy charges were filed in 1844, although Schaff was eventually acquitted. Along with colleague John Williamson Nevin, Schaff developed the controversial Mercersburg Theology. Mercersburg theologians sought a moderate and historically rooted Protestantism, avoiding experience-driven revivalism, scholastic Protestantism (as at Princeton), and rationalistic theologies of emerging liberalism. Critics believed this new evangelical catholicity was ritualistic and soft on Rome.

Schaff emphasized a Christ-centered approach to history. He believed that God was at work in history to bring greater Christian cooperation and the triumph of Christ's church. These convictions were intensely personal. The best defense against German higher criticism, Schaff said, was "an honest soul filled by Christ." A later work defended the divinity of Jesus Christ, which Schaff considered to be "the surest

[and] most sacred of all facts." Evangelical convictions are seen in Schaff's assurance that "Christ lives in me, and he is the only valuable part of my existence."

Schaff produced an enormous body of scholarship. His *History of the Christian Church* (eight volumes) covered church history through the Reformation. His *Creeds of Christendom* (three volumes) surveyed confessional and creedal statements. He helped edit two substantial series of Christian source materials in the *Nicene and Post-Nicene Fathers* (28 volumes). He edited the influential *Schaff-Herzog Encyclopedia of Religious Knowledge*. A long-term biblical project involved editing and translating Peter Lange's *Commentary on the Holy Scriptures* (25 volumes). Schaff also served as president of the committee that produced the American Standard Version of the Bible. Much of his work remains in print, a testimony to the enduring quality of it.

Roger Schultz

Bibliography

Clark, Elizabeth. *Founding the Fathers: Early Church History and Protestant Professors in Nineteenth-Century America.* Philadelphia: University of Pennsylvania Press, 2011.

Graham, Stephen R. *Cosmos in the Chaos: Philip Schaff's Interpretation of Nineteenth-Century American Religion.* Grand Rapids: Eerdmans, 1995.

Nichols, James. *The Mercersburg Theology.* Chicago: University of Chicago Press, 1966.

Pranger, Gary K. *Philip Schaff (1819–1893): Portrait of an Immigrant Theologian.* New York: Peter Lang, 1997.

Shriver, George H. *Philip Schaff: Christian Scholar and Ecumenical Prophet.* Macon, GA: Mercer University Press, 1987.

S

SCHLEIERMACHER, FRIEDRICH (1768–1834)

German theologian Friedrich Schleiermacher was born into a pietistic family. His father was a Reformed army chaplain who had been converted to Moravian Pietism. Schleiermacher's early education was pietistic until he moved to the University of Halle, where his intellectual curiosity was influenced by the philosophy of Immanuel Kant (Olson, 542-43). During this period of his life, he became a Reformed minister (1794), and two years later, he moved to Berlin, where he served as the chaplain at the Charité hospital.

Schleiermacher became friends with Karl Wilhelm Friedrich von Schlegel, Novalis, and other prominent figures. It was their challenge at his twenty-ninth birthday party that led to the writing of his revolutionary *On Religion: Speeches to Its Cultured Despisers* (1799). The writing of *Speeches* was Schleiermacher's answer to why religion was viable for the educated and cultured classes of Berlin at the turn of the nineteenth century. In *Speeches*, Schleiermacher argued that religion is not the problem per se. The cultured despisers were critical toward what Schleiermacher considered the peripheral issues of religion (Wilkens and Padgett, 50). He believed the essence of religion was found in feeling. *Gefühl*, the term that Schleiermacher used, can be described as "…the feeling of unity with the Whole, and the sense of wholeness that comes with this feeling" (Gonzalez, vol. 3, 349). Others have described this feeling as "of being totally and utterly dependent upon something infinite, which is nevertheless made known in and through finite things" (McGrath, 156).

In 1804, Schleiermacher joined the faculty at the University of Halle (university preacher and theological faculty), but due to the invasion by Napoleon's armies, he left Halle and became pastor of Trinity Church in Berlin, and married in 1809. In 1810, he was a founding faculty member of the University of Berlin. It is here that he remained till his death in 1834.

Schleiermacher's academic achievements during this period of his life were astounding. He wrote *Brief Outline on the Study of Theology* (1811) and lectured on a wide range of subjects that included ethics, dialectics, education, church history, philosophy of religion, theology, hermeneutics, political thought, psychology, aesthetics, and the New Testament.

The Christian Faith (1821–1822 and revised in 1831–1832) picked up where *Speeches* left off. If *Speeches* sought to argue for the validity of religion in general, *The Christian Faith* argued for Christianity in particular. The basic argument in *The Christian Faith* was that Christian doctrines "are second order expressions of its primary religious truth, which is the experience of redemption" (McGrath, 156-57). Schleiermacher made the point that key to Christianity was the feeling of absolute dependence on the work of Jesus Christ for a proper relationship with God.

However, due to his philosophical presuppositions, Schleiermacher took a phenomenological approach in laying the foundation of Christianity, which he said was expressed as the experience we have with God. Schleiermacher also redefined Christian doctrines. Three examples of his redefinitions can be seen in these assertions: the Bible is a record of religious experiences instead of an absolute authority; the doctrine of God is not a description of God based on his self-revelation but a description of our feeling of absolute dependence in relation to him; and Christology is redefined to the degree that the two natures of Christ are denied and the divinity of Christ is located in his God-consciousness.

Some have called Schleiermacher the most influential neo-Protestant theologian of the nineteenth century, while others have viewed him as laying the philosophical foundations of modern theology. For Schleiermacher, religious feelings became the standard for testing truth and knowing God. He viewed Christ as redeeming people from ignorance rather than sin. He also believed man's God-consciousness was sustained by Christ through the church, even though he denied the deity of Christ, whom he viewed as the ultimate spiritual ideal. Much of his thinking and influence lives on today in postmodern interpretations of Christianity.

Kevin L. King Sr.

Bibliography

Gonzalez, Justo. *A History of Christian Thought,* vol. 3. Nashville, TN: Abingdon, 1987.

McGrath, Alister. *Christian Theology: An Introduction.* 5th ed. Malden, MA: Wiley-Blackwell, 2011.

Olson, Roger. *The Story of Christian Theology.* Downers Grove, IL: IVP Academic, 1999.

Schleiermacher, Friedrich. *On Religion: Speeches to Its Cultured Despisers.* Translated by John Oman. London: K. Paul, Trench, Trubner, 1893.

Wilkens, Steve, and Alan G. Padgett. *Christianity and Western Thought,* vol. 2. Downers Grove, IL: InterVarsity, 2000.

S

SCHOLASTICISM

Scholasticism is "a development in thinking which comes between the world of the church fathers and the rise of the modern world" (Roy, 1085). What is commonly meant in the context of Christian thought is more technically Latin scholasticism, in which a comprehensive understanding of truth is attempted by integrating Scripture, liturgy, and reason (as it was inherited from the ancient Graeco-Roman world). The name derives from the Latin *schola*, and the Greek, *schole*, which referred generally to the teaching/learning context of a school as the term is used today. Johannes Scotus Eriugena, in the ninth century, had suggested that all truth is a theophany, and attempted to wed philosophy to theology in a comprehensive approach to the discovery of truth.

Historically, scholasticism refers to the subsequent development in the late medieval period with the rise of "sentence literature." Peter Lombard (ca. 1095–1169) is one of the best-known examples, with his work in placing sentences from Scripture, early Christian writers, and contemporary scholars together.

This had the effect of placing divergent and sometimes contrary opinions from what were considered authoritative sources side by side and inviting ways to resolve these tensions through various distinctions, definitions, and classifications derived from careful reasoning using the canons of logic inherited from ancient Greek and Latin philosophers and thinkers. These early scholastics were essentially seeking to arrive at a comprehensive and consistent understanding of truth.

This led to the next phase in the second half of the twelfth century. Running commentaries on the Scriptures were interspersed with questions raised by the text and theological commentary attempting to posit answers to the questions. Scholars would *lecture* on the text in the morning, and then in the afternoon employ the method of *disputation* to wrestle with the disputed questions. This "unitary vision of medieval scholars" culminated in the thirteenth-century *summas* (Roy, 1087). Albert Magus (the Great) and his student, Thomas Aquinas, stand out as the best exemplars of this period. Commenting on Paul's statement concerning the foolishness of the cross in 1 Corinthians 1, Thomas noted, "Something divine seems to be foolish, not because it lacks wisdom but because it transcends human wisdom. For men are wont to regard as foolish anything beyond their understanding." Such was the goal of "high scholasticism" as it attempted to integrate all knowledge in direct contact with Scripture, the fathers, Christian spirituality, and all other sources of rational inquiry. This would change in the fourteenth century as the scholastics became less interested in the Scriptures and more preoccupied with minutia increasingly irrelevant to Christian life experience.

Later Protestant scholastics followed this same trajectory. Calvin and Luther attempted a new synthesis by going back to the Scriptures and the early fathers of the church. Those who followed them increasingly went back to Calvin and Luther and the Protestant creeds instead of going to the writings of the New Testament, leading inexorably to the same result and becoming increasingly distant from authentic Christian living.

Daniel R. Mitchell

Bibliography

Pieper, Josef. *Scholasticism: Personalities and Problems of Medieval Philosophy*. New York: McGraw Hill, 1964.

Roy, Louise. "Scholasticism." *Encyclopedia of Christianity*. Edited by John Bowden. New York: Oxford University Press, 2005.

SCOTLAND, CHURCH OF

Scotland's national church is Presbyterian and consists of over one million members. The Westminster Confession of Faith has served as its doctrinal standard since 1647, although the earlier Scots Confession of 1560 drawn up under the influence of John Knox served as the original standard. Knox studied under John Calvin and Heinrich Bullinger in Geneva, where he published his treatise *On Predestination* in 1560, which influenced the English translation of the Geneva Bible, as well as a translation of Calvin's *Catechism*. Invited by the Protestant lords in Scotland, Knox returned to his homeland to establish the Protestant Church of Scotland and was later succeeded by Andrew Melville, who has been generally recognized as the father of Presbyterianism.

S

However, after the restoration of the monarchy in England in 1660, the Scottish Presbyterians, known as Covenanters, who had earlier signed the National Covenant of 1638, continued to maintain their insistence upon evangelical Presbyterianism and their opposition to the established Church of England. As a result of their determination, Presbyterianism was fully restored to Scotland by William III in 1690.

In 1843, one-third of the ministers left the Church of Scotland during what was called the Disruption over the relation of civil and religious authorities to form the Free Church of Scotland. The breach was healed in 1929 with the reunification of most of the congregations back into the Church of Scotland, with a minority still remaining outside the national church. The Church of Scotland maintains Presbyterian polity and is organized into 12 provincial synods and a general assembly. All ministers have equal status and are elected by individual congregations and are subject to ratification by the local presbytery.

Mal Couch

Bibliography

Douglas, J.D, ed. *The New International Dictionary of the Christian Church*. Grand Rapids: Zondervan, 1978.

Macleod, John. *Scottish Theology Since the Reformation*. Edinburgh: Free Church of Scotland, 1943.

Renwick, A.M. *The Story of the Scottish Reformation*. Grand Rapids: Eerdmans, 1960.

Smellie, Alexander. *Men of the Covenant*. Edinburgh: Banner of Truth, 1975.

SHAKERS

The Shakers were a religious movement that originated in mid-1700s England as an offshoot of the Quakers. By the early 1800s, they became successful practitioners of religious communal living in America. Early Shakers shook while they worshipped; hence the group's name. (In time, this spontaneous shaking gave way to formal religious dances.)

The Shaker movement began in 1747 under the leadership of the husband-and-wife team of James and Jane Wardley, and the practice of sharing leadership between the sexes continued throughout Shaker history. In 1774, Shaker convert Mrs. Ann Lee (1736–1784) led a small group of Shakers to America and promptly began establishing Shaker-only communities. At the height of their success, around 1840, such communities included about 6000 full members. By the late 1800s, however, these communities had begun to dwindle, and by 1900, fewer than 1000 Shakers remained. Since 1992, only one small Shaker community has survived, located at Sabbathday Lake, Maine.

Ann Lee appealed to Scripture to support her religious teachings, but she also claimed to receive direct revelation from God. As a result, the Shaker faith as she molded it bore little resemblance to historic Christianity. Viewing Adam's original sin as sexual, Lee concluded that sexual abstinence is a key to holy living. Accordingly, Shaker communities rejected marriage and imposed strict measures, such as separate men's and women's building entrances, to enforce separation of the sexes. Lee also valued ownership of property by the community rather than by individuals. Principles like celibacy, confession, and common ownership, then, and not the cross of Christ or any other Christian doctrine, stood at the center of Shaker faith.

Lee argued from Genesis 1:27 ("male and female created he them") that God is both male and female. This view helps explain the distinctive role that Lee herself played in Shaker theology. Identified as the "female principle in Christ"—with Jesus as the male principle in Christ—Lee was recognized as fulfilling Christ's second coming. The title of a Shaker-sponsored book exalts Lee as *Our Blessed Mother Ann Lee... Through Whom the Word of Eternal Life Was Opened in This Day of Christ's Second Appearing*.

Though never numerically significant, the Shakers have sparked great interest among students of modern political, philosophical, religious, and social trends—in part, perhaps, because the Shakers tried to implement so many of the ideas that have dominated the intellectual and popular landscape of the last few centuries, such as communism, continuing revelation, feminism, millenarianism (the Shakers viewed themselves as the vanguard of a new age), pacifism, simple living (as reflected, for instance, in Shaker furniture), speaking in tongues, spiritual healing, and utopianism.

Greg Enos

Bibliography

Kurian, G.T. "Shakers." *Nelson's Dictionary of Christianity.* Nashville, TN: Thomas Nelson, 2005.

Stein, Stephen J. *Alternative American Religions.* Oxford: Oxford University Press, 2000.

———. *The Shaker Experience in America: A History of the United Society of Believers.* New Haven, CT: Yale University Press, 1992.

Testimonies of the Life, Character, Revelations and Doctrines of Our Blessed Mother Ann Lee, and the Elders with Her; Through Whom the Word of Eternal Life Was Opened in This Day of Christ's Second Appearing: Collected from Living Witnesses, by Order of the Ministry, in Union with the Church. Hancock, MA: J. Tallcott & J. Deming, 1816.

S

SIMONS, MENNO (1496–1561)

Anabaptist Mennonite leader Menno Simons was born in 1496 in the town of Witmarsum, located in the Friesland province of the Netherlands. Little is known about his family or early life, but in 1524, at the age of 28, he was ordained a priest at Utrecht. According to a letter he wrote to Gellius Faber, it was during the early days of his priesthood that Menno began searching the Bible for answers to his questions concerning transubstantiation. In April of 1535, Simon's brother, Pieter, along with 300 other Anabaptists, were put to death at the Old Cloister near Bolsward. Up to this point in his life, Simons had given intellectual assent to Christian doctrine, but had not placed his faith in Christ. The distress caused by the events at the Old Cloister troubled his soul greatly and eventually led to his conversion. For the first nine months afterward, Simons attempted to preach the gospel in his old pulpit at Witmarsum but to no avail.

Simons sought out and joined the Anabaptists in January of 1536. By the following October, Simons was ordained by Anabaptists Obbe and Dirk Philips sometime in 1537. The Philips brothers were among the peaceful disciples of Melchior Hoffman, who stood against the Munster rebellion, which had been stirred by Hoffman's more radical adherents. The pacifist example set by Simons and the Philips brothers became one of the hallmarks of the later Mennonite movement.

Simons quickly became an influential figure within the Anabaptist movement, and eventually the Dutch Anabaptists were being called Mennonites. His popularity among the Anabaptists was largely due to his prolific writings. Between 1535 and 1560, Simons published at least 39 books, pamphlets, and tracts that were read and distributed among his followers. Simon's most influential work, *Foundation of Christian Doctrine*, was originally published in 1540 but later revised (1554) then translated into Dutch (1558) and German (1575). After a brief illness, Menno Simons died on January 31, 1561. Virtually every branch of Mennonites today traces its roots to Menno Simons.

Joseph Buchanan

Bibliography

Bender, Harold S. *Menno Simon's Life and Writings*. Eugene, OR: Wipf & Stock, 2003.

Estep, William. *The Anabaptist Story: An Introduction to Sixteenth-Century Anabaptism*. Grand Rapids: Eerdmans, 1996.

Horsch, John. *Menno Simons*. Scottdale, PA: Mennonite Publishing House, 1916.

Littell, Franklin Hamlin. *A Tribute to Menno Simmons*. Scottdale, PA: Herald Press, 1961.

Wenger, John Christian, ed. *The Complete Writings of Menno Simmons*. Translated by Leonard Verduin. Scottdale, PA: Mennonite Publishing House, 1956.

SMITH, CHARLES WARD "CHUCK" (1927–)

Charles Smith, popularly known as Chuck Smith, is the founder of the Calvary Chapel movement and senior pastor of Calvary Chapel, Costa Mesa, California. The author of more than two dozen books, Pastor Chuck's radio broadcast, *The Word for Today*, is heard in more than 350 cities worldwide. He is also the cohost of the live call-in question-and-answer show *Pastor's Perspective*. Smith attended LIFE Bible College (now Life Pacific College) in the Los Angeles area and originally served pastorates in the Foursquare denomination.

In 1965, Smith took over a small, struggling church in Santa Ana, California, called Calvary Chapel. By the late 1960s, the Vietnam War was at its height, the drug culture was pervasive up and down the California coast, and Eastern religions were being explored by discontented youth. Chuck and his wife, Kay, began to pray for these "hippies," as they were called. Shortly thereafter they met Lonnie Frisbee. Smith invited Frisbee to teach a Wednesday Bible study, which soon attracted thousands from the youth counterculture. Calvary Chapel began to grow until a large tent was needed to hold services before the current building was finished. The national press began to take notice and the movement was dubbed the Jesus People movement. Hundreds of young people came to Southern California, accepted Christ, and were baptized in the Pacific Ocean. Many who came to faith in Christ during this time were to become the church leaders of the next generation of Calvary Chapels worldwide. They played their own music at the church services, giving birth to contemporary praise and worship.

Calvary Chapel is known for its commitment to an expositional style of Bible teaching, contemporary music, and a church government that has been described as the "Moses model," where the pastor leads the church and has a board of elders for accountability. Calvary Chapel Bible College was founded in 1975 and has over two dozen affiliates. Today, there are over 1200 Calvary Chapels around the world.

Michael Brennan

Bibliography

MacIntosh, Mike, and Raul Ries. *A Venture in Faith: The History and Philosophy of the Calvary Chapel Movement.* Diamond Bar, CA: Logos Media Group, 1992.

Smith, Chuck. *Calvary Chapel Distinctives: The Foundational Principles of the Calvary Chapel Movement.* Costa Mesa, CA: The Word for Today, 2000.

———. *Harvest.* Costa Mesa, CA: The Word for Today, 2001.

———. *A Memoir of Grace.* Costa Mesa, CA: The Word for Today, 2009.

SMITH, OSWALD J. (1889–1986)

Canadian pastor and missionary statesman Oswald J. Smith has been called the greatest missionary statesman in the twentieth century. He planted The People's Church in Toronto, Canada, which is said to be the first church to give $1 million to missions. The church, which Smith built to more than 4000 in attendance, sent out 350 missionaries to 40 countries around the world. His church was innovative, not following the liturgical worship patterns of most Canadian churches. Rather, he emphasized gospel singing, evangelistic preaching, and special sermons for children using props long before the practice became popular among children's pastors.

Smith was born above a train station in Odessa, Ontario, in 1889; his father was a telegraph operator for the Canadian Pacific Railway. He was converted January 28, 1906. Smith did undergraduate studies at Toronto Bible College and pursued graduate education at McCormick Theological Seminary in Chicago. He held pastorates in several small churches in Toronto, Chicago, and Kentucky. During the winter of 1908, he spent time in Port Essington, British Columbia, ministering to the Indians at Hartley Bay. With only a few supplies, deep snow, and barren living conditions, it was the most difficult winter of his life. That experience drove him closer to the Lord and helped him empathize with missionaries and their problems. He developed a deep sensitivity for missionaries that lasted the rest of his life.

Smith published more than 35 books with cumulative sales of more than a million copies, and published *The People's Magazine*, which circulated worldwide. Smith has also written prose that has been set to music. Some of Smith's famous sayings are repeated often today, including, "Attempt great things for God; expect great things from God," and "Why should anyone hear the gospel twice before everyone has heard it once?"

Elmer Towns

Bibliography

Smith, Oswald J. *The Man God Uses.* New York: Christian Alliance, 1925.

———. *The Passion for Souls.* London: Marshall, Morgan & Scott, 1950.

———. *The Revival We Need.* New York: Christian Alliance, 1925.

SOCINIANISM

Socinianism is an anti-Trinitarian system named for Faustus Socinus (1539–1604) of Siena, Italy, who in turn was influenced by the teachings of Michael Servetus (1511–1553), the Spanish physician and theologian who was famously burned at the stake as a heretic at Geneva.

Socinus's education was limited to two uncles who tutored him. One of the uncles, Laelius Socinus, was active in the Protestant movement and also came to embrace anti-Trinitarian beliefs. His writings became the basis of Socinus's theological outlook and teachings. Many of these ideas came out of the Radical Reformation as it was developing in Venice in the 1540s and included a strong anti-Trinitarian element later to be identified with Unitarianism.

Socinus traveled through several European countries where he openly expressed his theological views. But it was among the Polish Brethren, an Arian Anabaptist sect, where he found himself most at home. In time he became their principal leader, shaping the theology of the movement in keeping with his uncles' ideas.

Socinian theology is summarized in the Racovian Catechism (Rees). Influenced by the humanism of the time, Socinus interpreted Scripture rationally. In regard to Christ, the Socinians rejected the eternal preexistence of the Son, positing instead that he only began to exist when conceived of the virgin Mary. Christ did not become God until the resurrection, at which time God gave to him some of the divine prerogatives. In regard to the condition of humanity and original sin, Socinians are essentially Pelagian. Adam and Eve were created mortal and would have died regardless of their sin. Regarding the atonement of Christ, the Socinians developed a view similar to that of Abelard. Christ was said to be an example. Faustus complained that we needed to get rid of the idea of justice in the atonement, which only served to perpetuate what he considered the fiction of Christ's satisfaction. Divine justice and mercy are matters of the will, and God has chosen to exercise mercy instead of justice (Allison, 401-2). Salvation is brought about through repentance and good works.

Socinianism rejects the idea that God knows all contingencies. His foreknowledge is limited to what human free will determines. Hell is a temporary punishment, after which it is imagined that there is a "universal restoration, which maintains that all men, however depraved…will be brought ultimately to goodness and consequently to happiness" (Rees, 368).

The influence of Socinian doctrine eventually spread to Holland and England and was felt among the Arminians and the English Unitarians, influencing such thinkers as Isaac Newton, John Locke, Voltaire, and Thomas Jefferson.

Daniel R. Mitchell

Bibliography

Allison, Greg. *Historical Theology*. Grand Rapids: Zondervan, 2011.

Kubricht, P. "Socinus, Faustus." *Evangelical Dictionary of Theology*. Edited by Walter A. Elwell. Grand Rapids: Baker, 1984.

Rees, Thomas. *The Racovian Catechism*. London: Longman, Hurst, Rees, Orme, & Brown, 1818.

SOLA FIDE, SOLA GRATIA, AND *SOLA SCRIPTURA*

As the early reformers contrasted their beliefs with the Roman Catholic Church from which they separated themselves, they crystallized their position with the following defining terms: *sola fide*, *sola gratia*, and *sola Scriptura*. These Latin phrases mean "faith alone," "grace alone," and "Scripture alone." Sometimes associated with these three interrelated concepts are two other Latin phrases—*solo Christo* ("through Christ alone") and *soli Deo gloria* ("glory to God alone"). To connect all of these five *sola* concepts, the reformers affirmed that salvation comes through faith alone, through Christ alone, by (God's) grace alone, as revealed in Scripture alone, to God's glory alone.

Sola Fide—In his Bible commentaries, Martin Luther utilized the phrase *faith alone* more than 20 times. Furthermore, he included an affirmation of *sola fide* in the doctrinal confession called the Smalcald Articles in 1537: "…it is clear and certain that this *faith alone* justifies us as St. Paul says, Rom. 3, 28: For we conclude that a man is justified by faith, without the deeds of the Law. Likewise v. 26: That He might be just, and the Justifier of him which believeth in Christ." The Roman Catholic Council of Trent, which was in large measure a response to Luther and other reformers, was somewhat ambiguous on *sola fide*, both affirming and denying it. And yet, in the official canons of the Council, *sola fide* was denied and declared anathema:

If any one saith, that by *faith alone* the impious is justified; in such wise as to mean, that nothing else is required to co-operate in order to the obtaining the grace of Justification, and that it is not in any way necessary, that he be prepared and disposed by the movement of his own will; let him be anathema (Council of Trent, Sixth Session, Canon IX).

Key early church fathers also affirmed salvation by faith alone:

Basil of Caesarea—"Now, this is the perfect and consummate glory in God: not to exult in one's own justice [righteousness], but recognizing oneself as lacking true justice [righteousness], to be justified *by faith in Christ alone*" (Basil, Homily 20, "Of Humility," 9:479).

John Chrysostom—"But what is the *law of faith*? It is, being saved by grace. Here too he shews God's power, in that He has not only saved, but has even justified, and led them to boasting, and this too without needing works, but looking for *faith only*" (Chrysostom, Homily VII, on Romans 3:9-18, in *The Homilies of St. John Chrysostom*).

Jerome—"God justifies by *faith alone*" (*Deus ex sola fide justificat*) (Jerome, commentary on Romans 10:3, in *Patrilogia Latina*, 30:722A).

Ambrose—"They are justified freely because they have not done anything nor given anything in return, but by faith alone [*sola fide*] they have been made holy by the gift of God" (Commentary on Romans 3:24, cited in *Ancient Christian Commentary on Scripture*, 101).

The concept of *sola fide*, then, was affirmed by the early church fathers, as well as the key leaders of the Reformation—primarily Martin Luther. Parallel to *sola fide* is the concept of *sola gratia*, or "grace alone."

Sola Gratia—Leaders of the Protestant Reformation were convinced that salvation is by faith alone (rather than by good works) and by grace alone (*sola gratia*) rather than by any human initiative. Salvation is not deserved or earned, but is a gift of grace, as affirmed in Ephesians 2:8-10. Since all have sinned and come short of the glory of God (Romans 3:23), no one is deserving of salvation. God has no obligation to save any sinner. Yet while we were sinners, he gave his Son, Jesus Christ, to provide atonement for our sin (Romans 5:6-10). Therefore, there is no place for boasting, pride, or self-righteousness by any Christian. The only appropriate response to the grace of God is thankfulness and gratitude. This was the strong emphasis of the reformers, against the works-righteousness they had experienced under Catholicism.

The Council of Trent appeared to embrace *sola gratia* in affirming that justification is "derived from the prevenient grace of God" (Council of Trent, Sixth Session, Chapter V). However, the canons of the Council appear to require good works for salvation:

> If any one saith, that justifying faith is nothing else but confidence in the divine mercy which remits sins for Christ's sake; or, that this confidence alone is that whereby we are justified; let him be anathema (Council of Trent, Sixth Session, Canon XXII).

Roman Catholicism thus continued to require a synergism of divine grace and human effort for salvation, rather than grace alone.

Sola Scriptura—The Roman Catholic faith tradition had placed the *ex cathedra* pronouncements of the Pope and other authoritative church traditions as being on the same plane of authority as Scripture. Roman Catholics qualified *sola Scriptura* at the Council of Trent in 1547 by asserting that both Scripture and the pronouncements of the Pope, church councils, church fathers, and other such teachings from the church were due "equal affection of piety, and reverence" (Council of Trent, Session 4, "Decree concerning the Holy Scriptures"). In contrast, the leaders of the Protestant Reformation enunciated the principle of *sola Scriptura*—"by Scripture alone." In *sola Scriptura,* the Bible is the only and final source of authority for religious beliefs. Luther appealed to *sola Scriptura* when he was called upon to defend his views before the Diet of Worms:

> Unless I am convinced by the testimony of the Holy Scriptures or by evident reason—for I can believe neither pope nor councils alone, as it is clear that they have erred repeatedly and contradicted themselves— I consider myself convicted by the testimony of Holy Scripture, which is my basis; my conscience is captive to the Word of God. Thus I cannot and will not recant, because acting against one's conscience is neither safe nor sound. God help me. Amen (Luther, cited in *Luther: Man between God and the Devil*, 36; Bainton, 180).

John Wesley suggested four main sources for Christian truth in the Methodist quadrilateral—Scripture, experience, tradition, and reason. Although many theologians affirm *sola Scriptura*, they also utilize experience, tradition, and reason as authorities to some degree. Although each of these sources can contribute to our knowledge of God, the Bible must unequivocally be the ultimate standard by which all our beliefs are measured. One might describe this primacy of Scripture as *suprema Scriptura*— that is, experience, church tradition, and reason must always be judged in the light of

Scripture. The Bible is our final and supreme authority, but we may learn from experience, church tradition, and reason if they are not contrary to Scripture (Garrett, *Systematic Theology,* 1:179-181).

Steve Lemke

Bibliography

Allison, Gregg R. *Historical Theology: An Introduction to Christian Doctrine.* Grand Rapids: Zondervan, 2011.

Bainton, Roland H. *Here I Stand: A Life of Martin Luther.* Peabody, MA: Hendrickson, 1950

Garrett, James Leo Jr. *Systematic Theology: Biblical, Historical, and Evangelical.* 2 vols, 1:179-181. Grand Rapids: Eerdmans, 1990.

Harm, F.R. "Solafidianism." *Evangelical Dictionary of Theology.* Edited by Walter A. Elwell. Grand Rapids: Baker, 1934.

McGrath, Alister E. *Christian Theology: An Introduction.* Oxford: Blackwell, 2011.

SOUTHERN BAPTIST CONVENTION

The Southern Baptist Convention (SBC) was organized in 1845 in Augusta, Georgia, due to disagreements with northern Baptists over the issues of slavery and missions funding. The SBC is a voluntary fellowship of autonomous Baptist churches that generally subscribe to the "Baptist faith and message" as a statement of beliefs regarding the authority of the Bible, the autonomy of the churches, the priesthood of believers, democratic church polity, religious liberty, and believers' baptism by immersion.

The new convention established the Board of Domestic Missions (now the North American Mission Board) and the Foreign Mission Board (now the International Mission Board). The foreign board commissioned its first missionaries the following year and soon had missionaries in China and Nigeria. The cooperative effort was helped by an annual Christmas offering begun in 1887 at the urging of a missionary to China named Lottie Moon. In 1925, Southern Baptists meeting in Memphis, Tennessee, adopted the Cooperative Program, which further centralized budgeting and fund-raising for the convention's many enterprises.

The SBC is composed of various state conventions, area associations, and local churches. The executive headquarters are in Nashville, Tennessee, as is Lifeway, the publishing arm of the SBC. SBC seminaries include Southern (Kentucky), Southwestern

(Texas), Southeastern (North Carolina), Midwestern (Missouri), Golden Gate (California), and New Orleans (Louisiana). The SBC also has five theological colleges associated with its seminaries—Boyce College (Kentucky), The College at Southwestern (Texas), The College at Southeastern (North Carolina), Midwestern Baptist College (Missouri), and Leavell College (Louisiana).

Numerous other schools with which the SBC maintains a cooperative relationship include Liberty University (Virginia) and Cedarville University (Ohio). Outstanding Southern Baptists have included Adrian Rogers, Charles Stanley, Jerry Falwell, and David Jeremiah. After several decades of spiritual decline, a conservative resurgence beginning in the 1970s returned the SBC to its conservative theological roots with an emphasis on evangelism, missions, and church planting.

Fred Smith

Bibliography

Baker, Robert A. *The Southern Baptist Convention and Its People: 1607–1972*. Nashville, TN: The Baptist Sunday School Board, 1972.

James Hefley, et al. *The Truth in Crisis: The Conservative Resurgence in the Southern Baptist Convention*. 6 vols. Hannibal, MO: Hannibal Books, 2005.

McBeth, Leon, *The Baptist Heritage: Four Centuries of Baptist Witness*. Nashville, TN: Broadman Press, 1987.

Sutton, Jerry. *The Baptist Reformation: The Conservative Resurgence in the Southern Baptist Convention*. Nashville, TN: Broadman & Holman, 2000.

SPURGEON, CHARLES HADDON (1834–1892)

English Baptist preacher Charles Haddon Spurgeon was born to John and Eliza Spurgeon in Kelvedon, Essex, on June 19, 1834. His Bible-saturated sermons, common-man wit, and unparalleled oratorical skills, all of which were apparent even in his youth, made him famous as a pulpiteer and earned him the nickname "the Prince of Preachers." Spurgeon's ministry was among the most fruitful and yet most controversial among nineteenth-century Baptists.

The oldest of 17 children (nine died in infancy), Spurgeon was the son and grandson of ministers. Although his upbringing was rich in Puritan piety and independent church life, he was not converted until he was a teen, which took place on a snowy January Sunday in 1850 at a Methodist church. One month later, the young Spurgeon became a convinced Baptist, a decision that would change his life forever.

Though he himself lacked any formal training, Spurgeon ventured to preach his first sermon at the age of 16. In 1851, he became pastor of the small Baptist church at Waterbeach. Word soon spread about his ability and, just two years later, he was called to serve the well-established New Park Street Church in London. While there, Spurgeon married Susannah Thompson on January 8, 1856. Together they had twin boys, Charles and Thomas.

In London, Spurgeon's notoriety caused the New Park Street congregation to outgrow its facility and begin building the famed Metropolitan Tabernacle. During that time, the church rented out exhibition halls, such as the Crystal Palace, where he once preached to over 23,000. In March 1861, the Tabernacle was completed and could seat 6000. Eventually it grew to a megachurch with a membership in excess of 14,000. Spurgeon's weekly penny pulpit sermons, preached during those years, are still among the most widely published writings in history.

The fruitfulness of Spurgeon's ministry, though, was not without difficulty. Theologically, Spurgeon was decidedly Calvinistic and Baptistic; both of which landed him, at times, in controversy. Not only did he come under criticism for ardently denouncing the Church of England's view on baptismal regeneration, but he was often attacked by some Baptists for being too Reformed and yet by hyper-Calvinists who deemed him too evangelistic.

Furthermore, Spurgeon's unwavering commitment to the authority of Scripture placed him at odds with the growing secular ideas of his era. In what became known as the Down Grade Controversy, Spurgeon battled his own Baptist brethren over the influence of Darwinian evolution and liberal higher criticism. In 1887, he withdrew from the Baptist Union, a painful decision in the midst of all the pressures and difficulties that the Down Grade Controversy had placed upon his already-failing health. Over the last few years of his life, Spurgeon struggled more and more frequently with serious illnesses, and during a trip to Mentone, France, while attempting to recover from poor health, Spurgeon died on January 31, 1892.

Beyond his ministry as a preacher, Spurgeon also established orphanages, a widely circulated periodical (*The Sword and the Trowel*), and his most beloved work, which was a training school for aspiring ministers (known today as Spurgeon's College). Charles Spurgeon was a prolific author who published numerous books still read by many today, including *Lectures to My Students* and *The Treasury of David*, and his still-popular devotional *Morning and Evening*.

J. Tyler Scarlett

Bibliography

Dallimore, Arnold. *Spurgeon: A New Biography*. Carlisle, PA: Banner of Truth, 1985.

Drummond, Lewis. *Spurgeon: Prince of Preachers*. Grand Rapids: Kregel, 1992.

Murray, Iain. *The Forgotten Spurgeon.* Carlisle, PA: Banner of Truth, 2009.

Spurgeon, Charles. *C.H. Spurgeon Autobiography: Volume 1, The Early Years, 1834–1859.* Carlisle, PA: Banner of Truth, 1962.

———. *C.H. Spurgeon Autobiography: Volume 2, The Full Harvest, 1860–1892.* Carlisle, PA: Banner of Truth, 1973.

SUNDAY, WILLIAM "BILLY" ASHLEY (1862–1935)

American evangelist William "Billy" Ashley Sunday, born on November 19, 1862, is considered one of the more preeminent evangelists in American history. Sunday's father died as a Union soldier in the Civil War, and because raising two boys proved to be too much for their mother, both William and his brother, Ed, were sent away to be raised in the Iowa Soldiers' Orphans' Home. Prior to his fame as an evangelist, Billy Sunday was a professional baseball player from 1883–1891, most of which was with the Chicago White Stockings. In 1886, during his baseball-playing days in Chicago, Sunday was converted to Christ through the street preaching ministry of the Pacific Garden Mission.

In 1891, Sunday retired from baseball and spent the next few years serving with the YMCA and assisting evangelist J. Wilbur Chapman. When Chapman abruptly returned to the pastorate in 1895, Sunday, who had very little formal education, took Chapman's place and remained as an evangelist for the rest of his life. Sunday generated an enormous following—he was known as a down-to-earth communicator who preached in a way that captured the imagination while condemning sin in no uncertain terms. One of his famous sermon targets was the consumption of alcohol, and one of his best known messages was his "booze sermon," entitled, "Get on the Water-wagon." It is believed that Billy Sunday greatly influenced the passage of the Eighteenth Amendment, also known as the Prohibition Amendment.

Sunday was also known for the phrase "hitting the sawdust trail." Sawdust was used in the aisles of churches and tabernacles during evangelistic meetings and assisted in lowering the noise of those walking the aisles in response to a message. The phrase, originally associated with lumberjacks who used sawdust trails to find their way home, was used metaphorically by Sunday in reference to those who found their way to Christ (Sunday, 158).

Billy Sunday died on November 6, 1935. His last sermon was entitled "What Must I Do to Be Saved?" It is estimated that more than 100 million people heard Billy

Sunday preach during his lifetime. He can be named, along with Charles Finney, D.L. Moody, and Billy Graham, as among the greatest evangelists in American history.

John Cartwright

Bibliography

Brown, E.P. *The Real Billy Sunday*. Whitefish, MT: Kessinger, 2007.

Dorsett, L.W. *Billy Sunday and the Redemption of Urban America*. Grand Rapids: Eerdmans, 1991.

Falwell, Jerry, ed. "Get on the Waterwagon." *25 of the Greatest Sermons Ever Preached*. Lynchburg, VA: Old-Time Gospel Hour, 1983.

Lockerbie, D.B. *Billy Sunday*. Waco, TX: Word, 1966.

Sunday, B. *"Billy" Sunday, the Man and His Message, with His Own Words which Have Won Thousands for Christ*. Philadelphia, PA: John C. Winston, 1914.

SUNDAY SCHOOL

Sunday school, or Bible instruction classes generally conducted in Protestant churches, is generally defined by four unique characteristics: (1) it includes both Christian and non-Christian children; (2) its curriculum is the Word of God rather than the catechism; (3) it is generally operated and taught by lay people; and (4) the purpose is to evangelize children for Christ, instruct them in the Word of God, and train them in Christian character.

Robert Raikes, of Gloucester, England, the founder of the Sunday school, was the publisher of *The Gloucester Journal*. In 1757, he went one Sunday afternoon to a rough slum district in search of a gardener and was jostled by a gang of ragged boys. He determined to do something about the condition of children, and collected the names of 90 children and paid a Mrs. Meredith to teach them reading, writing, arithmetic, and religion. Raikes's pupils learned by reading directly from the Bible. Raikes also wrote four textbooks used in Sunday school. These were large newspapers over 100 pages long, from which the pupils read out loud in unison.

Three years later, Raikes told the story of his Sunday school in his newspaper. His enthusiastic report caught the eyes of Christian leaders in other poverty-ridden areas of London, and they responded to Raikes's plea and started Sunday schools throughout the nation. John Wesley urged, "There must be a Sunday school wherever there is a Methodist Society."

In 1785, the Society for the Support and Encouragement of Sunday school throughout the British Dominions (understandably shortened to the Sunday School Society) was set up and was largely responsible for the rapid expansion of the movement. Robert Raikes reported that in four years, Sunday school enrollment had reached 250,000 children. Robert Raikes died in 1811. By the time a statue was erected in his memory in 1831, Sunday schools in Great Britain were ministering weekly to some 1,250,000 children.

The first record of a Sunday school in America is that of one held in 1785 at Oak Grove, Virginia, by William Elliot. Francis Asbury then established a Sunday school in Virginia in 1786. In rapid succession, Sunday schools sprang up in South Carolina, Maryland, Rhode Island, New York, and Pennsylvania. Within 11 years after Robert Raikes began the first Sunday school in England, a new Sunday school society was organized in Philadelphia in 1791. The Sunday schools that mushroomed over the United States were focused on evangelism, whereas the movement in England was focused on general education.

Around 1825, the Mississippi Valley enterprise captured the imagination of Sunday school leaders on the Eastern seaboard. Francis Scott Key (author of the national anthem) was president of the Sunday school association in May 1830 when a resolution was passed to start a Sunday school in every town in the Mississippi Valley. The area west of the Alleghenies to the Rocky Mountains had a population of 4 million people in 1.3 million square miles. Two thousand people voted unanimously and raised more than $17,000 for the project. Large gatherings in Boston, Washington, and Charleston also contributed to the project, including United States senators. More than 80 missionaries planted libraries throughout the Midwest, each costing $10 for 100 books. It has been estimated that more than one million volumes were thus placed in circulation, giving further momentum to the growth of literacy in the United States. From 1830 to 1874 there were 61,299 Sunday schools organized with 407,244 teachers and 2,650,784 pupils. The total amount spent on this endeavor was $2,133,364. As one observer noted, never had so much been accomplished for God with such a small down payment.

The Sunday school movement was spread by publications and conventions. John H. Vincent, a Methodist minister, published *The Sunday School Times*, which included a curriculum that comprehensively and consistently covered the Scripture in seven years. Known as the International Uniform Lesson, it had the largest circulation of any magazine in the United States. Massive Sunday school conventions also grew after the US Civil War. The first international convention was held in Baltimore in 1875, and recorded 71,272 Sunday schools in existence in America. In 1884, the conventions reported 8,712,511 Sunday school students in the United States alone.

Starting in the late nineteenth century and on through the twentieth century, in reaction to the growing influence of theological liberalism in mainline churches, inter-denominational publishing houses such as Scripture Press, Gospel Light Press, Union Gospel Press, and David C. Cook were established with innovative evangelistic fervor and doctrinal orthodoxy. They laid the foundation for a Sunday school revival after World War II. It was then that attendance took a new upturn in evangelical denominations. In addition, large Sunday school conventions were planned by the National Sunday School Association (NSSA).

Sunday school attendance reached a peak in evangelical churches during the 1970s and has been in decline since the 1990s with the growth of home Bible studies and home-based cell groups that also emphasize lay leadership and the application of biblical principles to practical living.

Elmer Towns

Bibliography

Benson, Clarence H. *A Popular History of Christian Education.* Chicago, IL: Moody, 1943.

Edge, Findley B. *The History of Christian Education.* Nashville, TN: B&H, 1998.

Towns, Elmer L. *Towns' Sunday School Encyclopedia.* Wheaton, IL: Tyndale House, 1993.

S

✠

TERTULLIAN
North African Latin Church Father
ca. 155–220

TERTULLIAN (CA. 155–220)

North African Latin church father Tertullian was one of the most significant and influential of the early Latin fathers. Tertullian was born at Carthage in North Africa (modern Tunisia) to pagan parents. Named Quintus Septimius Florens Tertullianus, he was sent to Rome, the imperial capital of the empire, to study law. The impact of his law studies, methodologically and often conceptually, remained throughout his life and can be observed in his later writings as a Christian. It was in Rome that Tertullian converted to Christianity and (like Augustine later) consequently rejected his prior sensuous lifestyle. Upon returning to Carthage he was an energetic and rigorous proclaimer and apologist for the Christian faith. However, because of what he believed to be a moral laxity, Tertullian broke away (ca. 200) and joined himself to the increasingly popular new Christian sect commonly known as Montanism (named after its founder and leader, Montanus). As a moral rigorist, Tertullian was especially attracted to austere Montanist asceticism with its strict moral codes, which he did not find in the Roman Church.

Highly educated and possessing great rhetorical skills with an excellent knowledge of prominent Greek and Latin authors, Tertullian put his rich background to effective use as a Christian theologian and apologist. Though at one level he rejected Christian tendencies to make prominent use of Greek philosophy for the purpose of explaining the Christian faith, especially via Plato and Aristotle ("What has Jerusalem to do with Athens?"), he himself made eclectic use of Greek thought, especially Stoicism, in order to give greater clarity to Christian doctrines against both pagans and heretics (for example, doctrines about the Trinity and Christ). His major works included *Apology* (197), *To the Martyrs* (197), *Testimony of the Soul* (198), *Prescription of Heretics* (203), *The Soul* (206), *Against Marion* (207), and *Against Praxeus* (210).

With the able help of fellow contemporary theologian Hippolytus, Tertullian greatly advanced the Christian understanding of God. The second-century church struggled with various attempts to give expression to such new covenant fulfillment via various "triadic" expressions of the Godhead. It was Tertullian who coined the word *Trinity* (Latin, *trinitas*) for use in Christian theology, and, whose formulations and succinct phrasing of the Godhead as "one substance consisting in the three persons" greatly advanced the church's thinking about God. Tertullian's ideas substantially led to the fuller trinitarian conclusions at Nicaea (325) and Constantinople (381). It was also Tertullian who, at this early stage, and against false teachings of the time, clarified the church's understanding of the person of Christ. He declared that Jesus Christ was composed "of two substances" (true deity and true humanity) in "one person, at once God and man." This insight greatly clarified the church's doctrine of Christ, thereby preparing the way for the decisive formulation at the Council of Chalcedon (451). In all his 30-plus extant works, Tertullian shows himself to be a passionate, careful, learned, faithful, and constructively innovative theologian who, as his faith caused him to seek understanding, helped the church increasingly to take hold of "the faith which was once for all delivered to the saints" (Jude 3).

John Douglas Morrison

Bibliography

Ante-Nicene Christian Library, vols. 7, 11, 15, 18. Boston: Adamant Media, 2001.

Roberts, Robert. *The Theology of Tertullian*. London: Epworth, 1924.

Warfield, B.B. *Studies in Tertullian and Augustine*. Grand Rapids: Baker, 2000.

TORREY, REUBEN ARCHER (1856–1928)

An American evangelist, pastor, educator, and writer, R.A. Torrey was born in Hoboken, New Jersey, to Reuben, a corporate banker, and Elizabeth. At age 15 he entered Yale, graduating in 1875. In his last year of college he experienced a spiritual crisis that brought him to his knees and led him to receive Christ. He later entered Yale Divinity School, graduating in 1878. Although Torrey was born to great wealth, his father's fortune was lost before both parents died in the summer of 1877. All he inherited was "a matchbox and a pair of sleeve buttons" (Reese).

In 1878, Torrey became pastor of the Congregational Church in Garrettsville, Ohio. The next year he married Clara Smith. Together they had five children. In 1882–1883, he studied at Leipzig and Erlangen universities. There, he was exposed to liberalism and higher criticism. Rejecting these teachings, Torrey became an even more convinced Fundamentalist. Returning to the United States, he organized the Open Door Church in Minneapolis. He pastored there for three years, then moved to the People's Church, where he served as pastor as well as the superintendent of the Congregational City Mission Society. He received no stated salary, relying on faith offerings for his support.

In 1889, when D.L. Moody was looking for someone to head his Chicago Evangelization Society (now Moody Bible Institute), Torrey, age 33, was highly recommended to him by his friend E.M. Williams. Torrey accepted the invitation, remaining as the CEO of the work until 1908. During this time he also led an evangelistic effort at the Chicago World's Fair (1893), and became pastor of the Chicago Avenue Church (1894), which was founded by Moody and later renamed The Moody Church (Moody, 100). Summers were spent at Northfield Bible Conference in Massachusetts with Moody.

When Moody collapsed during a crusade in Kansas City in 1899, it was Torrey who took up the mantle to continue the crusade. Upon Moody's death that same year, Torrey became the "Elisha" to continue Moody's evangelistic work (Reese). In 1902, adopting Moody's approach to evangelism, Torrey, along with with Charles Alexander, undertook a worldwide evangelistic ministry, holding services with crowds of thousands throughout America, Canada, Great Britain, China, Japan, Australia, and India. In 1907, Torrey was honored with a doctorate from Wheaton College.

Torrey wrote numerous articles and books, including *How to Work for Christ* and *The Person and Work of the Holy Spirit*. Like Moody, Torrey placed great emphasis on believers being filled with the Spirit. He also served as one of the main editors of *The Fundamentals*, a 12-volume work that set the tone for the fundamentalist movement in the earlier part of the twentieth century.

In 1912, Torrey went to Los Angeles to become the dean of the Bible Institute of Los Angeles (now Biola University), where the future radio preacher Charles E. Fuller was trained. Three years later he became the first pastor of the Church of the Open Door. In 1924 Torrey moved to Biltmore, North Carolina, and spent the next four years traveling, conducting Bible conferences, and lecturing. He died in 1928 in Asheville, North Carolina. An eloquent preacher, gifted educator, prolific writer, and aggressive soul-winner, Torrey was known chiefly as a man of prayer.

Daniel R. Mitchell

T

Bibliography

Kurian, G.T., ed. "Torrey, R.A." *Nelson's Dictionary of Christianity*. Nashville, TN: Thomas Nelson, 2005.

Moody, William. *D.L. Moody*. New York: Macmillan, 1930.

Reese, Ed. *The Life and Ministry of Reuben Torrey*. Knoxville, TN: Reese Publications, nd.

Torrey, R.A., ed. *The Fundamentals*. 4 vols. Grand Rapids: Baker, 1980 reprint of 1917 edition.

TOZER, AIDEN WILSON (1897–1963)

American pastor and author Aiden Wilson Tozer was more popularly known as A.W. Tozer by the multitudes who loved and read his many books and articles. Tozer was a pastor of Christian and Missionary Alliance churches, magazine editor, author, Bible conference speaker, and prayer warrior. But most will remember him as a deeper-life author. Tozer was born April 21, 1897, at a farm in Western Pennsylvania, and later moved to Akron, Ohio, where he was converted after hearing a street preacher proclaim how to become saved.

Tozer was called to pastor a small church in Nutter Ford, West Virginia, and he remained in the Christian and Missionary Alliance (CMA) denomination till his death in 1963. He pastored for 31 years in Chicago's Southside Alliance Church. He married Ada Cecelia Pfautz before taking his first church; they had six sons and one daughter. He was buried in Akron, Ohio, and his tombstone bears the epitaph "A Man of God."

Tozer's theology was a mild form of American Holiness that was a blend of Pietistic evangelicalism typical of the CMA and its founder A.B. Simpson. He sought to provoke his readers into examining their Christian professions of faith and urged a deeper walk with the Lord as an expression of true Christian discipleship.

In 1950, Tozer became editor of *The Alliance Weekly*, the newspaper arm of the CMA. His editorials reflected his longing for the person and presence of God. He wrote more than 40 books, and is remembered most for *The Knowledge of the Holy* and *The Pursuit of God*. While those two books are theological presentations about God, they also encourage the reader to seek a deeper relationship with God.

Elmer Towns

Bibliography

The Alliance Witness: Dr. A.W. Tozer Memorial Issue, July 24, 1963. http://www.cmalliance.org/resources/archives/alifepdf/AW-1963-07-24.pdf#search=pdf#search=%22Tozer%22. Accessed November 15, 2012.

Harris, Eleanor Lynn. *The Mystic Spirituality of A.W. Tozer*. San Francisco, CA: Mellen Research University Press, 1992.

Snyder, James L. *The Life of A.W. Tozer: In Pursuit of God*. Ventura, CA: Regal, 2009.

Tozer, A.W. *The Knowledge of the Holy*. New York: Harper & Row, 1961.

———. *The Pursuit of God*. Harrisburg, PA: Christian Publications, 1958.

TRENT, COUNCIL OF

The Council of Trent was an ecumenical council of the Roman Catholic Church, considered to be one of the Church's most important. It was the central event in what has generally been called the Counter-Reformation, but which many prefer to call the Catholic Reformation because it consisted of far more than merely a reaction to the Reformation. It was also an aggressive effort to deal with the issues and abuses that brought on the Reformation in the first place.

By the mid-sixteenth century, the spread of Protestantism and its putative "heresies" seemed unstoppable. "England and the Scandinavian kingdoms had broken with Rome, Protestantism was making strong inroads in France and the Netherlands, and also (especially among the nobility) in Poland, Austria and Hungary" (Marshall, 291). The issues were so complex that the council took 18 years to complete, spanning the pontificates of five Popes, while engaging in session for only four-and-a-half years. Pope Paul III convened the council in Trent, Italy, in 1545. The three sessions include the sessions in Trent, Italy, and later in Bologna 1545–1547 under Paul III, 1551–1552 under Julius III, and 1559–1563 under Pius IV.

While it was hoped by some that the Council of Trent would make concessions to the teachings of the Protestants (if only to reestablish political unity in countries split apart by religious factions), the first session did nothing of the sort. Instead, it established a theological beachhead to affirm traditional Catholic teachings on justification (the importance of works), the number of sacraments (seven), and the authority of tradition equal to that of Scripture. It was not until the later sessions that the issues of reform within the Roman Catholic Church came to be addressed. These included the condemnation of corruption within the administration of the Church, abuse of indulgences, and immorality among the priests and religious orders. The problem with uneducated clergy was addressed with the mandate to establish seminaries and to teach according to the scholastic method, not a biblical one. On the other hand, the teachings on purgatory, the priesthood as replacing the Levitical priesthood of the Old Testament, celibacy, the veneration of the saints, and especially of Mary, were upheld. The Vulgate was to be used in all public readings and the basis of all commentaries. The interpretation of the Scriptures was the prerogative of the Church, and anyone who held to a private interpretation was condemned.

The conservative shift within the Church was immediately felt and reflected in the leadership. Bishops became more pastorally minded. New religious orders were established to respond to the laxness of the late medieval religious orders such as the Capuchins, a breakaway from the Franciscans that sought to recapture the early vision of

Francis of Assisi (Marshall, 292). Trent established and normalized Catholic belief and practice for the next four centuries.

Daniel R. Mitchell

Bibliography

Marshall, Peter. "Counter-Reformation." *Encyclopedia of Christianity*. Edited by John Bowden. New York: Oxford University Press, 2005.

Mullett, M.A. *The Catholic Reformation*. New York: Routledge, 1999.

Piggin, F.S. "Trent, Council of." *The Evangelical Dictionary of Theology*, 2d ed. Edited by Walter A. Elwell. Grand Rapids: Baker Academic, 2006.

TYNDALE, WILLIAM (1494–1536)

English reformer and Bible translator William Tyndale, known as the father of the English Bible, was educated at Magdalen Hall and received both his BA and MA degrees at Oxford, where he was influenced by the humanism of Erasmus. In 1524, he traveled to Germany and met personally with Martin Luther. While in Wittenberg, he completed his English translation of the New Testament, which he later published at Worms. He was denounced by Thomas More as that "hell-hound of the devil's kennel," was eventually arrested in 1535 and held at Vilvoorde, near Brussels, and executed a year later by strangulation.

When Tyndale's original hopes to translate the Greek New Testament in England failed, he fled to Antwerp to continue the project on his own. However, once on the Continent, he found a valuable ally in Luther and came under his influence, which is reflected in his 1534 revision, which included marginal notes on the text of Revelation. Though Tyndale was strongly committed to the literal sense of Scripture and the polemic use of history, he tended to view the Apocalypse as allegorical.

Tyndale also wrote Old Testament commentaries and expositions on 1 John and Matthew 5–7. In 1528, he published *The Parable of the Wicked Mammon* and *The Obedience of a Christian Man*, emphasizing justification by faith alone and other Reformation doctrines. Duffield (990) notes, "His style was lucid, crisp, and concise, and above all appealed to ordinary people." Tyndale's amazing career included being shipwrecked, pursued by secret agents, and betrayed by his friends. His English New Testament became a standard for all other English Bibles to follow.

Some scholars estimate that up to 80 percent of the King James Version's New

Testament is based upon Tyndale's original translation, which included such phrases as "the salt of the earth," "let there be light," and "the spirit is willing." He was the first to translate Hebrew and Greek texts into English and print them in pocket volumes that could be easily obtained and read by the common people. Except for a few manuscripts translated into English from Latin, the Bible had been available only in Latin for 1000 years and few in England could read it. On one occasion when Tyndale was taunted by a Catholic priest who held that tradition was more important than Scripture, Tyndale responded, "If God spare my life, ere many years I will cause a boy that driveth the plough to know more of the Scripture than you."

Ed Hindson

Bibliography

Daniel, David. *William Tyndale: A Biography*. New Haven, CT: Yale University Press, 1994.

Duffield, G.E. "Tyndale, William." *The New International Dictionary of the Christian Church*. Edited by J.D. Douglas. Grand Rapids: Zondervan, 1978.

Edwards, Brian. *William Tyndale: Father of the English Bible*. Farmington Hills, MI: William Tyndale College, 1982.

McGoldrick, J.E. *Luther's English Connection: The Reformation Thought of Robert Barnes and William Tyndale*. Milwaukee, WI: Northwestern, 1979.

Wallis, N.H., ed. *The New Testament: Translated by William Tyndale 1534*. Cambridge: Cambridge University Press, 1938.

T

✠

WILLIAM TYNDALE
English Bible Translator
1494–1536

UNITARIANISM

Trinitarianism is the orthodox Christian belief in the one substance or essence of God in the three persons of Father, Son, and Holy Spirit. Some have accused Trinitarian belief of not satisfying the clear monotheistic teaching of Scripture, and others have implied that the teaching is grounded more in pagan philosophy than scriptural doctrine. Unitarians, who comprise an antitrinitarian religious movement, fall into this camp, stressing the oneness of God and ardently denying the deity of the Son and Holy Spirit. The earliest thoughts in this vein are found in third-century Monarchianism and a bit later in Arianism, both of which postulated the unity of God.

Michael Servetus (1511–1553) was executed in Geneva with the approval of John Calvin for his antitrinitarian beliefs, and is sometimes claimed as the first Unitarian martyr. This, however, did not stop movements toward Unitarianism as reactions against Calvinistic orthodoxy. This was a time rife with inquiry and open to rationalistic influences. With an increasing abandonment of historical creeds and confessions, the influences of reason and experience led some in England and Ireland to embrace Unitarian ideals. John Biddle (1615–1662) published Unitarian tracts that garnered him the title the "Father of English Unitarianism." He also was persecuted for his beliefs and eventually died in prison.

In 1791, Thomas Belsham (1750–1829) organized the first Unitarian Society. From this time Unitarianism developed theologically although it continued to encompass a wide variety of beliefs primarily committed to reason, freedom of the individual, piety, and social reform. During this same period, William Ellery Channing (1780–1842) became the best known American Unitarian. He grew up in Rhode Island under strict Calvinist preaching, but had a conversion experience as a Harvard undergraduate. In 1803, Channing became preacher of Boston's Federal Street Church. With his preaching influence and the teachings of liberal Harvard College, Boston became a center for Unitarian belief.

Through the nineteenth and twentieth centuries, Unitarianism's influence remained small but persistent. In 1961, the American Unitarian Association merged with the Universalist Church of America and formed the Unitarian Universalist Association of Congregations in North America. Though comprised of some Unitarians, the association has maintained no doctrinal standard, but rather a set of seven principles hinging on human dignity, social justice, acceptance, intellectual freedom, the democratic process, world peace, and mutual respect. Although these ideals are popular in secular circles, twenty-first century Unitarianism appears to be in a season of numerical decline because in its desire to include everyone, it may in fact turn out to include almost no one. Many see little difference between Unitarian Universalism and secularism in general.

Keith Church

Bibliography

Burke, Daniel. "Can Creedless Unitarians Make It Another 50 Years?" *Christian Century* 128 no. 15, July 26 (2011): 20-21.

Gow, Henry. *The Unitarians*. Garden City, NY: Doubleday, Doran, 1928.

Unitarian Universalists Association of Congregations. "Our Unitarian Universalist Principles." http://www.uua.org/beliefs/principles/index.shtml. Accessed September 6, 2012.

Wilbur, Earl Morse. *A History of Unitarianism, Socianism, and Its Antecedents*. Cambridge, MA: Harvard University Press, 1947.

Wright, Conrad. *The Beginnings of Unitarianism in America*. Boston: Starr King Press, 1955.

UNITY (UNITY SCHOOL OF CHRISTIANITY)

The Unity School of Christianity is a metaphysical and mystical blend of Christianity and pantheism. Unity, also known as the Unity School of Christianity, was founded by Charles (1854–1948) and Myrtle (1845–1931) Fillmore in 1889. Unity is a metaphysical system that believes the mind controls physical healing and produces prosperity. It is a merging of Eastern thought with Christian terminology and includes concepts such as pantheism and reincarnation. Consequently, biblical Christianity considers Unity a cult. Today, they are headquartered at Unity Village near Lee's Summit, Missouri.

When the Fillmores were married in 1881, Myrtle suffered from tuberculosis and Charles from a childhood leg injury. Engaged in various real estate ventures, they eventually settled in Kansas City, Missouri. In 1886, they attended New Thought classes held by Dr. E.B. Weeks, where Myrtle applied his teachings and allegedly was healed of her disease. Charles also claimed healing from his childhood injury. In 1889, Charles left the business world to begin Modern Thought. The name changed to Christian

Science Thought (1890), Thought (1891), and finally Unity in 1895. This final name reflected its synthesis of various ideas and philosophies. In 1906, Charles and Myrtle became ordained ministers of the organization, and they remained its driving force throughout their lives.

Unity believes that God is an impersonal principle, and not a personality. Moreover, God is in everything (panentheism), and sin is ignorance of one's indwelling divinity. To correct this error, Unity practices "affirmative prayer," positive affirmations to align one's words and thinking with the Universal God-Mind in order to receive such things as healing or prosperity. Concerning Christ, Unity separates Jesus from Christ in Gnostic-like manner. They claim Jesus was the man and Christ is the divine nature that lives in all of us. As in Hinduism, Unity's belief in reincarnation precludes judgment, hell, or the need for redemption. To achieve this metaphysical philosophy using Christian terms, Unity "spiritualizes" the Bible, wrenching the writing out of its historical context in an attempt to allegorize its message. The *Metaphysical Bible Dictionary* is their standard for biblical interpretation. Evangelicals reject almost all of the basic tenets of Unity School theology as heretical aberrations of Christian doctrine.

Unity teaches salvation through a series of reincarnations of the body, and that all people will eventually become like Christ by overcoming illness through correct personal thought.

Terry Barnes

Bibliography

Fillmore, Charles. *Metaphysical Bible Dictionary*. Unity, 1995. http://www.scribd.com/doc/23469146/Charles-Fillmore-Metaphysical-Bible-Dictionary. Accessed July 17, 2012.

Martin, Walter. *The Kingdom of the Cults*. Minneapolis: Bethany House, 1985.

McDowell, Josh, and Don Stewart. *Handbook of Today's Religions*. San Bernardino, CA: Here's Life Publishers, 1992.

Mead, Frank S. *Handbook of Denominations in the United States*. Nashville, TN: Abingdon, 1995.

U

UNIVERSALISM

Universalism is the doctrine of universal salvation. Universalists believe that all moral and rational beings—including humans, angels, and fallen angels—will ultimately be reconciled to God. Many universalists deduce their belief from other beliefs, such as the infinite love of God, and others attempt to find universalism in the Bible. For most of Christian history the belief in a literal, eternal hell has been prominent and universalism has been rare, with a few notable exceptions. For example, Origen (ca. AD 185–254) taught that creatures who have, of their own free will, fallen (to varying degrees) from God are destined to a process of purification. For humans who experience death, that process of purification begins in one's embodied life on earth and continues after the death of the body until the process is complete. Origen believed the soul may remain in hell for an indefinite period of time, but because every creature has free will, salvation is always a possibility.

A few notable Christian thinkers in the fourth and fifth centuries were clearly universalists, including one of the Cappadocian fathers, Gregory of Nyssa (335–394). Origin's view was condemned at the Second Council of Constantinople in 553, and universalism never was accepted in the Christian East or West, except among a few dissenters such as medieval theologian Johannes Scotus Eriugena (who lived during the ninth century).

Universalists can be found throughout Christian history, though they are never predominant. Those who deny universalism usually point to biblical passages that indicate the everlasting nature of the final resting place of the wicked (for example, see Matthew 25:46; Revelation 20:10).

Brian Goard

Bibliography

Ballou, Hosea. *Ancient History of Universalism: From the Time of the Apostles to the Fifth General Council*. Boston: Universalist Publishing House, 1872.

Ludlow, Morwenna. *Universal Salvation: Eschatology in the Thought of Gregory of Nyssa and Karl Rahner*. Oxford: Oxford University Press, 2009.

Parry, Robin A., and Christopher H. Partridge, eds. *Universalism: The Current Debate*. Grand Rapids: Eerdmans, 2003.

Scott, Mark S.M. *Journey Back to God: Origen on the Problem of Evil*. Oxford: Oxford University Press, 2012.

VAN TIL, CORNELIUS (1895–1987)

American Reformed theologian and revolutionary apologist Cornelius Van Til taught for more than 40 years at Westminster Theological Seminary in Philadelphia, Pennsylvania. Born in Grootegast, Holland, and emigrating to Highland, Indiana, with his family at age ten, he was raised in a devout Dutch Reformed community. Van Til was educated at Calvin College and Seminary, Princeton Seminary, and Princeton University (PhD, 1927) and taught apologetics for one year at Princeton Seminary (1928–1929). Ordained in the Christian Reformed Church (1927), he pastored for one year in Michigan. When J. Gresham Machen founded Westminster Seminary in 1929, Van Til was invited to become one of the founding faculty members as professor of apologetics and remained there his entire career (1929–1976). In 1936, he left the Christian Reformed denomination and joined Machen's newly formed Orthodox Presbyterian Church, where he remained for the rest of his life.

Van Til's apologetic system was built upon his acceptance of traditional Reformed theology as the best expression of biblical theology. Dutch Reformed influences included Herman Bavinck and Abraham Kuyper, who taught that there is no episte mological neutrality in any area of thought. The "traditional method" of apologetics, Van Til believed, wrongly allows reason, often disguised as "neutral," to sit in judgment over God and His Word. Because the Triune God of the Bible is the self-contained Creator, then man as creature must either start with submission to his self-disclosure in his Word or begin by rejecting the authority of that revelation. Thus denying neutrality, Van Til's apologetic clearly believes in the use of reason but it must be in submission to God's Word in order to think God's thoughts after him. Van Til attempted to prove that all human reasoning presupposes God and thus can be neither autonomous nor neutral.

Since there is no epistemological common ground with an unbeliever, one must defend the faith presuppositionally. The believer admits that all systems of thought are circular in that they all must presuppose an authority for their starting point. The unbeliever starts with fallen human reason, while the believer starts with the Triune God and his revelation, the Bible. In the process of interaction, the believer demonstrates that starting with man leads one to irrationality and meaninglessness, while starting with God's revelation one is able to interpret reality rationally in a way that results in meaning and purpose. According to Van Til, one defends the faith with the faith and in the process proclaims the gospel. His "transcendental approach" seeks to demonstrate that one must posit the truths of God's Word to have any hope for rationality, while the "traditional approach" wrongly attempts to defend the faith upon the presupposition of autonomous rationalism.

Van Til produced over 300 publications, including almost 40 books. Some of his more important works include *Why I Believe in God* (1948), *Christian Apologetics* (1975), *The Defense of Christianity and My Credo* (1971), and *The Defense of the Faith* (1955, 1963).

Thomas Ice

Bibliography

Bahnsen, Greg L. *Van Til's Apologetic: Readings and Analysis*. Phillipsburg, NJ: P&R Publishing, 1998.

Frame, John M. *Cornelius Van Til: An Analysis of His Thought*. Phillipsburg, NJ: P&R Publishing, 1995.

Muether, John R. *Cornelius Van Til: Reformed Apologist and Churchman*. Phillipsburg, NJ: P&R Publishing, 2008.

White, William. *Van Til—Defender of the Faith*. Nashville, TN: Thomas Nelson, 1979.

VATICAN COUNCILS

The two Vatican Councils are so named for their meeting location, in the Vatican Basilica. Vatican I convened under Pope Pius IX in December 1869 and adjourned October 1870. The previous Roman councils met in the Lateran Basilica, hence the name Lateran Councils. Both Vatican Councils met to confront the challenges of modernity to the authority and identity of the Roman Catholic Church.

While the primary purpose of Vatican I was to define the Catholic Church against the errors of rationalism, it was initially distracted with the issue of the infallibility of the bishop of Rome. The appeal to papal infallibility had been used by Pope Pius IX in his papal bull, *Ineffabilis Deus* in 1854 to define the dogma of the immaculate conception of Mary. However, papal infallibility itself, as dogma, had not been defined, and the attempt to do so was met with mixed responses. Few doubted the infallibility of the Pope, but not everyone agreed that this was the time to define it (McBrien, 1297).

V

Nevertheless, in the document *Pastor aeternus*, it was affirmed that the Pope has "full and supreme power of jurisdiction over the whole Church" (chapter 3:9); and that, when he speaks *ex cathedra*, he "possesses infallibility" (chapter 4:9). The meetings were suspended in 1870 when the Franco-Prussian War broke out and the kingdom of Italy captured Rome. Vatican I was not formally closed until 1960, prior to Vatican II.

Vatican II was convened by Pope John XXIII on October 1962 and closed December 1965 under Pope Paul VI. The overarching purpose of Vatican II was to complete the unfinished business of Vatican I concerning the nature and identity of the Roman Catholic Church in a modern world. By this time the challenges were only exacerbated by the advances in technology and the profound political, cultural, and religious changes worldwide. Of those who took part in the council's opening session, four to date have gone on to become Pope: cardinal Giovanni Battista Montini became Paul VI; bishop Albino Luciani became Pope John Paul I; bishop Karol Wojtyła became Pope John Paul II; and Father Joseph Ratzinger, who became Pope Benedict XVI, until his retirement in February 2013.

In his first charge to the council after the death of John XXIII, Pope Paul VI stated the mission of the council was to more fully define the nature of the Roman Catholic Church and the role of the bishop, to renew the Church, to restore unity among all Christians, and to start a dialogue with the contemporary world. Of the many documents produced, the Dogmatic Constitution on the Church, *Lumen Gentium*, is especially important. The first chapter, "The Mystery of the Church," affirms "the sole Church of Christ which in the Creed we profess to be one, holy, catholic and apostolic...as 'the pillar and mainstay of the truth.'" Yet in many ways Vatican II would break with the traditional view of the Catholic Church as standing "over against" the world and defined its role in solidarity with the world, its cultures, and its humanity.

This, in turn, would be seen as a new openness to "separated brethren" (Protestants, Eastern Catholics) and "anonymous Christians" (non-Christians of other faiths, or no faith at all), leading to a universalist view of the Church as the communion of all humanity.

Another important contribution of Vatican II was its repudiation of anti-Semitism and its previous teachings that the Church has replaced the Jews, who, in turn, remain under a curse. To mark the fiftieth anniversary of the beginning of Vatican II, Pope Benedict XVI declared the period from October 2012 to the end of November 2013 a "Year of Faith" in reaffirming the Apostles' Creed and the Niceno-Constantinopolitan Creed.

Daniel R. Mitchell

Bibliography

Faculty of Catholic University of America, ed. (1967). "Vatican Council II." *New Catholic Encyclopedia*, XIV. New York: McGraw-Hill, 1967.

Hasler, A. *How the Pope Became Infallible: Pius IX and the Politics of Persuasion*. New York: Doubleday, 1981.

Kelly, Joseph F. *The Ecumenical Councils of the Catholic Church: A History*. Collegeville, MN: Liturgical Press, 2009.

McBrien, Richard P. *The HarperCollins Encyclopedia of Catholicism*. San Francisco: HarperSanFrancisco, 1995 .

VULGATE

The Vulgate is the Latin version of the Bible translated by the church father Jerome between AD 384 and 405. The word *vulgate* means "common" and reflects its purpose as the translation in the Latin vernacular (common tongue) of the Western Roman Empire. It was commissioned by Pope Damasus, and much later at the Council of Trent it became the only version officially sanctioned by the Roman Catholic Church. As such, it has exercised considerable influence in Western Christendom.

Pope Damasus's concern over the many scribal errors in the copies of the Old Latin Version, the Itala (ca. AD 150–200), provided the impetus for asking Jerome, one of the ablest scholars of his day, to create an entirely new translation that would standardize the text utilized by the faithful in the Latin churches.

Jerome began his task in Rome and by 384 had translated the Gospels and Psalms, but after the death of Damasus, he lost favor in Rome and journeyed to Bethlehem, where he oversaw an order and completed his work on the Old Testament after having learned Hebrew. His translation of the Old Testament from the original Hebrew was met with much opposition from those, including Augustine, who favored the Greek translation, the Septuagint, as the inspired version. Jerome did not think highly of the apocryphal books and only reluctantly included some of them in his translation.

The impact of the Vulgate on Western Christendom was substantial. Jerome's effort created a version that influenced Western Christianity for more than a millennium, even figuring prominently in the debates between the reformers and the Roman clerics. As an updated Latin version in the language of the Roman Empire, it aided in the growth of the church by providing the Bible in a vernacular used across the empire. As the standard version, it provided a common court of appeal for ecclesiastical debates.

The Vulgate also enriched the language of theology with Anglicized Latin terms

V

such as *justification* and *sanctification*. Through the Latin renderings, Greek terms translated *apostle* and *baptism* have entered the vocabulary of the church. Fulfilling its role as the official Latin version of Roman Catholicism guarantees the influence of this ancient version on a large segment of Christendom for the foreseeable future.

David Pettus

Bibliography

Hartman, L.F., B.F. Peebles, and M. Stevenson. "Vulgate." *New Catholic Encyclopedia*, vol. 14. 2d ed. Detroit, MI: Gale, 2003.

Kelly, J.N.D. *Jerome: His Life, Writings and Controversies*. New York: Harper & Row, 1975.

Newton, William L. "Influences on St. Jerome's Translation of the Old Testament." *Catholic Biblical Quarterly* 5/1, January 1943.

Sparks, H.F.D. "Jerome as a Biblical Scholar." *The Cambridge History of the Bible*, vol. 1. Edited by P.R. Ackroyd and C.F. Evans. Cambridge: Harvard University Press, 1970.

Tkacz, Catherine Brown. "LABOR TAM UTILIS: The Creation of the Vulgate." *Vigilia christiana* 50/1, March, 1996.

V

✠

JOHN WESLEY
English Methodist Minister
1703–1791

WALDENSIANS

Founded by Peter Waldo, also known as Valdesius (ca. 1140–1220), the Waldensian movement suffered persecution during the first 500 years of its existence, and therefore is scattered, with most Waldensians living in Europe, then Canada, the United States of America, and some congregations in South America. Because the Waldensians are so scattered, and many merged with other denominations, the number of adherents is difficult to ascertain. Waldensian scholars point to the emergence of Waldensian, Hussite, Wycliffite, and Bohemian Brethren ideas as pre-Reformation protestations against Roman Catholicism.

Waldo was a wealthy merchant in Lyons, France, when, around 1160, he began teaching and preaching that one should live a simple life. He gave part of his wealth to his wife and the other part to the poor. As he traveled he preached about this simple life as well as against clerical excesses and certain Catholic dogmas, most notably purgatory and transubstantiation. He also taught the sole authority of the Bible. He attracted a following, and some of these individuals also traveled and preached throughout France and Italy.

In 1179, Waldo was able to meet with Pope Alexander III. Waldo's ideas were not accepted, and he was condemned at the Third Lateran Council in 1179. Waldo continued to travel and preach and gain followers. Because of this he was excommunicated in 1184. Eighty of his followers were executed by burning in Strasburg in 1211. The Waldensians were condemned in 1215, which is also the first time the name appears when it is listed as a heretical group at the Fourth Lateran Council. At this point the Catholic Church began systematically persecuting and killing Waldensians. In 1487, Pope Innocent VIII issued a bull calling for their extermination.

With the advent of the Protestant Reformation, the Waldensians found a home in the like-minded reformers in central Europe. Many Waldensians joined with the Reformed movement. Still, many Waldenians continued to be killed by Catholics, with an estimated 1700 brutally killed in one massacre in 1655. Thus, the persecuted Waldensians came to view themselves as the "Israel of the Alps."

By the late 1700s the persecutions had ended, but the Waldensians were widely scattered and displaced. Many remained in the Reformed movement and became part of Presbyterianism, others joined the Anabaptists or Mennonites, and still others joined the Methodists. By and large the Waldensians remained a self-governing group until the Reformation, when most joined the different branches of the Reformation at some point over time. For example, the Waldensian Presbyterian Church in Valdese, North Carolina, was built by Waldensians in 1899 but is now a part of the Presbyterian Church (USA).

Some small groups of Waldensians still exist. For example, the Waldensian Evangelical Church in Italy joined forces with the Italian Methodists to form the Union of Methodist and Waldensian Churches in 1979; they have approximately 30,000 members, with 15,000 more in Argentina and Uruguay. The American Waldensian Society was created in 1906 and supports the churches in Italy as well as elsewhere.

Mark Nickens

Bibliography

Arbuthnot, Charles W. *The Waldensians*. Turin, Italy: Claudiana, 1980.

Audisos, Gabriel. *The Waldensian Dissent: Persecution and Survival, c. 1170–c. 1570.*
    Cambridge: Cambridge University Press, 1999.

Tourn, Giorgio. *The Waldensians: The First 800 Years (1174–1974)*. Turin, Italy: Claudiana, 1980.

WALVOORD, JOHN F. (1910–1999)

American dispensational theologian John Walvoord served as president of Dallas Theological Seminary (DTS), in Dallas, Texas, from 1952–1986. He was born in Sheboygan, Wisconsin, in 1910, and graduated from Wheaton College in 1931. He then entered Dallas Seminary, completing the ThB, ThM, and ThD degrees by 1936. He also received an MA from Texas Christian University in 1945 and an honorary LittD from Liberty University in 1984. He initially served as a professor of systematic theology and assisted then President Lewis Sperry Chafer in editing his eight-volume *Systematic Theology*. Walvoord later became president of Dallas Seminary upon Chafer's death in 1952. Under his leadership, the school received full accreditation and grew into one of America's largest evangelical institutions.

W

Walvoord published 23 books, which mainly dealt with aspects of dispensational eschatology. These included commentaries on Revelation (1966), Daniel (1971), and Matthew (1974); and *The Millennial Kingdom* (1959), *Israel in Prophecy* (1962), and *Major Bible Prophecies* (1991). From 1983–1985 he served as coeditor of the two-volume *Bible Knowledge Commentary* and for several years as the executive editor of the *Bibliotheca Sacra* theological journal.

Under Walvoord's leadership, DTS spawned dozens of Bible colleges and hundreds of independent Bible churches that emphasized expository preaching and dispensational eschatology. Walvoord combined academic excellence with personal humility and piety and served as an excellent role model for the many scholars and pastors whom he trained in his more than 60 years of service at DTS.

Mal Couch

Bibliography

Couch, Mal, ed. *Dictionary of Premillennial Theology*. Grand Rapids: Kregel, 1996.

Elwell, Walter, and J. Weaver, *Bible Interpreters of the 20th Century*. Grand Rapids: Baker, 1999.

Walvoord, John F., with Mal Couch. *Blessed Hope: The Autobiography of John F. Walvoord*. Chattanooga, TN: AMG, 2001.

WARFIELD, BENJAMIN BRECKINRIDGE (1851–1921)

Benjamin Breckinridge Warfield was a Presbyterian minister, apologist, and theologian at Princeton Theological Seminary. Standing in the line of Archibald Alexander and Charles Hodge, Warfield represented the best of Old Princeton.

Warfield was raised in a genteel Presbyterian family in Kentucky. He was educated at Princeton, where he was deeply influenced by Hodge before undertaking additional studies in Europe at the University of Leipzig. When he came back to the States, he served as a Presbyterian minister and a professor at Western Seminary (1878–1887), but the bulk of his career was spent at Princeton Seminary, where he served as professor of theology (1887–1921). Warfield's theology was conservative, biblical, and Calvinistic. He stressed the theology of Augustine, Calvin, and the Westminster Standards. His theology was anchored in Scripture, and he provided an able theological defense of biblical authority.

Warfield published widely. He edited *The Presbyterian and Reformed Review* and frequently contributed to *The Princeton Theological Review*. The Oxford edition of his works includes ten volumes, and there are other collections of his articles and reviews. Unable to travel or be involved with denominational service because of his wife's health, Warfield instead defended the faith through his extensive writings.

W

Warfield carefully observed new theological trends. He was concerned about tendencies toward subjectivism and emotionalism, perfectionism and modernism. He provided careful assessments of theological developments in Europe. He wrote from a biblical worldview perspective, noting that liberal authors started with different presuppositions, having rejected a supernatural worldview.

Warfield championed biblical inerrancy. In articles on "Inspiration" (1881) and "The Inerrancy of the Original Autographs" (1893), Warfield defended the reliability of the Scriptures. While open to analysis and criticism of the transmission of biblical manuscripts, Warfield insisted that the original autographs, as given to the apostles under the inspiration of the Holy Spirit, were inerrant. In the late nineteenth century, the Presbyterian Church emphasized this high view of Scripture in multiple theological trials. The Princeton doctrine of inerrancy was a crucial theological standard for American Fundamentalists.

Warfield's relationship with the Fundamentalist movement was ambiguous. He emphasized biblical inspiration and contributed an article titled "The Deity of Christ" for *The Fundamentals*. But he did not affirm dispensational premillennialism, as most Fundamentalists commonly did. His position on evolution firmly rejected Darwin's view of natural selection, but was open to the idea of progressive evolution, provided that it was governed by the providence of God. Warfield also stressed Christian devotion. While the Princetonians had a reputation for scholastic orthodoxy, recent scholarship notes their emphasis on piety. Warfield's writings included *The Lord of Glory*, *The Plan of Salvation*, *Counterfeit Miracles*, *Revelation and Inspiration*, *Calvin and Calvinism*, and two volumes titled *Perfectionism*.

Roger Schultz

Bibliography

Helseth, Paul. *Right Reason and the Princeton Mind: An Unorthodox Proposal.* Phillipsburg, NJ: P&R Publishing, 2010.

Hoeffecker, Andrew. *Piety and the Princeton Theologians: Archibald Alexander, Charles Hodge, and Benjamin Warfield.* Phillipsburg, NJ: P&R Publishing, 1981.

Johnson, Gary, ed. *B.B. Warfield: Essays on His Life and Thought.* Phillipsburg, NJ: P&R Publishing, 2007.

Noll, Mark, ed. *The Princeton Theology: 1812–1921.* Grand Rapids: Baker, 1984.

Zaspel, Fred. *The Theology of B.B. Warfield: A Systematic Summary.* Wheaton, IL: Crossway, 2010.

W

WATTS, ISAAC (1674–1748)

Isaac Watts was an English hymn writer as well as a philosopher, theologian, and pastor. With possibly as many as 750 hymns to his name, he has been called the father of English hymnody. But his published works, in addition to three volumes of sermons, included books on grammar, pedagogy, logic, ethics, psychology, astronomy, and geography. His *Logic* became the standard text on logic at Oxford, Cambridge, Harvard, and Yale for nearly a century thereafter.

Isaac was the oldest of nine children born to a dissenter from the Anglican Church at Southampton, England. In 1690, he entered the dissenting academy located at Stoke Newington. Later he joined a large independent church in London, where he eventually became the pastor. However, ill-health soon forced him to leave the rigors of pastoral work. Subsequently he was invited to live with Sir Thomas Abney, who, together with his wife, Mary, became Isaac's patron for the remainder of his life.

From his earliest years, Watts demonstrated a high intelligence and aptitude for learning. He was studying Latin at age four. He later studied Hebrew, Greek, and French at the King Edward VI School. He had a natural talent for rhyme almost to the point of distraction. The story is told that when his father threatened him with corporal punishment for interrupting evening prayers with a rhyme, the lad cried out, "O father, do some pity take, and I will no more verses make."

Some of Watts's better-known hymns include "Come Ye that Love the Lord," "Come Holy Spirit," "Jesus Shall Reign Where'er the Sun," and "When I Survey the Wondrous Cross." His most-published book was his *Psalms of David* (1719), consisting of poetic paraphrases of the Psalms. These were adapted to express New Testament truths of Christianity as they were fulfilled in Jesus Christ. Examples of this are his paraphrase of Psalm 90, "O God, Our Help in Ages Past," and Psalm 98, "Joy to the World."

Music scholar Stephen Marini suggests that Watts broke with the older tradition of the Calvinists, who limited their hymns to the poetry of the Bible. Watts introduced original songs from Christian experience and spirituality, while at the same time articulating objective affirmations of Christian doctrine. For example, "When I Survey the Wondrous Cross" articulates solid doctrinal content while, at the same time, articulating a personal reflection of confident faith (Marini, 71-76). Following Watts in this tradition are many of the great names associated with evangelical Christianity, such as Charles Wesley, Ann Steele, Augustus Toplady, John Newton, William Cowper, Timothy Dwight, John Leland, and Peter Cartwright (Marini, 71-76).

Benjamin Franklin was responsible for publishing the American edition of Watts's

W

Psalms of David in 1729. Watts's hymns were later published in Boston and were well known to Americans by the time of the Revolution. After his death in 1748, his papers were donated to Yale in Connecticut.

Daniel R. Mitchell

Bibliography

Marini, Stephen. *Sacred Son in America; Religion, Music and Public Culture*. Urbana, IL: University of Illinois Press, 2003.

WESLEY, CHARLES (1707–1788)

Charles Wesley was born in Epworth, England, the son of an Anglican clergyman. While at Oxford, he formed a small group of fellow students devoted to Bible study and spiritual development. His brother, John Wesley, later joined, and a few others had formed similar groups, which constituted the early beginnings of Methodism. In May 1738, though already an ordained Anglican deacon, he experienced an intensely personal conversion during a period of fellowship with the Moravians.

While not usually remembered as the churchman or theologian that his brother John was, Charles nevertheless made his own contributions to Methodism and Protestant Christianity in general. He is perhaps best known for his hymns, many of which were a means of personal devotion and sermon preparation. The estimates of how many he wrote number between 6000 to 9000, and they include, "Hark, the Herald Angels Sing," "O for a Thousand Tongues to Sing," "Christ the Lord Is Risen Today," and "Love Divine, All Loves Excelling." Over 400 of his hymns are still found in contemporary hymnals (Tyson, vii-viii).

Wesley's hymnody reflects a deep theological understanding on both intellectual and emotional levels, with lyrics often inspired by his own life experiences. "O for a Thousand Tongues to Sing," for example, was originally a poem written to commemorate the one-year anniversary of his conversion. Many of his songs also encapsulate the gospel in its entirety, in many ways mirroring sermons by an evangelist. They tell the story of a person struggling with sin, accepting God's grace by faith, and rejoicing in new life. Set in context, these musical works expounded Methodist theology and Wesleyan views on the atonement, the new birth, and conversion. They also helped fuel the fires of revival both in England and in the United States.

Charles Wesley was more than a song writer. He was a devout Anglican, and was committed to Methodism as a true reform movement within the church, laboring for

W

more than 50 years to keep the movement firmly within the Anglican communion. This put him increasingly at odds with a growing number of lay preachers in England who pushed for separation from the Church of England. Even his brother John came to favor more autonomy for Methodism, and Charles began to clash with him as well. The ordination of preachers for America was a particular point of contention and for a time deeply saddened Charles. He continued to support and pray for the Church of England even after it became clear Methodism would split from the mother church.

Charles married Sarah Gwynne in 1749 at a ceremony officiated by his brother. The marriage was a happy one, but it did play a role in Charles eventually giving up the itineracy that characterized early Methodist preachers. By 1771, he had settled in London and primarily ministered to urban congregations. Frail health also limited his preaching ministry. Yet he continued to write hymns until his death, in his last days dictating to his wife a final verse praising God for salvation. With his family by his side, he died at his home in London.

Joseph Super

Bibliography

Bailsford, Mabel. *A Tale of Two Brothers: John and Charles Wesley.* New York: Oxford, 1954.

Heitzenrater, Richard P. *Wesley and the People Called Methodists.* Nashville, TN: Abingdon, 1995.

Osborn, George. *The Poetical Works of John and Charles Wesley.* London: London Wesleyan-Methodist Conference Office, 1868.

Newport, Kenneth G.C., ed. *The Sermons of Charles Wesley: A Critical Edition with Introduction and Notes.* New York: Oxford, 2001.

Tyson, John R. *Assist Me to Proclaim: The Life and Hymns of Charles Wesley.* Grand Rapids: Eerdmans, 2007.

W

WESLEY, JOHN (1703–1791)

English founder of Methodism and brother of Methodist hymn writer Charles Wesley (1707–1788), John Wesley was born the fifteenth child in 1703 of Samuel and Susanna Wesley. His father was reactor of the Epworth, Church of England congregation. At age five he was rescued from the burning rectory and that experience stayed with him the rest of his life because he described himself as a "brand plucked from the fire" (Zechariah 3:2). John was educated at Christ Church and Lincoln College, receiving his MA degree in 1727. The seeds of the Methodist Church were planted while Wesley was a student at Oxford when he joined a group called the Holy Club begun by his brother Charles Wesley (and which included George Whitefield). Others sarcastically called the members of this group *methodists* because of their methodical commitment to holiness.

John Wesley is the founder of what have become the United Methodist Church of the United States, the Methodist Church of Great Britain, and the African Methodist Episcopal Church. He traveled widely, walking or riding on horseback, preaching three or four times each day, building chapels, and ordaining lay preachers. It is estimated he rode 250,000 miles, preached 40,000 sermons, and gave £30,000 to charity. Within one generation after his death, Methodism had spread around the world. By 1776, during the Revolutionary War, there were 243 Methodist churches in the United States, and by the War of 1812, there were more than 5000 churches.

John Wesley spent almost two years in Savannah, Georgia (1735–1737), with the purpose of establishing a Church of England among the colonists and evangelizing the American Indians. During this time Wesley wrote of his experiences and personal failures in his journal, including the statement, "I went to America to convert the Indians, but who will convert me?" While in America, Wesley met 21 German Moravians who talked to him about the matter of personal conversion. Returning to England, he had his Aldersgate conversion experience May 24, 1738, when at a Moravian meeting he heard the reading of Martin Luther's preface to his *Commentary on Romans,* "I felt my heart strangely warmed," he later wrote. A few weeks later he preached a sermon on the necessary doctrine of personal salvation, which reflected his conversion and kindled a "fire" in his soul, which he said, "I trust will never be extinguished."

George Whitefield had established a ministry in Bristol, England, and wanted John Wesley to take it over because Whitefield was going to minister in Georgia. Wesley was horrified when he saw Whitefield preach in the open air to miners at Kingswood, a nearby village, but had a change of mind when he read that Jesus preached in the open fields. Many miners professed faith in Christ, and thus began a Methodist revival. So Wesley began to preach wherever a crowd gathered, and on occasions he stood on his father's tomb at Epworth to preach.

As Wesley preached throughout England, his message of personal salvation and sanctification was rejected by the established clergy and most pulpits were closed to him. There were many physical altercations from mobs and ecclesiastical attacks from Anglican pulpits, and Wesley's critics claimed he taught strange doctrines and led people astray.

As a result of this opposition, Wesley began providing chapels in which his followers could worship, establishing the Bristol Chapel in 1739. From then on, Wesley became a fervent evangelist who conducted open air services and formed Methodist societies to preserve the results of his preaching missions. Eventually, the chapels and societies would become the Methodist Churches of England.

John Wesley began ordaining ministers and appointing lay preachers to make a circuit of preaching. Many of them did not have university educations, but Wesley felt what was important was that these men had the Holy Spirit. Most of these lay preachers began and each preached at 20 to 40 Methodist chapels.

After England lost the American Revolution, Wesley was concerned that Methodists in America could no longer have communion, so he ordained Thomas Coke, who was the bishop of the movement in America. Coke, along with Francis Asbury, helped spread Methodism in America during the eighteenth and nineteenth centuries.

John Wesley had ongoing controversies with Calvinism and wrote against that viewpoint. He believed in free will and preached unlimited atonement. He often mentioned "prevenient grace"—that is, that all persons were capable of personal salvation by faith in Christ. He did not derive faith from reason, but taught that reason, church tradition, and personal experiences must be subservient to Scripture.

Wesleyan theology basically rests on the foundation of Arminian theology. John Wesley's view of sanctification meant that a Christian could be made "perfect in love." He rejected eradication of the old nature and sinless perfection. For Wesley, "perfect love" was the expression of the soul in perfect obedience to Christ. Sin was disobedience to a known law of God. For Wesley, the sinfulness of humans resulted from their deliberate choosing of sin, which, in turn, corrupted their sinful human nature.

John Wesley's influence is felt in the United Methodist Church, the Free Methodist Church, the Church of the Nazarene, the Wesleyan Church, and the Christian and Missionary Alliance Church, among others. As well, his doctrine of entire sanctification as a second work of grace has influenced many Pentecostal and Charismatic churches.

Elmer Towns

W

Bibliography

Ayling, Stanley. *John Wesley*. New York: Collins, 1980.

Baker, F., ed. *The Works of John Wesley*. 34 vols. Nashville, TN: Abingdon, 1984.

Cox, L.G. *John Wesley's Concept of Perfection*. Kansas City, MO: Beacon Hill, 1964.

Monk, R.C. *John Wesley: His Puritan Heritage*. Nashville, TN: Abingdon, 1966.

Tuttle, R.G. *John Wesley: His Life and Theology*. Grand Rapids: Zondervan, 1978.

WESTMINSTER CONFESSION

The Westminster Confession is a doctrinal statement of Presbyterian Calvinism drawn up at Westminster in London between 1643 and 1646. The Westminster assembly was convened in 1643 during the English Civil War to write a statement of doctrine and church polity that would be "more agreeable to God's word…and Reformed churches." The original assembly summoned by Parliament consisted of 121 theologians ("divines"), 10 lords, and 20 commoners, along with 4 ministers and 2 elders of the Church of Scotland. The assembly first met July 1, 1643, and continued to meet over a period of years, during which time they wrote the Westminster Confession of Faith and the Larger and Shorter Catechisms. Originally published as *Confessio Fidei* in Latin and *The Humble Advice of the Assembly of Divines…Sitting at Westminster* in English, the doctrinal confession later became known simply as the Westminster Confession. Strongly influenced by Calvinist English Puritans and Scottish Presbyterians, the confession later became the standard doctrinal statement of most English-speaking Presbyterian churches in England, Scotland, and America. The Westminster Confession also influenced the development of the Savoy Declaration of Congregational Churches (1658), and the Philadelphia Confession of Baptists (1688).

Ed Hindson

Bibliography

Jellama, Dirk. "Westminster Confession." *The New International Dictionary of the Christian Church*. Edited by J.D. Douglas. Grand Rapids: Zondervan, 1978.

Murray, Ian. *The Reformation of the Church: A Puritan and Reformed Anthology*. London: Banner of Truth, 1965.

Schaff, Philip. *The Creeds of Christendom*. 3 vols. Grand Rapids: Baker, 1966.

Warfield, B.B. *The Westminster Assembly and Its Work*. Grand Rapids: Baker, 1981.

W

WHITE, ELLEN GOULD (1827–1915)

Seventh-day Adventist (SDA) leader Ellen White was born in Gorham, Maine, and she received very little formal education because of poor health as a child. Her parents embraced the Adventist teachings of William Miller, who predicted the return of Christ on October 22, 1844. When this did not occur, Adventists claimed Miller's visions as prophetic messages indicating that Jesus Christ had entered the Holy of Holies of the heavenly sanctuary to begin his investigative judgment in 1844. Adventists also point to Ellen White's claim to have seen a halo of glory around the Sabbath commandment on the Ten Commandments as evidence that affirmed the importance of the Sabbath doctrine.

Ellen Gould Harmon married elder James White in 1846, and in 1855, they moved the headquarters of the SDA Church and its publishing arm to Battle Creek, Michigan. Ellen is revered by the SDA as a "true prophetess" and inspired leader and messenger. She authored 64 works, including *The Great Controversy Between Christ and Satan* (1888), *The Desire of Ages* (1898), *The Ministry of Healing* (1905), and numerous works published posthumously.

Mrs. White toured Europe for two years and spent nearly ten years in Australia and spent her later years in California, where she died of a fall in 1915 when she was 88 years of age.

White's theology included a strong emphasis on biblical creation, health reforms, a historicist view of eschatology, and a strong anti-Catholic view of church history. Adventists repudiate Sunday worship as the "mark of the Beast" and adhere to strict Saturday Sabbath worship. In 1903, the SDA headquarters moved to Washington, DC.

Ed Hindson

Bibliography

Froom, L.E. *The Prophetic Faith of Our Fathers*. 4 vols. Washington, DC: Review and Herald, 1954.

Hoekema, Anthony. *The Four Major Cults*. Grand Rapids: Eerdmans, 1984.

Martin, Walter. *The Kingdom of the Cults*. Rev. ed. Minneapolis: Bethany House, 2003.

White, Ellen G. *Christ in His Sanctuary*. Mountain View, CA: Pacific Press, 1969.

W

WHITEFIELD, GEORGE (1714–1770)

Great Awakening evangelist George Whitefield was the youngest of seven children. He was only two when his father died, leaving care of the family to his mother, who maintained the Bell Inn in Gloucester, Britain. Whitefield later described his youth as being wasted by filthy talking, lying, and stealing. On the brighter side of things, he also loved the theater and spent much of his time reading plays and acting them out. He listened carefully to the preachers of his day and imagined what it would be like to be one himself.

Whitefield entered Pembroke College at Oxford when he was seventeen as a *servitor,* the lowest level of the students admitted. He joined the Wesley brothers' Holy Club there, and not long after he repented of his sin, put his faith in Jesus Christ, and received the forgiveness that only God can give. The next year he was ordained by the Church of England, and began preaching. His preaching was so well received among the lay people that he was immediately and extensively requested to preach in various churches in Bristol and London. His close friendship with the Wesley brothers resulted in his going to Savannah, Georgia, to continue the work they had begun there. His preaching was received every bit as enthusiastically in Georgia as in Britain, but his heart yearned for the orphans he met in Georgia, and he founded an orphanage there.

When Whitefield returned to Britain, he was not as welcome by church leaders as by the people. His preaching style was very energetic and dramatic. Because he was not invited to speak in pulpits, he began to preach outdoors in the streets, fields, and anywhere else a congregation would gather. His preaching brought about responses of repentance, faith, and joy in knowing people had been forgiven.

Over time, Whitefield and the Wesleys had a falling out. Whitefield was an unapologetic Calvinist whose preaching struck a chord with the Presbyterian and Reformed Christians in Scotland, South Wales, and America. The Wesleys, by contrast, took a turn toward Arminianism. Wesley was the better organizer, so his Methodist congregations flourished in England and America. Whitefield was the better preacher, so he traveled extensively, being the main figure of the First Great Awakening in America and its counterpart in Britain. He befriended Benjamin Franklin in Pennsylvania, who was one of his many supporters and helped toward building an orphanage in Georgia. Whitefield also befriended Selina, Countess of Huntingdon, who funded the building of a chapel and a tabernacle in Britain. Whitefield's schedule of preaching at least three or four times per day eventually wore him down, but not before he established the Calvinist Methodist Church, which particularly flourished in Wales.

Whitefield's zeal and success was contagious. Not only did God use Whitefield's ministry to turn thousands toward Christ, but many preachers followed his example in Britain and America. In America, Whitefield's influence crossed denominational barriers among Baptists, Congregationalists, and Presbyterians. Many would come to refer to him as the father of the First Great Awakening.

Kenneth Cleaver

Bibliography

Dallimore, Arnold A. *George Whitefield: God's Anointed Servant in the Great Revival of the Eighteenth Century.* Wheaton, IL: Crossway, 1990.

Philip, Robert. *Life and Times of George Whitefield.* Edinburgh: Banner of Truth Trust, 2007.

Stout, Harry S. *The Divine Dramatist: George Whitefield and the Rise of Modern Evangelicalism.* Grand Rapids: Baker, 1991.

WILBERFORCE, WILLIAM (1759–1833)

William Wilberforce's early life was typical of a boy raised in a wealthy home in England until the death of his father in 1768. After this, Wilberforce's mother sent him away to live with his uncle and aunt. However, because of the Methodist influences of his extended family, he was returned home at the age of 12. At age 14 he wrote a letter to the York newspaper about the evils of the slave trade. By the time he attended college at the age of 17, he was independently wealthy due to family inheritances (Pollock, 1-9).

Wilberforce, while still a student at St. John's College, was elected to Parliament at the age of 21. During this time he maintained a social life that included drinking and gambling. In 1785, Wilberforce converted to Christianity while on a trip to Europe with Isaac Milner. He was also influenced greatly by John Newton, who by this time had long since left the slave trade to become a minister. In addition, Newton counseled Wilberforce to remain in public service, advice that was contrary to the view evangelicals held at the time. Heeding Newton's counsel, Wilberforce joined the Clapham Sect, a group of evangelicals who were active in public life.

Wilberforce largely focused the remainder of his career in Parliament on efforts to abolish the slave trade. According to Wilberforce's own words, he viewed the abolition of the slave trade as a call of God in his life (Pollock, 69). For two decades, Wilberforce labored unsuccessfully for the abolition of British slave trading. But finally, in February 1807, a bill to abolish the slave trade was passed. Wilberforce continued

W

to work toward the complete abolition of slavery in England even after his retirement from Parliament in 1826. In 1833, just a few days before he died, the *Slavery Abolition Act* had passed a third reading in the Commons, which guaranteed its passage. Wilberforce died on July 29, 1833, knowing that the slavery in England would be abolished, a cause for which he fought his entire adult life.

John Cartwright

Bibliography

Furneaux, R. *William Wilberforce*. London: Hamilton, 1974.

Pollock, John Charles. *Wilberforce*. New York: St. Martin's Press, 1978.

Wilberforce, William. *A Letter on the Abolition of the Slave Trade*. Yorkshire: T. Cadell & W. Davies, & J. Hatchard, 1807.

WILLIAMS, ROGER (1603–1683)

English colonial Baptist Roger Williams was born in London and attended Cambridge University, where his studies were supported by a prominent lawyer of that time, Sir Edward Coke, who had been impressed with Williams's shorthand skills. Coke often defended those who were persecuted for religious cause by the established Church of England. Thus, Williams developed sympathy for the persecuted, and became an advocate of religious freedom. He completed his MA studies for the ministry but was not ordained, since that required that he receive Anglican ordination. He became a private chaplain on Sir William Masham's estate, where he met and married Mary Barnard.

When Williams's Puritanism developed into Separatism, he fled England for America, as did many Separatists. Upon his arrival in Boston in 1631, Williams was asked to serve the Boston church (Puritan), but refused, stating that he was not willing to serve an "unseparated" people. His ministry over the next five years was divided between Salem and Plymouth. While at Plymouth, he established a trading post that did business with the Narragansett Indians and began efforts toward evangelizing them. While at Salem, Williams's views against civil enforcement of religious uniformity brought him into conflict with the Boston court. He felt that religious persecution had no biblical sanction. Under the threat of banishment back to England, Williams fled into the wilderness in January 1636 and spent the winter in the teepee of Massasoit, his Indian friend.

W

In the spring of 1636, Williams established Providence Plantations on land he had purchased from the Indians, and he drew up a government to deal with civil matters only, thus separating church and state. He later helped to found the first Baptist church in America in 1639. He engaged in a pamphlet war with John Cotton, pastor of a church in Boston, writing *The Bloody Tenet of Persecution*, to which Cotton responded with his *The Bloody Tenet of Persecution Washed White in the Blood of the Lamb*. Because Providence (Rhode Island) came under the threat of domination by the Massachusetts Bay Colony, Williams and his good friend, John Clarke, pastor of the Baptist church at Newport, traveled to England seeking a parliamentary charter in 1644, which they received. They sought a parliamentary charter rather than a royal charter because England at that time was engaged in a civil war between the king and Parliament, and it seemed unlikely that a colony practicing religious freedom would be able to secure support from King Charles I.

When the monarchy was restored in England in 1660, it became necessary to seek a royal charter, which was granted by Charles II in 1663. Charles called Rhode Island a "lively experiment" to see if in fact a government could survive in which church and state were separated. Thus, Williams provided the first example of Baptist convictions placed under trial, and set the pattern that later generations would implement in the first amendment to the United States Constitution, which established the separation of church and state.

Carl Diemer

Bibliography

Gammell, William. *Life of Roger Williams: The Founder of the State of Rhode Island.* Np: Forgotten Books, 2010.

Gaustad, Edwin S. *Roger Williams (Lives & Legacies).* New York: Oxford University Press, 2005.

Miller, Perry. *Roger Williams: His Contribution to the American Tradition.* Paris, AR: The Baptist Standard Bearer, 1962.

W

WINTHROP, JOHN (1588–1649)

American Puritan John Winthrop was born in Suffolk, England, and attended Trinity College, Cambridge, and studied law at Gray's Inn. He was chosen governor of the Puritans and led their exodus to Massachusetts in 1630. A firm believer in covenant theology, he modeled the new colony after the pattern of Israel in the Old Testament. He laid down his principles of Christian government in *A Model of Christian Charity* (1630), which called for both moral purity and theological conformity. In 1643, he became the first president of the New England Confederation.

Ed Hindson

Bibliography
Marsden, George. "Winthrop, John." *The New International Dictionary of the Christian Church*. Edited by J.D. Douglas. Grand Rapids: Zondervan, 1978.

WITHERSPOON, JOHN (1723–1794)

Scottish-American Presbyterian minister John Witherspoon had an enormous impact on American education, religion, and politics. His greatest influence was as the president of the College of New Jersey, now Princeton University, from 1768 to 1794. Witherspoon was born and educated in Scotland. His early career was as a minister in the Presbyterian Church, where he was a leader of the evangelical Popular Party, which opposed the liberal Moderate faction. Witherspoon's *Ecclesiastical Characteristics*, a religious satire about liberal churchmen, made him famous on both sides of the Atlantic.

Witherspoon was president of Princeton for nearly 30 years, providing continuity for a school whose earliest presidents had short tenures and untimely deaths. His students had outstanding careers in the church, law, medicine, and especially politics, and they included a president and vice president of the United States, 9 cabinet officers, 21 United States senators, 39 congressmen, 3 justices of the Supreme Court, 12 state governors, 56 state legislators, 30 state judges, and 13 college presidents. His most famous student was James Madison, father of the US Constitution.

Witherspoon was an American patriot and served in the New Jersey legislature and in the Continental Congress (Collins, 776-82), contributing to vital committees. His *Dominion of Providence over the Passions of Men*, written in 1776, made a passionate

W

case for American independence. He was a signer of the Declaration of Independence, the only clergyman who signed the document. The British considered Witherspoon a driving force in the Revolution and Princeton a "seedbed of sedition."

Witherspoon was a philosopher, advocating the Scottish Common Sense Realism. While some criticize Witherspoon for this assumed Enlightenment influence, it is likely that he used Scottish Realism to combat the radical, skeptical enlightenment. Recent scholarship has stressed Witherspoon's Scottish Christian roots. He was a committed churchman, and he played a key role in creating a national Presbyterian General Assembly in 1789, drafting foundational documents and serving as the first moderator. Many Presbyterian ministers in the Assembly had been Witherspoon's students, and Princeton became a model for church-related Presbyterian academies and colleges that sprang up around the country.

Above all, Witherspoon was a committed evangelical. In the *Dominion of Providence*, for instance, before ever discussing politics, Witherspoon emphasized the gospel. He stressed the need for all to be born again, noting that there was no hope of heaven without accepting Jesus Christ as personal Savior. Though politically active, Witherspoon emphasized the primacy of spiritual and eternal matters. For future generations of evangelicals, Witherspoon was a faithful minister engaged in vital political causes.

Roger Schultz

Bibliography

Collins, Varnum Lansing. *President Witherspoon: A Biography.* 2 vols. New York: Arno Press, 1925, repr. 1969.

Mailer, Gideon. "Anglo-Scottish Union and John Witherspoon's American Revolution." *The William and Mary Quarterly* 67:4 (October, 2010).

Miller, Thomas. *The Selected Writings of John Witherspoon.* Carbondale, IL: University of Southern Illinois Press, 1990.

Morrison, Jeffrey H. *John Witherspoon and the Founding of the American Republic.* South Bend, IN: University of Notre Dame Press, 2007.

Tait, L. Gordon. *The Piety of John Witherspoon: Pew, Pulpit, and Public Forum.* Louisville, KY: Geneva Press, 2000.

W

WORD OF LIFE FELLOWSHIP

Word of Life Fellowship is an international youth ministry committed to the evangelization and discipleship of youth. Although Word of Life was not officially an organization until 1942, the roots of this ministry began as a Bible study with four men in Jack Wyrtzen's home. Wyrtzen (1913–1996) eventually surfaced as Word of Life's natural and later selected leader. Under Wyrtzen's leadership, Word of Life (WOL) Fellowship became known for its effective evangelistic rallies held in New York City in places like Times Square, Carnegie Hall, Madison Square Garden, and Yankee Stadium. During this time, WOL also began radio broadcasting from coast to coast.

In 1947, WOL acquired a 45-acre island in the middle of Schroon Lake (located in upstate New York). This island became an oasis for teenage evangelism. Under the leadership of Wyrtzen, an adult conference center was established (Word of Life Inn), a children's camp began (Ranch and Ranger Camp), the Family Campground was formed, and later, the Word of Life Florida Youth Camp and Conference Center was built. Also a two-year, college-level Bible institute began (Word of Life Bible Institute) as well as a program of evangelism and discipleship for the local church (Student Ministries).

In 1950, WOL became an international organization and sent its first missionaries, Harry Bollback and Harold Reimer, to Brazil. By the time Jack Wyrtzen died in 1996, WOL was in 37 countries. George Theis (WOL missionary to Brazil), prior to Jack's death, was selected as WOL's next director. He was followed by Joe Jordan (a WOL missionary to Argentina). Under their leadership, Word of Life continued to increase its influence and gospel witness around the world, and WOL expanded into another 29 countries.

The reins of leadership were then passed on to Donald H. Lough Jr. in 2011. Today Word of Life Fellowship continues to be known for its camps, student ministries (discipleship programs under the auspices of local churches), and Bible institutes, all of which are found across the globe. As of 2012, Word of Life was ministering in 66 countries, their camps were being attended by over 100,000 youth a year, its mission board had 1138 missionaries, and young people were studying at its 13 Bible institutes.

Paul Weaver

W

Bibliography

Bollback, Harry. *The House that God Built: The Story of Jack Wyrtzen.* Rev. ed. Schroon Lake, NY: Word of Life Fellowship, 2005.

Jackson, Dave, and Neta Jackson, eds. *Celebration: Fifty Faithful Years.* Schroon Lake, NY: Word of Life Fellowship, 1989.

Sweeting, George. *The Jack Wyrtzen Story.* Grand Rapids: Zondervan, 1960.

Wyrtzen, David. "Words of Life: Jack Wyrtzen." *More Than Conquerors*. Chicago: Moody Press, 1992.

WORLD COUNCIL OF CHURCHES

Officially founded in 1948 at Amsterdam, the World Council of Churches (WCC) united 147 churches from 44 countries in a concerted effort to unify the Christian witness. The origin of a global church movement is generally credited to the Edinburgh Missionary Conference of 1910 and subsequent conferences on Faith and Order at Lausanne in 1927, Edinburgh in 1937, and Oxford in 1937, which led to a call for a world council of churches. By the end of the twentieth century, the WCC had 322 member churches with its headquarters at Geneva, Switzerland.

The Roman Catholic Church began sending observers in 1968 but has remained outside the WCC as have almost all evangelical church bodies. The official basis of membership is stated as "a fellowship of churches which confess the Lord Jesus Christ as God and Saviour according to the scriptures, and therefore seek to fulfil together their common calling to the glory of the one God, Father, Son and Holy Spirit." However, the WCC has since adopted the dictum, "Doctrine divides, but service unites."

With the increasing trend of liberal theological bias in the mainline denominations, the WCC has tended to advocate liberal theological, social, and political positions in an effort to maximize ecumenical cooperation, often at the expense of biblical Christianity. Issues such as globalism, feminism, and homosexuality have dominated the life and work emphasis of the WCC. The Peace Commission has been especially critical of Israel and focused on Palestinian rights. Much of what the WCC defines as ministry is really more about socialist political and economic agendas that are often completely divorced from the gospel. As a result, most evangelicals have continued to remain outside the WCC.

Mal Couch

Bibliography
Buchanan, C. "World Council of Churches." *The New International Dictionary of the Christian Church*. Edited by J.D. Douglas. Grand Rapids: Zondervan, 1978.

Hoekstra, Harvey Thomas. *The World Council of Churches and the Demise of Evangelism*. Carol Stream, IL: Tyndale House, 1979.

W

WYCLIFFE, JOHN (1329–1384)

English reformer and Bible translator John Wycliffe (or Wyclif) became known as "the Morning Star of the Reformation" because many of his views were similar to those of the later reformers. He denied transubstantiation, urged the abolition of religious orders, repudiated indulgences, and suggested the Pope was the Antichrist. He received his Doctorate in Theology from Oxford (1372), where he was a lecturer at the university, in addition to serving as a rector in parish ministry at Lutterworth. His teachings were condemned by the Pope in 1377, and he and his followers were expelled from Oxford by the Catholic Bishop Courtenay in 1382. Wycliffe retired to his Lutterworth parish, where he died of a stroke in 1384 and was buried in the church graveyard. Later, in a posthumous attack by the Roman Catholic Church in 1428, Wycliffe's body was exhumed, burned, and his ashes thrown into the Swift River.

During the final years of his life, Wycliffe wrote extensively despite constant trials and hearings to deal with his supposed heresies. These writings included his *Summa Theologiae*, *Trialogus*, *De Potestate Papae* (in which he identified the Pope as the Antichrist), and his English translation of the Vulgate. Wycliffe has been not only identified as a proto Reformer, but also as the father of the English Bible. Since he was the first to identify the Roman Catholic Church in general, and the Pope in particular, as the Antichrist, he is also generally viewed as the father of the Protestant apocalyptic tradition. Many of his ideas influenced the Lollards in England and the followers of Jan Huss (Hussites) in Bohemia.

Wycliffe's views were extremely popular with the Puritans, and his system of eschatology was well accepted by them. Wycliffe himself was greatly influenced by the hermeneutical principles developed by Nicholas of Lyra and his followers, who interpreted biblical prophecies as a picture of the continual conflict between Christ and the Antichrist. Like many scholars of the late Middle Ages, Wycliffe viewed the 1000 years of the binding of Satan as predicting the age of the church from the edicts of Constantine (325) until the loosing of Satan in the fourteenth century (ca. 1325). Thus, it became a matter of logical deduction to assume that the papacy was indwelt by Satan during Wycliffe's lifetime.

Wycliffe received popular support from the people, scholars, and many of the nobles of England because of his outspoken opposition to papal authority, clerical abuses, and foreign encroachment upon the English churches. His emphasis on the Bible alone as the sole source of truth provided a new stimulus of genuine gospel preaching by a group of Oxford graduates known as the Poor Priests and later identified as the

Lollards. Despite opposition from the Roman Catholic Church hierarchy, Wycliffe lit the first flames of what would later become the Protestant Reformation.

Ed Hindson

Bibliography

Clouse, Robert. "Wycliffe." *The New International Dictionary of the Christian Church*. Edited by J.D. Douglas. Grand Rapids: Zondervan, 1978.

Fristedt, S.L. *The Wycliffe Bible*. Stockholm: Fristedt, 1953.

Parker, G.H.W. *The Morning Star: Wycliffe and the Dawn of the Reformation*. Exeter: Paternoster Press, 1968.

Winn, H.E., ed. *Wyclif: Select English Writings*. Oxford: Oxford University Press, 1929.

WYRTZEN, JACK (1913–1996)

Casper John von Wyrtzen, popularly known as "Jack," was a passionate evangelist as well as the founder and director of Word of Life Fellowship, an international ministry devoted to the evangelization and discipleship of youth. Jack was raised in Brooklyn, New York. As a child his family occasionally attended a Unitarian church, but his father was hostile toward the gospel. At the age of 19, Jack came to faith in Christ after the persistent witness and consistent testimony of George Schilling. Eventually, Jack and George, along with two others, began meeting to study the Bible in Wyrtzen's bedroom. They formed what they called the Chi Beta Alpha (XBA), which stood for Christians Born Again. Their group quickly grew and other accommodations had to be found. In 1942, XBA became Word of Life Fellowship.

During the 1940s and 1950s, Wyrtzen led many evangelistic rallies. Masses of people attended, and thousands made professions of faith in Christ. Some of the more notable locations at which these rallies were held include the Old Alliance Gospel Tabernacle on Times Square, Carnegie Hall, Madison Square Garden, Yankee Stadium, Boston Garden, and the Philadelphia Convention Center.

Next, Wyrtzen began a coast-to-coast radio broadcast. Then in 1947, he turned his attention to setting up a camp ministry after Word of Life acquired a 45-acre island (renamed Word of Life Island) in the middle of Schroon Lake in upstate New York. The Word of Life ministry later developed an adult conference center (Word of Life Inn), then built the Word of Life Florida Youth Camp and Conference Center near

W

Tampa Bay. Also, a two-year, college-level Word of Life Bible Institute was added in 1971. Today, Word of Life operates 13 Bible institutes and camping programs in 66 countries reaching over 100,000 people each year.

Paul Weaver

Bibliography

Billy Graham Center Archives, transcripts of personal interview with Jack Wyrtzen by Robert Shuster on October 5, 1991. http://www2.wheaton.edu/bgc/archives/GUIDES/446.htm#3. Accessed August 29, 2012.

Bollback, Harry. *The House that God Built: The Story of Jack Wyrtzen.* Rev. ed. Schroon Lake, NY: Word of Life Fellowship, 2005.

Jackson, Dave, and Neta Jackson, eds. *Celebration: Fifty Faithful Years.* Schroon Lake, NY: Word of Life Fellowship,1989.

Sweeting, George. *The Jack Wyrtzen Story.* Grand Rapids: Zondervan, 1960.

Wyrtzen, David. "Words of Life: Jack Wyrtzen." *More Than Conquerors.* Chicago: Moody Press, 1992.

W

XAVIER, FRANCIS (1506–1552)

Francis Xavier was a pioneer Jesuit Catholic missionary to India and Japan in the sixteenth century. Born in the Kingdom of Navarre (modern Spain), Xavier went on to study at the University of Paris. In Paris, he came into contact with Ignatius of Loyola and became a founding member of the Society of Jesus or the Jesuits—the most innovative missions movement within the Roman Catholic Church from the sixteenth to eighteenth centuries.

In 1542, Xavier arrived in southern India as a representative of the Portuguese king. His ministry was centered on teaching the Parava, a newly converted and largely illiterate people who worked as fishermen. Though Xavier did not master the Tamil language, a simple liturgy was developed and the Parava were organized into 16 villages for teaching and spiritual discipline. While coordinating these ministries, Xavier had a particular focus on evangelizing children.

In 1549, after meeting a Japanese man named Yajiro, who had fled his country, Xavier and two Jesuits made the commitment to go to Japan. There, they encountered a number of challenges. First, Yajiro proved not to be a very helpful cultural guide. Second, the Jesuits struggled to translate many Christian ideas and terms into Japanese; so they opted to use transliterated Portuguese words instead. Despite these difficulties, after two years, they reported some 100 Japanese converts. After Xavier's death in 1552, the Jesuits continued to carry on a fruitful ministry and many Japanese people had been evangelized by 1600.

Xavier is important to church and missions history. First, despite his clear challenges with understanding language and culture, his pioneering spirit and willingness to go to India and Japan set the stage for a long-standing Jesuit missions presence in those regions. Second, he was an innovator in contextualizing the gospel. After coming into contact with the Japanese and admiring some noble aspects of their culture, he rejected the prevailing Roman Catholic missions presupposition that nothing of value could be found within a non-Christian culture. In short, Xavier led the way in looking for appropriate cultural bridges to clarifying the gospel—a practice continued by Protestant pioneer missionaries William Carey and Hudson Taylor.

Edward Smither

Bibliography

Coleridge, Henry James. *The Life and Letters of St. Francis Xavier*. Toronto: University of Toronto, 2011.

Neill, Stephen. *A History of Christian Missions*. London: Penguin, 1991.

O'Malley, John W. *The First Jesuits*. Cambridge, MA: Harvard University Press, 1995.

Tucker, Ruth A. *From Jerusalem to Irian Jaya: A Biographical History of Christian Missions*. Grand Rapids: Zondervan, 2004.

X

YOUNG MEN'S CHRISTIAN ASSOCIATION (YMCA)

The Young Men's Christian Association (YMCA) is recognized to be one of the oldest and largest youth movements in the world, currently reaching 119 countries and touching the lives of nearly 58 million people. The YMCA, founded by George Williams in 1844, had its beginnings in London, England. He and 11 other men agreed to form a society for the sole purpose of evangelism, winning others to faith in Jesus Christ. In a short period of time, Williams was able to establish other YMCA branches throughout the British Isles.

In 1851, Thomas Valentine Sullivan, a retired sea merchant, observed the needs of merchants and sailors and desired to establish a "safe-haven" ministry near the Boston harbor. Encouraged by the success of the YMCAs in England, he established the first YMCA in the United States. The rapid expansion of this organization resulted in the formation of the World Alliance of YMCAs in Paris in 1855, just 11 years after its founding by Williams. The delegates attending this conference adopted a clear mission statement to evangelize and disciple young men in their Christian faith.

The early success of the YMCA could be attributed to these factors: (1) the large number of young people moving to the industrialized cities; (2) the growing influence of the evangelical movement; (3) the ecumenical appeal of the organization; and (4) the involvement of lay volunteers. Sidney Ahlstrom (742) noted that the YMCA in the United States entered "upon their half-century of greatest vitality and usefulness during the 1870s."

In the twentieth century, the YMCA in the United States became more focused on social service programs. The effects of World War I and the Great Depression caused this organization to evaluate its mission and modify its programs to meet the needs of society. During this time, there was a marked increase in enrollment in the education, vocational training, and physical exercise classes. Therefore, there was an increase in cooperation with social welfare agencies. The World Alliance of YMCAs reaffirmed its Christian heritage by adopting the Kampala Principles in July 1973 and Challenge 21 in 1998, which stated that the YMCA is "a world-wide Christian, ecumenical, voluntary movement for women and men with special emphasis on the genuine involvement of young people and that it seeks to share the Christian ideal of building a human community of justice with love, peace and reconciliation for the fullness of life for all creation."

John Durden

Bibliography

Ahlstrom, Sydney E. *A Religious History of the American People*. 2d ed. New Haven, CT: Yale University Press, 2004.

Gaustad, Edwin, and Leigh Schmidt. *The Religious History of America*. New York: HarperCollins, 2002.

Latourette, Kenneth Scott. *A History of Christianity: Reformation to the Present*, vol. 2. Rev. ed. San Francisco: Harper & Row, 1975.

YOUTH FOR CHRIST

Youth for Christ is an international evangelical Christian youth movement. All across America during the early 1940s, dozens of evangelists were conducting rallies to reach the large number of young people going out on the weekend as well as the young servicemen who were home from duty. These meetings were often held in a hall or neutral location on a Saturday night and had similar programs that utilized radio broadcasts, exciting testimonies, upbeat music, and a lively message. To describe the rally, a banner was hung out front, and "Youth for Christ" went from being a slogan to the name of an emerging movement. With the popularity of these rallies increasing, it became clear that more than just a common strategy was needed; there should be an organization based on a shared vision.

Torrey Johnson, director of Chicagoland for Christ and coauthor of *Reaching Youth for Christ*, was the catalyst for forming a national Youth for Christ in 1944. A year later he led the movement to become Youth for Christ International. Johnson was elected president at the organization's first annual meeting and helped shape its early identity. He was also responsible for hiring Billy Graham as Youth for Christ's first full-time evangelist.

Traveling across America, to Canada, and throughout Europe, Graham brought Youth for Christ (YFC) unprecedented attention. His most notable campaign of this era was the Christ for Los Angeles campaign in 1949. The meetings were scheduled to last three weeks but were extended to eight weeks because of the size of the crowds. In total, more than 350,000 people came to the tent and listened to Graham preach in Los Angeles.

Y

By the early 1950s, Graham had moved on from YFC to his own Billy Graham Evangelistic Association. In addition, Johnson had declined another term as president. Bob Cook, who had been with YFC from the beginning, became the next president. Cook helped facilitate a change in operations that emphasized clubs over rallies. This new strategy allowed the movement to grow further. Jack Hamilton had the title of Bible Club Director, and by the end of his tenure, YFC had more than 2500 clubs.

Eventually the youth of the 1940s became the parents of the 1960s. Baby Boomers were now the teens. In response, YFC adopted a Campus Life approach that had an equal emphasis on evangelism and discipleship. Since that time YFC has done some further restructuring and has developed more personalized ministries. The influence of these newer specializations can be seen in the number of church youth groups in America that mirror the YFC style.

YFC emerged from a network of evangelists who had a common strategy to reach the youth of their day. Over time, the organization's methods changed from rallies to clubs, then shifted to Campus Life, and ultimately became the spectrum of personalized ministries that exist today.

Dan Russell

Bibliography

Carpenter, Joel. "Geared to the Times, but Anchored to the Rock." *Christianity Today*, November 1985.

Graham, Billy. *Just As I Am: The Autobiography of Billy Graham*. New York: Harper Collins, 1997.

Johnson, Torrey, and Robert Cook. *Reaching Youth for Christ*. Chicago: Moody Press, 1944.

Larson, Mel. *Young Man on Fire: The Story of Torrey Johnson and Youth for Christ*. Chicago: Youth Publications, 1945.

Shelley, Bruce. "The Young and the Zealous." *Christian History and Biography*, Fall 2006.

Youth For Christ. "History." http://www.yfc.net/about/history/.

Y

YOUTH WITH A MISSION

Youth With A Mission (YWAM, popularly pronounced "y-wàm") is an international nondenominational mission agency that has been sending young people across the globe to fulfill the Great Commission since 1960. Established by Loren Cunningham and originally based out of his parents' California home, YWAM has grown into the largest, youth-specific mission organization in the world. With its decentralized structure, YWAM has over 18,000 full-time staff working in over 1000 locations scattered across 180 countries worldwide. Each year, YWAM trains and sends out approximately 25,000 short-term missions volunteers.

The concept of YWAM came to Cunningham in a vision he had as a 20-year-old Assemblies of God college student. In the vision, he saw scores of teenagers like ocean waves crashing onto the shores of every country to share the good news of Christ. Cunningham then began planning and mobilizing a youth-driven strategy for faith-based, parachurch global missions. In 1960, YWAM organized its first missions trip, sending two young men to a leper colony in Liberia.

Over the next few decades, YWAM grew in its popularity and reach—increasing in staff, property, and volunteers. Early in its formation, Cunningham was asked to integrate YWAM into the mission structure of the Assemblies of God denomination, but he preferred to retain the agency's interdenominational focus. Today, YWAM regularly partners with a broad range of missions organizations, including Cru (formerly Campus Crusade for Christ), the International Mission Board of the Southern Baptist Convention, United Bible Societies, and Wycliffe Bible Translators, among others.

Rather than maintaining a centralized headquarters, YWAM characterizes itself as a "family of ministries"—allowing each operating center to determine its program and work. Even so, YWAM has maintained a three-pronged strategy for missionary activity: evangelism, training, and mercy ministries. In addition to conducting short-term trips, YWAM engages in evangelistic efforts through Olympic outreaches (since 1972) as well as youth rallies, which utilize drama, music, art, and door-to-door evangelism.

YWAM's training is primarily offered through its Discipleship Training School—a six-month study and service program available at numerous locations worldwide. Furthermore, its unaccredited University of the Nations—which has branch campuses in 600 locations, providing classes in over 100 languages—offers Associate's, Bachelor's, and Master's degree programs.

In terms of mercy ministry, YWAM engages in humanitarian aid, disaster relief work, women's rights protection in developing countries, as well as medical work.

Y

Though established in the United States, today more than half of YWAM's staff comes from non-Western countries. YWAM's purpose statement is to "know God and to make Him known."

J. Tyler Scarlett

Bibliography

Cannister, Mark W. "Youth Ministry Pioneers of the 20th Century, Part II: Jack Wyrtzen, Jim Rayburn, Torrey Johnson, Don McClanen, and Loren Cunningham." *Christian Education Journal*, Fall 2003: 176-88.

Cunningham, Loren. *Is That Really You, God?* Seattle, WA: YWAM Publishing, 1984.

Kennedy, John W. "Youth with a Passion." *Christianity Today*, December 2010.

Youth With A Mission. www.ywam.org. Accessed August 2012.

Y

✠

ULRICH ZWINGLI
Swiss Reformer
1483–1531

ZINZENDORF, NICHOLAS VON (1700–1760)

Zinzendorf was a wealthy German nobleman who helped set the stage for the modern Protestant missions movement. After the untimely death of his father and his mother's subsequent remarriage, he was raised by a Pietist grandmother. The Pietists were a movement within German Lutheranism that valued a heartfelt relationship with God as much as a commitment to sound doctrine.

While at university, Zinzendorf was a part of the Order of the Grain of Mustard Seed, a fraternity committed to Christian love and proclaiming the gospel. Initially on course for a career in state service, the expected vocation for a nobleman, Zinzendorf sensed a greater call for the ministry. In 1722, he began to invite Protestant refugees from Moravia to his estate at Berthelsdorf, which he called Herrnhutt ("the Lord's watch"). After five years of living, worshipping, and praying together, the group, later referred to as Moravians, experienced a revival. One habit that developed in the community was a 24-hour prayer chain that would continue for the next 100 years.

In 1731, Zinzendorf attended the coronation of King Christian VI of Denmark, a Pietist monarch who had a great burden for global missions. During the ceremonies, Christian shared with Zinzendorf about the great spiritual needs of Greenland, which prompted the nobleman-pastor to appoint Moravians to serve there. Over the next decade, Moravians began serving in the Virgin Islands, South America, Canada, South Africa, and among native North Americans. They were also instrumental in witnessing to John Wesley, the founder of Methodism. Eventually, about one out of every 60 Moravians served as a full-time, cross-cultural missionary, and the Moravian Church adopted the slogan "Every Christian is a missionary," meaning that everyone in the body of Christ had something to contribute (for example, prayer, financial giving) to the global task. The Moravians were also innovative in that they were both evangelists and tentmakers. They emphasized God's love and salvation, and supported themselves as carpenters and skilled laborers. Though Zinzendorf's wealth was helpful in launching missions efforts, the Moravians were committed to developing skills that would enable them to sustain themselves.

In short, Zinzendorf was a Pietist Christian whose convictions led him to forsake the typical path of nobility to serve as a pastor and missions mobilizer. He was willing to use his wealth and influence to place missionaries in needy places around the world. Ultimately, the Moravian story anticipated the nineteenth-century work of William Carey and others in the "great century" of missions.

Edward Smither

Bibliography

James, R. Alton. "Post-Reformation Missions Pioneers." *Discovering the Mission of God.* Edited by Mike Barnett and Robin Martin. Downers Grove, IL: InterVarsity, 2012.

Neill, Stephen. *A History of Christian Missions.* London: Penguin, 1991.

Tucker, Ruth A. *From Jerusalem to Irian Jaya: A Biographical History of Christian Missions.* Grand Rapids: Zondervan, 1983, 2004.

ZWINGLI, ULRICH (1483–1531)

Swiss Reformer Ulrich Zwingli, one of the three magisterial reformers, is perhaps less well known than Martin Luther or John Calvin, but as Roger Olson observes, Zwingli is "the true father of Reformed Protestant theology" (Olson, 397). Zwingli was a pastor, patriot, and scholar who died in battle at age 47.

Zwingli studied at Vienna and Basel, and received his MA degree in 1506. He was influenced by humanists, especially Erasmus, and became proficient in Greek and Hebrew. The meeting with Erasmus was so profound that Zwingli could be "considered an unreserved Erasmian" and would become an "outstanding adherent of biblical humanism" (Olson, 399). He served as parish priest at Glarus for ten years, during which time he accompanied the young men of Switzerland into battle as they served as mercenaries for foreign interests.

Zwingli then served as a pastor in Einsiedeln (1516–1518), a pilgrimage town. While there, he preached against the Roman Catholic notion that activities like pilgrimages could gain salvation for an individual. His authority for such a bold proclamation was the New Testament, which he declared offered no support for such teachings (Gonzalez, 59). He applied his considerable exegetical and linguistic skills to the preaching task, vehemently calling his hearers to repentance.

The next major chapter in Zwingli's life occurred upon his becoming the "people's priest" at the Grossmünster in Zurich. It is here that the Swiss Reformation began to flower in full. Zwingli took the pulpit in Zurich on January 1, 1519, and initiated a

Z

preaching ministry that ushered in spiritual reform as he taught through the Gospel of Matthew. Zwingli's governing principle was that the Bible must be obeyed wherever it led. Consequently, virtually all vestiges of Roman Catholicism were stripped from the churches.

In 1523, the city council called for a disputation to determine if Zurich would continue with the reforms of Zwingli or return to the Catholic fold. In preparation for the disputation, Zwingli wrote the 67 Articles, considered by some to be the first document that articulated Reformation principles. Zwingli won the first disputation and Zurich embraced the reforms. A second disputation was later called for as some of Zwingli's followers, called the Brethren, pressed Zwingli to increase the speed of these reforms. The principle issue was believer's baptism. The decision of the council was that children were to be baptized and that rebaptism could not be practiced, under penalty of death. Felix Manz and three others were executed, and all others who held to Brethren views were expelled from Zurich or fled.

Aside from his prolific writings, Zwingli, wrote what is generally considered the first Reformed dogmatics, titled *On True and False Religion* (Olson, 401). Two other important events that involved Zwingli were the Marburg Colloquy (1529) and the Second Battle of Kappel (1531). Philipp I of Hessen called a meeting of the leading Protestant reformers to Marburg in an attempt to settle the dispute between Luther and Zwingli over the presence of Christ in the Lord's Supper. At the meeting there were 15 points of difference. Luther and Zwingli agreed on 14, but could not reach an agreement on the fifteenth point, or the meaning of the presence of Christ in the Supper. Luther held to the opinion that there was a real presence of Christ in the Supper, whereas Zwingli's view was that the Supper was a memorial meal (Olson, 406-7). Today, many evangelicals trace their view of the Lord's Supper to Zwingli's position.

Kevin L. King Sr.

Bibliography

Gonzalez, Justo. The *Story of Christianity*, vol. 2. New York: Harper One, 2010.

Grob, Jean. *The Life of Ulrich Zwingli*. New York: Funk & Wagnalls, 1883.

Old, Hughes Oliphant. *The Reading and Preaching of the Scriptures in the Worship of the Christian Church*, vol. 4. Grand Rapids: Eerdmans, 1998.

Olson, Roger. *The Story of Christian Theology*. Downers Grove, IL: IVP Academic, 1999.

Stitzinger, James. "The History of Expository Preaching." *The Master's Seminary Journal 3/1* (Spring 1992): 5-32.

Z

APPENDIX

✠

CLASSIC SERMONS

1.

JOHN WESLEY
God's Love to Fallen Man

2.

C.H. SPURGEON
The Cross Our Glory

3.

D.L. MOODY
What Think Ye of Christ?

"Not as the offence, so also is the free gift" (Romans 5:15).

1. How exceeding common, and how bitter, is the outcry against our first parent for the mischief which he not only brought upon himself, but entailed upon his latest posterity! It was by his willful rebellion against God that "sin entered into the world." "By one man's disobedience," as the apostle observes, the many, *hoi polloi*, as many as were then in the loins of their forefather, "were made," or constituted, "sinners": Not only deprived of the favour of God, but also of this image, of all virtue, righteousness, and true holiness; and sunk, partly into the image of the devil—in pride, malice, and all other diabolical tempers ; partly into the image of the brute, being fallen under the dominion of brutal passions and groveling appetites. Hence also death entered into the world, with all his forerunners and attendants—pain, sickness, and a whole train of uneasy, as well as unholy passions and tempers.

2. "For all this we may thank Adam," has echoed down from generation to generation. The self-same charge has been repeated in every age and every nation, where the oracles of God are known; in which alone this grand and important event has been discovered to the children of men. Has not *your* heart, and probably *your* lips too, joined in the general charge? How few are there of those who believe the scriptural relation of the fall of man that have not entertained the same thought concerning our first parent; severely condemning him that, through willful disobedience to the sole command of his Creator,

Brought death into the world,
and all our woe!

3. Nay it were well if the charge rested here: But it is certain it does not. It cannot be denied that it frequently glances from Adam to his Creator. Have not thousands even of those that are called Christians, taken the liberty to call his mercy, if not his justice also, into question on this very account? Some, indeed, have done this a little more modestly, in an oblique and indirect manner; but others have thrown aside the mask, and asked, "Did not God foresee that Adam would abuse his liberty? And did he not know the baneful consequences which this must naturally have on all his posterity? And why, then, did he permit that disobedience? Was it not easy for the Almighty to have prevented it?" He certainly did foresee the whole. This cannot be denied: For "known unto God are all his works from the beginning of the world"; rather, from all eternity, as the words *ap aivnos* properly signify. And it was undoubtedly in his power to prevent it; for he hath all power both in heaven and earth. But it was known to him, at the same time, that it was best, upon the whole, not to prevent it. He knew that "not as the transgression, so is the free gift"; that the evil resulting from the former was not as the good resulting from the latter—not worthy to be compared with it. He saw that to permit the fall of the first man was far best for mankind in general; that abundantly more good than evil would accrue to the posterity of Adam by his fall; that if "sin abounded" thereby over all the earth, yet grace "would much more abound"; yea, and that to every individual of the human race, unless it was his own choice. 4. It is exceeding strange that

hardly anything has been written or at least published, on this subject; nay that it has been so little weighed or understood by the generality of Christians; especially considering that it is not a matter of mere curiosity, but a truth of the deepest importance; it being impossible, on any other principle,

To assert a gracious Providence,
And justify the ways of God with men;

and considering withal how plain this important truth is to all sensible and candid inquirers. May the Lover of men open the eyes of our understanding, to perceive clearly that, by the fall of Adam, mankind in general have gained a capacity,

I. First, of being more holy and more happy on earth, and,

II. Secondly, of being more happy in heaven, than otherwise they could have been!

....

I.

1. And, first, mankind in general have gained, by the fall of Adam, a capacity of attaining more holiness and happiness on earth than it would have been possible for them to attain if Adam had not fallen. For if Adam had not fallen, Christ had not died. Nothing can be more clear than this; nothing more undeniable: The more thoroughly we consider the point the more deeply shall we be convinced of it. Unless all the partakers of human nature had received that deadly wound in Adam, it would not have been needful for the Son of God to take our nature upon him. Do you not see that this was the very ground of his coming into the world? "By one man sin entered into the world, and death by sin: And thus death passed upon all," through him in whom all

men sinned (Rom. 5:12). Was it not to remedy this very thing that "the Word was made flesh," that "as in Adam all died, so in Christ all" might "be made alive"? Unless, then, many had been made sinners by the disobedience of one, by the obedience of one many would not have been made righteous (Rom. 5:19). So there would have been no room for that amazing display of the Son of God's love to mankind: There would have been no occasion for his being "obedient unto death, even the death of the cross." It could not then have been said, to the astonishment of all the hosts of heaven "God so loved the world," yea, the ungodly world, which had no thought or desire of returning to him, "that he gave his Son" out of his bosom, his only-begotten Son, "to the end that whosoever believeth on him should not perish, but have everlasting life." Neither could we then have said, "God was in Christ reconciling the world to himself"; or, that he "made him to be sin," that is, a sin-offering, "for us, who knew no sin, that we might be made the righteousness of God through him." There would have been no such occasion for such "an Advocate with the Father," as "Jesus Christ the righteous"; neither for his appearing "at the right hand of God, to make intercession for us."

2. What is the necessary consequence of this? It is this: There could then have been no such thing as faith in God thus loving the world, giving his only Son for us men, and for our salvation. There could have been no such thing as faith in the Son of God, as "loving us and giving himself for us." There could have been no faith in the Spirit of God, as renewing the image of God in our hearts, as raising us from the death of sin unto the life of righteousness. Indeed the whole privilege of justification by faith could have had no existence; there could have been no redemption in the blood of Christ; neither

could Christ have been "made of God unto us," either "wisdom, righteousness, sanctification" or "redemption."

3. And the same grand blank which was in our faith must likewise have been in our love. We might have loved the Author of our being, the Father of angels and men as our Creator and Preserver. We might have said, "O Lord our Governor, how excellent is thy name in all the earth!" But we could not have loved him under the nearest and dearest relation—as delivering up his Son for us all. We might have loved the Son of God, as being "the brightness of his Father's glory, the express image of his person" (although this ground seems to belong rather to the inhabitants of heaven than earth), but we could not have loved him as "bearing our sins in his own body on the tree," and "by that one oblation of himself once offered, making a full sacrifice, oblation, and satisfaction for the sins of the whole world." We could not have been "made conformable to his death," nor have known "the power of his resurrection." We could not have loved the Holy Ghost, as revealing to us the Father and the Son; as opening the eyes of our understanding; bringing us out of darkness into his marvelous light; renewing the image of God in our soul, and sealing us unto the day of redemption. So that, in truth, what is now "in the sight of God, even the Father," not of fallible men, "pure religion and undefiled," would then have had no being; inasmuch as it wholly depends on those grand principles—"By grace ye are saved through faith"; and, "Jesus Christ is of God made unto us wisdom, and righteousness, and sanctification and redemption."

4. We see then, what unspeakable advantage we derive from the fall of our first parent with regard to faith—faith both in God the Father, who spared not his own Son, his only Son, but "wounded him for our transgressions," and "bruised him for our iniquities": and in God the Son, who poured out his soul for us transgressors, and washed us in his own blood. We see what advantage we derive therefrom with regard to the love of God; both of God the Father and God the Son. The chief ground of this love, as long as we remain in the body, is plainly declared by the apostle: "We love Him, because He first loved us." But the greatest instance of his love had never been given, if Adam had not fallen.

5. And as our faith both in God the Father and the Son, receives an unspeakable increase, if not its very being, from this grand event, as does also our love both of the Father and the Son; so does the love of our neighbour also, our benevolence to all mankind, which cannot but increase in the same proportion with our faith and love of God. For who does not apprehend the force of that inference drawn by the loving apostle: "Beloved, if God so loved us, we ought also to love one another?" If God *SO* loved us—observe, the stress of the argument lies on this very point: *SO loved us,* as to deliver up his only Son to die a cursed death for our salvation. Beloved, what manner of love is this wherewith God hath loved us; so as to give his *only Son,* in glory equal with the Father, in Majesty co-eternal? What manner of love is this wherewith the only begotten Son of God hath loved us so as to *empty himself,* as far as possible, of his eternal Godhead; as to divest himself of that glory which he had with the Father before the world began; as to take upon him the form of a servant, being found in fashion as a man; and then, to humble himself still further, "being obedient unto death, even the death of the cross"! If God *SO* loved us, how ought we to love one another! But this motive to brotherly love had been totally wanting if Adam had not fallen. Consequently, we could not then

have loved one another in so high a degree as we may now. Nor could there have been that height and depth in the command of our blessed Lord, "As I have loved you, so love one another."

6. Such gainers may we be by Adam's fall, with regard both to the love of God and of our neighbour. But there is another grand point, which, though little adverted to, deserves our deepest consideration. By that one act of our first parent, not only "sin entered into the world," but pain also, and was alike the justice but the unspeakable goodness of God. For how much good does he continually bring out of this evil! How much holiness and happiness out of pain!

7. How innumerable are the benefits which God conveys to the children of men through the channel of sufferings!—so that it might well be said, "What are termed afflictions in the language of men, are in the language of God styled blessings." Indeed, had there been no suffering in the world, a considerable part of religion, yea, and, in some respects, the most excellent part, could have had no place therein; since the very existence of it depends on our suffering; so that had there been no pain, it could have had no being. Upon this foundation, even our suffering, it is evident all our passive graces are built; yea, the noblest of all Christian graces—love enduring all things. Here is the ground for resignation to God, enabling us to say from the heart in every trying hour, "It is the Lord: Let him do what seemeth him good." "Shall we receive good at the hand of the Lord, and shall we not receive evil!" And what a glorious spectacle is this! Did it not constrain even a heathen to cry out, *Ecce spectaculum Deo dignum!* "See a sight worthy of God"; a good man struggling with adversity, and superior to it. Here is the ground for confidence in God, both with regard to what we feel, and with regard to what we should

fear, were it not that our soul is calmly stayed on Him. What room could there be for trust in God if there was no such thing as pain or danger? Who might not say then, "The cup which my Father hath given me, shall I not drink it?" It is by sufferings that our faith is tried, and, therefore, made more acceptable to God. It is in the day of trouble that we have occasion to say, "Though he slay me, yet will I trust him." And this is well pleasing to God, that we should own him in the face of danger: in defiance of sorrow, sickness, pain, or death.

8. Again: Had there been neither natural nor moral evil in the world, what must have become of patience, meekness, gentleness, longsuffering? It is manifest they could have had no being; seeing all these have evil for their object. If, therefore, evil had never entered into the world, neither could these have had any place in it. For who could have returned good for evil, had there been no evil-doer in the universe? How had it been possible, on that supposition, to "overcome evil with good"? Will you say, "But all these graces might have been divinely infused into the hearts of men"? Undoubtedly they might: But if they had, there would have been no use or exercise for them. Whereas in the present state of things we can never long want occasion to exercise them: And the more they are exercised, the more all our graces are strengthened and increased. And in the same proportion as our resignation, our confidence in God, our patience and fortitude, our meekness, gentleness, and longsuffering, together with our faith, and love of God and man, increase, must our happiness increase, even in the present world.

9. Yet again: As God's permission of Adam's fall gave all his posterity a thousand opportunities of suffering, and thereby of exercising all those passive graces which increase both their holiness and happiness;

so it gives them opportunities of doing good in numberless instances; of exercising themselves in various good works, which otherwise could have had no being. And what exertions of benevolence, of compassion, of godlike mercy, had then been totally prevented! Who could then have said to the Lover of men—

> *Thy Mind throughout my life be shown,*
> *While listening to the wretch's cry,*
> *The widow's or the orphan's groan,*
> *On mercy's wings I swiftly fly,*
> *The poor and needy to relieve;*
> *Myself, my all for them to give?*

It is the just observation of a benevolent man—

> *All worldly joys are less*
> *Than that one joy of doing kindnesses.*

Surely in "keeping this commandment," if to no other, "there is great reward." "As we have time, let us do good unto all men"; good of every kind, and in every degree. Accordingly, the more good we do (other circumstances being equal), the happier we shall be. The more we deal our bread to the hungry, and cover the naked with garments—the more we relieve the stranger and visit them that are sick or in prison—the more kind offices we do to those that groan under the various evils of human life—the more comfort we receive even in the present world, the greater the recompense we have in our own bosom.

10. To sum up what has been said under this head: As the more holy we are upon earth the more happy we must be (seeing there is an inseparable connection between holiness and happiness), as the more good we do to others, the more of present reward redounds into our own bosom; even as our sufferings for God lead us to rejoice in him "with joy unspeakable and full of glory"; therefore, the fall of Adam—first, by giving us an opportunity of being far more holy; secondly, by giving us the occasions of doing innumerable good works, which otherwise could not have been done; and, thirdly, by putting it into our power to suffer for God, whereby "the Spirit of glory and of God resteth upon us"—may be of such advantage to the children of men, even in the present life, as they will not thoroughly comprehend till they attain life everlasting.

....

II.

1. It is then we shall be enabled fully to comprehend, not only the advantages which accrue at the present time to the sons of men by the fall of their first parent, but the infinitely greater advantages which they may reap from it in eternity. In order to form some conception of this, we may remember the observation of the apostle: As "one star differeth from another star in glory, so also is the resurrection of the dead." The most glorious stars will undoubtedly be those who are the most holy, who bear most of that image of God wherein they were created; the next in glory to these will be those who have been most abundant in good works; and next to them, those that have suffered most, according to the will of God. But what advantages, in every one of these respects, will the children of God receive in heaven, by God's permitting the introduction of pain upon earth in consequence of sin! By occasion of this they attained many holy tempers, which otherwise could have had no being— resignation to God; confidence in him, in times of trouble and danger; patience, meekness, gentleness, longsuffering, and the whole train of passive virtues. And

on account of this superior holiness, they will then enjoy superior happiness. Again: Everyone will then "receive his own reward, according to his own labour." Every individual will be "rewarded according to his work." But the fall gave rise to innumerable good works, which could otherwise never have existed; such as ministering to the necessities of saints; yea, relieving the distressed in every kind: And hereby innumerable stars will be added to their eternal crown. Yet again: There will be an abundant reward in heaven for *suffering* as well as for *doing* the will of God: "These light afflictions, which are but for a moment, work out for us a far more exceeding and eternal weight of glory." Therefore that event which occasioned the entrance of suffering into the world, has thereby occasioned to all the children of God an increase of glory to all eternity. For although the sufferings themselves will be at an end; although

The pain of life shall then be o'er,
The anguish and distracting care;
There sighing grief shall weep no more;
And sin shall never enter there—

Yet the joys occasioned thereby shall never end, but flow at God's right hand forevermore.

2. There is one advantage more that we reap from Adam's fall, which is not unworthy our attention. Unless in Adam all had died, being in the loins of their first parent, every descendant of Adam, every child of man, must have personally answered for himself to God. It seems to be a necessary consequence of this, that if he had once fallen, once violated any command of God, there would have been no possibility of his rising again; there was no help, but he must have perished without remedy. For that covenant knew not to show mercy: The word

was, "The soul that sinneth, it shall die." Now who would not rather be on the footing he is now—under a covenant of mercy? Who would wish to hazard a whole eternity upon one stake? Is it not infinitely more desirable to be in a state wherein, though encompassed with infirmities, yet we do not run such a desperate risk, but if we fall, we may rise again? Wherein we may say,

My trespass is grown up to heaven;
But far above the skies,
In Christ abundantly forgiven,
I see thy mercies rise!

3. *In Christ!* Let me entreat every serious person once more to fix his attention here. All that has been said, all that can be said, on these subjects, centers in this point: The fall of Adam produced the death of Christ. Hear, O heavens, and give ear, O earth! Yea,

Let earth and heaven agree,
Angels and men be join'd,
To celebrate with me
The Saviour of mankind;
To adore the all-atoning Lamb,
And bless the sound of Jesus' name!

If God had prevented the fall of man, "the Word" had never been "made flesh"; nor had we ever "seen his glory, the glory as of the only-begotten of the Father." Those mysteries never had been displayed "which the" very "angels desire to look into." Methinks this consideration swallows up all the rest, and should never be out of our thoughts. Unless "by one man judgment had come upon all men to condemnation," neither angels nor men could ever have known "the unsearchable riches of Christ."

4. See, then, upon the whole, how little reason we have to repine at the fall of our first parent; since herefrom we may derive

such unspeakable advantages, both in time and eternity. See how small pretense there is for questioning the mercy of God in permitting that event to take place; since therein mercy, by infinite degrees, rejoices over judgment. Where then is the man that presumes to blame God for not preventing Adam's sin? Should we not rather bless him from the ground of the heart, for therein laying the grand scheme of man's redemption, and making way for that glorious manifestation of his wisdom, holiness, justice, and mercy? If, indeed, God had decreed, before the foundation of the world, that millions of men should dwell in everlasting burnings, because Adam sinned hundreds or thousands of years before they had a being. I know not who could thank him for this, unless the devil and his angels: Seeing, on this supposition, all those millions of unhappy spirits would be plunged into hell by Adam's sin, without any possible advantage from it. But, blessed be God, this is not the case. Such a decree never existed. On the contrary, every one born of a woman may be an unspeakable gainer thereby: And none ever was or can be a loser but by his own choice.

5. We see here a full answer to that plausible account of the origin of evil, published to the world some years since, and supposed to be unanswerable: That it "necessarily resulted from the nature of matter, which God was not able to alter." It is very kind in this sweet-tongued orator to make an excuse for God! But there is really no occasion for it: God hath answered for himself. He made man in his own image; a spirit endued with understanding and liberty. Man, abusing that liberty, produced evil, brought sin and pain into the world. This God permitted, in order to a fuller manifestation of his wisdom, justice, and mercy, by bestowing on all who would receive it an infinitely greater happiness than they could possibly have attained if Adam had not fallen.

6. "O the depth of the riches both of the wisdom and knowledge of God!" Although a thousand particulars of "his judgments and of his ways are unsearchable" to us, and past our finding out; yet may we discern the general scheme running through time into eternity. "According to the counsel of his own will," the plan he had laid before the foundation of the world, he created the parent of all mankind in his own image; and he permitted all men to be made sinners, by the disobedience of that one man, that, by the obedience of one, all who receive the free gift may be infinitely holier and happier to all eternity.

"But God forbid that I should glory, save in the cross of our Lord Jesus Christ, by whom the world is crucified unto me, and I unto the world" (Galatians 6:14).

Almost all men have something wherein to glory. Every bird has its own note of song. It is a poor heart that never rejoices: it is a dull packhorse that is altogether without bells. Men usually rejoice in something or other, and many men so rejoice in that which they choose that they become boastful and full of vain glory. It is very sad that men should be ruined by their glory; and yet many are so. Many glory in their shame, and more glory in that which is mere emptiness. Some glory in their physical strength, in which an ox excels them; or in their gold, which is but thick clay; or in their gifts, which are but talents with which they are entrusted. The pounds entrusted to their stewardship are thought by men to belong to themselves, and therefore they rob God of the glory of them.

O my hearers, hear ye the voice of wisdom, which crieth, "He that glorieth, let him glory only in the Lord." To live for personal glory is to be dead while we live. Be not so foolish as to perish for a bubble. Many a man has thrown his soul away for a little honor, or for the transient satisfaction of success in trifles. O men, your tendency is to glory in somewhat; your wisdom will be to find a glory worthy of an immortal mind.

The apostle Paul had a rich choice of things in which he could have gloried. If it had been his mind to have remained among his own people, he might have been one of their most honored rabbis. He saith in his epistle to the Philippians, in the third chapter, "If any other man thinketh that he hath whereof he might trust in the flesh, I more: circumcised the eighth day, of the stock of Israel, of the tribe of Benjamin, an Hebrew of the Hebrews; as touching the law, a Pharisee; concerning zeal, persecuting the church; touching the righteousness which is in the law, blameless." He says that he profited in the Jews' religion above many, his equals in his own nation; and he stood high in the esteem of his fellow-professors. But when he was converted to the faith of the Lord Jesus, he said, "What things were gain to me, those I counted loss for Christ. Yea doubtless, and I count all things but loss for the excellency of the knowledge of Christ Jesus my Lord." As soon as he was converted he forsook all glorying in his former religion and zeal, and cried, "God forbid that I should glory in my birth, my education, my proficiency in Scripture, or my regard to orthodox ritual. God forbid that I should glory, save in the cross of our Lord Jesus Christ."

Paul might also, if he had so chosen, have gloried in his sufferings for the cross of Christ; for he had been a living martyr, a perpetual self-sacrifice to the cause of the crucified. He says, "Are they ministers of Christ? (I speak as a fool) I am more; in labors more abundant, in stripes above measure, in prisons more frequent, in deaths oft. Of the Jews five times received I forty stripes save one. Thrice was I beaten with rods, once was I stoned, thrice I suffered shipwreck, a night and a day I have been in the deep; in journeyings often, in perils of waters, in perils of robbers, in perils by mine own countrymen, in perils by the heathen, in perils in the city, in perils in the wilderness, in perils in the sea, in perils among false brethren; in weariness and painfulness, in watchings often, in hunger and thirst, in fastings often, in cold and nakedness." He was once driven to give a summary of these sufferings to establish his apostleship; but before he did so he wrote, "Would to God ye could bear with me a little in my folly." In his heart he was saying all the while, "God forbid that I should glory, save in the cross of our Lord Jesus Christ."

The great apostle had yet another reason for glorying, if he had chosen to do so; for he could speak of visions and revelations of the Lord. He says, "I knew a man in Christ above fourteen years ago...caught up to the third heaven. And I knew such a man...how that he was caught up into Paradise, and heard unspeakable words, which it is not lawful for a man to utter." He was in danger of being exalted above measure by reason of the abundance of these revelations, and hence he was humbled by a painful thorn in the flesh. Paul, when hard driven by the necessity to maintain his position in the Corinthian church, was forced to mention these things—but he liked not such glorying, he was most at ease when he said, "God forbid that I should glory, save in the cross of our Lord Jesus Christ."

Brethren, notice that Paul does not here say that he gloried in Christ, though he did so with all his heart; but he declares that he gloried most in "the cross of our Lord Jesus Christ," which in the eyes of men was the very lowest and most inglorious part of the history of the Lord Jesus. He could have gloried in the incarnation: angels sang of it, wise men came from the Far East to behold it. Did not the new-born King awake the song from heaven of "Glory to God in the highest"? He might have gloried in the life

of Christ: was there ever such another, so benevolent and blameless? He might have gloried in the resurrection of Christ: it is the world's great hope concerning those that are asleep. He might have gloried in our Lord's ascension; for he "led captivity captive," and all his followers glory in his victory. He might have gloried in his Second Advent, and I doubt not that he did; for the Lord shall soon descend from heaven with a shout, with the voice of the archangel and the trump of God, to be admired in all them that believe.

Yet the apostle selected beyond all these that center of the Christian system, that point which is most assailed by its foes, that focus of the world's derision—the cross, and, putting all else somewhat into the shade, he exclaims, "God forbid that I should glory, save in the cross of our Lord Jesus Christ." Learn, then, that the highest glory of our holy religion is the cross. The history of grace begins earlier and goes on later, but in its middle point stands the cross. Of two eternities this is the hinge: of past decrees and future glories this is the pivot. Let us come to the cross this morning, and think of it, till each one of us, in the power of the Spirit of God, shall say, "God forbid that I should glory, save in the cross of our Lord Jesus Christ."

I. First, as the Lord shall help me (for who shall describe the cross without the help of him that did hang upon it?) WHAT DID PAUL MEAN BY THE CROSS? Did he not include under this term, first, the fact of the cross: secondly, the doctrine of the cross: and thirdly, the cross of the doctrine? I think he meant, first of all, the fact of the cross. Our Lord Jesus Christ did really die upon a gibbet, the death of a felon. He was literally put to death upon a tree, accursed in the esteem of men. I beg you to notice how the apostle puts it—"the cross of our Lord Jesus Christ." In his epistles he sometimes saith "Christ," at another time "Jesus," frequently "Lord," oftentimes "our Lord"; but here he saith "our Lord Jesus Christ." There is a sort of pomp of words in this full description, as if in contrast to the shame of the cross. The terms are intended in some small measure to express the dignity of him who was put to so ignominious a death. He is Christ the anointed, and Jesus the Savior; he is the Lord, the Lord of all, and he is "our Lord Jesus Christ." He is not a Lord without subjects, for he is "our Lord"; nor is he a Savior without saved ones, for he is "our Lord Jesus"; nor has he the anointing for himself alone, for all of us have a share in him as "our Christ": in all he is ours, and was so upon the cross.

But, next, I said that Paul gloried in the doctrine of the cross, and it was so. What is that doctrine of the cross, of which it is written that it is "to them that perish foolishness, but unto us who are saved it is the power of God and the wisdom of God"? In one word, it is the doctrine of the atonement, the doctrine that the Lord Jesus Christ was made sin for us, that Christ was once offered to bear the sins of many and that God hath set him forth to be the propitiation for our sins. Paul saith, "When we were yet without strength, in due time Christ died for the ungodly": and again, "Now once in the end of the world hath he appeared to put away sin by the sacrifice of himself." The doctrine of the cross is that of sacrifice for sin: Jesus is "the Lamb of God that taketh away the sin of the world." "God so loved the world, that he gave his only begotten Son, that whosoever believeth in him should not perish, but have everlasting life."

The doctrine is that of a full atonement made, and the utmost ransom paid. "Christ hath redeemed us from the curse of the law, being made a curse for us: for it is written, Cursed is every one that hangeth on a tree." In Christ upon the cross we see the Just dying for the unjust, that he might bring us to God, the innocent bearing the crimes of the guilty, that they might be forgiven and accepted. That is the doctrine of the cross, of which Paul was never ashamed. This also is a necessary part of the doctrine: that whosoever believeth in him is justified from all sin; that whosoever trusts in the Lord Jesus Christ is in that moment forgiven, justified, and accepted in the Beloved. "As Moses lifted up the serpent in the wilderness, even so must the Son of man be lifted up; that whosoever believeth in him should not perish, but have eternal life." Paul's doctrine was, "It is not of him that willeth, nor of him that runneth, but of God that showeth mercy"; and it was his constant teaching that salvation is not of doings, nor of ceremonies, but simply and alone by believing in Jesus. We are to accept by an act of trust that righteousness which is already finished and completed by the death of our blessed Lord upon the cross. He who does not preach atonement by the blood of Jesus does not preach the cross; and he who does not declare justification by faith in Christ Jesus has missed the mark altogether. This is the very bowels of the Christian system. If our ministry shall be without blood it is without life, for "the blood is the life thereof." He that preacheth not justification by faith knows not the doctrine of grace; for the Scripture saith, "Therefore it is of faith that it might be by grace; to the end the promise might be sure to all the seed." Paul gloried both in the fact of the cross and in the doctrine of the cross.

But the apostle also gloried in the cross of the doctrine, for the death of the Son of God upon the cross is the crux of

Christianity. Here is the difficulty, the stumbling block, and rock of offense. The Jew could not endure a crucified Messiah: he looked for pomp and power. Multitudinous ceremonies and diverse washings and sacrifices, were these all to be put away and nothing left but a bleeding Savior? At the mention of the cross the philosophic Greek thought himself insulted, and vilified the preacher as a fool. In effect he said, "You are not a man of thought and intellect; you are not abreast of the times, but are sticking in the mire of antiquated prophecies. Why not advance with the discoveries of modern thought?" The apostle, teaching a simple fact which a child might comprehend, found in it the wisdom of God. Christ upon the cross working out the salvation of men was more to him than all the sayings of the sages. As for the Roman, he would give no heed to any glorying in a dead Jew, a crucified Jew! Crushing the world beneath his iron heel, he declared that such romancing should never win him from the gods of his fathers. Paul did not blench before the sharp and practical reply of the conquerors of the world. He trembled not before Nero in his palace. Whether to Greek or Jew, Roman or barbarian, bond or free, he was not ashamed of the gospel of Christ, but gloried in the cross. Though the testimony that the one all-sufficient atonement was provided on the cross stirs the enmity of man, and provokes opposition, yet Paul was so far from attempting to mitigate that opposition, that he determined to know nothing save Jesus Christ and him crucified. His motto was "We preach Christ crucified." He had the cross for his philosophy, the cross for his tradition, the cross for his gospel, the cross for his glory, and nothing else.

II. But, secondly, WHY DID PAUL GLORY IN THE CROSS? He did not do so because he was in want of a theme; for, as I have shown you, he had a wide field for boasting if he had chosen to occupy it. He gloried in the cross from solemn and deliberate choice. He had counted the cost, he had surveyed the whole range of subjects with eagle eye, and he knew what he did, and why he did it. He was master of the art of thinking. As a metaphysician, none could excel him; as a logical thinker, none could have gone beyond him. He stands almost alone in the early Christian church as a master mind. Others may have been more poetic, or more simple, but none were more thoughtful or argumentative than he. With decision and firmness Paul sets aside everything else, and definitely declares, throughout his whole life, "I glory in the cross." He does this exclusively, saying, "God forbid that I should glory, save in the cross." There are many other precious things, but he puts them all upon the shelf in comparison with the cross. He will not even make his chief point any of the great scriptural doctrines, nor even an instructive and godly ordinance. No, the cross is to the front. This constellation is chief in Paul's sky. The choice of the cross he makes devoutly, for although the expression used in our English version may not stand, yet I do not doubt that Paul would have used it, and would have called upon God to witness that he abjured all other ground of glorying save the atoning sacrifice.

> Forbid it, Lord, that I should boast,
> Save in the death of Christ, my God;
> All the vain things that charm me most,
> I sacrifice them to his blood.

He would have called God to witness that he knew no ambition save that of bringing glory to the cross of Christ. As I think of this I am ready to say, "Amen" to Paul, and bid you sing that stirring verse—

It is the old cross still,
Hallelujah! hallelujah!
Its triumphs let us tell,
Hallelujah! hallelujah!
The grace of God here shone
Through Christ, the blessed Son,
Who did for sin atone;
Hallelujah for the cross!

Why did Paul thus glory in the cross? You may well desire to know, for there are many nowadays who do not glory in it, but forsake it. Alas that it should be so! But there are ministers who ignore the atonement; they conceal the cross, or say but little about it. You may go through service after service, and scarce hear a mention of the atoning blood; but Paul was always bringing forward the expiation for sin: Paul never tried to explain it away. Oh the number of books that have been written to prove that the cross means an example of self-sacrifice, as if every martyrdom did not mean that. They cannot endure a real substitutionary sacrifice for human guilt, and an effectual purgation of sin by the death of the great substitute. Yet the cross means that or nothing. Paul was very bold: although he knew this would make him many enemies, you never find him refining and spiritualizing: the cross and the atonement for sin is a plain matter of fact to him. Neither does he attempt to decorate it by adding philosophical theories. He pronounces an anathema on all who propose a rival theme—"But though we, or an angel from heaven, preach any other gospel unto you than that which we have preached unto you, let him be accursed."

I take it that this was so, first, because Paul saw in the cross a vindication of divine justice. Where else can the justice of God be seen so clearly as in the death of God himself, in the person of his dear Son? If the Lord himself suffers on account of broken law, then is the majesty of the law honored to the full. Some time ago, a judge in America was called upon to try a prisoner who had been his companion in his early youth. It was a crime for which the penalty was a fine, more or less heavy. The judge did not diminish the fine; the case was clearly a bad one, and he fined the prisoner to the full. Some who knew his former relation to the offender thought him somewhat unkind thus to carry out the law, while others admired his impartiality. All were surprised when the judge quitted the bench and himself paid every farthing of the penalty. He had both shown his respect for the law and his goodwill to the man who had broken it; he exacted the penalty, but he paid it himself.

So God hath done in the Person of his dear Son. He has not remitted the punishment, but he has himself endured it. His own Son, who is none other than God himself—for there is an essential union between them—has paid the debt which was incurred by human sin. I love to think of the vindication of divine justice upon the cross; I am never weary of it. Some cannot bear the thought; but to me it seems inevitable that sin must be punished, or else the foundations of society would be removed. If sin becomes a trifle, virtue will be a toy. Society cannot stand if laws are left without penal sanction, or if that sanction is to be a mere empty threat. Men in their own governments every now and then cry out for greater severity. When a certain offense abounds, and ordinary means fail, they demand exemplary punishment; and it is but natural that they should do so; for deep in the conscience of every man there is the conviction that sin must be punished to secure the general good. Justice must reign, even benevolence demands it. If there could have been salvation without an atonement it would have been a calamity; righteous men, and even benevolent men, might deprecate the setting aside of law in order to save the guilty from the natural result of their crimes.

For my own part I value a just salvation: an unjust salvation would never have satisfied the apprehensions and demands of my conscience. No, let God be just, if the heavens fall; let God carry out the sentence of his law, or the universe will suspect that it was not righteous; and when such a suspicion rules the general mind, all respect for God will be gone. The Lord carries out the decree of his justice even to the bitter end, abating not a jot of its requirements. Brethren, there was an infinite efficacy in the death of such a one as our Lord Jesus Christ to vindicate the law. Though he is man, yet is he also God; and in his passion and death he offered to the justice of God a vindication not at all inferior to the punishment of hell. God is just indeed when Jesus dies upon the cross rather than that God's law should be dishonored. When our august Lord himself bore the wrath that was due for human sin, it was made evident to all that law is not to be trifled with. We glory in the cross, for there the debt was paid, our sums on Jesus laid.

But we glory because on the cross we have an unexampled display of God's love. "God commendeth his love toward us, in that, while we were yet sinners, Christ died for us." Oh to think of it, that he who was offended takes the nature of the offender, and then bears the penalty due for wanton transgression. He who is infinite, thrice holy, all glorious, forever to be worshipped, yet stoopeth to be numbered with the transgressors, and to bear the sin of many. The mythology of the gods of high Olympus contains nothing worthy to be mentioned in the same day with this wondrous deed of supreme condescension and infinite love. The ancient Shastras and Vedas have nothing of the kind. The death of Jesus Christ upon the cross cannot be an invention of men; none of the ages have produced aught like it in the poetic dreams of any nation. If we did not hear of it so often, and think of it so little, we should be charmed with it beyond expression. If we now heard of it for the first time, and seriously believed it, I know not what we should not do in our glad surprise; certainly we should fall down and worship the Lord Jesus, and continue to worship him forever and ever.

I believe again, thirdly, that Paul delighted to preach the cross of Christ as the removal of all guilt. He believed that the Lord Jesus on the cross finished transgression, made an end of sin, and brought in everlasting righteousness. He that believeth in Jesus is justified from all things from which he could not be justified by the law of Moses. Since sin was laid on Jesus, God's justice cannot lay it upon the believing sinner. The Lord will never punish twice the same offense. If he accepts a substitute for me, how can he call me to his bar and punish me for that transgression, for which my substitute endured the chastisement? Many a troubled conscience has caught at this and found deliverance from despair. Wonder not that Paul gloried in Christ, since it is written, "In the Lord shall all the seed of Israel be justified, and shall glory." This is the method of salvation which completely and eternally absolves the sinner, and makes the blackest offender white as snow. Transgression visited upon Christ has ceased to be, so far as the believer is concerned. Doth not faith cry, "Thou wilt cast all their sins into the depths of the sea"? O sirs, there is something to glory in in this, and those who know the sin-removing power of the cross will not be hindered in this glorying by all the powers of earth or hell.

He glories in it, again, as a marvel of wisdom. It seemed to him the sum of perfect wisdom and skill. He cried, "O the depths of the riches both of the wisdom and knowledge of God!" The plan of salvation by vicarious suffering is simple, but sublime. It would have been impossible for human or angelic wisdom to have invented it. Men already so hate it and fight against it that they never would have devised it. God alone out of the treasury of His infinite wisdom brought forth this matchless project of salvation for the guilty through the substitution of the innocent. The more we study it, the more we shall perceive that it is full of teaching.

It is only the superficial thinker who regards the cross as a subject soon to be comprehended and exhausted: the most lofty intellects will here find ample room and verge enough. The profoundest minds might lose themselves in considering the splendid diversities of light which compose the pure white light of the cross. Everything of sin and justice, of misery and mercy, of folly and wisdom, of force and tenderness, of rage and pity, on the part of man and God, may be seen here. In the cross may be seen the concentration of eternal thought, the focus of infinite purpose, the outcome of illimitable wisdom. Of God and the cross we may say:

> *Here I behold his inmost heart,*
> *Where grace and vengeance strangely join;*
> *Piercing his Son with sharpest smart*
> *To make the purchased pleasures mine.*

I believe that Paul gloried in the cross, again, because it is the door of hope, even to the vilest of the vile. The world was very filthy in Paul's time. Roman civilization was of the most brutal and debased kind, and the masses of the people were sunken in vices that are altogether unmentionable. Paul felt that he could go into the darkest places with light in his hand when he spoke of the cross. To tell of pardon bought with the blood of the Son of God is to carry an omnipotent message. The cross uplifts the fallen and delivers the despairing. Today, my brethren, the world's one and only remedy is the cross. Go, ye thinkers, and get up a mission to the fallen in London, leaving out the cross! Go, now, ye wise men, reclaim the harlots, and win to virtue the degraded by your perfumed philosophies! See what you can do in the slums and alleys without the cross of Christ! Go talk to your titled reprobates, and win them from their abominations by displays of art! You will fail, the most cultivated of you, even to win the rich and educated to anything like purity, unless your themes be drawn from Calvary, and the love which there poured out its heart's blood. This hammer breaks rocky hearts, but no other will do it. Pity itself stands silent. Compassion bites her lip and inwardly groans she has nothing to say till she has learned the story of the cross; but, with that on her tongue, she waxes eloquent; with tears she entreats, persuades, prevails. She may but stammer in her speech; like Moses, she may be slow of utterance; but the cross is in her hand, as the rod of the prophet. With this she conquers the Pharaoh of tyrannic sin; with this she divides the Red Sea of guilt; with this she leads the host of God out of the house of bondage into the land of promise which floweth with milk and honey. The cross is the standard of victorious grace. It is the lighthouse whose cheering ray gleams across the dark waters of despair and cheers the dense midnight of our fallen race, saving from eternal shipwreck, and piloting into everlasting peace.

Again, Paul, I believe, gloried in the cross, as I often do, because it was the source of rest to him and to his brethren. I make this confession, and I make it very boldly, that I never knew what rest of heart truly meant till I understood the doctrine of the substitution of our Lord Jesus Christ. Now, when I see my Lord bearing away my sins as my scapegoat, or dying for them as my sin-offering, I feel a profound peace of heart and satisfaction of spirit. The cross is all I ever want for security and joy. Truly, this bed is long enough for a man to stretch himself on it. The cross is a chariot of salvation, wherein we traverse the high road of life without fear. The pillow of atonement heals the head that aches with anguish. Beneath the shadow of the cross I sit down with great delight, and its fruit is sweet unto my taste. I have no impatience even to haste to heaven while resting, beneath the cross, for our hymn truly says:

Here it is I find my heaven,
While upon the cross gaze.

Here is perfect cleansing, and hence a divine security, guarded by the justice of God; and hence a "peace of God, which passeth all understanding." To try to entice me away from the truth of substitution is labor in vain. Seduce me to preach the pretty nothings of modern thought! This child knows much better than to leave the substance for the shadow, the truth for the fancy. I see nothing that can give to my heart a fair exchange for the rest, peace and unutterable joy which the old fashioned doctrine of the cross now yields me. Will a man leave bread for husks, and quit the home of his love to dwell in a desolate wilderness? I dare not renounce the truth in order to be thought cultured. I am no more a fool than the most of my contemporaries, and

if I could see anything better than the cross I would willingly grasp it as they; for it is a flattering thing to be thought a man of light and leading; but whither shall I go if I quit the rock of the atoning sacrifice? I cannot go beyond my simple faith that Jesus stood in my stead, and bore my sin, and put my sin away. This I must preach; I know nothing else. God help me I will never go an inch beyond the cross, for to me all else is vanity and vexation of spirit. Return unto thy rest, O my soul! Where else is there a glimpse of hope for thee but in him who loved thee and gave himself for thee?

I am sure Paul gloried in the cross yet again because he saw it to be the creator of enthusiasm. Christianity finds its chief force in the enthusiasm which the Holy Ghost produces; and this comes from the cross. The preaching of the cross is the great weapon of the crusade against evil. In the old times vast crowds came together in desert places, among the hills, or on the moors, at peril of their lives, to hear preaching. Did they come together to hear philosophy? Did they meet at dead of night when the harriers of persecution were hunting them, to listen to pretty moral essays? I trow not. They came to hear of the grace of God manifest in the sacrifice of Jesus to believing hearts. Would your modern gospel create the spirit of the martyrs? Is there anything in it for which a man might go to prison and to death? The modern speculations are not worth a cat's dying for them much less a man. A something lies within the truth of the cross which sets the soul aglow; it touches the preacher's lips as with a live coal, and fires the hearer's hearts as with flame from the alter of God. We can on this gospel live, and for this gospel die. Atonement by blood, full deliverance from sin, perfect safety in Christ given to the believer, call a man to joy, to gratitude, to consecration, to decision, to patience, to holy living, to all-consuming zeal. Therefore in the doctrine of the cross we glory, neither will we be slow to speak it out with all our might.

III. My time has gone, or else I had intended to have enlarged upon the third head, of which I must now give you the mere outline. One of Paul's great reasons for glorying in the cross was its action upon himself. WHAT WAS ITS EFFECT UPON HIM?

The cross is never without influence. Come where it may, it worketh for life or for death. Wherever there is Christ's cross there are also two other crosses. On either side there is one, and Jesus is in the midst. Two thieves are crucified with Christ; and Paul tells us their names in his case: "the world is crucified to me, and I unto the world." Self and the world are both crucified when Christ's cross appears and is believed in. Beloved, what does Paul mean? Does he not mean just this—that ever since he had seen Christ he looked upon the world as a crucified, hanged up, gibbeted thing, which had no more power over Paul than a criminal hanged upon a cross. What power has a corpse on a gibbet? Such power had the world over Paul. The world despised him, and he could not go after the world if he would, and would not go after it if he could. He was dead to it, and it was dead to him; thus there was a double separation.

How does the cross do this? To be under the dominion of this present evil world is horrible; how does the cross help us to escape? Why, brethren, he that has ever seen the cross looks upon the world's pomp and glory as a vain show. The pride of heraldry and the glitter of honor fade into meanness before the Crucified One. O ye great ones, what are your silks, and your furs, and your jewelry, and your gold, your stars and your garters, to one who has learned to glory in Christ crucified! The old clothes which belong to the hangman are quite as precious. The world's light is darkness when the Sun of Righteousness shines from the tree. What care we for all the kingdoms of the world and the glory thereof when once we see the thorn-crowned Lord? There is more glory about one nail of the cross than about all the scepters of all kings. Let the knights of the Golden Fleece meet in chapter, and all the Knights of the Garter stand in their stalls, and what is all their splendor? Their glories wither before the inevitable hour of doom, while the glory of the cross is eternal. Everything of earth grows dull and dim when seen by cross light. So was it with the world's approval. Paul would not ask the world to be pleased with him, since it knew not his Lord, or only knew him to crucify him. Can a Christian be ambitious to be written down as one of the world's foremost men when that world cast out his Lord? They crucified our Master; shall his servants court their love? Such approval would be all distained with blood. They crucified my Master, the Lord of glory; do I want them to smile on me, and say to me, "Reverend Sir" and "Learned Doctor"? No, the friendship of the world is enmity with God, and therefore to be dreaded. Mouths that spit on Jesus shall give me no kisses. Those who hate the doctrine of the atonement hate my life and soul, and I desire not their esteem.

Paul also saw that the world's wisdom was absurd. That age talked of being wise and philosophical! Yes, and its philosophy brought it to crucify the Lord of glory. It did not know perfection, nor perceive the beauty of pure unselfishness. To slay the Messiah was the outcome of the culture of the Pharisee, to put to death the greatest teacher of all time was the ripe fruit of Sadducean thought. The cogitations of the present age have performed no greater feat than to deny the doctrine of satisfaction for sin. They have crucified our Lord afresh by their criticisms and their new theologies; and this is all the world's wisdom ever does. Its wisdom lies in scattering doubt, quenching hope, and denying certainty; and therefore the wisdom of the world to us is sheer folly. This century's philosophy will one day be spoken of as an evidence that softening of the brain was very usual among its scientific men. We count the thought of the present moment to be methodical madness, bedlam out of doors; and those who are furthest gone in it are credulous beyond imagination. God hath poured contempt upon the wise men of this world; their foolish heart is blinded, they grope at noonday.

So, too, the apostle saw the world's religion to be nought. It was the world's religion that crucified Christ, the priests were at the bottom of it; the Pharisees urged it on. The church of the nation, the church of many ceremonies, the church which loved the traditions of the elders, the church of phylacteries and broad-bordered garments—it was this church, which, acting by its officers, crucified the Lord. Paul therefore looked with pity upon priests and altars, and upon all the attempts of a Christless world to make up by finery of worship for the absence of the Spirit of God. Once see Christ on the cross, and architecture and fine display become meretricious, tawdry things. The cross calls for worship in spirit and in truth, and the world knows nothing of this.

And so it was with the world's pursuits. Some ran after honor, some toiled after learning, others labored for riches; but to Paul these were all trifles since he had seen Christ on the cross. He that has seen Jesus die will never go into the toy business; he puts away childish things. A child, a pipe, a little soap, and many pretty bubbles: such is the world. The cross alone can wean us from such play.

And so it was with the world's pleasures and with the world's power. The world, and everything that belonged to the world, had become as a corpse to Paul, and he was as a corpse to it. See where the corpse swings in chains on the gibbet. What a foul, rotten thing! We cannot endure it! Do not let it hang longer above ground to fill the air with pestilence. Let the dead be buried out of sight. The Christ that died upon the cross now lives in our hearts. The Christ that took human guilt has taken possession of our souls, and henceforth we live only in him, for him, by him. He has engrossed our affections. All our ardours burn for him. God make it to be so with us, that we may glorify God and bless our age. Paul concludes this epistle by saying, "From henceforth let no man trouble me: for I bear in my body the marks of the Lord Jesus." He was a slave, branded with his Master's name. That stamp could never be got out, for it was burned into his heart. Even thus, I trust, the doctrine of the atonement is our settled belief, and faith in it is part of our life. We are rooted and grounded in the unchanging verities. Do not try to convert me to your new views; I am past it. Give me over. You waste your breath. It is done: on this point the wax takes no farther impress. I have taken up my standing, and will never quit it. A crucified Christ has taken such possession of my entire nature, spirit, soul, and body, that I am henceforth beyond the reach of opposing arguments.

Brethren, sisters, will you enlist under the conquering banner of the cross? Once rolled in the dust and stained in blood, it now leads on the armies of the Lord to victory! Oh that all ministers would preach the true doctrine of the cross! Oh that all Christian people would live under the influence of it, and we should then see brighter days than these! Unto the Crucified be glory forever and ever. Amen.

✠ WHAT THINK YE OF CHRIST? ✠
Dwight Lyman Moody (1837–1899)

I suppose there is no one here who has not thought more or less about Christ. You have heard about him, and read about him, and heard men preach about him. For eighteen hundred years men have been talking about him and thinking about him; and some have their minds made up about who he is, and doubtless some have not. And although all these years have rolled away, this question comes up, addressed to each of us, today, "What think ye of Christ?"

I do not know why it should not be thought a proper question for one man to put to another. If I were to ask you what you think of any of your prominent men, you would already have your mind made up about him. If I were to ask you what you thought of your noble queen, you would speak right out and tell me your opinion in a minute.

If I were to ask about your prime minister, you would tell me freely what you had for or against him. And why should not people make up their minds about the Lord Jesus Christ, and take their stand for or against him? If you think well of him, why not speak well of him and range yourselves on his side? And if you think ill of him, and believe him to be an impostor, and that he did not die to save the world, why not lift up your voice and say you are against him? It would be a happy day for Christianity if men would just take sides—if we could know positively who was really for him and who was against him.

It is of very little importance what the world thinks of anyone else. The queen and the statesmen, the peers and the princes, must soon be gone. Yes; it matters little, comparatively, what we think of them. Their lives can interest only a few; but every living soul on the face of the earth is concerned with this Man. The question for the world is, "What think ye of Christ?"

I do not ask you what you think of the Established Church, or of the Presbyterians, or the Baptists, or the Roman Catholics;

I do not ask you what you think of this minister or that, of this doctrine or that; but I want to ask you what you think of the living person of Christ?

I should like to ask: Was he really the Son of God—the great God-Man? Did he leave heaven and come down to this world for a purpose? Was it really to seek and to save? I should like to begin with the manger, and follow him up through the thirty-three years he was here upon earth.

I should ask you what you think of his coming into this world and being born in a manger when it might have been a palace; why he left the grandeur and the glory of heaven, and the royal retinue of angels; why he passed by palaces and crowns and dominion and came down here alone? I should like to ask you what you think of him as a teacher. He spake as never man spake. I should like to take him up as a preacher. I should like to bring you to that mountainside, that we might listen to the words as they fall from his gentle lips. Talk about the preachers of the present day! I would rather a thousand times be five minutes at the feet of Christ than listen a lifetime to all the wise men in the world. He used just to hang truth upon anything. Yonder is a sower, a fox, a bird, and he just gathers the truth round them, so that you cannot see a sower, a fox, or a bird without thinking what Jesus said. Yonder is a lily of the valley; you cannot see it without thinking of his words, "They toil not, neither do they spin."

He makes the little sparrow chirping in the air preach to us. How fresh those wonderful sermons are; how they live today! How we love to tell them to our children; how the children love to hear! "Tell me a story about Jesus"—how often we hear it; how the little ones love his sermons! No storybook in the world will ever interest them like the stories that he told. And yet how profound he was; how he puzzled the wise men; how the scribes and the Pharisees could never fathom him! Oh, do you not think he was a wonderful preacher?

If you want to find out what a man is nowadays, you inquire about him from those who know him best. I do not wish to be partial; we will go to his enemies, and to his friends. We will ask them, What think ye of Christ? We will ask his friends and his enemies.

First, among the witnesses, let us call upon the Pharisees. We know how they hated him. Let us put a few questions to them. "Come, Pharisees, tell us what you have against the Son of God. What do you think of Christ?" Hear what they say! "This man receiveth sinners." What an argument to bring against him! Why, it is the very thing that makes us love him. It is the glory of the gospel. He receives sinners. If he had not, what would have become of us? Have you nothing more to bring against him than this? Why, it is one of the greatest compliments that was ever paid him. Once more: "When he was hanging on the tree, you had this to say of him, 'He saved others, but he could not save himself and save us, too.'" So he laid down his own life for yours and mine. Yes, Pharisees, you have told the truth for once in your lives! He saved others. He died for others. He was a ransom for many; so it is

quite true what you think of him—he saved others, himself he cannot save.

Now, let us call upon Caiaphas. Let him stand up here in his flowing robes; let us ask him for his evidence. "Caiaphas, you were chief priest when Christ was tried; you were president of the Sanhedrin; you were in the council-chamber when they found him guilty; you yourself condemned him. Tell us; what did the witnesses say? On what grounds did you judge him? What testimony was brought against him?" "He hath spoken blasphemy," says Caiaphas. "He said, 'Hereafter shall ye see the Son of Man sitting on the right hand of power, and coming in the clouds of heaven.' When I heard that, I found him guilty of blasphemy; I rent my mantle and condemned him to death." Yes, all that they had against him was that he was the Son of God; and they slew him for the promise of his coming for his bride!

Now let us summon Pilate. Let him enter the witness-box.

"Pilate, this man was brought before you; you examined him; you talked with him face to face; what think you of Christ?"

"I find no fault in him," says Pilate. "He said he was the King of the Jews [just as he wrote it over the cross], but I find no fault in him." Such is the testimony of the man who examined him! And, as he stands there, the center of a Jewish mob, there comes along a man, elbowing his way in haste. He rushes up to Pilate, and, thrusting out his hand, gives him a message. He tears it open; his face turns pale as he reads, "Have thou nothing to do with this just man, for I have suffered many things this day in a dream because of him." It is from Pilate's wife—her testimony to Christ. You want to know what his enemies thought of him? You want to know what a heathen thought? Well, here it is: "no fault in him"; and the wife of a heathen: "this just man"!

And now, look—in comes Judas. He ought to make a good witness. Let us address him. "Come, tell us, Judas, what think you of Christ? You knew the master well; you sold him for thirty pieces of silver; you betrayed him with a kiss; you saw him perform those miracles; you were with him in Jerusalem. In Bethany, when he summoned up Lazarus, you were there. What think you of him?" I can see him as he comes into the presence of the chief priests; I can hear the money ring as he dashes it upon the table with, "I have betrayed innocent blood!" Here is the man who betrayed him, and this is what he thinks of him! Yes, those who were guilty of his death put their testimony on record that he was an innocent man.

Let us take the centurion who was present at the execution. He had charge of the Roman soldiers. He had told them to make him carry his cross; he had given orders for the nails to be driven into his feet and hands, for the spear to be thrust in his side. Let the centurion come forward. "Centurion, you had charge of the executioners; you saw that the order for his death was carried out; you saw him die; you heard him speak upon the cross. Tell us, what think you of Christ?" Hark! Look at him; he is smiting his breast as he cries, "Truly, this was the Son of God!"

I might go to the thief upon the cross, and ask what he thought of him. At first he railed upon him and reviled him. But then he thought better of it. "This man hath done nothing amiss," he says.

I might go further. I might summon the very devils themselves and ask them for their testimony. Have they anything to say of him? Why, the very devils called him the Son of God! In Mark we have the unclean spirit crying, "Jesus, thou Son of the Most High God." Men say, "Oh, I believe Christ to be the Son of God, and because I believe it intellectually I shall be saved." I tell you, the devils did that. And they did more than that; they trembled.

Let us bring in his friends. We want you to hear their evidence. Let us call that prince of preachers. Let us hear the forerunner; none ever preached like this man—this man who drew all Jerusalem and all Judea into the wilderness to hear him; this man who burst upon the nations like the flash of a meteor. Let John the Baptist come with his leathern girdle and his hairy coat, and let him tell us what he thinks of Christ. His words, though they were echoed in the wilderness of Palestine, are written in the Book for ever: "Behold the Lamb of God which taketh away the sin of the world!" This is what John the Baptist thought of him. "I bear record that he is the Son of God." No wonder he drew all Jerusalem and Judea to him, because he preached Christ. And whenever men preach Christ, they are sure to have plenty of followers.

But I shall go still further. I shall go away from earth into the other world. I shall summon the angels and ask what they think of Christ. They saw him in the bosom of the Father before the world was. Before the dawn of creation, before the morning stars sang together, he was there. They saw him leave the throne and come down to the manger. What a scene for them to witness! Ask these heavenly beings what they thought of him then. For once they are permitted to speak; for once the silence of heaven is broken. Listen to their song on the plains of Bethlehem, "Behold, I bring you good tidings of great joy, which shall be to all people. For unto you is born this day, in the city of David, a Savior, which is Christ the Lord." He leaves the throne to save the world. Is it a wonder the angels thought well of him?

Then there are the redeemed saints— they that see him face to face. Here on earth he was never known, no one seemed really to be acquainted with him; but he was known in that world where he had been from the foundation. What do they think of him there? If we could hear from heaven we should hear a shout which would glorify and magnify his name. We are told that when John was in the Spirit on the Lord's Day, and being caught up, he heard a shout around him, ten thousand times ten thousand, and thousands and thousands of voices, "Worthy is the Lamb that was slain, to receive power, and riches, and wisdom, and strength, and honor, and glory, and blessing!" Yes, he is worthy of all this. Heaven cannot speak too well of him. Oh, that earth would take up the echo and join with heaven in singing, "Worthy to receive power, and riches, and wisdom, and strength, and honor, and glory, and blessing!"

But there is still another witness—a higher still. Some think that the God of the Old Testament is the Christ of the New. But when Jesus came out of Jordan, baptized by John, there came a voice from heaven. God the Father spoke. It was his testimony to Christ: "This is my beloved Son, in whom I am well pleased." Ah, yes! God the Father thinks well of the Son. And if God is well pleased with him, so ought we. If the sinner and God are well pleased with Christ, then the sinner and God can meet. The moment you say, as the Father said, "I am well pleased with him," and accept him, you are wedded to God. Will you not believe the testimony? Will you not believe this witness, this last of all, the Lord of hosts, the King of kings himself? Once more he repeats it, so that all may know it. With Peter and James and John, on the mount of transfiguration, he cries again, "This is my beloved Son; hear him." And that voice went echoing and reechoing through Palestine, through all the earth from sea to sea; yes, that voice is echoing still, Hear him! Hear him!

My friend, will you hear him today? Hark! what is he saying to you? "Come unto me, all ye that labor and are heavy laden, and I will give you rest. Take my yoke upon you and learn of me; for I am meek and lowly in heart, and ye shall find rest unto your souls. For my yoke is easy, and my burden is light." Will you not think well of such a Savior? Will you not believe in him? Will you not trust in him with all your heart and mind? Will you not live for him? If he laid down his life for us, is it not the least we can do to lay down ours for him? If he bore the cross and died on it for me, ought I not to be willing to take it up for him? Oh, have we not reason to think well of him? Do you think it is right and noble to lift up your voice against such a Savior? Do you think it is just to cry, "Crucify him! Crucify him!" Oh, may God help all of us to glorify the Father by thinking well of his only begotten Son.

OTHER GOOD HARVEST HOUSE
REFERENCE RESOURCES

-✝-

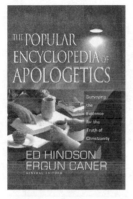

The Popular Encyclopedia of Apologetics
Ed Hindson and Ergun Caner, General Editors

As a Christian, are you ready to answer the questions people have about God, Jesus Christ, and your faith? That's not an easy task in today's world. You'll find *The Popular Encyclopedia of Apologetics* a helpful guide to responding to even the most difficult questions with clarity and confidence. Includes 175 articles from 55 expert contributors, with Christian responses to major world religions, cults, and secular philosophies.

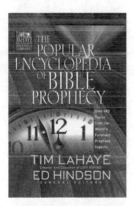

The Popular Encyclopedia of Bible Prophecy
Tim LaHaye and Ed Hindson, General Editors

This volume brings together an outstanding team of more than 40 premillennial prophecy and theology experts who examine the key players, pivotal events, and time line of God's still-unfolding plan for the ages. Includes more than 400 pages of fascinating facts, information, and charts about the last days.

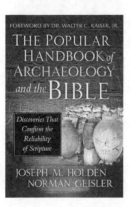

The Popular Handbook of Archaeology and the Bible
Joe Holden and Norm Geisler

Here is a fascinating survey of the most important Old and New Testament archaeological discoveries through the ages, written in a user-friendly format and popular style. This book examines the latest finds and explains their significance, and includes numerous photographs.